# PHP 6/MySQL® Programming for the Absolute Beginner

Andy Harris

**Course Technology PTR**

*A part of Cengage Learning*

COURSE TECHNOLOGY
CENGAGE Learning™

Australia • Brazil • Japan • Korea • Mexico • Singapore • Spain • United Kingdom • United States

# COURSE TECHNOLOGY
## CENGAGE Learning™

**PHP 6/MySQL Programming for the Absolute Beginner:** Andy Harris

**Publisher and General Manager, Course Technology PTR:** Stacy L. Hiquet

**Associate Director of Marketing:** Sarah Panella

**Manager of Editorial Services:** Heather Talbot

**Marketing Manager:** Mark Hughes

**Acquisitions Editor:** Mitzi Koontz

**Project Editor:** Jenny Davidson

**Technical Reviewer:** Matt Telles

**PTR Editorial Services Coordinator:** Erin Johnson

**Interior Layout Tech:** Value Chain

**Cover Designer:** Mike Tanamachi

**CD-ROM Producer:** Brandon Penticuff

**Indexer:** Larry Sweazy

**Proofreader:** Sara Gullion

For product information and technology assistance, contact us at **Cengage Learning Customer & Sales Support, 1-800-354-9706**

For permission to use material from this text or product, submit all requests online at **cengage.com/permissions** Further permissions questions can be emailed to **permissionrequest@cengage.com**

Library of Congress Control Number: 2008928831

ISBN-13: 978-1-59863-798-4
ISBN-10: 1-59863-798-3

**Course Technology**
25 Thomson Place
Boston, MA 02210
USA

Cengage Learning is a leading provider of customized learning solutions with office locations around the globe, including Singapore, the United Kingdom, Australia, Mexico, Brazil, and Japan. Locate your local office at: **international.cengage.com/region**

Cengage Learning products are represented in Canada by Nelson Education, Ltd.

For your lifelong learning solutions, visit **courseptr.com**

Visit our corporate website at **cengage.com**

Printed in the U.S.A.
2 3 4 5 6 7 16 15 14 13

*To Heather, Elizabeth, Matthew, Jacob, and Benjamin, and to all those who have called me Teacher.*

# ACKNOWLEDGMENTS

First, I thank my Lord and Savior Jesus Christ.

Heather, you always work harder on these books than I do. Thank you for your love and your support. Thank you Elizabeth, Matthew, Jacob, and Benjamin for understanding why Dad was typing all the time.

Thanks to the Open Source community for creating great free software like PHP and MySQL.

Thank you, Stacy Hiquet, for your continued support and encouragement on this and other projects. Thanks to Mitzi Koontz, for seeing this project through, and to Jenny Davidson for your work as the project editor. Special thanks to Matt Telles for the outstanding technical edit. You made the book far better than it would have been before.

Thanks to all who worked on the previous two editions. Your hard work was the foundation for something that might be even better.

Thank you to the many members of the Course Technology PTR team who worked on this book.

A huge thanks goes to my students throughout the years and the many people who sent in comments and advice from the first two editions. Thank you for being patient with my manuscript, for helping me spot many errors, and for providing invaluable advice. I learned as much from you as you did from me.

# ABOUT THE AUTHOR

**A**ndy Harris began his teaching career as a high-school special education teacher. During that time, he taught himself enough computing to do part-time computer consulting and database work. He began teaching computing at the university level in the late 1980s as a part-time job. Since 1995 he has been a full-time lecturer in the Computer Science Department of Indiana University/Purdue University–Indianapolis, where he serves as a senior lecturer and teaches classes in several programming languages. His primary interests are web development, PHP, Java, game programming, virtual reality, portable devices, and streaming media. He has written numerous books on these and other technology topics.

# TABLE OF CONTENTS

## Chapter 3    CONTROLLING YOUR CODE WITH CONDITIONS AND FUNCTIONS............................................................... 57

# INTRODUCTION

Computer programming has often been seen as a difficult and arcane skill. Programming languages are difficult and complicated, out of the typical person's reach. However, the advent of the World Wide Web changed that to some extent. It's reasonably easy to build and post a web page for the entire world to see. The languages of the web are reasonably simple, and numerous applications are available to assist in the preparation of static pages. At some point, every web author begins to dream of pages that actually do something useful. The simple HTML language that builds a page offers the tantalizing ability to build forms, but no way to work with the information that users type into these forms.

Often, a developer has a database or some other dynamic information they wish to somehow attach to a web page. Even languages such as JavaScript are not satisfying in these cases. The CGI interface was designed as an early solution to this problem, but CGI itself can be confusing and the languages used with CGI (especially Perl) are very powerful, but confusing to beginners.

PHP is an amazing language. It is meant to work with web servers, where it can do the critical work of file management and database access. It is reasonably easy to learn and understand, and can be embedded into web pages. It is as powerful as more-difficult languages, with a number of impressive extensions that add new features to the language.

In this book, I teach you how to write computer programs. I do not expect you to have any previous programming experience. You learn to program using the PHP language. Although PHP itself is a very specialized language (designed to enhance web pages), the concepts you learn through this language can be extended to a number of other programming environments.

Whenever possible, I use games as example programs. Each chapter begins by demonstrating a simple game or diversion. I show you all the skills you need to write that game through a series of simple example programs. At the end of the chapter, I show the game again, this time by looking at the code, which at that point you will understand. Games are motivating and often present special challenges to the programmer. The concepts presented are just as applicable in real-world applications.

I've updated this third edition to keep up with important trends in web development and languages.

First, I've changed all the web pages to be fully compliant to the XHTML 1.0 strict standard. This makes the pages more likely to work in multiple browsers, and simplifies the PHP coding, as the layout is entirely done in Cascading Style Sheets (CSS), and the PHP output tends to be much simpler than it was in earlier editions.

I've also added new features from PHP 6, including extensive use of the filter techniques for safe data retrieval. I've removed all the PHP functions that are no longer supported by PHP. I've also modified the SQL code to take advantage of some new features of MySQL 5.0.

Programming is not a skill you can learn simply by reading about it. You have to write code to really understand what's going on. I encourage you to play along at home. Look at the code on the accompanying CD. Run the programs yourself. Try to modify the code and see how it works. Make new variations of the programs to suit your own needs.

# CHAPTER 1

# EXPLORING THE ENVIRONMENT

eb pages are interesting, but on their own, they are simply documents. You can use PHP to add code to your web pages so they can do more. A scripting language like PHP can convert your website from a static document to an interactive application. In this chapter, you learn how to add basic PHP functionality to your web pages. You also learn how to do these things:

- Download and install Apache
- Download and install PHP
- Configure Apache to recognize PHP 6.0
- Configure PHP to run extensions used in this book (including MySQL and XML)
- Ensure PHP is on your system
- Run a basic diagnostic check of your PHP installation
- Add PHP code to a web page

Your first program probably won't win any web awards, but it takes you beyond what you can do with regular HTML. Figure 1.1 illustrates the Tip of the Day page, which offers friendly, helpful advice.

**FIGURE 1.1**

The tip of the day might look simple, but it is a technological marvel. It features HTML, cascading style sheets, and PHP code.

You could write this kind of page without using a technology like PHP, but the program is a little more sophisticated than it might look on the surface. The tip isn't actually embedded in the web page at all, but it is stored in a completely separate file. The program integrates this separate file into the HTML page. The page owner can change the tip of the day very easily by editing the text file that contains the tips.

## IN THE REAL WORLD

The Tip of the Day page illustrates one of the hottest concepts in web programming today: the content management system. This kind of structure allows programmers to design a website's general layout, but it isolates the contents from the page design. The page owners (who might not know how to modify a web page directly) can easily change a text file without risk of exposing the code that holds the site together. You'll learn how to build a full-blown content management system in Chapter 8, "XML and Content Management Systems."

You should begin by reviewing your XHTML skills. Soon enough, you're going to be writing programs that write web pages, so you need to be very secure with your HTML/XHTML coding.

If you usually write all your web pages with a plain text editor, you should be fine. If you tend to rely on higher-end tools like Microsoft FrontPage or Macromedia Dreamweaver, you should put those tools aside for a while and make sure you can write solid HTML by hand. You should know how to build standard web pages using modern standards (XHTML 1.0 strict is preferred), including form elements and cascading style sheets (CSS). If you need a refresher, please see the examples on my website: http://www.aharrisbooks.net.

Earlier editions of this text used HTML 4.0, but for this edition, I've switched entirely to XHTML 1.0 strict. This standard is a big improvement for a number of reasons:

- If you use a validator like the one at `validator.w3.org`, you'll know instantly if your page has any XHTML errors that could cause you big problems later on.
- XHTML disallows any formatting tags (like `<font>` and `<center>`). All formatting is done in the CSS code.
- The XHTML that your program creates will be cleaner, because it won't have formatting tags.
- Tables are no longer used for layout, so your PHP programs will be a lot easier to write.

## PROGRAMMING ON THE WEB SERVER

The Internet is all about various computers communicating with each other. The prevailing model of the Internet is the notion of clients and servers. You can understand this better by imagining a drive-through restaurant. As you drive to the little speaker, a barely intelligible voice asks for your order. You ask for your cholestoburger supreme and the teenager packages your food. You drive up, exchange money for the meal, and drive away. Meanwhile, the teenager waits for another customer to appear.

The Internet works much like this model. Large permanent computers called web servers host web pages and other information. They are much like the drive-through restaurant. Users drive up to the web server using a web browser. The data is exchanged and the user can read the information on the web browser.

What's interesting about this model is the interaction doesn't have to stop there. Since the client (user's) machine is a computer, it can be given instructions. Commonly, the JavaScript language stores special instructions in a web page. These instructions (like the HTML code itself) don't mean anything on the server. Once the page gets to the client machine, the browser interprets the HTML code and any other JavaScript instructions.

While much of the work is passed to the client, there are some disadvantages to this client-side approach. Programs designed to work inside a web browser are usually greatly restricted in the kinds of things they can do. A client-side web program usually cannot access the user's printer or disk drives. This limitation alone prevents such programs from doing much of the most useful work of the Internet, such as database connectivity and user tracking.

The server is also a computer; it's possible to write programs designed to operate on the server rather than the client. This arrangement has a number of advantages:

- Server-side programs run on powerful web server computers.
- The server can freely work with files and databases.
- The code returned to the user is plain XHTML, which can be displayed on any web browser.

## Installing PHP and Apache

PHP is only interesting when it runs on a computer configured as a web server. One way or another, you need access to a computer with at least three components on it: The PHP interpreter, a web server (such as Apache or Microsoft IIS), and some sort of database management system (usually MySQL).

## Using an Existing Server

For most people, there's no need to run your own active web server from home. There are many free and inexpensive web hosts available that provide PHP hosting. There are a number of reasons to take advantage of these services:

- **Installing a server can be a pain.** As you'll see in this chapter, there's a lot to putting together a web server, and it's great to let somebody else do the work if you can.
- **Most broadband agreements forbid servers**. If you're using a standard home-based broadband service (DSL or cable), you probably agreed not to run a web server as part of the contract. (Often the upload speeds are slowed on these connections to discourage running a server.)
- **A server requires a permanent address**. When a computer is attached to the Internet, it is given a special number called an IP address. Home-based connections often change this address, which is fine if you're a web client, but unacceptable for server applications.
- **Running a server opens some security risks**. It's not terribly dangerous to run a web server, but you are adding vulnerability. As a beginner, you may not want to worry about that risk yet.
- **Running a web server is a 24/7 commitment**. People will become dependent on your server always being available. You can't just turn it off when you want to play a game or something. You probably shouldn't run a working web server on a machine that does other things, too.

- **Professional web hosting is a bargain (often free).** Do a search for free PHP hosting and you'll find dozens of sites offering free PHP and MySQL hosting. Some of these services don't even embed advertisements. You can upgrade to a commercial site for a very low price (often less than $10/month) for more features. Hosting services are a bargain.
- **You'll eventually want a domain name.** You'll probably want some sort of domain name for your service (so people can type it in instead of an IP address), and the hosting services usually include domain searching and registration services.

As of this writing (May 2008) there are no commercial servers using PHP 6, but if you find one running PHP 5, it should still be able to run all the code in this book.

You'll be running database applications as you advance in this book, so you'll also want the MySQL database installed. Look for MySQL 5.0 or greater, as it has some important features not available in earlier versions.

It is also useful if the service supports phpMyAdmin, a database management system described in Chapter 9, "Using MySQL to Create Databases." (Almost all servers that offer mySQL support use this tool.)

## Installing Your Own Development Environment

Even if you have access to an online web server, you may want to build a practice server for development. This approach has many advantages:

- You can control exactly how the server you install is configured. You can tune it so all the options you want are turned on, and things you don't need are disabled. (I describe how to do this later in this chapter in the section called "Telling Apache about PHP.")
- You can test your programs without exposing them to the entire world. When you install a local server, you usually do not expose it to anyone but yourself. That way people won't snoop around your work until you're ready to expose it.
- It's easier to configure development environments to work with local servers than to work with remote ones.
- You don't have to be connected to the web while you work. This is especially important if you don't have a high-speed connection.

Most PHP developers create their programs on a local (development) server that is not exposed to the Internet, and then transfer working programs to a remote (production) server to launch the application.

However, installing a web server (and its related programs) can be complex. There are a lot of variables and many things that can go wrong.

You need several components to build your own PHP development system. PHP development is often done with either a system called LAMP (Linux, Apache, MySQL, and PHP) or WAMP (Windows, Apache, MySQL, and PHP).

> **HINT** If you're running Linux, there's a good chance everything is already installed on your system and you need only configure and turn things on. For that reason, I'm presuming for this discussion that you're working on a Windows XP system. Please look at the various Help documents that came with the software components for assistance installing on other operating systems.

To get your system up and running, you need the following components.

## A Web Server

The web server is software that allows a computer to host web pages. The most popular web server as of this writing is Apache, an open-source offering that runs on Windows, Linux, and just about every other operating system. The web server lets you write and test programs running from your local computer exactly the same way they will be seen on the Internet.

## The PHP Environment

The PHP environment is a series of programs and library files. These programs are unusual because the user never runs them directly. Instead, a user requests a PHP program from a web server and the server calls upon PHP to process the instructions in the file. PHP then returns HTML code, which the user sees in the browser. This book was written using PHP 6.0, although most of the code works well on earlier versions of PHP.

Although the code in this book will generally work on earlier versions of PHP, code written in earlier versions of PHP won't always work on PHP 6. This is unusual, as many languages strive to be backwards compatible. PHP 6 fixes a large number of security vulnerabilities; so much of the code written in earlier versions needs to be modified. I'll point out these changes as they come up in the book.

## A Database Environment

Interacting with databases is one of PHP's most powerful uses. For that reason, you need at least one database engine installed with your system. For this book, you use MySQL and SQLite. I cover the installation and use of these packages more fully in Chapter 9, because you won't need them until then.

## An Editor

Have some sort of editor to manipulate your code. You can use Notepad, but you probably want something more substantial. A number of freeware and commercial PHP editors are available. Several excellent free editors are available for PHP, including:

- **Aptana**—An open-source program based on the famous eclipse Java editor. Comes with a very solid PHP plugin with syntax coloring, syntax completion, and the ability to preview your programs directly in the editor. Especially useful for AJAX development, as it includes support for XHTML, CSS, JavaScript, and many popular AJAX libraries out of the box.

- **Maguma Open Studio**—Another incredible PHP editor with many professional features. Can be linked directly to your local server, or used to edit PHP files on a remote server. Syntax coloring and completion, and other nice features are also part of the default setup.

- **DevPHP**—An open-source IDE with the built-in integration of the PHP documentation, page preview, syntax coloring and completion, and many other very useful tools.

Of course, you can use any plain text editor to build your PHP files. Notepad does the job, but it doesn't have many support features. If you prefer a text editor, consider an enhanced programmer's editor like notepad++ or the old standbys: VI/VIM and EMACS.

I've included copies of all these editors on the CD-ROM that accompanies this book.

## Installing with XAMPP

It's possible to install all the features you need by hand, but the process is painful and time-consuming. It's much easier to use one of the pre-configured installation packages. My favorite is XAMPP, which is released under the GPL license. The Windows version includes the following features:

- Apache web server
- PHP programming language
- MySQL relational data manager
- PHPMyAdmin database management package
- Mercury Mail email server
- A control panel application that helps you configure and run the software
- Some additional languages and packages

There are versions of XAMPP available for all major platforms. Each contains a similar set of programs, but the exact details vary by platform. There is a version of XAMPP for Mac that works very well.

XAMPP installs just like any other application. It has an installation script that guides you through the entire process. Once you've finished, everything is installed, and the various components are already configured to talk to each other.

 As I write this book, PHP 6 is still in beta, so it is not currently included in XAMPP. Look for a version of XAMPP that includes PHP 6. If it is not yet available, install the latest version (with PHP 5). Most of the programs in this book run perfectly fine on PHP 5. See the section "upgrading to PHP 6" if you really must have PHP 6 on your system before it's out of beta testing.

XAMPP can be found at http://www.apachefriends.org/en/xampp.html.

## Starting Your Server

Once you've got XAMPP installed, locate the XAMP controller (xamp-control.exe) in the directory where you installed XAMPP. You'll use this program a lot, so you may want to make a shortcut to it on your desktop. It looks like Figure 1.2.

FIGURE 1.2

The XAMPP controller application.

Start your web server by clicking the Start button next to Apache. If you want Apache to be running all the time, click on the "Svc" checkbox. If all goes well, the Start button's caption will change to "Stop" and you'll see a little label that says "Running." You can turn all the major features of XAMPP on and off with this application. For now, all you really need is Apache, but it doesn't hurt to have MySQL on too.

To test your server, open up a web browser, and type the following URL:

```
http://localhost
```

If all goes well, you will see a page like Figure 1.3.

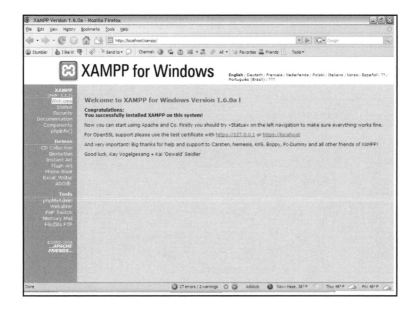

FIGURE 1.3

The XAMPP
welcome screen
after selecting the
English language.

## Checking Your Security Settings

There is a security link on the main XAMPP page. Use this link to investigate the current
security settings of your server. Figure 1.4 shows this in process.

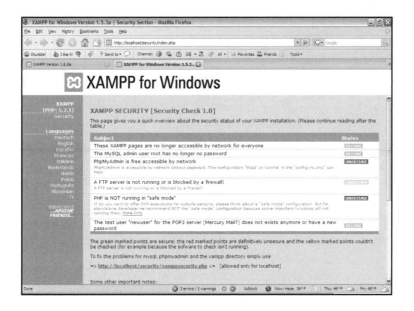

FIGURE 1.4

Checking the
security of the
server.

You can have XAMPP fix two common security problems automatically by using the provided link. This allows you to change the default password of your MySQL database and add a password to your XAMPP directory. It is a very good idea to perform both of these basic security steps, as shown in Figure 1.5.

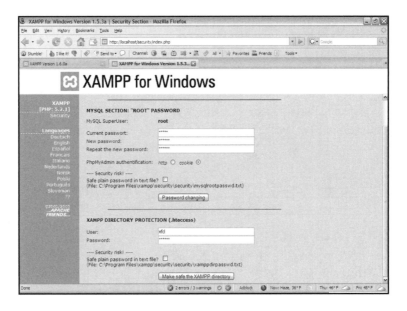

FIGURE 1.5

Adding passwords to the server.

In addition to these basic changes, you should run a firewall on your machine (the one that comes with Windows is a bare minimum) to prevent any external access to your server. Remember, the local server is used only for development. You don't want people to be able to access it from the outside and potentially change your data or cause grief in your name.

HINT

When I'm running a development server, I usually take out the index page so I can see a directory listing and navigate the htdocs directory through the server. Typically, I add an index.html page when I'm ready to release the project to the world.

## Configuring Apache

Apache is configured through a series of heavily commented text files. Look in the conf directory of your Apache directory for a file called httpd.conf. This is the main configuration file for Apache. You shouldn't have to change this file much, but this is the file to modify if you want, for example, to add a domain name.

## RUNNING YOUR LOCAL SERVER

The XAMPP directory has an `htdocs` subdirectory. Any files you want displayed on your local server must be in this directory or its subdirectories.

**CAUTION** You might normally double-click a file in your file manager to display it in a browser, or you may drag it to the browser from your file-management system. This works for plain HTML files, but PHP programs must run through a web server Dragging a PHP file to the browser will bypass the server, and the PHP programs will not work correctly. PHP code must be called through a formal http call, even if it's localhost. All PHP code will be in an `htdocs` directory's subdirectory, unless you specifically indicate in your `httpd.conf` file that you want another directory to be accessible to your web server. If you place your code anywhere but in `htdocs` (or a subdirectory of `htdocs`), it will not be accessible to your server and it will not work correctly.

## Adding PHP to Your Pages

Now that you've got PHP installed, it's time to add some code.

See that PHP is installed and run a quick diagnostic check to see how it is configured. You should do this whether you're installing your own web server or using an existing server for your programs.

The easiest way to determine if PHP exists on your server is this: Write a simple PHP program and see if it works. Here's a very simple PHP program that greets the user and displays all kinds of useful information about the development system. To try it yourself, type it in and save it as "hello.php" in your server's `htdocs` directory.

### Adding PHP Commands to an HTML Page

```
<!DOCTYPE html PUBLIC "-//W3C//DTD XHTML 1.0 Strict//EN"
"http://www.w3.org/TR/xhtml1/DTD/xhtml1-strict.dtd">
<html lang="EN" dir="ltr" xmlns="http://www.w3.org/1999/xhtml">
<head>
<title>Hello in PHP</title>
</head>
<body>
<h1>Hello in PHP</h1>

<?php
 print "Hello, world!";
  phpInfo();
```

```
?>

</body>
</html>
```

Since this is the first PHP code you've seen in this book, I need to go over some basic concepts.

A page written in PHP begins much like an ordinary HTML page. Both are written with a plain text editor and stored on a web server. What makes a PHP program different is the embedded `<script>` elements. When the user requests a PHP page, the server examines the page and executes any script elements before sending the resulting HTML to the user.

 The `<? ?>` sequence was formerly used to indicate PHP, but this mechanism is discouraged (still allowed but disabled by default) in PHP 6. The preferred way to indicate PHP code is with a longer version, like this: `<?php ?>`. You can also specify your code with normal HTML tags much like JavaScript: `<script language = "php"></script>`. Some PHP servers are configured to prefer one type of script tag over another so you may need to be flexible. However, all these variations work in exactly the same way.

A PHP program looks a lot like a typical HTML page. The difference is the special `<?PHP ?>` tag, which specifies the existence of PHP code. Any code inside the tag is read by the PHP interpreter and then converted into HTML code. The code written between the `<?PHP` and `?>` symbols is PHP code. I added two commands to the page. Look at the output of the program shown in Figure 1.6. You might be surprised.

## Examining the Results

This page has three distinct types of text.

- `Hello in PHP` is ordinary HTML. I wrote it just like a regular HTML page, and it was displayed just like regular HTML.
- `Hello, world!` was written by the PHP program embedded in the page.
- The rest of the page is a bit mysterious. It contains a lot of information about the particular PHP engine being used. It actually stretches on for several pages. The `phpInfo()` command generated all that code. This command displays information about the PHP installation.

**FIGURE 1.6**

This is a fancy page
for so little code.

It isn't that important to understand all the information displayed by the phpInfo() command. It's much more critical to appreciate that when the user requests the hello.html web page, the text is first run through the PHP interpreter. This program scans for any PHP commands, executes them, and prints HTML code in place of the original commands. All the PHP code is gone by the time a page gets to the user.

For proof of this, point your browser at hello.php and view the source code. It looks something like this:

```
<!DOCTYPE html PUBLIC "-//W3C//DTD XHTML 1.0 Strict//EN"
"http://www.w3.org/TR/xhtml1/DTD/xhtml1-strict.dtd">
<html lang="EN" dir="ltr" xmlns="http://www.w3.org/1999/xhtml">
<head>
<title>Hello in PHP</title>
</head>
<body>
<h1>Hello in PHP</h1>

Hello, world!<!DOCTYPE html PUBLIC "-//W3C//DTD XHTML 1.0 Transitional//EN"
"DTD/xhtml1-transitional.dtd">
<html><head>
<style type="text/css">
```

```
body {background-color: #ffffff; color: #000000;}
body, td, th, h1, h2 {font-family: sans-serif;}
pre {margin: 0px; font-family: monospace;}
a:link {color: #000099; text-decoration: none; background-color: #ffffff;}
a:hover {text-decoration: underline;}
table {border-collapse: collapse;}
.center {text-align: center;}
.center table { margin-left: auto; margin-right: auto; text-align: left;}
.center th { text-align: center !important; }
td, th { border: 1px solid #000000; font-size: 75%; vertical-align: baseline;}
h1 {font-size: 150%;}
h2 {font-size: 125%;}
.p {text-align: left;}
.e {background-color: #ccccff; font-weight: bold; color: #000000;}
.h {background-color: #9999cc; font-weight: bold; color: #000000;}
.v {background-color: #cccccc; color: #000000;}
.vr {background-color: #cccccc; text-align: right; color: #000000;}
img {float: right; border: 0px;}
hr {width: 600px; background-color: #cccccc; border: 0px; height: 1px; color:
#000000;}
</style>
<title>phpinfo()</title><meta name="ROBOTS" content="NOINDEX,NOFOLLOW,NOARCHIVE"
/></head>
<body><div class="center">
<table border="0" cellpadding="3" width="600">
<tr class="h"><td>
<a href="http://www.php.net/"><img border="0"
src="/php6/ph01/hello.php?=PHPE9568F34-D428-11d2-A769-00AA001ACF42" alt="PHP
Logo" /></a><h1 class="p">PHP Version 6.0.0-dev</h1>
</td></tr>
</table><br />
<table border="0" cellpadding="3" width="600">
<tr><td class="e">System </td><td class="v">Windows NT AHARRIS_LT 5.1 build 2600
</td></tr>
<tr><td class="e">Build Date </td><td class="v">Mar 4 2008 10:04:48 </td></tr>
<tr><td class="e">Configure Command </td><td class="v">cscript /nologo
configure.js &quot;--enable-snapshot-build&quot; &quot;--with-gd=shared&quot;
</td></tr>
```

```
<tr><td class="e">Server API </td><td class="v">Apache 2.0 Handler </td></tr>
<tr><td class="e">Virtual Directory Support </td><td class="v">enabled
</td></tr>
<tr><td class="e">Configuration File (php.ini) Path </td><td
class="v">C:\WINDOWS </td></tr>
<tr><td class="e">Loaded Configuration File </td><td class="v">C:\Program
Files\xampp\php6\php.ini </td></tr>
<tr><td class="e">PHP API </td><td class="v">20070116 </td></tr>
<tr><td class="e">PHP Extension </td><td class="v">20070729 </td></tr>
<tr><td class="e">Zend Extension </td><td class="v">320070729 </td></tr>
<tr><td class="e">Debug Build </td><td class="v">no </td></tr>
<tr><td class="e">Thread Safety </td><td class="v">enabled </td></tr>
<tr><td class="e">Zend Memory Manager </td><td class="v">enabled </td></tr>
<tr><td class="e">Unicode Support </td><td class="v">Based on Copyright (C)
2005, International Business Machines Corporation and others. All Rights
Reserved. . ICU Version 3.4. </td></tr>
<tr><td class="e">IPv6 Support </td><td class="v">enabled </td></tr>
<tr class="v"><td>Registered PHP Streams</td><td>php, file, glob, data, http,
ftp, compress.zlib</td></tr>
<tr class="v"><td>Registered Stream Socket Transports</td><td>tcp, udp</td></tr>
<tr class="v"><td>Registered Stream Filters</td><td>unicode.*, string.rot13,
string.toupper, string.tolower, string.strip_tags, convert.*, consumed,
zlib.*</td></tr>
</table><br />
```

Note that I showed only a small part of the code generated by the phpInfo() command. Also, note that the code details might be different when you run the program on your own machine. The key point is that the PHP code that writes Hello, World! (print "Hello, World!") is replaced with the actual text Hello, World! More significantly, a huge amount of HTML code replaces the very simple phpInfo() command.

A small amount of PHP code can very efficiently generate large and complex HTML documents. This is one significant advantage of PHP. Also, by the time the document gets to the web browser, it's plain-vanilla HTML code, which can be read easily by any browser. These two features are important benefits of server-side programming in general, and of PHP programming in particular.

As you progress through this book, you learn about many more commands for producing interesting HTML, but the basic concept is always the same. Your PHP program is simply an HTML page that contains special PHP markup. The PHP code is examined by a special program on the server. The results are embedded into the web page before it is sent to the user.

Typically I take great pains to ensure all code in this book is XHTML 1.0 strict compliant. This first program is not, because the phpInfo() directive assumes there's no other HTML or XHTML around. It doesn't cause any problems in this case, but as you'll see, it's often best to aim for XHTML strict unless you have a good reason otherwise.

## Configuring Your Version of PHP

PHP comes in a reasonable form out of the box (at least if you install it with XAMPP), but there are a few configuration options you should be aware of, because your production server (the one the universe can really see) may be set differently than your development server (the one on your personal machine). Sometimes it's nice to configure the machine at home just like the production machine so you aren't too surprised.

You can modify your PHP configuration by editing a text file called php.ini. In the standard XAMPP installation, it's found in the xampp/php directory. You can edit it with a standard text editor.

You can cause a lot of problems tinkering with configuration files you don't completely understand. Make a backup before you start messing with this file, and change only one thing at a time. Restart PHP and check your PHPInfo() page to see if the change has taken place. Use the XAMPP control panel to turn Apache off then back on, and Apache will restart with the new configuration in place.

In particular, think about the following elements.

## Display Errors

When you make a mistake in your code, the error message is not (at least in some installations) displayed to the browser. Malicious users can use error messages to find security loopholes in your system. Error messages are sent to a log file instead, which you can view with a text editor. While this is a reasonable solution in production (where errors will be rare), it is too complicated for development. On a development server, I prefer to turn display_errors on. When you're testing a program, if there's an error, you'll see the error right away rather than having to dig around in an error log. Check PHPinfo() to see if this particular setting is currently on or off. If it's off, here's how to turn it on.

1. Find the line in php.ini that says display_errors.
2. Change the text of that line from display_errors = off to display_errors = on.
3. Restart Apache to ensure the changes are permanent.
4. Check PHPInfo (in your hello.php program) to ensure the change has been made.

## Windows Extensions

PHP comes with a number of extensions that allow you to modify its behavior. You can add functionality to your copy of PHP by adding new modules. To find the part of `php.ini` that describes these extensions, look for `windows extensions` in the `php.ini` file.

You'll see some code that looks like this:

```
;Windows Extensions
;extension=php_bz2.dll
;extension=php_ctype.dll
;extension=php_cpdf.dll
;extension=php_curl.dll
;extension=php_cybercash.dll
;extension=php_db.dll
;extension=php_dba.dll
;extension=php_dbase.dll
;extension=php_dbx.dll
;extension=php_domxml.dll
;extension=php_dotnet.dll
;extension=php_exif.dll
;extension=php_fbsql.dll
;extension=php_fdf.dll
;extension=php_filepro.dll
;extension=php_gd.dll
;extension=php_gettext.dll
;extension=php_hyperwave.dll
;extension=php_iconv.dll
;extension=php_ifx.dll
;extension=php_iisfunc.dll
;extension=php_imap.dll
;extension=php_ingres.dll
;extension=php_interbase.dll
;extension=php_java.dll
;extension=php_ldap.dll
;extension=php_mbstring.dll
;extension=php_mcrypt.dll
;extension=php_mhash.dll
;extension=php_mssql.dll
```

```
;extension=php_oci8.dll ;extension=php_openssl.dll ;extension=php_oracle.dll
;extension=php_pdf.dll ;extension=php_pgsql.dll ;extension=php_printer.dll
;extension=php_sablot.dll ;extension=php_shmop.dll ;extension=php_snmp.dll
;extension=php_sockets.dll ;extension=php_sybase_ct.dll ;extension=php_xslt.dll
;extension=php_yaz.dll ;extension=php_zlib.dll
;;;;; I added gd2 extension extension=php_gd2.dll
;;; I added ming support extension=php_ming.dll
;;;;;I added mysql extension extension=php_mysql.dll
```

Most of the extensions begin with a semicolon. This character acts like a comment character and causes the line to be ignored. To add a particular extension, simply eliminate the semicolon at the beginning of the line. I usually put a comment in the code to remind myself that I added this extension.

XAMPP has default support for MySQL built in, but if not, you can fix this yourself as well.

Since I wrote this book before PHP 6 was standardized, I had to do more configuration than you should have to do. I added the php_mysql.dll extension. This allows support for the MySQL database language used in the second half of this book. Add support for that library by removing the semicolon characters from the beginning of the mysql line.

You can determine whether PHP added support for MySQL by looking again at the results of the phpInfo() function. If exposing the php_mysql.dll extension didn't work on its own, you may have to locate the libmysql.dll file and move it to the C:\Windowsdirectory.

I also added support for two graphics libraries that I occasionally use. The gd2 library allows me to build and modify graphics, and ming allows me to create Flash movies. Don't worry about exposing these files until you're comfortable with basic PHP programming. However, when you're ready, it's really nice to know that you can easily add to the PHP features by supporting new modules.

Take a look at the extension_dir variable in php.ini to see where PHP expects to find all your extension files. Any .dll file in that directory can be an extension. You can also download new extensions and install them when you are ready to expand PHP's capabilities. If something isn't working correctly, copy the DLLs from the PHP directory to the directory indicated by extension_dir.

There's no urgent need to add the extensions yet. Don't risk messing up your configuration unless you have a good reason. The configurations in XAMPP are a pretty good starting place.

## Changes in PHP 6

If you've worked in PHP 5, there are a few options that no longer exist. They reflect a change in the security approach of PHP 6.

## Safe Mode

This mode was a master setting that allows you to choose between ease of programming and server safety.

It never really made you that safe, and most programmers used parts of it and ignored others. Now there's no setting for safe mode. Just turn on and off the parts that matter to you.

## Register Globals

This setting was used to allow PHP to automatically determine variables from a web form. (It's really OK if you don't know what I'm talking about.) It was very convenient, but it caused a lot of security headaches, so it is no longer an option in PHP6. See Chapter 2 for information on how to extract data from HTML forms in safer ways.

## CREATING THE TIP OF THE DAY PROGRAM

Way back at the beginning of this chapter, I promised that you would be able to write the featured Tip of the Day program. This program requires HTML, CSS, and one line of PHP code. The code shows a reasonably basic page:

```
<!DOCTYPE html PUBLIC "-//W3C//DTD XHTML 1.0 Strict//EN"
"http://www.w3.org/TR/xhtml1/DTD/xhtml1-strict.dtd">
<html lang="EN" dir="ltr" xmlns="http://www.w3.org/1999/xhtml">
<head>
<title>Tip of the day</title>
</head>

<body>


<h1>Tip of the day</h1>
<?php

print "<h3>Here's your tip:</h3>";
?>

<div style = "border-color:green; border-style:groove; border-width:2px">
<?php
readfile("tips.txt");
```

```
?>
</div>
```

```
</body>
</html>
```

The page is basic HTML. It contains one div element with a custom style setting up a border around the day's tip. Inside the div element, I added PHP code with the <?php and ?> devices. This code calls one PHP function called readFile(). The readFile() command takes as an argument the name of some file. It reads that file's contents and displays them on the page as if it were HTML. As soon as that line of code stops executing (the text in the tips.txt file has been printed to the web browser), the ?> symbol indicates that the PHP coding is finished and the rest of the page will be typical HTML.

 This program assumes you have a plain text file called "tips.txt" in the same directory as your program with a tip inside it. If you don't have this file, you'll get an error.

## SUMMARY

You've already come a very long way. You've learned or reviewed all the main HTML objects. You installed a web server on your computer. You added PHP. You changed the Apache configuration to recognize PHP. You saw how PHP code can be integrated into an HTML document. You learned how to change the configuration file for PHP to incorporate various extensions. Finally, you created your first page, which includes all these elements. You should be proud of your efforts already. In the next chapter, you more fully explore the relationship between PHP and HTML and learn how to use variables and input to make your pages do interesting things.

---

### CHALLENGES

1. Find a web server with PHP support and create an account on it.
2. Install Apache, PHP, and MySQL on your own system.
3. Create a PHP page that displays phpInfo() results.
4. Review XHTML and CSS standards. Build a sample page using XHTML strict and CSS (especially if you are unfamiliar with these technologies).

# USING VARIABLES AND INPUT

I n Chapter 1, "Exploring the PHP Environment," you learned the foundations of all PHP programming. If you have your environment installed, you're ready to write some PHP programs. Computer programs are ultimately about data.

In this chapter, you begin looking at the way programs store and manipulate data in variables. Specifically, you learn how to:

- Create a variable in PHP
- Recognize the main types of variables
- Name variables appropriately
- Output the values of variables in your scripts
- Perform basic operations on variables
- Read variables from an HTML form

## INTRODUCING THE STORY PROGRAM

By the end of this chapter, you'll be able to write the program, called Story, featured in Figures 2.1 and 2.2.

**FIGURE 2.1**

The program begins by asking the user to enter some information.

The program asks the user to enter some values into an HTML form and then uses those values to build a custom version of a classic nursery rhyme. The Story program works like most server-side programs. It has two distinctive parts: a form for user input, and a PHP program to read the input and produce some type of feedback. First, the user enters information into a plain HTML form and hits the Submit button. The PHP program doesn't execute until after the user has submitted a form. The program takes the information from the form and does something to it. Usually, the PHP program returns an HTML page to the user.

**FIGURE 2.2**

I hate it when the
warthog's in the
kohlrabi.

## USING VARIABLES IN YOUR SCRIPTS

The most important new idea in this chapter is the notion of a variable. A variable is a container for holding information in the computer's memory. To make things easier for the programmer, every variable has a name. You can store information in and get information out of a variable.

### Introducing the Hi Jacob Program

The program featured in Figure 2.3 uses a variable, although you might not be able to tell simply by looking at the output.

You can't really see anything special about this program from the web page itself (even if you look at the HTML source). To see what's new, look at the hiJacob.php source code.

```
<!DOCTYPE html PUBLIC "-//W3C//DTD XHTML 1.0 Strict//EN"
"http://www.w3.org/TR/xhtml1/DTD/xhtml1-strict.dtd">
<html lang="EN" dir="ltr" xmlns="http://www.w3.org/1999/xhtml">
<head>
<title>Hi Jacob</title>
</head>
<body>
<h1>Hi Jacob</h1>
```

```
<h3>Demonstrates using a variable</h3>
<div>
<?php

$userName = "Jacob";

print "Hi, $userName";
?>
</div>
</body>
</html>
```

**FIGURE 2.3**

The word Jacob is
stored in a variable
in this page.

**TRAP** In regular HTML and JavaScript programming, you can use the web browser's view source command to examine your program code. For server-side languages, this is not sufficient; the result of the view source command has no PHP at all. Remember that the actual program code never gets to your web browser. Instead, the program is executed on the server and the program results are sent to the browser as ordinary HTML. Look at the actual PHP source code on the server when examining these programs. On a related note, you cannot simply use your browser's File menu to load a PHP page. Instead, run it through a server.

The helloJacob page is mainly HTML with a small patch of PHP code in it. That code does a lot of very important work.

## Creating a String Variable

The line $userName = "Jacob"; does two major things. First, it creates a variable named $userName. Second, it will assign the value "Jacob" to the variable. In PHP, all variables begin with a dollar sign to distinguish them from other program elements. The variable's name is significant.

## Naming Your Variables

As a programmer, you frequently get to name things. Experienced programmers have learned some tricks about naming variables and other elements.

- Make the name descriptive. It's much easier to figure out what $userName means than something like $myVariable or $r. When possible, make sure your variable names describe the kind of information they contain.

- Use an appropriate length. Your variable name should be long enough to be descriptive, but not so long that it becomes tedious to type.

- Don't use spaces. Most languages (including PHP) don't allow spaces in variable names.

- Don't use symbols. Most of the special characters such as #, *, and / already have meaning in programming languages. Of course, every variable in PHP begins with the $ character, but otherwise you should avoid using punctuation. One exception to this rule is the underscore (_) character, which is allowed in most languages, including PHP.

- Be careful about case. PHP is a case-sensitive language, which means that it considers $userName, $USERNAME, and $UserName to be three different variables. The convention in PHP is to use all lowercase except when separating words. (Note the uppercase N in $userName.) This is a good convention to follow, and it's the one I use throughout this book.

- Watch your spelling! Every time you refer to a variable, PHP checks to see if that variable already exists somewhere in your program. If so, it uses that variable. If not, it quietly makes a new variable for you. PHP will not catch a misspelling. Instead, it makes a whole new variable, and your program probably won't work correctly.

## Assigning a Value to a Variable

The equals sign (=) is special in PHP. It does not mean equality (at least in the present context). The equals sign is used for assignment. If you read the equals sign as the word "gets," you are closer to the meaning PHP uses for this symbol. For example, look at this line of code:

```
$userName = "Jacob"
```

It should be read as "The variable $userName gets the value Jacob."

Usually when you create a variable in PHP, you also assign some value to it. Assignment flows from right to left, so the value "Jacob" is being passed into the variable $userName. If you have a statement like $a = $b, the contents of variable $b are copied into variable $a.

The $userName variable has been assigned the value "Jacob". Computers are picky about what type of information goes into a variable, but PHP automates this process for you by determining the data type of a variable based on its context. Still, it's important to recognize that Jacob is a text value, because text is stored and processed a little bit differently in computer memory than numeric data.

**TRICK** Computer programmers almost never refer to text as text. Instead, they prefer the more esoteric term string. The word string actually has a somewhat poetic origin, because the underlying mechanism for storing text in a computer's memory reminded early programmers of making a chain of beads on a string.

## Printing a Variable's Value

The next line of code prints a message to the screen. You can print any text to the screen you want. Text (also called string data) is usually encased in quotation marks. If you want to print the value of a variable, simply place the variable name in the text you want printed. Examine the following line:

```
print "Hi, $userName";
```

It actually produces this output:

```
Hi, Jacob
```

It produces this because when the server encounters the variable $userName, it's replaced with that variable's value, which is "Jacob". The PHP program output is sent directly to the web browser, so you can even include HTML tags in your output, simply by including them inside the quotation marks.

**TRICK** The ability to print the value of a variable inside other text is called *string interpolation*. That's not critical to know, but it could be useful information on a trivia show or something.

## USING THE SEMICOLON TO END A LINE

PHP is a more formal language than HTML and, like most programming languages, has some strict rules about the syntax used when writing. Each unique instruction is expected to end with a semicolon. If you look at the complete code for the helloJacob program, you see that each line of PHP code ends with said semicolon. If you forget to do this, you get an error that looks like the one in Figure 2.4.

 An instruction sometimes is longer than a single line on the editor. The semicolon goes at the end of the instruction, which often (but not always) corresponds with the end of the line. You'll see an example of this shortly as you build long string variables. In general, though, you end each line with a semicolon.

 **FIGURE 2.4**

This error occurs if you go sans semicolon to the end of every line.

 Don't panic if you get an error message or two. Errors are a completely normal part of programming. Even experienced programmers expect to see many error messages while building and testing programs.

Usually the resulting error code gives you important clues about what went wrong. Make sure you look carefully at whatever line of code is reported. Although the error isn't always on that line, you can often get a hint. In many cases (particularly a missing semicolon), a syntax error indicates an error on the line that actually follows the real problem. If you get a syntax error on line 14, and the problem is a missing semicolon, the problem line is actually line 13.

**TIP** It's possible you won't see error messages even if something went wrong. Some servers are set up to suppress error messages for security reasons. If this is the case, you'll have a file on the server called `error_log` that will hold all the error messages. Use this to determine what went wrong. See Chapter 1 for information on configuring PHP to display error messages with the `display_errors` setting.

## USING VARIABLES FOR MORE COMPLEX PAGES

While the `Hello Jacob` program was interesting, there is no real advantage in that particular program to using a variable. Check out another use for variables.

### Building the Row Your Boat Page

Figure 2.5 shows the `Row Your Boat` page.

<table>
<tr><td>

**FIGURE 2.5**

This program shows the words to a popular song. They sure repeat a lot.
</td></tr>
</table>

I chose this song in particular because it repeats the same verse three times. If you look at the original code for the rowBoat.php program, you see I used a trick to save some typing:

```
<!DOCTYPE html PUBLIC "-//W3C//DTD XHTML 1.0 Strict//EN"
"http://www.w3.org/TR/xhtml1/DTD/xhtml1-strict.dtd">
<html lang="EN" dir="ltr" xmlns="http://www.w3.org/1999/xhtml">
<head>
<title>Row Your Boat</title>
</head>
<body>
<h1>Row Your Boat</h1>
<h3>Demonstrates use of long variables</h3>

<?php

$verse = <<<HERE

<p>
Row, Row, Row, your boat<br />
Gently Down the stream<br />
Merrily, Merrily, Merrily, Merrily<br />
Life is but a dream!<br />
</p>
HERE;

print "<h3>Verse 1:</h3>";
print $verse;

print "<h3>Verse 2:</h3>";
print $verse;
print "<h3>Verse 3:</h3>";
print $verse;

?>


</body>
</html>
```

## Creating Multi-Line Strings

You find yourself wanting to print several lines of HTML code at once. It can be very tedious to use quotation marks to indicate such strings (especially because HTML also often uses the quotation mark symbol). PHP provides a special quoting mechanism, which is perfect for this type of situation. The following line begins assigning a value to the $verse variable:

```
$verse = <<<HERE
```

The <<<HERE segment indicates this is a special multi-line string that ends with the symbol HERE. You can use any phrase you want, but I generally use the word HERE because I think of the <<< symbols as "up to." In other words, you can think of the following as meaning "verse gets everything up to HERE."

```
$verse = <<<HERE
```

You can also think of <<<HERE as a special quote sign, which is ended with the value HERE.

You can write any amount of text between <<<HERE and HERE. You can put variables inside the special text and PHP replaces the variable with its value, just like in ordinary (quoted) strings. The ending phrase (HERE) must be on a line by itself, and there must be no leading spaces in front of it.

You might wonder why the $verse = <<<HERE line doesn't have a semicolon after it. Although this is one line in the editor, it begins a multi-line structure. Technically, everything from that line to the end of the HERE; line is part of the same logical line, even though the code takes up several lines in the editor. Everything between <<<HERE and HERE is a string value.

The semicolon doesn't have any special meaning inside a string. At a minimum, you should know that a line beginning a multi-line quote doesn't need a semicolon, but the line at the end of the quote does.

If your heredocs aren't working, check these common problems:

- Use the <<< symbol. Sometimes I get sloppy and use >>> instead. It doesn't work. Silly mistake, but it's cost me hours before.
- Be sure the ending symbol is unindented. The symbol (usually HERE) that ends the phrase needs to be all the way to the left margin. This does interrupt your indentation scheme, but that's a small price to pay for the advantages of the heredoc approach.

- Be sure the symbols match. If you misspelled one of the symbols or didn't match the capitalization, PHP will never see the end of your quote, and will report an error.

  If you just can't get it working, delete the offending code and re-type it. Often there will be a mistake you can't see, but when you re-type, the mistake is gone.

Once the multi-line string is built, it is very easy to use. It's actually harder to write the captions for the three verses than the verses themselves. The `print` statement simply places the value of the `$verse` variable in the appropriate spots of the output HTML.

## Working with Numeric Variables

Computers ultimately store information in on/off impulses. You can convert these very simple data values into a number of more convenient kinds of information. The PHP language makes most of this invisible to you, but it's important to know that memory handles string (text) differently than it does numeric values, and that there are two main types of numeric values: integers and floating-point real numbers.

### Making the ThreePlusFive Program

As an example of how PHP works with numbers, consider the `ThreePlusFive.php` program illustrated in Figure 2.6.

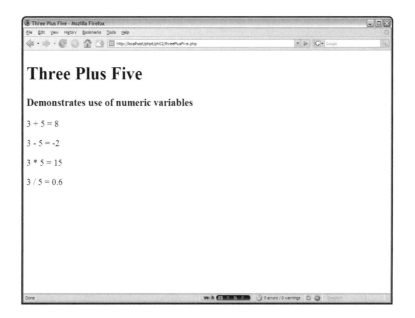

**Figure 2.6**

This program does basic math on variables containing the values 3 and 5.

All the work in the `ThreePlusFive` program is done with two variables called $x and $y. (I know, I recommended that you assign variables longer, descriptive names, but these variables are commonly used in arithmetic problems, so these very short variable names are okay in this instance.) The code for the program looks like this:

```
<!DOCTYPE html PUBLIC "-//W3C//DTD XHTML 1.0 Strict//EN"
"http://www.w3.org/TR/xhtml1/DTD/xhtml1-strict.dtd">
<html lang="EN" dir="ltr" xmlns="http://www.w3.org/1999/xhtml">
<head>
<title>Three Plus Five</title>
</head>
<body>
<h1>Three Plus Five</h1>
<h3>Demonstrates use of numeric variables</h3>

<?php

$x = 3;
$y = 5;

$sum = $x + $y;
$dif = $x - $y;
$prod = $x * $y;
$quotient = $x / $y;

print <<< HERE

<p>$x + $y = $sum</p>
<p>$x - $y = $dif</p>
<p>$x * $y = $prod</p>
<p>$x / $y = $quotient</p>

HERE;

?>

</body>
</html>
```

## Assigning Numeric Values

You create a numeric variable like any other variable in PHP: Simply assign a value to a variable. Notice that numeric values do not require quotation marks. I created variables called $x and $y and assigned appropriate values to these variables.

## Using Mathematical Operators

For each calculation, I want to print the problem as well as its solution. This line prints out the values of the $x and $y variables with the plus sign between them:

```
print "$x + $y = ";
```

In this particular case (since $x is 3 and $y is 5), it prints out this literal value: 3 + 5 =

Because the plus and the equals signs are inside quotation marks, they are treated as ordinary text elements. PHP doesn't do any calculation (such as addition or assignment) with them.

The next line does not contain any quotation marks:

```
print $x + $y;
```

It calculates the value of $x + $y and prints the result (8) to the web page.

---

### IN THE REAL WORLD

Numbers without any decimal point are called integers and numbers with decimal values are called real numbers. Computers store these two types differently, and this distinction sometimes leads to problems. PHP does its best to shield you from this type of issue.

For example, since the values 3 and 5 are both integers, the results of the addition, subtraction, and multiplication problems are also guaranteed to be integers. However, the quotient of two integers is often a real number. Many languages would either refuse to solve this problem or give an incomplete result. They might say that 3 / 5 I 0, rather than 0.6. PHP tries to convert things to the appropriate type whenever possible, and it usually does a pretty good job.

You sometimes need to control this behavior, however. The setType() function lets you force a particular variable into a particular type. You can look up the details in the online Help for PHP (at http://www.php.net).

Most of the math symbols you are familiar with also work with numeric variables. The plus sign (+) is used for addition, the minus sign (-) indicates subtraction, the asterisk (*) multiplies, and the forward slash (/) divides. The remainder of the program illustrates how PHP does subtraction, multiplication, and division.

It's important to recognize that two different pages are involved in the transaction. In this section, you learn how to link an HTML page to a particular script and how to write a script that expects certain form information.

## CREATING A FORM TO ASK A QUESTION

It's very typical for PHP programs to be made of two or more separate documents. An ordinary HTML page contains a form, which the user fills out. When the user presses the Submit button, the information in all the form elements is sent to a program specified by a special attribute of the form. This program processes the information from the form and returns a result, which looks to the user like an ordinary web page. To illustrate, look at the whatsName.html page in Figure 2.7.

**FIGURE 2.7**

This ordinary HTML page contains a form.

The `whatsName.html` page does not contain any PHP at all. It's simply an HTML page with a form on it. When the user clicks the Submit Query button, the page sends the value in the text area to a PHP program called `hiUser.php`. Figure 2.8 shows what happens when the `hiUser.php` program runs.

It's important to recognize that two different pages are involved in the transaction. In this section, you learn how to link an HTML page to a particular script and how to write a script that expects certain form information.

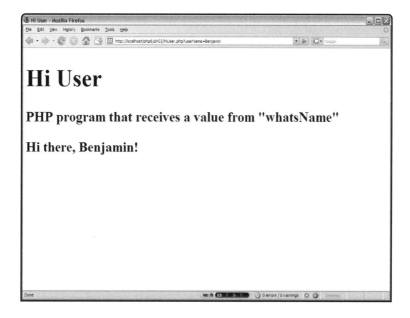

The resulting page uses the value from the original HTML form.

## Building an HTML Page with a Form

Forms are very useful when you want to get information from the user. To illustrate how this is done, look at the `whatsName.html` code:

```
<!DOCTYPE html PUBLIC "-//W3C//DTD XHTML 1.0 Strict//EN"
"http://www.w3.org/TR/xhtml1/DTD/xhtml1-strict.dtd">
<html lang="EN" dir="ltr" xmlns="http://www.w3.org/1999/xhtml">
<head>
<title>What's your name?</title>
<link rel = "stylesheet"
      type = "text/css"
      href = "whatsName.css" />
</head>
```

```
<body>
<h1>What's your name?</h1>
<h3>Writing a form for user input</h3>
<form method = "get"
      action = "hiUser.php">
  <fieldset>
    <label>
      Please type your name:
    </label>
    <input type = "text"
           name = "userName"
           value = "" />
    <input type = "submit" />
  </fieldset>
</form>
</body>
</html>
```

If you're familiar with XHTML forms, there is only one element of this page that may not be familiar to you. Take a careful look at the `form` tag. It contains two new attributes. `action` is one of those attributes. The other, `method`, indicates how the data is sent to the browser. `get` and `post` are the two primary methods. `post` is the most powerful and flexible, so it is the one I use most often in this book. However, you see some interesting ways to use `get` later in this chapter in "Sending Data without a Form." For that reason, I show the `get` technique first.

**TIP** If you've spent more time in HTML than XHTML, there may be some other unfamiliar elements in this code. Note that I'm using the `fieldset` and `label` tags to describe the organization of the form. This allows me to use an external CSS file to describe exactly how the page should look.

Please see my website at `http://www.aharrisbooks.net` for plenty of resources on how to build XHTML pages with CSS formatting.

## Setting the Action Attribute to a Script File

The other attribute of the `form` tag is the `action` attribute. It determines the URL of a program, designed to read the page and respond with another page. The URL can be an absolute reference (which begins with http:// and contains the entire domain name of the response program), or a relative reference (meaning the program is in the same directory as the original web page). When possible, I prefer relative references because they are cleaner and easier to manage.

The `whatsName.html` page contains a form with its `action` attribute set to `hiUser.php`. Whenever the user clicks the Submit button, the values of all the fields (only one in this case) are packed up and sent to a program called `hiUser.php`, which is expected to be in the same directory as the original `whatsName.html` page.

## Writing a Script to Retrieve the Data

The code for `hiUser.php` expects to be run from `whatsName.html`. The form that called the `hiUser.php` code is expected to have an element called `userName`. Take a look at the code for `hiUser.php` and see what I mean.

```
<!DOCTYPE html PUBLIC "-//W3C//DTD XHTML 1.0 Strict//EN"
"http://www.w3.org/TR/xhtml1/DTD/xhtml1-strict.dtd">
<html lang="EN" dir="ltr" xmlns="http://www.w3.org/1999/xhtml">
<head>
<title>Hi User</title>
</head>
<body>
<h1>Hi User</h1>
<h3>PHP program that receives a value from "whatsName"</h3>

<?php

$userName = filter_input(INPUT_GET, "userName");
print "<h3>Hi there, $userName!</h3>";

?>

</body>
</html>
```

Like many PHP pages, `hiUser.php` is mainly HTML. The only thing that's different is the two new lines of code. One creates a variable called `$userName`, and the other uses that variable in a `print` statement.

The first line extracts the user name from the previous form. When the form is sent to the server, all the form data is passed to the server, which can extract the data. The `filter_input()` function is one way to retrieve that data.

When you call `filter_input()`, you need at least two parameters. The first indicates where PHP should look for the data. `INPUT_GET` is a predefined value, meaning the data was sent through the `GET` mechanism. (Of course, you can also use `INPUT_POST` if that's how the data was sent.) The second parameter is the name of the value. It corresponds to the `name` attribute in the previous form. In this case, the form had one input element named "`userName`." The value of that text field is now extracted and stored into a PHP variable named `$userName`. Almost all PHP and HTML interactions work this way; you build an HTML form with a bunch of input elements, and write PHP code to extract those elements into variables.

---

### IRW

If this technique is so common, you might wonder why it isn't automatic. In the early days of PHP, it was. You could simply refer to a variable called `$userName` and if the previous form had an element with that name, the value of that element would "magically" be in the variable with no other work at all. Cool as this sounds, it opened up a lot of security problems, and now the option to automatically cull data from forms (called `register_globals`) is no longer available in PHP 6.

Often you'll also see another approach that looks like this:

```
$userName = $_REQUEST["userName"];
```

Or

```
$userName = $_GET["userName"];
```

These are very similar techniques for data retrieval, which are perfectly acceptable ways to perform the same task (retrieving data from a web form.) I explain how $_REQUEST and $_GET work in detail in Chapter 5, where I describe associative arrays. Throughout this book I tend to use the `filter_input()` technique described in this chapter instead, as it is slightly more secure and the preferred technique in PHP 6.

## SENDING DATA WITHOUT A FORM

It can be very handy to send data to a server-side program without using a form. This little-known trick can really enhance your web pages without requiring a lick of PHP programming. The Link Demo page (linkDemo.html) shown in Figures 2.9 and 2.10 illustrate this phenomenon.

### Understanding the get Method

All the links in the linkDemo.html page use a similar trick. As you recall from earlier in the chapter, form data can be sent to a program through two different methods. The post method is the technique usually in your forms, but you've been using the get method all along, because normal HTML requests actually are get requests. The get mechanism encodes all the data from the form into the URL before sending the request to the server. The server-side program can then pull all the information it needs from the URL. The interesting thing is that you can send form data to any program that knows how to read get requests by embedding the request in your URL. You don't really need a form!

**FIGURE 2.9**

The links on this page appear ordinary, but they are unusually powerful.

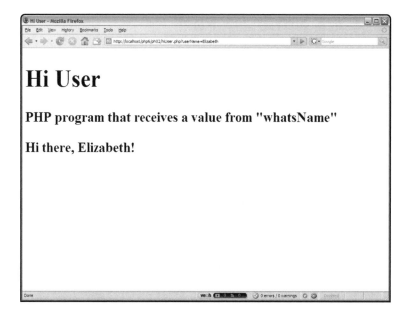

**FIGURE 2.10**

When I clicked the
Hi Elizabeth
link, I was taken to
the hiUser
program with the
value Elizabeth
automatically
sent to the
program!

Run the page again and take a look at the address bar. The URL of the resulting page looks like this (presuming you said the user's name is Andy):

```
http://localhost/ph02/hiUser.php?userName=Andy
```

The get method stashes all the form information into the URL using a special code. If you go back to the whatsName page and put in Andy Harris, you get a slightly different result:

```
http://12localhost/ph02/hiUser.php?userName=Andy+Harris
```

The space between Andy and Harris was converted to a plus sign because space characters cause a lot of confusion. When form data is transmitted, it often undergoes a number of similar transformations. All the translation is automatic in PHP programming, so you don't have to worry about it.

## Using a URL to Embed Form Data

If you understand how embedded data in a URL works, you can use a similar technique (sometimes called URL encoding) to harness any server-side program on the Internet (presuming it's set up to take get method data). When I examined the URLs of Google searches, I could see my search data in a field named q (for query, I suppose). I took a gamble that all the other fields would have default values, and wrote a hyperlink that incorporates a query. My link looked like this:

```
<li><a href = "http://www.google.com/search?q=php">
Google search for "php"</a></li>
```

Whenever the user clicks this link, it sets up a `get` method query to Google's search program. The result is a nifty Google search. One fun thing you might want to do is figure out how to set up canned versions of your most common queries in various search engines, so you can get updated results with one click. Figure 2.11 illustrates what happens when the user clicks the `Google search for "php"` link in the `linkDemo` page.

Figure 2.12 shows the results of this slightly more complex search.

```
<li><a href =
    "http://www.google.com/search?q=php beginner&num=50">
    50 "php beginner" sites</a> from google</li>
```

This approach has a down side. The program owner can change the program without telling you, and your link will no longer work correctly. Most web programmers assume that their programs are called only by the forms they originally built.

The other thing to consider is that people can do this with your programs. Just because you intend for your program to be called only by a form, doesn't mean that's how it always works. Such is the vibrant nature of the free-form Internet.

FIGURE 2.11

The link runs a search on
`www.google.com`
for the term "php."

FIGURE 2.12

The Google search
for "php beginner"
shows some really
intriguing book
offerings!

## Working with Multiple Field Queries

The second Google search has another interesting feature. Note that this search returned 50 results rather than the normal 20. The URL actually has two fields:

```
http://www.google.com/search?q=php beginner&num=50
```

The q field stands for the query, and the ampersand (&) is used to indicate there is another form element called num with a value of 50.

Of course, the question is how I knew I could set this value. I looked at the advanced search form and viewed the HTML to see what fields it sends. The number of pages is sent in a list called num, so it's natural to assume that the program is expecting a variable called num.

## Building a Pre-formatted Query

As one more practical example, the code for the National Weather Service link looks like this:

```
<li><a href =
    "http://forecast.weather.gov/zipcity.php?inputstring=46038">
    National Weather Service Forecast</a> for my neighborhood.</li>
```

While this link looks a little more complex, it doesn't require any special knowledge. I simply searched the National Weather Service (NWS) website until I found a search script where I can enter a zip code. With a little detective work (looking at the HTML source), I was able to determine that a single field named inputstring was being sent to a script called zipcity.php.

Apparently, NWS uses PHP. Interestingly, it doesn't really matter what type of server language is being used for this type of example, as long as it can read data sent through the GET mechanism.

I tested the link directly in my browser, then copied it and incorporated it into `linkDemo.html`. The weather page is automatically created by a PHP program based on the zip code. Any time I want to see the local weather, I can recall the same query even though the request doesn't come directly from the National Weather Service. This is a really easy way to customize your web page.

I've never actually seen the program at the weather service, but I know the PHP program requires a field named `inputstring`, because I figured it out from the form.

## Reading Input from Other Form Elements

A PHP program can read the input from any type of HTML form element. You can use the `filter_input()` function to extract any field from a form and convert it to a variable in PHP. The initial value of that variable will be passed from the original form.

## INTRODUCING THE borderMaker PROGRAM

To examine most of the various form elements, I built a simple page to demonstrate various attributes of cascading style sheet (CSS) borders. The HTML program is shown in Figure 2.13.

**FIGURE 2.13**

The `borderMaker` `.html` page uses a text area, two list boxes, and a select group.

## Building the borderMaker.html Page

The borderMaker.html page contains a very typical form with most of the major input elements in it. The code for this form follows:

```
<!DOCTYPE html PUBLIC "-//W3C//DTD XHTML 1.0 Strict//EN"
"http://www.w3.org/TR/xhtml1/DTD/xhtml1-strict.dtd">
<html lang="EN" dir="ltr" xmlns="http://www.w3.org/1999/xhtml">
<head>
<title>Border Maker</title>
<style type = "text/css">
h1, h2, h3 {
  text-align:center;
}
textarea, button {
  display: block;
  margin-left: auto;
  margin-right: auto;
  margin-bottom: 1em;
}

table {
  margin-left: auto;
  margin-right: auto
}

</style>
</head>
<body>

<h1>Border Maker</h1>
<h3>Demonstrates how to read HTML form elements</h3>

<form method = "post"
      action = "borderMaker.php">

<div id = "input">
<h3>Text to modify</h3>
```

```
<textarea name = "basicText"
         rows = "10"
         cols = "40">
Four score and seven years ago our fathers brought forth on this
continent a new nation, conceived in liberty and dedicated to the
proposition that all men are created equal. Now we are engaged in a
great civil war, testing whether that nation or any nation so
conceived and so dedicated can long endure.
</textarea>
</div>

<table border = "2">
<tr>
  <td><h3>Border style</h3></td>
  <td colspan = "2"><h3>Border Size</h3></td>
</tr>

<tr>
<td>
<select name = "borderStyle">
  <option value = "ridge">ridge</option>
  <option value = "groove">groove</option>
  <option value = "double">double</option>
  <option value = "inset">inset</option>
  <option value = "outset">outset</option>
</select>
</td>
<td>


<select size = "5"
        name = "borderSize">
  <option value = "1">1</option>
  <option value = "2">2</option>
  <option value = "3">3</option>
  <option value = "5">5</option>
  <option value = "10">10</option>
</select>
</td>
```

```
<td>
<input type = "radio"
       name = "sizeType"
       value = "px"
       checked = "checked" />pixels<br />
<input type = "radio"
       name = "sizeType"
       value = "pt" />points<br />
<input type = "radio"
       name = "sizeType"
       value = "cm" />centimeters<br />
<input type = "radio"
       name = "sizeType"
       value = "in" />inches<br />
</td>
</tr>
</table>

<div>
<button type = "submit">
  show me
</button>
</div>
</form>

</body>
</html>
```

The `borderMaker.html` page is designed to interact with a PHP program called `borderMaker.php`, as you can see by inspection of the `action` attribute. Note that I added a `value` attribute for each option element, and the radio buttons all have the same name but different values. The `value` attribute becomes very important when your program is destined to be read by a program. Finally, the Submit button is critical, because nothing interesting happens until the user submits the form.

 **TRICK**     I didn't include checkboxes in this particular example. I show you how checkboxes work in Chapter 3, "Controlling Your Code with Conditions and Functions," because you need conditional statements to work with them. Conditional statements allow your programs to make choices.

## Reading the Form Elements

The `borderMaker.php` program expects input from `borderMaker.html`. When the user submits the HTML form, the PHP program produces results like those shown in Figure 2.14.

In general, it doesn't matter what type of element you use on an HTML form. The PHP interpreter simply looks at each element's name and value. By the time the information gets to the server, it doesn't matter what type of input element was used. PHP automatically creates a variable corresponding to each form element. The value of that variable is the value of the element. The code used in `borderMaker.php` illustrates:

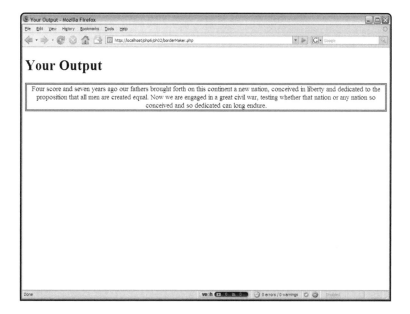

**FIGURE 2.14**

The `borderMaker .php` code reacts to all the various input elements on the form.

```
<!DOCTYPE html PUBLIC "-//W3C//DTD XHTML 1.0 Strict//EN"
"http://www.w3.org/TR/xhtml1/DTD/xhtml1-strict.dtd">
<html lang="EN" dir="ltr" xmlns="http://www.w3.org/1999/xhtml">
<head>
<title>Your Output</title>
</head>
<body>
<h1>Your Output</h1>
<div style = "text-align: center">
<?php
```

```
//retrieve all the variables
$basicText = filter_input(INPUT_POST, "basicText");
$borderSize = filter_input(INPUT_POST, "borderSize");
$sizeType = filter_input(INPUT_POST, "sizeType");
$borderStyle = filter_input(INPUT_POST, "borderStyle");


$theStyle = <<<HERE
"border-width:$borderSize$sizeType;
border-style:$borderStyle;
border-color:green"
HERE;

print "<div style = $theStyle>";
print $basicText;
print "</div>";


?>
</div>

</body>
</html>
```

In the case of text boxes and text areas, the user types in the value directly. In borderMaker.html, there is a text area called basicText. The PHP interpreter creates a variable called $basicText. Anything typed into that text box (as a default, the first few lines of the Gettysburg Address) becomes the value of the $basicText variable.

 Note that if you run this program on its own (without running the HTML page first) you'll get a blank screen and probably some HTML errors, because the PHP program is expecting to find variables that aren't there. PHP programs are usually run directly from HTML programs. I show a great trick for eliminating this problem in Chapter 3, where you learn to build PHP programs that create their own forms when they need them.

## Reading Select Elements

Recall that both drop-down lists and list boxes are created with the select object. That object has a name attribute. Each of the possible choices in the list box is an option object. Each option object has a value attribute.

The name of the select object becomes the variable name. For example, border-Maker.html has two select objects: borderSize and borderStyle. The PHP program must retrieve two corresponding variables: $borderSize and $borderStyle. Because the user has nowhere to type a value into a select object, the values it can return must be encoded into the structure of the form itself. The value of whichever option the user selected is sent to the PHP program as the value of the corresponding variable. For example, if the user chose groove as the border style, the $borderStyle variable has the value "groove" in it.

---

### IN THE REAL WORLD

The options value doesn't necessarily have to be what the user sees on the form. This "hidden value" is handy if you want to show the user one thing but send something else to the server. For example, you might want to let the user choose from several colors. In this case, you might want to create a list box that shows the user several color names, but the value property corresponding to each of the option objects might have the actual hexadecimal values. Similar tricks are used in online shopping environments, where you might let the user choose an item by its name, but the value associated with that item might be its catalog number, which is easier to work with in a database environment.

---

 You can have multiple selections enabled in a list box. In that case, the variable contains a list of responses. While managing this list is not difficult, it is a topic for another chapter (Chapter 4, "Loops and Arrays," to be specific). For now, concentrate on the singular list box style.

## Reading Radio Groups

CSS allows the developer to indicate sizes with a variety of measurements. This is an ideal place for a group of radio buttons because only one unit of measure is appropriate at a time. Even though there are four different radio buttons on the borderDemo.html page with the name sizeType, the PHP program will only extract one $sizeType variable. The value associated with whichever option is selected will become the value of the $sizeType variable. Note that like option elements, it is possible for the value of a radio button to be different than the text displayed beside it. Also keep in mind that it's best to set the checked property of one radio button to guarantee that the variable always has a value.

## DECIDING ON A FORM ELEMENT

You might wonder if all these form elements are necessary, since they all boil down to a name and value by the time they get to the PHP interpreter. The various kinds of user interface elements do make a difference in a few ways:

- It's easier (for many users) to use a mouse than to type. Whenever possible, it is nice to add lists, checks, and options so the user can navigate your forms more quickly. Typing is often much slower than the kinds of input afforded by the other elements.

- Interface elements (especially the drop-down list box) are extremely efficient in terms of screen space. You can pack a lot of choices on a small screen by using drop-downs effectively. While you might not think space is an issue, take a look at how many people are now surfing the web with PDAs and cell phones.

- Your life as a programmer is much easier if you can predict what the user will send. When users type things, they make spelling and grammar mistakes, use odd abbreviations, and are just unpredictable. If you limit choices whenever possible, you are less likely to frustrate users.

## RETURNING TO THE STORY PROGRAM

The Story program introduced at the beginning of this chapter is an opportunity to bring together all the new elements you learned. The program doesn't introduce anything new, but it helps you see a larger context.

## Designing the Story

Even though this is not an especially difficult program to write, you run into problems if you simply open your text editor and start blasting away. It really pays to plan ahead. The most important thinking happens before you write a single line of code.

Start by thinking about your story. You can write your own story or modify some existing text for humorous effect. I raided a nursery rhyme book for my story. Regardless of how you come up with a story, have it in place before you start writing code. I wrote the original unmodified version of "Little Boy Blue" in my text editor first so I could admire its artistic genius—and then mangle it beyond recognition.

As you look over the original prose, look for key words you can take out, and try to find a description that hints at the original word without giving anything away. For example, I printed my story, circled the word blue in the original poem, and wrote color on another piece of paper. Keep doing this until you've found several words you can take out of the original story. You should have a document with a bunch of holes in it, and a list of hints. Mine looked like Figure 2.15.

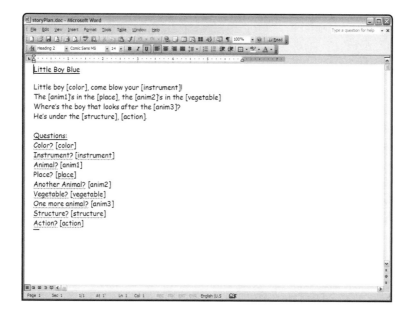

FIGURE 2.15

I thought through the story and the word list before writing any code.

## IN THE REAL WORLD

Figure 2.15 shows the plan written as a Word document. Although things are sometimes done this way (especially in a professional programming environment), I really wrote the plan on paper. I reproduced it in a cleaner format because you don't deserve to be subjected to my handwriting.

I usually plan my programs on paper, chalkboard, or dry erase board. I avoid planning programs on the computer, because it's too tempting to start programming immediately. It's important to make your plan describe what you want to do in English before you worry about how you'll implement the plan. Most beginners (and a lot of pros) start programming way too early, and get stuck as a result. You'll see, throughout the rest of this chapter, how this plan evolves into a working program.

## Building the HTML Page

With the basic outline from Figure 2.15, it becomes clear how the Story program should be created. It should have two parts. The first is an HTML page that prompts the user for all the various words. Here's the code for my version:

```
<!DOCTYPE html PUBLIC "-//W3C//DTD XHTML 1.0 Strict//EN"
"http://www.w3.org/TR/xhtml1/DTD/xhtml1-strict.dtd">
<html lang="EN" dir="ltr" xmlns="http://www.w3.org/1999/xhtml">
<head>
<title>Story</title>
<link rel = "stylesheet"
      type = "text/css"
      href = "story.css" />

</head>
<body>
<h1>Story</h1>
<h3>Please fill in the blanks below, and I'll tell
    you a story</h3>
<form method = "post"
      action = "story.php">

<fieldset>
  <label>color:</label>
  <input type = "text"
         name = "color" />

  <label>instrument</label>
  <input type = "text"
         name = "instrument" />

  <label>animal</label>
  <input type = "text"
         name = "anim1" />

  <label>another animal</label>
  <input type = "text"
         name = "anim2" />
```

```
<label>one more animal:</label>
<input type = "text"
       name = "anim3" />

<label>place: </label>
<input type = "text"
       name = "place" />

<label>vegetable: </label>
<input type = "text"
       name = "vegetable" />

<label>structure: </label>
<input type = "text"
       name = "structure" />

<label>action: </label>
<select name = "action">
  <option value = "fast asleep">fast asleep</option>
  <option value = "drinking cappuccino">drinking cappuccino</option>
  <option value = "wandering around aimlessly">wandering around
aimlessly</option>
  <option value = "doing nothing in particular">doing nothing in
particular</option>
</select>

<button type = "submit">
  Tell me the story
</button>
</fieldset>

</form>
</body>
</html>
```

There's nothing terribly exciting about the HTML. In fact, since I had the plan, I knew exactly what kinds of things I was asking for and created form elements to ask each question. I used a list box for the last question so I could put in some interesting suggestions. Note that I changed the order a little bit just to throw the user off.

You might also note that I'm depending on a CSS file for the formatting. If you just type this HTML in your editor, it won't look very nice. You'll need the CSS file (included on the CD-ROM) if you want things to look nice.

Check a few things when you're writing a page that connects to a script:

- Make sure you've added an action attribute.
- Ensure you've got the correct action attribute in the form tag.
- Make sure each form element has an appropriate name attribute.
- If you have radio or option objects, make sure each one has an appropriate value.
- Be sure there is a Submit button somewhere in your form.
- Don't forget to end your form tag. Your browser may work fine if you forget to include </form>, but you don't know how the users' browsers will act.
- Be sure the form validates as XHTML strict. This can prevent many other difficult-to-find errors.

## Building the Story

The story itself is very simple to build if you've planned and ensured that the variables are working right. All I had to do was write out the story as it was written in the plan, with the variables incorporated in the appropriate places. Here's the code for the finished story.php page:

```
<!DOCTYPE html PUBLIC "-//W3C//DTD XHTML 1.0 Strict//EN"
"http://www.w3.org/TR/xhtml1/DTD/xhtml1-strict.dtd">
<html lang="EN" dir="ltr" xmlns="http://www.w3.org/1999/xhtml">
<head>
<title>Little Boy Who?</title>
<style type = "text/css">
  h1, h2 {
    text-align: center;
  }
</style>

</head>
<body>

<h1>Little Boy Who?</h1>
```

```php
<?php

$color = filter_input(INPUT_POST, "color");
$instrument = filter_input(INPUT_POST, "instrument");
$anim1 = filter_input(INPUT_POST, "anim1");
$anim2 = filter_input(INPUT_POST, "anim2");
$anim3 = filter_input(INPUT_POST, "anim3");
$place = filter_input(INPUT_POST, "place");
$vegetable = filter_input(INPUT_POST, "vegetable");
$structure = filter_input(INPUT_POST, "structure");
$action = filter_input(INPUT_POST, "action");

print <<<HERE
<h2>
Little Boy $color, come blow your $instrument!<br />
The $anim1's in the $place, the $anim2's in the $vegetable.<br />
Where's the boy that looks after the $anim3?<br />
He's under the $structure, $action.
</h2>
HERE;
?>



</body>
</html>
```

Once you have created the story, set up the variables, and ensured that all the variables are sent correctly, the story program itself turns out to be almost trivial. Most of the story.php code is plain HTML. The only part that's in PHP is one long print statement, which uses the print <<<HERE syntax to print a long line of HTML text with PHP variables embedded inside. The story itself is this long concatenated text.

 Check the results of your PHP scripts with an HTML validator, too. This is most easily done with the HTML validator extension for Firefox. The validator can help you find small errors in your HTML that you would not have located otherwise (but that would eventually cause you problems).

## SUMMARY

In this chapter, you learned some incredibly important concepts: what variables are, and how to create them in PHP; how to connect a form to a PHP program with modifications to the form's method and `action` attributes; and how to write normal links to send values to server-side scripts. You built programs that respond to various kinds of input elements, including drop-down lists, radio buttons, and list boxes. You went through the process of writing a program from beginning to end, including the critical planning stage, creating a form for user input, and using that input to generate interesting output.

---

### CHALLENGES

1. Write a web page that asks the user for his first and last name and then uses a PHP script to write a form letter to that person. Inform the user he might be a millionaire.
2. Write a custom web page that uses embedded data tricks to generate custom links for your favorite web searches, local news and weather, and other elements of interest to you.
3. Write your own story game. Find or write some text to modify, create an appropriate input form, and output the story with a PHP script.

---

# CHAPTER 3

# CONTROLLING YOUR CODE WITH CONDITIONS AND FUNCTIONS

Most of the really interesting things you can do with a computer involve letting it make decisions. Actually, the computer only appears able to decide things. The programmer generates code that tells the computer exactly what to do in different circumstances. In this chapter, you learn how to control the flow of a program; specifically, how to:

- Create a random integer
- Use the `if` structure to change the program's behavior
- Write conditions to evaluate variables
- Work with the `else` clause to provide instructions when a condition is not met
- Use the `switch` statement to work with multiple choices
- Build functions to better manage code
- Write programs that can create their own forms

## EXAMINING THE PETALS AROUND THE ROSE GAME

The `Petals Around the Rose` game, featured in Figure 3.1, illustrates all the new skills you learn in this chapter.

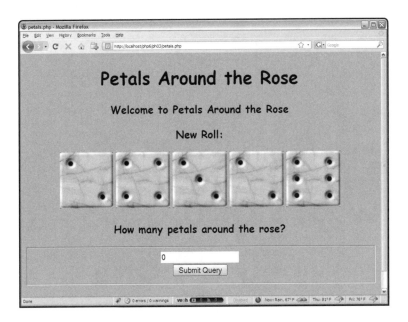

**FIGURE 3.1**

This is a new twist on an old dice puzzle.

The premise of the Petals game is very simple. The computer rolls a set of five dice and asks the user to guess the number of petals around the rose. The user enters a number and presses the button. The computer indicates whether this value is correct, and provides a new set of dice. Once the user understands the secret, it's a very easy game, but it can take a long time to figure out how it works. Try the game before you learn how it's done.

If you're having a hard time figuring out the puzzle, don't feel too bad. According to *Personal Computing* magazine, this game was shown to a number of software executives on a plane trip in the late '70s. Most of the people present figured it out, but the person who took the longest time to come to the solution was Bill Gates.

## CREATING A RANDOM NUMBER

The dice game, like many other games, relies on random number generation to make things interesting. Most programming languages have at least one way to create random numbers. PHP's rand() function makes it easy to create random numbers.

### Viewing the Roll Em Program

The Roll Em program shown in Figure 3.2 demonstrates how the rand function can generate virtual dice.

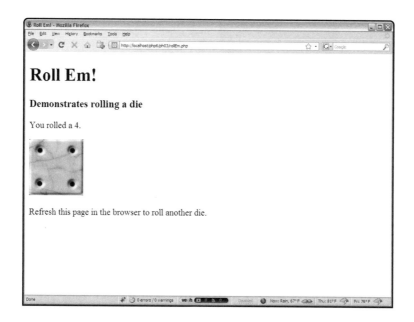

**FIGURE 3.2**

The die roll is randomly generated by PHP.

The code for the Roll Em program shows how easy random number generation is:

```
<!DOCTYPE html PUBLIC "-//W3C//DTD XHTML 1.0 Strict//EN"
"http://www.w3.org/TR/xhtml1/DTD/xhtml1-strict.dtd">
<html lang="EN" dir="ltr" xmlns="http://www.w3.org/1999/xhtml">
<head>
<title>Roll Em!</title>
</head>
<body>
<h1>Roll Em!</h1>
<h3>Demonstrates rolling a die</h3>

<?php

$roll = rand(1,6);

print <<< HERE

<p>You rolled a $roll.</p>
<p>
  <img src = "die$roll.jpg"
       alt = "die: $roll" />
```

```
</p>

HERE;

?>

<p>
Refresh this page in the browser to roll another die.
</p>

</body>
</html>
```

The rand function generates a random number between 1 and 6 (including the values 1 and 6) and stores the resulting value in the $roll variable. The rand function expects two parameters: The first value is the lowest number and the second value represents the highest number.

Since I want to replicate an ordinary six-sided die, I told the rand() function to return a value between 1 and 6. Since I knew that rand() would return a value, I assigned that resulting value to the variable $roll. By the time the following line has finished executing, the $roll variable has a random value in it:

```
$roll = rand(1,6);
```

The lowest possible value is 1, the highest possible value is 6, and the value will not have a decimal part. (In other words, it will never be 1.5.)

**TRICK** If you're coming from another programming language, you might be surprised at the way random numbers are generated in PHP. Most languages allow you to create a random floating-point value between 0 and 1, and then require you to transform that value to whatever range you want. PHP allows—in fact, requires—you to create random integers within a range, which is usually what you want anyway. If you really want a value between 0 and 1, you can generate a random number between 0 and 1,000 and then divide that value by 1,000.

## Printing a Corresponding Image

Notice the sneaky way I used variable interpolation in the preceding code. I carefully named my first image die1.jpg, the second die2.jpg, and so on. When I was ready to print an image to the screen, I used an ordinary HTML image tag with the source set to die$roll.jpg. If $roll is 3, the image shows die3.jpg.

**NOTE**  Note that this example expects files with the specific names in the same directory as the PHP program, so you must have a file called die3.jpg in the same directory as your program or things will not work correctly.

Variable interpolation can be a wonderful trick if you know how the filenames are structured. You might recall from Chapter 2, "Using Variables and Input," that interpolation is the technique that allows you to embed a variable in a quoted string by simply using its name.

## Using the if Statement to Control Program Flow

One of the most interesting things computers do is appear to make decisions. The decision-making ability is an illusion. The programmer stores very specific instructions inside a computer, and it acts on those instructions. The simplest form of this behavior is a structure called the if statement.

---

### In the Real World

The dice games in this chapter demonstrate the power of graphical images to make your programs more interesting and fun. You can get graphics for your programs a number of ways. The easiest is to find an existing image on the web. Although this is technically very simple, many of the images on the web are owned by somebody. Respect the intellectual property rights of the original owners. Get permission for any images you use.

Another alternative is to create the graphics yourself. Even if you don't have any artistic talent at all, modern software and technology make it quite easy to generate passable graphics. You can do a lot with a digital camera and a freeware graphics editor. Even if you hire a professional artist to do graphics for your program, you might still need to be able to sketch what you are looking for. This book's CD has a couple of very powerful freeware image-editing programs, including Gimp (http://www.gimp.org) and IrfanView (http://www.irfanview.com).

---

### Introducing the Ace Program

You can improve the Roll Em program with an if structure. Enter the Ace program. Figure 3.3 shows the result when the program rolls any value except 1.

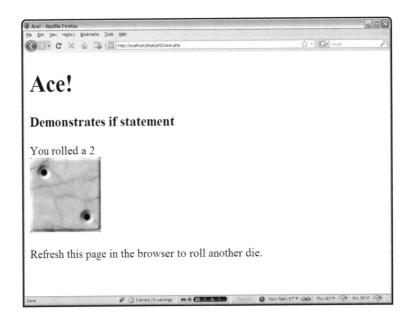

**FIGURE 3.3**

When the roll is not a 1, nothing interesting happens.

However, this program does something exciting (okay, moderately exciting), when it rolls a 1, as you can see from Figure 3.4.

**FIGURE 3.4**

An ace produces an extravagant multimedia event. I'll add the dancing hippos later..

## Creating a Condition

On the surface, the behavior of the Ace program is very straightforward: It does something interesting only if the die roll is 1, and it doesn't do that interesting thing in any other case. While it is a simple idea, the implications are profound. The same simple mechanism in the Ace program is the foundation of all complicated computer behavior, from flight simulators to heart monitors. Look at the code for the Ace program and see if you can spot the new element:

```
<!DOCTYPE html PUBLIC "-//W3C//DTD XHTML 1.0 Strict//EN"
"http://www.w3.org/TR/xhtml1/DTD/xhtml1-strict.dtd">
<html lang="EN" dir="ltr" xmlns="http://www.w3.org/1999/xhtml">
<head>
  <title>Ace!</title>
</head>
<body>
<h1>Ace!</h1>
<h3>Demonstrates if statement</h3>
<div>
<?php
$roll = rand(1,6);
print "You rolled a $roll";

if ($roll == 1){
  print "<h1>That's an ace!!!!!</h1>";
} // end if

print "<br />";
print "<img src = \"die$roll.jpg\" alt = \"die: $roll\" />";
?>
</div>
<p>
Refresh this page in the browser to roll another die.
</p>
</body>
</html>
```

The secret to this program is the segment that looks like this:

```
if ($roll == 1){
  print "<h1>That's an ace!!!!!</h1>";
} // end if
```

The line that prints "That's an ace!!!!!" doesn't happen every time the program is run. It only happens if a certain condition is true. The if statement sets up a condition for evaluation. In this case, the condition is read "$roll is equal to 1." If that condition is true, all the code between the left brace ({) and the right brace (}) evaluates. If the condition is not true, the code between the braces is skipped altogether.

A condition can be thought of as an expression that can be evaluated as true or false. Any expression that can return a true or false value can be used as a condition. Most conditions look much like the one in the Ace program. This condition checks the variable $roll to see if it is equal to the value 1.

Note that equality is indicated by two equals signs (==).

This is important, because computer programs are not nearly as flexible as humans. We humans often use the same symbol for different purposes. While computer languages can do this, it often leads to problems. The single equals sign is reserved for assignment. You should read this line as x gets five, indicating that the value 5 is being assigned to the variable $x:

```
$x = 5;
```

The following code fragment should be read as "x is equal to five", as it is testing equality.

```
$x == 5;
```

It is essentially asking whether x is equal to 5. A condition such as $x == 5 does not stand on its own. Instead, it is used inside some sort of other structure, such as an if statement.

## Exploring Comparison Operators

Equality (==) is not the only type of comparison PHP allows. You can compare a variable and a value or two variables using a number of comparison operators. Table 3.1 describes comparison operators.

These comparison operators work on any type of data, although the results might be a little strange when you use these mathematical operators on non-numeric data. For example, if you have a condition like the following, you get the result true:

```
"a" < "b"
```

## TABLE 3.1    COMPARISON OPERATORS

| Operator | Description |
| --- | --- |
| == | equal to |
| < | less than |
| > | greater than |
| <= | less than or equal to |
| >= | greater than or equal to |
| != | not equal to |

You get that result because alphabetically, the letter a is earlier than b, so it has a "smaller" value.

## Creating an if Statement

An if statement begins with the keyword if followed by a condition inside parentheses. After the closing parenthesis is a left brace: {. You can put as many lines of code between the left brace and right brace as you wish. Any code between the braces is executed only if the condition is true. If the condition is false, program control flows to the next line after the right brace.

It is not necessary to put a semicolon on a line ending with a brace. It is customary to indent all the code between the left and right braces.

## CODE STYLE

The PHP processor ignores the spaces and carriage returns in your PHP code, so you might wonder if it matters to pay such attention to how code is indented, where the braces go, and so on. While the PHP processor doesn't care how you format your code, human readers do. Programmers have passionate arguments about how you should format your code.

If writing code with a group (for instance, in a large project or for a class), you are usually given a style guide you are expected to follow. When working on your own, the specific style you adopt is not as important as being consistent in your coding. The particular stylistic conventions I adopted for this book are reasonably common, relatively readable, and easily adapted to a number of languages.

If you don't have your own programming style, the one in this book is a good starting place. However, if your team leader or teacher requires another style, adapt to it. Regardless of the specific style guidelines you use, it makes a lot of sense to indent your code, place comments liberally throughout your program, and use whitespace to make your program easier to read and debug.

**TRAP**

Do not put a semicolon at the end of the `if` line. The following code prints "we must be near a black hole."

```
if ("day" == "night") ; {
print "we must be near a black hole";
} // end if
```

When the processor sees the semicolon following ("day" = = "night"), it thinks there is no code to evaluate if the condition is true. The condition is effectively ignored. Essentially, the braces indicate that an entire group of lines is to be treated as one structure, and that structure is part of the current logical line.

## WORKING WITH NEGATIVE RESULTS

The `Ace` program shows how to write code that handles a condition. Much of the time, you want the program to do one thing if the condition is true, and something else if it's false. Most languages include a special variant of the `if` statement to handle exactly this type of contingency.

## DEMONSTRATING THE ACE OR NOT PROGRAM

The `Ace or Not` program is built from the `Ace` program, but it has an important difference, as you can see from Figures 3.5 and 3.6.

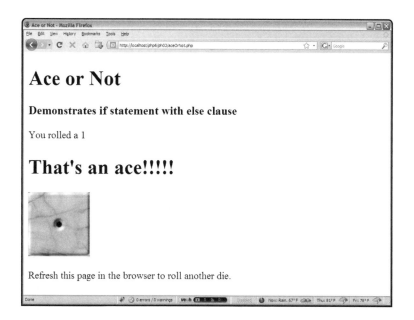

FIGURE 3.5

If the program rolls a 1, it still hollers out "That's an ace!!!!!"

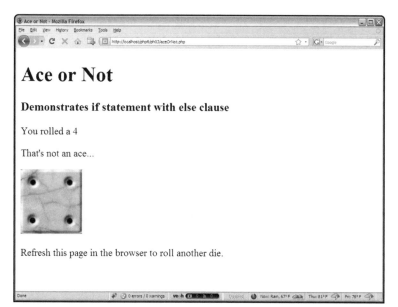

FIGURE 3.6

If the program rolls anything but a 1, it still has a message for the user.

The program does one thing when the condition is true and something else when the condition is false.

## Using the else Clause

The code for the Ace or Not program shows how the else clause can allow for multiple behaviors based on different conditions:

```
<!DOCTYPE html PUBLIC "-//W3C//DTD XHTML 1.0 Strict//EN"
"http://www.w3.org/TR/xhtml1/DTD/xhtml1-strict.dtd">
<html lang="EN" dir="ltr" xmlns="http://www.w3.org/1999/xhtml">
<head>
<title>Ace or Not</title>
</head>
<body>
<h1>Ace or Not</h1>
<h3>Demonstrates if statement with else clause</h3>
<div>
<?php

$roll = rand(1,6);
print "<p>You rolled a $roll</p> \n";

if ($roll == 1){
  print "<h1>That's an ace!!!!!</h1> \n";
} else {
  print "<p>That's not an ace...</p> \n";
} // end if

print "<img src = \"die$roll.jpg\" alt = \"$roll\" />";
?>

<p>Refresh this page in the browser to roll another die.</p>

</div>
</body>
```

The interesting part of this code comes near the if statement:

```
if ($roll == 1){
  print "<h1>That's an ace!!!!!</h1> \n";
} else {
  print "<p>That's not an ace...</p> \n";
} // end if
```

If the condition $roll == 1 is true, the program prints "That's an ace!!!!!." If the condition is not true, the code between else and the end of the if structure is executed instead.

Notice the structure and indentation. One chunk of code (between the condition and the else statement, encased in braces) occurs if the condition is true. If the condition is false, the code between else and the end of the if structure (also in braces) is executed. You can put as much code as you wish in either segment. Only one of the segments runs (based on the condition), but you are guaranteed that one will execute.

## WORKING WITH MULTIPLE VALUES

Often you find yourself working with more complex data. For example, you might want to respond differently to each of the six possible die rolls. The Binary Dice program illustrated in Figures 3.7 and 3.8 demonstrates just such a situation by showing the base two representation of the die roll.

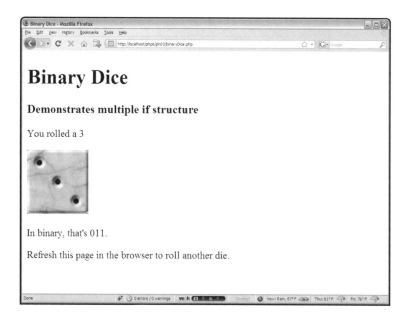

**FIGURE 3.7**

The roll is a 3, and the program shows the binary representation of that value.

## Writing the Binary Dice Program

The Binary Dice program has a slightly more complex if structure than the others, because the binary value should be different for each of six possible outcomes.

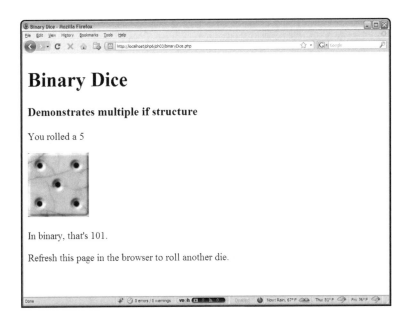

**FIGURE 3.8**

After rolling again, the program reports the binary representation of the new roll.

```
<!DOCTYPE html PUBLIC "-//W3C//DTD XHTML 1.0 Strict//EN"
"http://www.w3.org/TR/xhtml1/DTD/xhtml1-strict.dtd">
<html lang="EN" dir="ltr" xmlns="http://www.w3.org/1999/xhtml">
<head>
<title>Binary Dice</title>
</head>
<body>
<h1>Binary Dice</h1>
<h3>Demonstrates multiple if structure</h3>

<?php

$roll = rand(1,6);

if ($roll == 1){
  $binValue = "001";
} else if ($roll == 2){
  $binValue = "010";
} else if ($roll == 3){
  $binValue = "011";
} else if ($roll == 4){
```

```
  $binValue = "100";
} else if ($roll == 5){
  $binValue = "101";
} else if ($roll == 6){
  $binValue = "110";
} else {
  print "I don't know that one...";
} // end if

print <<< HERE
<p>You rolled a $roll</p>

<p>
  <img src = "die$roll.jpg"
       alt = "die: $roll" />
</p>

<p>
  In binary, that's $binValue.
</p>

HERE;
?>
<p>
Refresh this page in the browser to roll another die.
</p>
</body>
</html>
```

## Using Multiple else if Clauses

The Binary Dice program has only one if structure, but that structure has multiple else clauses. The first condition simply checks to see if $roll is equal to 1. If it is, the appropriate code runs, assigning the binary representation of 1 to the $binValue variable. If the first condition is false, the program looks at all the successive else if clauses until it finds a condition that evaluates to TRUE. If none of the conditions are true, the code in the else clause is executed.

**TRICK**

You may be surprised that I even put an else clause in this code. Since you know the value of $roll must be between 1 and 6 and you checked each of those values, the program should never need to evaluate the else clause. Things in programming don't always work out the way you expect, so it's a great idea to have some code in an else clause even if you don't expect to ever need it. It's much better to get a message from your program explaining that something unexpected occurred than to have your program blow up inexplicably while your users are using it.

The indentation for a multiple-condition if statement is useful so you can tell which parts of the code are part of the if structure, and which parts are meant to be executed if a particular condition turns out to be true.

## USING THE SWITCH STRUCTURE TO SIMPLIFY PROGRAMMING

The situation in the Binary Dice program happens often enough that another structure is designed for when you are comparing one variable to a number of possible values. The Switch Dice program in Figure 3.9 looks identical to the Binary Dice program as far as the user is concerned, except Switch Dice shows the roll's Roman numeral representation.

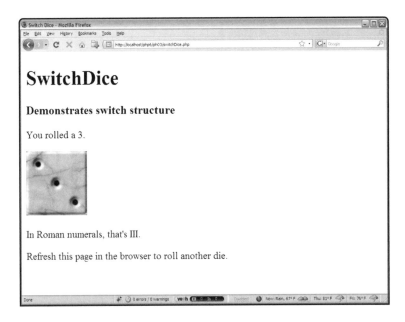

**FIGURE 3.9**

This version shows a die roll in Roman numerals.

While the outward appearance of the last two programs is extremely similar, the underlying code is changed to illustrate a very handy device called the switch structure. This device begins by defining an expression, and then defines a series of branches based on the value of that expression.

## Building the Switch Dice Program

The Switch Dice program code looks different from the Binary Dice code, but the results are essentially the same—except this program speaks Latin rather than Geek (sorry for the terrible pun):

```
<!DOCTYPE html PUBLIC "-//W3C//DTD XHTML 1.0 Strict//EN"
"http://www.w3.org/TR/xhtml1/DTD/xhtml1-strict.dtd">
<html lang="EN" dir="ltr" xmlns="http://www.w3.org/1999/xhtml">
<head>
<title>Switch Dice</title>
</head>
<body>
<h1>SwitchDice</h1>
<h3>Demonstrates switch structure</h3>

<?php
$roll = rand(1,6);

switch ($roll){
  case 1:
    $romValue = "I";
    break;
  case 2:
    $romValue = "II";
    break;
  case 3:
    $romValue = "III";
    break;
  case 4:
    $romValue = "IV";
    break;
  case 5:
    $romValue = "V";
    break;
  case 6:
```

```
    $romValue = "VI";
    break;
  default:
    print "This is an illegal die!";
} // end switch


print <<< HERE

<p>You rolled a $roll.</p>

<p>
  <img src = "die$roll.jpg"
       alt = "die: $roll" />
</p>

<p>In Roman numerals, that's $romValue.</p>

HERE;

?>
<p>
Refresh this page in the browser to roll another die.
</p>
</body>
</html>
```

## Using the switch Structure

The switch structure is optimal for when you have one variable to compare against a number of possible values. Use the switch keyword followed, in parentheses, by the name of the variable you wish to evaluate. A set of braces indicates that the next block of code focuses on evaluating this variable's possible values.

For each possible value, use the case statement, followed by the value, followed by a colon. End each case with a break statement, which indicates the program should stop thinking about this particular case and get ready for the next one.

**TRAP** The use of the `break` statement is probably the trickiest part of using the `switch` statement—especially if you are familiar with a language such as Visual Basic, which does not require such a construct. It's important to add the `break` statement to the end of each case, or the program flow simply "falls through" to the next possible value, even if that value would not otherwise evaluate to true. As a beginner, you should always place the `break` statement at the end of each case.

The last case, which works just like the `else` clause of the multi-value `if` statement, is called `default`. It defines code to execute if none of the other cases are active; it's smart to test for a `default` case even if you think it is impossible for the computer to get to this default option. Crazy things happen. It's good to be prepared for them.

## COMBINING A FORM AND ITS RESULTS

Most of your PHP programs up to now have had two distinct files. An HTML file has a form, which calls a PHP program. It can be tedious to keep track of two separate files. Use the `if` statement to combine both functions into one page.

The `Hi User` program shown in Figures 3.10 and 3.11 looks much like its counterpart in Chapter 2, "Using Variables and Input," but it has an important difference. Rather than being an HTML page and a separate PHP program, the entire program resides in one file on the server.

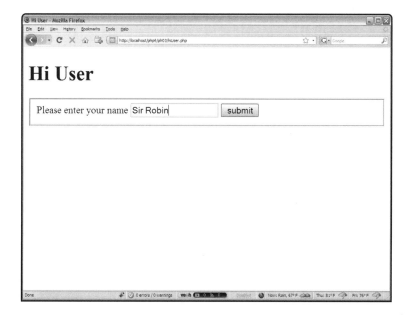

**FIGURE 3.10**

The HTML page is actually produced through the "Hi User" PHP code.

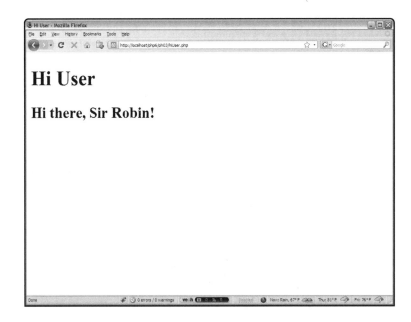

**FIGURE 3.11**

The result is
produced by
exactly the same
"Hi User"
program.

The code for the new version of hiUser shows how to achieve this trick:

```
<!DOCTYPE html PUBLIC "-//W3C//DTD XHTML 1.0 Strict//EN"
"http://www.w3.org/TR/xhtml1/DTD/xhtml1-strict.dtd">
<html lang="EN" dir="ltr" xmlns="http://www.w3.org/1999/xhtml">
<head>
<title>Hi User</title>
</head>
<body>
<h1>Hi User</h1>

<?php

if (filter_has_var(INPUT_POST, "userName")){

  // the form exists, so work with it
  $userName = filter_input(INPUT_POST, "userName");
  print "<h2>Hi there, $userName!</h2> \n";

} else {
```

```
    //there's no input. Create the form
    print <<< HERE
    <form action = ""
         method = "post">
    <fieldset>
      <label>Please enter your name</label>
      <input type = "text"
            name = "userName" />
      <button type = "submit">
        submit
      </button>
    </fieldset>
    </form>
HERE;


} // end 'value exists' if


?>


</body>
</html>
```

This program begins by looking for the existence of a variable called $userName. There is no $userName variable the first time the program is called, because the program was not called from a form. I anticipate this problem by checking first for the existence of the variable:

```
if (filter_has_var(INPUT_POST, "userName")){
  // the form exists, so work with it
```

The filter_has_var() function is very similar to the filter_input() function. It expects an input type (usually INPUT_POST or INPUT_GET) and a variable name. However, filter_has_var() is a Boolean function, which means it returns either true or false. If the previous form had a userName field, the function returns true (even if that field is empty). If the field does not exist, the function returns the value false.

Testing for the existence of a variable really tests to see if this is the first pass through the program (there will be more than one). If the program has never been called before, the variable doesn't exist. If the variable doesn't exist yet, the program creates the appropriate form to get the data from the user. If the variable does exist, the program branches over to code that manipulates that data.

The key idea here is that the program runs more than once. When the user first links to hiUser.php, the program creates a form. The user enters a value on the form, and presses the Submit button. This causes exactly the same program to be run again on the server. This time, though, the $userName variable is not empty, so rather than generating a form, the program uses the variable's value in a greeting.

Server-side programming frequently works in this way. It isn't uncommon for a user to call the same program many times in succession as part of solving a particular problem. You often use branching structures such as the if and switch statements to direct the program flow based on the user's current state of activity.

**TIP** If you're using a very old version of PHP (prior to 5.2), you may not have access to filter_has_var(). In this case, extract the value from the form using $_REQUEST, and then use the empty() function to determine if that variable has a value. See Chapter 5 for more on using the $_REQUEST technique.

## RESPONDING TO CHECKBOXES

Now that you know how to use the if structure and the input_has_vars() function, you can work with checkboxes. Take a look at the following HTML code:

```
<!DOCTYPE html PUBLIC "-//W3C//DTD XHTML 1.0 Strict//EN"
"http://www.w3.org/TR/xhtml1/DTD/xhtml1-strict.dtd">
<html lang="EN" dir="ltr" xmlns="http://www.w3.org/1999/xhtml">
<head>
<title>Checkbox Demo</title>
<link rel = "stylesheet"
      type = "text/css"
      href = "checkDemo.css" />
</head>
<body>
<h1>Checkbox Demo</h1>

<h2>Demonstrates checkboxes</h2>

<form action = "checkDemo.php"
      method = "post">

<fieldset>
  <legend>What would you like with that?</legend>
  <input type = "checkbox"
```

```
        name = "chkFries"
        value = "1.00" /><label>Fries</label>
  <input type = "checkbox"
        name = "chkSoda"
        value = ".85" /><label>Soda</label>
  <input type = "checkbox"
        name = "chkShake"
        value = "1.30" /><label>Shake</label>
  <input type = "checkbox"
        name = "chkKetchup"
        value = ".05" /><label>Ketchup</label>

  <button type = "submit">
    place order
  </button>
</fieldset>
</form>

</body>
</html>
```

This code generates the printout shown in Figure 3.12.

FIGURE 3.12

This page has a series of checkboxes.

When the user submits this form, it calls checkDemo.php, which looks like Figure 3.13.

**FIGURE 3.13**

Notice that checkbox variables have a value or don't exist.

Checkboxes are a little different from other form elements, which consistently return a name/value pair. Checkboxes also have a name and a value, but the checkbox variable is sent to the server only if the box has been checked. As an example, compare Figures 3.12 and 3.13. You can see that only two of the checkboxes were selected. These checkboxes report values. If a checkbox isn't selected, its name and value are not reported to the program.

Take a look at the code for the checkDemo.php program to see how this works:

```
<!DOCTYPE html PUBLIC "-//W3C//DTD XHTML 1.0 Strict//EN"
"http://www.w3.org/TR/xhtml1/DTD/xhtml1-strict.dtd">
<html lang="EN" dir="ltr" xmlns="http://www.w3.org/1999/xhtml">
<head>
<title>checkDemo.php</title>
</head>

<body>
<?php
$total = 0;

if (filter_has_var(INPUT_POST, "chkFries")){
```

```
    print "<p>You wanted fries</p> \n";
    $total += filter_input(INPUT_POST, "chkFries");
}

if (filter_has_var(INPUT_POST, "chkSoda")){
  print "<p>You wanted a soda</p> \n";
    $total += filter_input(INPUT_POST, "chkSoda");
}

if (filter_has_var(INPUT_POST, "chkShake")){
  print "<p>You wanted a shake</p> \n";
    $total += filter_input(INPUT_POST, "chkShake");
}

if (filter_has_var(INPUT_POST, "chkKetchup")){
  print "<p>You wanted ketchup</p> \n";
    $total += filter_input(INPUT_POST, "chkKetchup");
}

print "<p>The total cost is: \$$total</p> \n";
?>
</body>
</html>
```

**TRAP** Checkboxes are a little different from other form elements. If you try to read the value of the checkbox with `filter_input()` and the checkbox wasn't checked, you'll get an error.

If a form has checkboxes, you must first check for the presence of the variable, then work with it if it exists.

The first part of the program simply prints out the expected variables. As you can see, if the checkbox has not been selected, the associated variable is never created. You can use the `filter_has_var()` function to determine if a checkbox has been checked. I tallied the values associated with all the selected checkboxes to get a grand total.

## USING FUNCTIONS TO ENCAPSULATE PARTS OF THE PROGRAM

It hasn't taken long for your programs to get complex. As soon as the code gets a little bit larger than a screen in your editor, it gets much harder to track. Programmers like to break up code into smaller segments called functions to help keep everything straight. A function is like a miniature program. It is designed to do one job well. Look at Figure 3.14 for an example.

## Examining the This Old Man Program

Song lyrics often have a very repetitive nature. The "This Old Man" song shown in Figure 3.14 is a good example. Each verse is different, but the chorus is always the same. You write each verse when you write the lyrics to such a song, but only write the chorus once. After that, you simply write "chorus." This works very much like functions in programming language. The code for the This Old Man program illustrates:

**FIGURE 3.14**

This song has a straightforward pattern: verse, chorus, verse, chorus.

```
<!DOCTYPE html PUBLIC "-//W3C//DTD XHTML 1.0 Strict//EN"
"http://www.w3.org/TR/xhtml1/DTD/xhtml1-strict.dtd">
<html lang="EN" dir="ltr" xmlns="http://www.w3.org/1999/xhtml">
<head>
<title>This Old Man</title>
</head>
<body>
<h1>This Old Man</h1>
<h3>Demonstrates use of functions</h3>
<?php
```

```
verse1();
chorus();
verse2();
chorus();

function verse1(){
  print <<<HERE
  <p>
  This old man, he played 1<br />
  He played knick-knack on my thumb
  </p>
HERE;
} // end verse1

function verse2(){
  print <<<HERE
  <p>
  This old man, he played 2<br />
  He played knick-knack on my shoe
  </p>
HERE;
} // end verse1

function chorus(){
  print <<<HERE
  <p>
  ...with a knick-knack<br />
  paddy-whack<br />
  give a dog a bone<br />
  this old man came rolling home<br />
  </p>
HERE;
} // end chorus

?>
</body>
</html>
```

Careful examination of this code shows how it works. The main part of the program is extremely simple:

```
verse1();
chorus();
verse2();
chorus();
```

## Creating New Functions

The `This Old Man` code appears to have some new PHP functions. I called the `verse1()` function, then the `chorus()` function, and so on. These new functions weren't shipped with PHP. Instead, I made them as part of the page. You can take a set of instructions and store them with a name. This essentially builds a new temporary command in PHP, so you can combine simple commands to do complex things.

Building a function is simple. Use the keyword `function` followed by the function's name and a set of parentheses. Keep the parentheses empty for now; you learn how to use this feature in the next section. Use a pair of braces (`{}`) to combine a series of code lines into one function. Don't forget the right brace (`}`) to end the function definition. It's smart to indent everything between the beginning and end of a function.

TRICK    When you look at my code, you note there's one line I never indent: the HERE token used for multi-line strings. The word HERE acts like a closing quotation mark and must be all the way to the left side of the screen, so it can't be indented.

TRAP    You can use any function name you like (as long as you avoid spaces and punctuation). Careful, though: If you try to define a function that already exists, you're bound to get confused. PHP has a large number of functions already built in. If you're having strange problems with a function, look at the online help to see if that function already exists.

The `chorus()` function is especially handy in this program because it can be reused. It isn't necessary to rewrite the code for the chorus each time, when you can simply call a function instead.

## USING PARAMETERS AND FUNCTION VALUES

Functions are meant to be self-contained. This is good because the entire program can be too complex to understand. If you break the complex program into smaller functions, each function can be set up to work independently. When you work inside a function, you don't have to worry about anything outside the function. If you create a variable inside a function, that variable dies as soon as you leave the function. This prevents many errors that can otherwise creep into your code.

The bad side of functions being so self-contained is evident when you want them to work with data from the outside. You can accomplish this a couple of ways.

- Send a parameter to a function, which allows you to determine one or more values sent to the function as it starts.
- Give a function a return value.

The `param` program shown in Figure 3.15 illustrates another form of the "This Old Man" song. Although again the user might be unaware, some important differences exist between this more sophisticated program and the first `This Old Man` program.

## Examining the Param.php Program

You can create functions that are more efficient. Figure 3.15 shows another version of the "This Old Man" song that seems the same to the user but uses a more efficient structure underneath.

**FIGURE 3.15**

This looks like the same old man, but this one is better..

Notice that the output of Figure 3.15 is longer than that of 3.14, but the code that generates this longer output is shorter.

```
<!DOCTYPE html PUBLIC "-//W3C//DTD XHTML 1.0 Strict//EN"
"http://www.w3.org/TR/xhtml1/DTD/xhtml1-strict.dtd">
<html lang="EN" dir="ltr" xmlns="http://www.w3.org/1999/xhtml">
<head>
<title>Param Old Man</title>
</head>
<body>
<h1>Param Old Man </h1>
<h3>Demonstrates use of function parameters</h3>
<?php

print verse(1);
print chorus();
print verse(2);
print chorus();
print verse(3);
print chorus();
print verse(4);
print chorus();


function verse($stanza){
  switch ($stanza){
    case 1:
      $place = "thumb";
      break;
    case 2:
      $place = "shoe";
      break;
    case 3:
      $place = "knee";
      break;
    case 4:
      $place = "door";
      break;
    default:
      $place = "I don't know where";
  } // end switch
```

```
   $output = <<<HERE
<p>
  This old man, he played $stanza<br />
  He played knick-knack on my $place
</p>
HERE;
   return $output;
} // end verse

function chorus(){
   $output = <<<HERE
<p>
  ...with a knick-knack<br />
  paddy-whack<br />
  give a dog a bone<br />
  this old man came rolling home<br />
</p>
HERE;
   return $output;
} // end chorus

?>
</body>
</html>
```

## Looking at Encapsulation in the Main Code Body

This code features a number of improvements over the previous version. First, look at the main body of the code, which looks like this:

```
print verse(1);
print chorus();
print verse(2);
print chorus();
print verse(3);
print chorus();
print verse(4);
print chorus();
```

The program is to print the first verse, then the chorus, then the second verse, then the chorus, and so on. The details of how all these things are to be generated is left to the individual functions. This is an example of encapsulation. Encapsulation is good, because it allows you to think about problems in multiple levels. At the highest level, you're interested in the main ideas (print the verses and chorus) but you're not so concerned about the exact details. You use the same technique when you talk about your day: "I drove to work, had some meetings, went to lunch, and taught a class." You don't usually describe each detail of each task. Each major task can be broken down into its component tasks later. (If somebody asks, you could really describe the meeting: "I got some coffee, appeared to be taking notes furiously on my PDA, got a new high score on Solitaire while appearing to take notes, scribbled on the agenda, and dozed off during a presentation.")

## Returning a Value: The chorus() Function

Another interesting thing about the code's main section code is the use of the print() function. In the last program, I simply said chorus() and the program printed the verse. In this program, I did it a little differently. The chorus() function doesn't actually print anything to the screen. Instead, it creates the chorus as a big string and sends that value back to the program, which can do whatever it wants with it.

This behavior isn't new to you. Think about the rand() function. It always returns a value to the program. The functions in this program work the same way. Take another look at the chorus() function to see what I mean:

```
function chorus(){
  $output = <<<HERE
<p>
  ...with a knick-knack<br />
  paddy-whack<br />
  give a dog a bone<br />
  this old man came rolling home<br />
</p>
HERE;
  return $output;
} // end chorus
```

I began the function by creating a new variable called $output. You can create variables inside functions by mentioning them, just like you can in the main part of the program. However, a variable created inside a function loses its meaning as soon as the function is finished. This is good, because it means the variables inside a function belong only to that function. You don't have to worry about whether the variable already exists somewhere else in your program. You also don't have to worry about all the various things that can go wrong if you mistakenly modify an existing variable. I assigned a long string (the actual chorus of the song) to the $output variable with the <<<HERE construct.

The last line of the function uses the return statement to send the value of $output back to the program. Any function can end with a return statement. Whatever value follows the keyword return is passed to the program. This is one way your functions can communicate information back to the main program.

## Accepting a Parameter in the verse() Function

The most efficient part of the newer This Old Man program is the verse() function. Rather than having a different function for each verse, I wrote one function that can work for all the verses. After careful analysis of the song, I noticed that each verse is remarkably similar to the others. The only thing that differentiates each verse is what the old man played (which is always the verse number) and where he played it (which is something rhyming with the verse number). If I can indicate which verse to play, it should be easy enough to produce the correct verse.

Notice that when the main body calls the verse() function, it always indicates a verse number in parentheses. For example, it makes a reference to verse(1) and verse(3). These commands both call the verse function, but they send different values (1 and 3) to the function. Take another look at the code for the verse() function to see how the function responds to these inputs:

```
function verse($stanza){
  switch ($stanza){
    case 1:
      $place = "thumb";
      break;
    case 2:
      $place = "shoe";
      break;
    case 3:
      $place = "knee";
      break;
    case 4:
      $place = "door";
      break;
```

```
   default:
     $place = "I don't know where";
 } // end switch

 $output = <<<HERE
<p>
  This old man, he played $stanza<br />
  He played knick-knack on my $place
</p>
HERE;
   return $output;
} // end verse
```

In this function, I indicated $stanza as a parameter in the function definition. A parameter is simply a variable associated with the function. If you create a function with a parameter, you are required to supply some sort of value whenever you call the function. The parameter variable automatically receives the value from the main body. For example, if the program says verse(1), the verse function is called and the $stanza variable contains the value 1. I then used a switch statement to populate the $place variable based on the value of $stanza. Finally, I created the $output variable using the $stanza and $place variables and returned the value of $output.

You can create functions with multiple parameters. Simply declare several variables inside the parentheses of the function definition, and be sure to call the function with the appropriate number of arguments. Make sure to separate parameters with commas.

## MANAGING VARIABLE SCOPE

You have learned some ways to have your main program share variable information with your functions. In addition to parameter passing, sometimes you want your functions to have access to variables created in the main program. This is especially true because all the variables automatically created by PHP (such as those coming from forms) are generated at the main level. You must tell PHP when you want a function to use a variable created at the main level. These program-level variables are also called global variables.

If you've programmed in another language, you're bound to get confused by the way PHP handles global variables. In most languages, any variable created at the main level is automatically available to every function. In PHP, you must specify within a function that a variable will be shared outside the function.

## Looking at the Scope Demo

To illustrate the notion of global variables, take a look at the Scope Demo, shown in Figure 3.16.

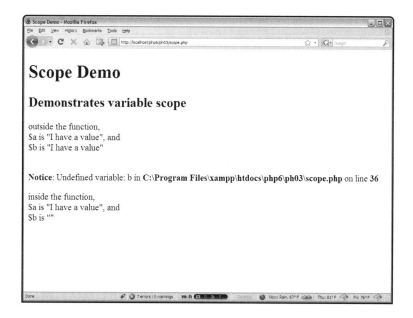

**FIGURE 3.16**

Variable $a keeps its value inside a function, but $b does not.

Note that the warning message in this program is intentional. If you do not explicitly set the scope of a variable, you may get errors like this one.

Take a look at the code for the Scope Demo and see how it works:

```
<!DOCTYPE html PUBLIC "-//W3C//DTD XHTML 1.0 Strict//EN"
"http://www.w3.org/TR/xhtml1/DTD/xhtml1-strict.dtd">
<html lang="EN" dir="ltr" xmlns="http://www.w3.org/1999/xhtml">
<head>
<title>Scope Demo</title>
</head>
<body>
<h1>Scope Demo</h1>
<h2>Demonstrates variable scope</h2>

<?php

$a = "I have a value";
```

```
$b = "I have a value";

print <<<HERE
  <p>
  outside the function, <br />
  \$a is "$a", and<br />
  \$b is "$b"
  </p>
HERE;

myFunction();

function myFunction(){

  //make $a global, but not $b
  global $a;

  print <<<HERE
    <p>
    inside the function, <br />
    \$a is "$a", and<br />
    \$b is "$b"
    </p>
HERE;
} // end myFunction

?>

</body>
</html>
```

I created two variables for this demonstration: $a and $b. I gave them both the value I have a value. As a test, I printed out the values for both $a and $b.

**TRICK**

Notice the trick I used to make the actual dollar sign show up in the quotation mark in the following line:

```
\$a is "$a", and<br />
```

When PHP sees a dollar sign inside quotation marks, it usually expects to be working with a variable. Sometimes (as in this case) you really want to print a dollar sign. You can precede a dollar sign with a backslash to have the sign appear. So, `print $a` prints the value of the variable $a, but `print \$a` prints the value "$a".

## RETURNING TO THE PETALS GAME

At the beginning of this chapter, I showed you the `Petals Around the Rose` game. This game uses all the skills you have learned so far, including the new concepts from this chapter. If you haven't already done so, play the game now so you can see how it works.

Here's the basic plan of the `Petals` game: Each time the page is drawn, it randomly generates five dice and calculates the correct number of petals based on a super-secret formula. The page includes a form that has a text area called `guess` for the user to enter the answer. The form also includes a hidden field called `numPetals`, which tells the program what the correct answer was.

---

### CAN'T THE PROGRAM REMEMBER THE RIGHT ANSWER?

Since the program generated the correct answer in the first place, you might be surprised to learn that the right answer must be hidden in the web page and then retrieved by the same program that generated it. Each contact between the client and the server is completely new.

When the user first plays the game, the page is sent to the browser and the connection is completely severed until the user hits the Submit button. When the user submits the form, the `Petals` program starts over again. It's possible the user plays the game right before he goes to bed, then leaves the page on the computer overnight. Meanwhile, a hundred other people might use the program. For now, use hidden data to help keep track of the user's situation. Later in this book, you learn some other clever methods for keeping track of the users' situations.

---

The Petals game doesn't introduce anything new, but it's a little longer than any of the other programs you've seen so far. I introduce the code in smaller chunks. All the code is shown in order, but not in one long code sample. Look on the CD for the program in its entirety.

## Starting HTML

Like most PHP programs, the Petals game uses some HTML to set everything up. The HTML is pretty basic because PHP code creates most of the interesting HTML.

```
<!DOCTYPE html PUBLIC "-//W3C//DTD XHTML 1.0 Strict//EN"
"http://www.w3.org/TR/xhtml1/DTD/xhtml1-strict.dtd">
<html lang="EN" dir="ltr" xmlns="http://www.w3.org/1999/xhtml">
<head>
<title>petals.php</title>
<link rel = "stylesheet"
      type = "text/css"
      href = "petals.css" />
</head>
<body>
<h1>Petals Around the Rose</h1>
```

The petals.css stylesheet contains all the style information to get the look and feel I want.

## Main Body Code

The main PHP code segment has three main jobs: print a greeting, print the dice, and print the form for the next turn. These jobs are (appropriately enough) stored in three different functions. One goal of encapsulation is to make the main code body as clean as possible. This goal is achieved in the Petals game.

```
<?php

printGreeting();
printDice();
printForm();
```

All the real work is passed off to the various functions, which are described shortly. Even before you see the functions themselves, you have a good idea what each function does and a good sense of the program's overall flow. Encapsulating your code and naming your functions well makes your code much easier to read and repair. The one line of code not in a function attempts to load in the $numPetals variable from the form.

## The printGreeting() Function

The printGreeting() function prints one of three possible greetings to the user. If the user has never called this program before, the program should provide a welcome. If the user has been here before, she has guessed the number of petals. That guess might be correct (in which case a congratulatory message is appropriate) or incorrect, requiring information about what the correct answer was. The printGreeting() function uses a switch statement to handle the various options.

```
function printGreeting(){
  global $numPetals;
  $guess = filter_input(INPUT_POST, "guess");
  $numPetals = filter_input(INPUT_POST, "numPetals");

  if (!filter_has_var(INPUT_POST, "guess")){
    print "<h3>Welcome to Petals Around the Rose</h3>";
  } else if ($guess == $numPetals){
    print "<h3>You Got It!</h3>";
  } else {

    print <<<HERE

      <h3>from last try: </h3>
      <p>
        you guessed: $guess
      </p>
      <p>
        -and the correct answer was: $numPetals petals around the rose
      </p>
HERE;

  } // end if

} // end printGreeting
```

This function refers to both the $guess and $numPetals variables. Since both may be needed by other functions, they are defined in a global statement. Note that you can assign global status to more than one variable in a single global command.

I used `filter_has_var()` to determine if the `$guess` variable is empty. This will be the case if it is the first time the user has come to the program. If `$guess` is empty, I print a welcoming greeting. If `$guess` is equal to `$numPetals`, the user has guessed correctly, so I print an appropriate congratulations. If neither of these conditions is true (which is most of the time), the function prints out a slightly more complex string indicating the user's last guess and the correct answer. This should give the user enough information to eventually solve the riddle.

The `else if` structure turns out to be the easiest option for handling the three possible conditions I want to check.

## The printDice() Function

After the program prints a greeting, it does the important business of generating the random dice. It's relatively easy to generate random dice, as you saw earlier in this chapter. However, I also wanted to be efficient and calculate the correct number of petals. To make the `printDice()` function more efficient, it calls some other custom functions.

```
function printDice(){
  global $numPetals;

  print "<h3>New Roll:</h3> \n";
  $numPetals = 0;

  $die1 = rand(1,6);
  $die2 = rand(1,6);
  $die3 = rand(1,6);
  $die4 = rand(1,6);
  $die5 = rand(1,6);

  print "<p> \n";
  showDie($die1);
  showDie($die2);
  showDie($die3);
  showDie($die4);
  showDie($die5);
  print "</p> \n";

  calcNumPetals($die1);
  calcNumPetals($die2);
  calcNumPetals($die3);
```

```
  calcNumPetals($die4);
  calcNumPetals($die5);

} // end printDice
```

The printDice() function is very concerned with the $numPetals variable, but doesn't need access to $guess. It requests access to $numPetals from the main program. After printing out the "New Roll" message, it resets $numPetals to 0. The value of $numPetals is recalculated each time the dice are rolled.

I got new dice values by calling the rand(1, 6) function six times. I stored each result in a different variable, named $die1 to $die6. To print out an appropriate graphic for each die, I called the showDie() function. I then called the calcNumPetals() function once for each die.

## The showDie() Function

The showDie() function is used to simplify repetitive code. It accepts a die value as a parameter and generates the appropriate HTML code for drawing a die with the corresponding number of dots.

```
function showDie($value){
  print <<<HERE
  <img src = "die$value.jpg"
      height = "100"
      width = "100"
      alt = "die: $value" />

HERE;
} // end showDie
```

 **TRICK** One advantage of using functions for repetitive HTML code is the ease with which you can modify large sections of code. For example, if you wish to change image sizes, change the img tag in this one function. All six die images are changed at once!

## The calcNumPetals Function

The printDice() function also calls calcNumPetals() once for each die. This function receives a die value as a parameter. It also references the $numPetals global variable. The function uses a switch statement to determine how much to add to $numPetals based on the current die's value.

Here's the trick: The center dot of the die is the rose. Any dots around the center dot are the petals. The value 1 has a rose but no petals; 2, 4, and 6 have petals, but no rose; 3 has two petals; 5 has four. If the die roll is 3, $numPetals should be increased by 2; if the roll is 5, $numPetals should be increased by 4.

```
function calcNumPetals($value){
  global $numPetals;

  switch ($value) {
    case 3:
      $numPetals += 2;
      break;
    case 5:
      $numPetals += 4;
      break;
  } // end switch

} // end calcNumPetals
```

The += code is a shorthand notation. The line shown here

```
$numPetals += 2;
```

is exactly equivalent to this line:

```
$numPetals = $numPetals + 2;
```

The first style is much shorter and easier to type, so it's the form most programmers prefer.

## The printForm() Function

The purpose of the printForm() function is to print the form at the bottom of the HTML page. This form is pretty straightforward except for the need to place the hidden field for $numPetals.

```
  global $numPetals;

  print <<<HERE

<h3>How many petals around the rose?</h3>

<form action = ""
      method = "post">
```

```
<fieldset>
<input type = "text"
       name = "guess"
       value = "0" />
<input type = "hidden"
       name = "numPetals"
       value = "$numPetals" />
<br />
<input type = "submit" />
</fieldset>
</form>
<p>
  <a href = "petalHelp.html">
  give me a hint</a>
</p>
HERE;
```

```
} // end printForm
```

This code places the form on the page. I could have done most of the form in plain HTML without needing PHP for anything but the hidden field. However, when I start using PHP, I like to have much of my code in PHP. It helps me see the flow of things more clearly (print greeting, print dice, and print form, for example).

## The Ending HTML Code

The final set of HTML code closes everything up. It completes the PHP segment, the font, the centered text, the body, and finally, the HTML itself.

```
?>
</body>
</html>
```

## SUMMARY

You learned a lot in this chapter. You learned several kinds of branching structures, including the if clause, else statements, and the switch structure. You know how to write functions, which make your programs much more efficient and easier to read. You know how to pass parameters to functions and return values from them. You can access global variables from inside functions. You put all these things together to make an interesting game. You should be very proud! In the next chapter, you learn how to use looping structures to make your programs even more powerful.

## CHALLENGES

1. Write a program that generates 4-, 10-, or 20-sided dice.
2. Write a program that lets the user choose how many sides a die has and print a random roll with the appropriate maximum values. (Don't worry about using images to display the dice.)
3. Write a Loaded Dice program that half the time generates the value 1 and half the time generates some other value.
4. Modify the Story game from Chapter 2, "Using Variables and Input," so the form and the program are one file.
5. Create a web page generator. Make a form for the page caption, background color, font color, and text body. Use this form to generate an XHTML page.

# LOOPS AND ARRAYS

You know a program's basic parts, but your programs can be much easier to write and more efficient when you know some other things. In this chapter, you learn about two very important tools: arrays and looping structures.

Arrays are special variables that form lists. Looping structures repeat certain code segments. As you might expect, arrays and loops often work together. You learn how to use these new elements to make programs that are more interesting. Specifically, you do these things:

- Use the `for` loop to build basic counting structures
- Modify the `for` loop for different kinds of counting
- Use a `while` loop for more flexible looping
- Identify the keys to successful loops
- Create basic arrays
- Write programs that use arrays and loops
- Use session variables to store data
- Store information in hidden fields

## INTRODUCING THE POKER DICE PROGRAM

The main program for this chapter is a simplified dice game. In this game, you are given $100 of virtual money. On each turn, you bet two dollars. The computer rolls five dice. You can elect to keep each die or roll it again. On the second roll, the computer checks for various combinations. You can earn money back for rolling pairs, triples, four or five of a kind, and straights (five numbers in a row). Figures 4.1 and 4.2 illustrate the game in action.

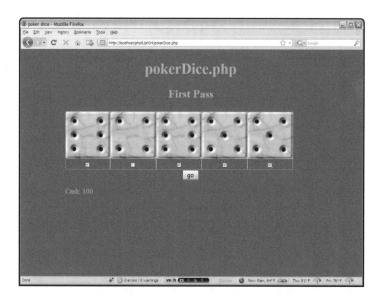

**FIGURE 4.1**

After the first roll, you can keep some of the dice by selecting the checkboxes underneath each die.

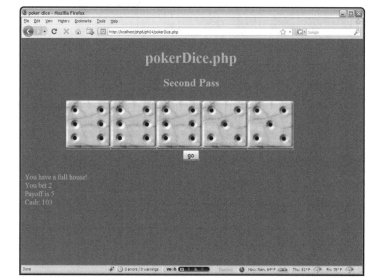

**FIGURE 4.2**

The player has earned back some money with a full house!

The basic concepts of this game are much like the ones you use in other chapters' programs. Keeping track of all five dice can get complicated, so this program uses arrays and loops to manage all the information.

## COUNTING WITH THE FOR LOOP

You might want the computer to repeat some sort of action multiple times. Good thing computers excel at repetitive behavior. For example, look at the `simpleFor.php` program shown in Figure 4.3.

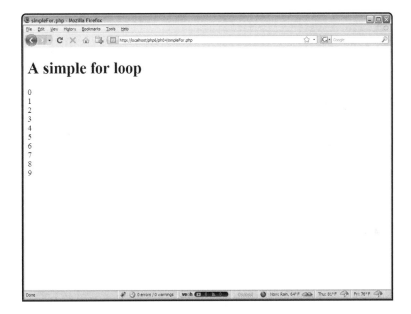

FIGURE 4.3

This program counts from zero to nine.

While the output of the `simpleFor.php` program doesn't look all that interesting, it has a unique characteristic. It has only one `print` statement in the entire program, which is executed 10 different times. Look at the source code to see how it works:

```
<!DOCTYPE html PUBLIC "-//W3C//DTD XHTML 1.0 Strict//EN"
"http://www.w3.org/TR/xhtml1/DTD/xhtml1-strict.dtd">
<html lang="EN" dir="ltr" xmlns="http://www.w3.org/1999/xhtml">

<head>
<title>
simpleFor.php
</title>
```

```
</head>

<body>

<h1>A simple for loop</h1>
<div>
<?php

for ($i = 0; $i < 10; $i++){
  print "$i <br />\n";
} // end for loop


?>
</div>

</body>
</html>
```

Each number is printed in the line that looks like this:

```
  print "$i <br />\n";
```

This line can print only one value, but it happens 10 times. The key to this behavior is the for statement. The for structure has three main parts: a variable declaration, a condition, and an increment statement.

**TIP**

The \n character signifies a newline or carriage return. This means that the program's HTML source code places each number on a separate line. The <br /> tag ensures that the HTML output also places each number on its own line. While carriage returns in the HTML source don't have much to do with how the output looks, I like my programs' code to be written as carefully as the stuff I build by hand.

## Initializing a Sentry Variable

For loops usually involve an integer (non-decimal) variable. Sometimes the key variable in a loop is referred to as a sentry variable, because it acts like a gatekeeper to the loop. The first part of a for loop definition is a line of code that identifies and initializes the sentry variable to some starting value. In the simple for loop demo, the initialization segment looks like this:

```
$i = 0;
```

It specifies that the sentry variable be called $i and its starting value be 0.

---

## IN THE REAL WORLD

You might wonder why the sentry variable is called $i. Like most variables, it's best if sentry variables have a name that suits their purpose. Sometimes, however, a for loop sentry is simply an integer and doesn't have any other meaning. In those situations, an old programming tradition is often called into play.

In the Fortran language (one of the earliest common programming languages), all integer variables had to begin with the letters i, j, and a few other characters. Fortran programmers would commonly use I as the name of generic sentry variables. Even though most modern programmers have never written a line of Fortran code, the tradition remains. It's amazing how much folklore exists in such a relatively new activity as computer programming.

---

Computer programs frequently begin counting with zero, so I initialized $i to 0 as well.

 **NOTE** Although the $i = 0; segment looks like (and is) a complete line of code, it is usually placed on the same line as the other parts of the for loop construct.

## Setting a Condition to Finish the Loop

Getting a computer to repeat behavior is the easy part. The harder task comes when trying to get the computer to stop correctly. The second part of the for loop construct is a condition. When this condition is evaluated as TRUE, the loop should continue. The loop should exit as soon as the condition is evaluated to FALSE. In this case, I set the condition as $i < 10. This means that as long as the variable $i has a value less than 10, the loop continues. As soon as the program detects that $i has a value equal to or larger than 10, the loop exits. Usually a for loop's condition checks the sentry variable against some terminal or ending value.

## Changing the Sentry Variable

The final critical element of a for loop is some mechanism for changing the value of the sentry variable. At some point the value of $i must become 10 or larger or the loop continues forever. In the basicLoop program, the part of the for structure that makes this happen looks like

$i++. The notation $i++ is just like saying add one to $i or $i = $i + 1. The ++ symbol is called an increment operator because it provides an easy way to increment (add 1) to a variable.

## Building the Loop

Once you've set up the parts of the for statement, the loop itself is easy to use. Place braces ({}) around your code and indent all code that's inside the loop. You can have as many lines of code as you wish inside a loop, including branching statements and other loops.

The sentry variable has special behavior inside the loop. It begins with the initial value. Each time the loop repeats, it is changed as specified in the for structure, and the interpreter checks the condition to ensure that it's still true. If so, the code in the loop occurs again.

In the case of the basicArray program, $i begins as 0. The first time the print statement occurs, it prints 0 because that is the current value of $i. When the interpreter reaches the right brace that ends the loop, it increments $i by 1 (following the $i++ directive in the for structure) and checks the condition ($i < 10).

Because 0 is less than 10, the condition is true and the code inside the loop occurs again. Eventually, the value of $i becomes 10, so the condition ($i < 10) is no longer true. Program control then reverts to the next line of code after the end of the loop, which ends the program.

Although the sentry variable is an ordinary variable, it should not be changed inside the loop. Let the for loop instructions do all the work.

## Modifying the for Loop

Once you understand for loop structure basics, you can modify it in a couple of interesting ways. You can build a loop that counts by fives or that counts backwards.

### Counting by Fives

The countByFive.php program shown in Figure 4.4 illustrates a program that counts by fives.

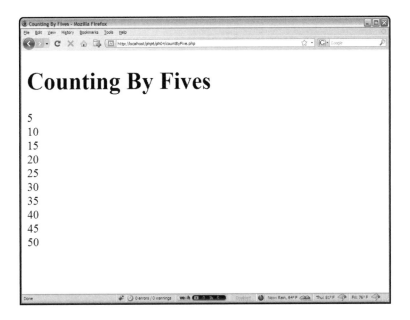

**FIGURE 4.4**

This program counts by fives using only one print statement.

The program is very much like the basicArray program, but with a couple of twists.

```
<!DOCTYPE html PUBLIC "-//W3C//DTD XHTML 1.0 Strict//EN"
"http://www.w3.org/TR/xhtml1/DTD/xhtml1-strict.dtd">
<html lang="EN" dir="ltr" xmlns="http://www.w3.org/1999/xhtml">

<head>
<title>
Counting By Fives
</title>
</head>

<body>

<h1>Counting By Fives</h1>

<?php
print "<p> \n";
for ($i = 5; $i <= 50; $i+= 5){
  print "$i <br />\n";
} // end for loop
```

```
print "</p> \n";

?>



</body>
</html>
```

The only thing I changed was the various parameters in the `for` statement. Since it seems silly to start counting at 0, I set the initial value of $i to 5. I decided to stop when $i reached 50 (after 10 iterations). Each time through the loop, $i is incremented by five.

The += syntax in the following code increments a variable:$i += 5;

The above is the same thing as this:

```
$i = $i + 5;
```

### Counting Backwards

It is fairly simple to modify a `for` loop so it counts backwards. Figure 4.5 illustrates this feat.

FIGURE 4.5

This loop now counts backwards.

Once again, the basic structure is just like the basic `for` loop program, but changing the `for` structure parameters alters the program's behavior. The code for this program shows how it is done:

```
<!DOCTYPE html PUBLIC "-//W3C//DTD XHTML 1.0 Strict//EN"
"http://www.w3.org/TR/xhtml1/DTD/xhtml1-strict.dtd">
<html lang="EN" dir="ltr" xmlns="http://www.w3.org/1999/xhtml">

<head>
<title>
Counting Backwards
</title>
</head>

<body>

<h1>Counting Backwards</h1>

<?php
print "<p> \n";
for ($i = 10; $i > 0; $i--){
  print "$i <br />\n";
} // end for loop
print "</p> \n";

?>



</body>
</html>
```

If you understand how `for` loops work, the changes all make sense. I'm counting backwards this time, so `$i` begins with a large value (in this case 10). The condition for continuing the loop is now `$i > 0`, which means the loop continues as long as `$i` is greater than 0. The loop ends as soon as `$i` is 0 or less.

Note that rather than adding a value to `$i`, this time I decrement by 1 each time through the loop. If you're counting backwards, be very careful that the sentry variable has a mechanism for getting smaller. Otherwise, the loop never ends. Recall that `$i++` adds 1 to `$i`; `$i--` subtracts 1 from `$i`.

## USING A WHILE LOOP

PHP, like most languages, provides another kind of looping structure even more flexible than the for loop. You can use the while loop when you know how many times something will happen, just like a for loop. Figure 4.6 shows how a while loop can work much like a for loop.

### Repeating Code with a while Loop

The code for the while.php program is much like the for loop example, but you can see that the while loop is a little bit simpler:

```
<!DOCTYPE html PUBLIC "-//W3C//DTD XHTML 1.0 Strict//EN"
"http://www.w3.org/TR/xhtml1/DTD/xhtml1-strict.dtd">
<html lang="EN" dir="ltr" xmlns="http://www.w3.org/1999/xhtml">

<head>
<title>
A simple While Loop
</title>
</head>

<body>

<h1>A simple while loop</h1>
<div>
<?php

$i = 1;

while ($i <= 10){
  print "$i <br />\n";
   $i++;
} // end while

?>
</div>

</body>
</html>
```

The while loop shown in Figure 4.6 requires only one parameter, which is a condition. The loop continues as long as the condition is evaluated as TRUE. As soon as the condition is evaluated as FALSE, the loop exits.

**FIGURE 4.6**

Although this program's output looks a lot like the basic for loop, it uses a different construct to achieve the same result.

This particular program starts by initializing the variable $i, then checking to see if it's greater than or equal to 10 in the while statement. Inside the loop body, the program prints the current value of $i and increments $i.

## Recognizing Endless Loops

The flexibility of the while construct gives it power, but with that power comes potential for problems. while loops are easy to build, but a loop that works improperly can cause a lot of trouble. It's possible that the code in the loop will never execute at all. Even worse, you might have some sort of logical error that causes the loop to continue indefinitely. As an example, look at the badWhile.php code:

```
<!DOCTYPE html PUBLIC "-//W3C//DTD XHTML 1.0 Strict//EN"
"http://www.w3.org/TR/xhtml1/DTD/xhtml1-strict.dtd">
<html lang="EN" dir="ltr" xmlns="http://www.w3.org/1999/xhtml">

<head>
<title>
```

```
A bad While Loop
</title>
</head>

<body>

<h1>A bad while loop</h1>
<h3 style = "color: red">
NOTE:  This page has a deliberate error!
</h3>
<div>
<?php

$i = 1;

while ($i <= 10){
   print "$i <br />\n";
   $j++;
} // end while

?>
</div>

</body>
</html>
```

 The badWhile.php program shows what happens when you have an endless loop in your code. If you run this program, it may temporarily slow down your web server. Be sure your server is configured to stop a PHP process when the user presses the stop button on the browser. (This is a default setting on most PHP installations.)

The badWhile.php program has a subtle but deadly error. Look carefully at the source code and see if you can spot it. The code is just like the first while program, except instead of incrementing $i, I incremented $j. The variable $j has nothing to do with $i and $i never changes. The loop keeps going on forever, because it cannot end until $i is greater than or equal to 10, which never happens. This program is an example of the classic endless loop. Every programmer alive has written them accidentally, and you will too.

Usually the culprit of an endless loop is a sloppy variable name, spelling, or capitalization. If you use a variable like $myCounter as the sentry variable but then increment $MyCounter, PHP tracks two entirely different variables. Your program won't work correctly. This is another reason to be consistent on your variable naming and capitalization conventions.

## Building a Well-Behaved Loop

Fortunately, you have guidelines for building a loop that behaves as you wish. Even better, you've already learned most of the important ideas, because these fundamental concepts are built into the for loop's structure. When you write a while loop, you are responsible for these three things:

- Creating a sentry variable
- Building a condition
- Ensuring the loop can exit

I discuss each of these ideas in the following sections.

### Creating and Initializing a Sentry Variable

If your loop is based on a variable's value (there are alternatives), make sure you do these three things:

- Identify the variable.
- Ensure the variable has appropriate scope.
- Make sure the variable has a reasonable starting value.

You might also check the value to ensure the loop runs at least one time (at least if that's your intent). Creating a variable is much like the initialization stage of a for construct.

### Building a Condition to Continue the Loop

Your condition usually compares a variable and a value. Make sure you have a condition that can be met and be broken. The hard part is ensuring that the program gets out of the loop at the correct time. This condition is much like the condition in the for loop.

### Ensuring the Loop Can Exit

There must be some trigger that changes the sentry variable so the loop can exit. This code must exist inside the code body. Be sure it is possible for the sentry variable to achieve the value necessary to exit the loop by making the condition false.

---

## DECIDING WHICH TYPE OF LOOP TO USE

So far, all the `while` loops I showed you worked just like `for` loops, counting a certain number of times. Generally, when you want something to happen a certain number of times, you'll use a `for` loop. `while` loops are more useful when you don't know exactly how many times your loop will execute, but you want the loop to execute based on some kind of condition. For example you might write a loop that reads data from a text file and continues until there are no more lines in the text file to read. This would be an ideal setting for a `while` loop.

---

## WORKING WITH BASIC ARRAYS

Programming is about the combination of control structures (like loops) and data structures (like variables). You know the very powerful looping structures. Now it's time to look at a data structure that works naturally with loops.

Arrays are special variables made to hold lists of information. PHP makes it quite easy to work with arrays. Look at Figure 4.7, whose `basicArray.php` program demonstrates two arrays.

**FIGURE 4.7**

The data in this program is stored in arrays.

First look over the entire program, then see how it does its work.

```
<!DOCTYPE html PUBLIC "-//W3C//DTD XHTML 1.0 Strict//EN"
"http://www.w3.org/TR/xhtml1/DTD/xhtml1-strict.dtd">
<html lang="EN" dir="ltr" xmlns="http://www.w3.org/1999/xhtml">
<head>
<title>
Basic Array
</title>
</head>

<body>

<h1>Basic Array</h1>

<?php

//simply assign values to array
$camelPop[1] = "Somalia";
$camelPop[2] = "Sudan";
$camelPop[3] = "Mauritania";
$camelPop[4] = "Pakistan";
$camelPop[5] = "India";

//output array values
print "<h3>Top Camel Populations in the World</h3>\n";
print "<p> \n";
for ($i = 1; $i <= 5; $i++){
  print "$i: $camelPop[$i]<br />\n";
} // end for loop
print "</p> \n";

print <<< HERE
  <p style = "text-decoration: italic">
    Source:
  <a href = "http://www.fao.org/ag/aga/glipha/index.jsp">
Food and Agriculture Organization of the United Nations</a>
 </p>

HERE;
```

```
//use array function to load up array
$binary = array("000", "001", "010", "011");

print "<h3>Binary numbers</h3>\n";
print "<p> \n";
for ($i = 0; $i < count($binary); $i++){
  print "$i: $binary[$i]<br />\n";
} // end for loop
print "</p> \n";
?>
</body>
</html>
```

## Generating a Basic Array

Look at the lines that describe $camelPop:

```
//simply assign values to array
$camelPop[1] = "Somalia";
$camelPop[2] = "Sudan";
$camelPop[3] = "Mauritania";
$camelPop[4] = "Pakistan";
$camelPop[5] = "India";
```

The $camelPop variable is a variable meant to hold the five countries with the largest camel populations in the world. (If this array stuff isn't working for you, at least you've learned something in this chapter!) Since $camelPop is going to hold the names of five different countries, it makes sense that this is an array (computer geek lingo for list) rather than an ordinary variable.

The only thing different about $camelPop and all the other variables you've worked with so far is $camelPop can have multiple values. To tell these values apart, use a numeric index in square brackets.

**TIP**  Apparently, the boxer George Foreman has several sons also named George. I've often wondered what Mrs. Foreman does when she wants somebody to take out the trash. I suspect she has assigned a number to each George, so there is no ambiguity. This is exactly how arrays work. Each element has the same name, but a different numerical index so you can tell them apart.

Many languages require you to explicitly create array variables, but PHP is very easygoing in this regard. Simply assign a value to a variable with an index in square brackets and you've created an array.

 **TIP** Even though PHP is good natured about letting you create an array variable on the fly, you might get a warning about this behavior on those web servers that have error reporting set to E_ALL. If that's the case, you can create an empty array with the array() function described in the following sections and then add values to it.

## Using a Loop to Examine an Array's Contents

Arrays go naturally with for loops. Very often when you have an array variable, you step through all of its values and do something to each one. In this example, I want to print the index and the corresponding country's name. Here's the for loop that performs this task:

```
for ($i = 1; $i <= 5; $i++){
  print "$i: $camelPop[$i]<br />\n";
} // end for loop
```

Because I know the array indices will vary between 1 and 5, I set up my loop so the value of $i will go from 1 to 5. Inside the loop, I simply print the index ($i) and the corresponding country ($camelPop[$i]). The first time through the loop, $i is 1, so $camelPop[$i] is $camelPop[1], which is Somalia. Each time through the loop, the value of $i is incremented, so eventually every array element is displayed.

The advantage of combining loops and arrays is convenience. If you want to do something with each element of an array, you only have to write the code one time, then put that code inside a loop. This is especially powerful when you start designing programs that work with large amounts of data. If, for example, I want to list the camel population of every country in the UN database rather than simply the top five countries, all I have to do is make a bigger array and modify the for loop.

## Using the array() Construct to Preload an Array

Often you start out knowing exactly which values you want placed in an array. PHP provides a shortcut for loading an array with a set of values.

```
//use array function to load up array
$binary = array("000", "001", "010", "011");
```

In this example, I create an array of the first four binary digits (starting at zero). The `array` keyword can assign a list of values to an array. Note that when you use this technique, the indices of the elements are created for you.

 Most computer languages automatically begin counting things with zero rather than one (the way humans tend to count). This can cause confusion. When PHP builds an array for you, the first index is 0 automatically, not 1.

## Detecting the Size of an Array

Arrays are meant to add flexibility to your code. You don't actually need to know how many elements are in an array, because PHP provides a function called `count()`, which can determine how many elements an array has. In the following code, I use the `count()` function to determine the array size:

```
for ($i = 0; $i < count($binary); $i++){
  print "$i: $binary[$i]<br />\n";
} // end for loop
```

Note that my loop sentry goes from 0 to 1 less than the number of elements in the array. If you have four elements in an array and the array begins with 0, the largest index is 3. This is a standard way of looping through an array.

 Since it is so common to step through arrays, PHP provides another kind of loop that makes this even easier. You get a chance to see that looping structure in Chapter 5, "Better Arrays and String Handling." For now, understand how an ordinary `for` loop is used with an array.

## IMPROVING THIS OLD MAN WITH ARRAYS AND LOOPS

The `basicArray.php` program shows how to build arrays, but it doesn't illustrate the power of arrays and loops working together. To see how these features can help you, revisit an old friend from Chapter 3, "Controlling Your Code with Conditions and Functions." The version of the `This Old Man` program featured in Figure 4.8 looks a lot like it did in Chapter 3, but the code is quite a bit more compact.

FIGURE 4.8

The improved
This Old Man
program in action.

The Fancy Old Man program uses a more compact structure than This Old Man.

The improvements in this version are only apparent when you look under the hood:

```
<!DOCTYPE html PUBLIC "-//W3C//DTD XHTML 1.0 Strict//EN"
"http://www.w3.org/TR/xhtml1/DTD/xhtml1-strict.dtd">
<html lang="EN" dir="ltr" xmlns="http://www.w3.org/1999/xhtml">
<head>
<title>
Fancy Old Man
</title>
</head>
<body>
<h1>This Old Man with Arrays</h1>
<?php
$place = array(
  "",
  "on my thumb",
  "on my shoe",
  "on my knee",
  "on a door");
```

```
//print out song
for ($verse = 1; $verse <= 4; $verse++){
print <<<HERE
 <p>
 This old man, He played $verse <br />
 He played knick-knack $place[$verse] <br />
 ...with a knick, knack, paddy-whack <br />
 give a dog a bone <br />
 This old man came rolling home
 </p>
HERE;
   } // end for loop

?>


</body>
</html>
```

This improved version takes advantage of the fact that the only things that change from verse to verse are the verse number and the place where the old man plays paddy-whack (whatever that means). Organizing the places into an array greatly simplifies writing out the song lyrics.

## Building the place Array

I notice that each place is a string value associated with some number. I use the array() directive to preload the $place array with appropriate values. Zero has no corresponding place, so I simply left the 0 element blank.

```
$place = array(
   "",
   "on my thumb",
   "on my shoe",
   "on my knee",
   "on a door");
```

Like most places in PHP, carriage returns don't matter when you're writing the source code. I put each place on a separate line, just because it looked neater that way. Commas do matter. Don't forget them, or the code will either crash or combine elements in a way you don't expect.

## Writing Out the Lyrics

The song itself is incredibly repetitive. Each verse is identical except for the verse number and place. For each verse, the value of the $verse variable is the current verse number. The corresponding place is stored in $place[$verse]. A large print statement in a for loop prints the entire code.

```
//print out song
for ($verse = 1; $verse <= 4; $verse++){
print <<<HERE
 <p>
 This old man, He played $verse <br />
 He played knick-knack $place[$verse] <br />
 ...with a knick, knack, paddy-whack <br />
 give a dog a bone <br />
 This old man came rolling home
 </p>
HERE;
 } // end for loop
```

The Fancy Old Man program illustrates very nicely the tradeoff associated with using arrays. Creating a program that uses arrays correctly often takes a little more planning than using control structures alone (as in This Old Man). However, the extra work up front pays off because the program is easier to modify and extend.

## USING ARRAYS IN FORMS

Sometimes your programs will need to pass an array of data from an HTML form. Figure 4.9 illustrates one such example.

The form is designed so all elements form an array, which can be read by the program when the user clicks the Submit button. The result of this program is shown in Figure 4.10.

The `readArray` program shown in Figures 4.9 and 4.10 is a simple example of this type of behavior. The code begins by detecting whether this is the first time the user has come to the form:

```
<!DOCTYPE html PUBLIC "-//W3C//DTD XHTML 1.0 Strict//EN"
"http://www.w3.org/TR/xhtml1/DTD/xhtml1-strict.dtd">
<html lang="EN" dir="ltr" xmlns="http://www.w3.org/1999/xhtml">
 <head>
<meta http-equiv="content-type" content="text/xml; charset=utf-8" />
    <link rel = "stylesheet"
          type = "text/css"
          href = "readArray.css" />


  <title>Read Array</title>
 </head>
 <body>


<?php


if (filter_has_var(INPUT_POST, "people")){
 showPeople();
} else {
 printForm();
} // end if
```

After the ordinary preliminaries of creating an XHTML page and importing a stylesheet, the program uses the `filter_has_var()` function to check for the existence of the `people` variable (which will be the only variable produced by the page). If this variable exists, control is passed to the `showPeople()` function, which will display the contents of the `people` array. If the variable does not exist, this must be the first pass through the program, so the `printForm()` method creates the user input form.

 **TIP**  This is a pattern you'll frequently see in PHP. Check to see if it's the first time you've gotten to a program by looking for the existence of a variable. If the variable exists, process the form; otherwise, create the form and present it to the user. In this way, PHP programs often create their own forms.

## Arranging an HTML Form to Create an Array

The printForm() function basically creates an HTML form. It's nothing but a huge hereDoc:

```
function printForm(){

  print <<< HERE
  <h2>Type in your people here...</h2>
<form action = ""
     method = "post">
   <fieldset>
    <input type = "text"
          name = "people[0]"
     value = "Andy" />
    <input type = "text"
          name = "people[1]"
     value = "Heather" />
    <input type = "text"
          name = "people[2]"
     value = "Elizabeth" />
    <input type = "text"
          name = "people[3]"
     value = "Matthew" />
    <input type = "text"
          name = "people[4]"
     value = "Jacob" />
    <input type = "text"
          name = "people[5]"
     value = "Benjamin" />
    <button>
      submit
    </button>
   </fieldset>
  </form>
HERE;

} // end printForm
```

Note that all the text boxes have a similar name attribute, but they use the array syntax (people[4] for example). When all these elements are read by a PHP function, they will automatically be combined into a single array variable, with all the individual elements in the assigned place. Since the action attribute of the form is left blank, the program will call itself when it is submitted.

## Reading an Array from a Form

To read an array of data, use a slight variation of the `filter_input()` function. The `filter_input_array()` function reads all the elements of a form into an array. You can then extract any of the variables from this array. Look at the code and then I'll explain how it works.

```
function showPeople(){
  $formData = filter_input_array(INPUT_POST);
  $people = $formData["people"];

  print "<h2>Your People</h2> \n";
  print "<pre>";
  print_r($people);
  print "</pre>";

  print "<ul> \n";
  for ($i = 0; $i < count($people); $i++){
    print "  <li>$people[$i] </li> \n";
  } // end for loop
  print "</ul> \n";
} // end showPeople
?>
```

The `filter_input_array()` function pulls all of the form elements into a single variable. This can be used with any type of data, but it's especially handy with arrays.

```
$formData = filter_input_array(INPUT_POST);
```

You can then extract any of these elements into their own variables. In this case, I isolate the `people` array and pass it to its own variable:

```
$people = $formData["people"];
```

 The mechanism used here is called an `associative array`. This extremely powerful array variant will be explained in full in the next chapter, but for now just understand you can use this mechanism to extract an element from the form data.

Now that you have access to the $people array, you can extract all the elements for it. One very handy trick for debugging array data is used in this code:

```
print "<pre>";
print_r($people);
print "</pre>";
```

The print_r() function is used to print out complex variables (like arrays) in a human-readable format. When testing forms that work with arrays, I often temporarily put this debugging code (a print_r() command) inside <pre> tags to make sure my arrays contain what I think they do. Once you are confident the variable contains the appropriate content, you can remove the debugging code.

The rest of the code uses a for loop to print out all the names in an unordered list.

```
print "<ul> \n";
for ($i = 0; $i < count($people); $i++){
  print " <li>$people[$i] </li> \n";
} // end for loop
print "</ul> \n";
```

## Keeping Persistent Data

Most traditional kinds of programming presume that the user and the program are engaging in a continual dialog. A program begins running, might ask the user some questions, responds to these inputs, and continues interacting with the user until he indicates an interest in leaving the program.

Programs written on a web server are different. The PHP programs you are writing have an incredibly short life span. When the user makes a request to your PHP program through a web browser, the server runs the PHP interpreter (the program that converts your PHP code into the underlying machine language your server understands). The result of the program is a web page that is sent back to the user's browser. Once your program sends a page to the user, the PHP program shuts down because its work is done. Web servers do not maintain contact with the browser after sending a page. Each request from the user is seen as an entirely new transaction.

The Poker Dice program at the beginning of this chapter appears to interact with the user indefinitely. Actually, the same program is being called repeatedly. The program acts differently in different circumstances. Somehow it needs to keep track of what state it's currently in.

**IN THE REAL WORLD**

The underlying web protocol (HTTP) that web servers use does not keep connections open any longer than necessary. This behavior is referred to as being a stateless protocol. Imagine if your program were kept running as long as anybody anywhere on the web were looking at it. What if a person fired up your program and went to bed? Your web server would have to maintain a connection to that page all night. Also, remember that your program might be called by thousands of people all at the same time.

It can be very hard on your server to have all these concurrent connections open. Having stateless behavior improves your web server's performance, but that performance comes at a cost. Essentially, your programs have complete amnesia every time they run. You need a mechanism for determining the current state.

## Counting with Form Fields

You can store information a couple of ways, including files, XML, and databases. The second half of this book details these important ideas. The easiest approach to achieving data permanence is to hide the data in the user's page using a special trick called *session variables*. The first example shows how to use hidden form data. To illustrate, take a look at Figures 4.11 and 4.12.

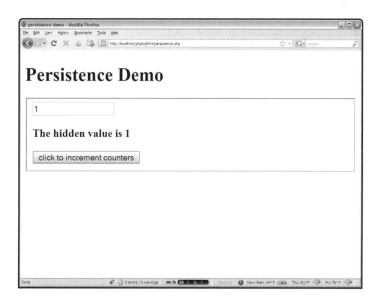

FIGURE 4.11

The program has two counters that read 1 when the program is run the first time.

**FIGURE 4.12**

Both values are
incremented after
the user clicks the
Submit button.

Each time you click the `Persistence` program's Submit button, the counters increment by one. The program behavior appears to contradict the basic nature of server-side programs because it seems to remember the previous counter value. In fact, if two users were accessing the `Persistence` program at the same time, each would count correctly. Look at the source code to see how it works:

```
<!DOCTYPE html PUBLIC "-//W3C//DTD XHTML 1.0 Strict//EN"
"http://www.w3.org/TR/xhtml1/DTD/xhtml1-strict.dtd">
<html lang="EN" dir="ltr" xmlns="http://www.w3.org/1999/xhtml">
<head>
<title>
persistence demo
</title>
</head>

<body>

<h1>Persistence Demo</h1>
<form action = ""
      method = "post">

<?php
```

```
//load up variables
$txtBoxCounter = filter_input(INPUT_POST, "txtBoxCounter");
$hdnCounter = filter_input(INPUT_POST, "hdnCounter");

//increment the counters
$txtBoxCounter++;
$hdnCounter++;

print <<<HERE
<fieldset>
<input type = "text"
       name = "txtBoxCounter"
       value = "$txtBoxCounter" />

<input type = "hidden"
       name = "hdnCounter"
       value = "$hdnCounter" />

<h3>The hidden value is $hdnCounter</h3>
<input type = "submit"
       value = "click to increment counters" />
HERE;

?>
</fieldset>
</form>
</body>
</html>
```

## Storing Data in the Text Box

The program has two variables: $txtBoxCounter and $hdnCounter. For now, concentrate on $txtBoxCounter, which is related to the text box. When the program begins, it grabs the value of $txtBoxCounter (if it exists) and adds one to it. When the program prints the text box, it automatically places the $txtBoxCounter value in the text box.

Since the form's action attribute is set to null (""), the program automatically calls itself when the user clicks the Submit button. This time, $txtBoxCounter has a value (1). When the program runs again, it increments $txtBoxCounter and stores the new value (now 2) in the text box. Each time the program runs, it stores in the text box the value it needs on the next run.

## Using a Hidden Field for Persistence

The text box is convenient for this example because you can see it, but using a text box this way in real programs causes serious problems. Text boxes are editable by the user, which means she could insert any kind of information and really mess up your day.

Hidden form fields are the unsung heroes of server-side programming. Look at `$hdnCounter` in the source code. This hidden field also has a counter, but the user never sees it. However, the value of the `$hdnCounter` variable is sent to the PHP program indicated by the form's `action` attribute. That program can do anything with the attribute, including printing it in the HTML code body.

A simple way to track information between pages is to store the information in hidden fields on the user's page.

The hidden fields technique shown here works fine for storing small amounts of information, but it is very inefficient and insecure when you are working with more serious forms of data.

## USING A SESSION VARIABLE TO STORE DATA

The other common technique for keeping data persistent between runs of a program is called the *session variable*. These are special variables you can set, and PHP uses a variety of mechanisms for ensuring the data is preserved between calls of the program. When you use a session variable, you can use a variable in multiple calls of a program without using hidden fields.

Figure 4.13 shows a variation of the counting program using a session variable to store the counter.

When you create a session variable, PHP does some interesting things under the hood. Essentially, it creates a file on the server containing whatever information is in the session variable, and it creates a random identifier of the session, which is stored in a *cookie* on the client's machine. A cookie is a small text file stored by the browser.

When you use a session variable, PHP uses the cookie identifier from the client to look up the data from the server file. Fortunately, all this is done automatically, so you don't need to worry too much about the details.

FIGURE 4.13

A session variable keeps track of the counter.

## AREN'T COOKIES BAD?

Cookies have gotten a bad reputation, which is largely undeserved. It's true that websites often use cookies to store data on a user's machine without explicit permission, but that's not always a bad thing. Cookies can only store plain text; they can only be modified by the website that created them, and they automatically expire, so they can't be used to directly create viruses or cause other mischief.

Like any other kind of powerful tool, cookies can be used for good or for evil. The particular application of cookies we're using here (automatic generation of cookies for session data) is very respectful of the user's resources (all the data is stored on the server except a small identifier used to determine the cookie). The cookies you build using session variables will not cause users any problems.

Still, there is some superstition around, and some people have completely turned off cookies. In such cases, PHP tries to use a workaround, but it's not always as effective. Fortunately, the hidden field trick (while not as elegant as session variables) works even if cookies are disabled in the user's browser.

Take a look at the code for session.php and you can see how it all works:

```php
<?php session_start() ?>

<!DOCTYPE html PUBLIC "-//W3C//DTD XHTML 1.0 Strict//EN"
"http://www.w3.org/TR/xhtml1/DTD/xhtml1-strict.dtd">
<html lang="EN" dir="ltr" xmlns="http://www.w3.org/1999/xhtml">
<head>
<title>
persistence demo
</title>
</head>

<body>

<h1>session.php</h1>

<?php
  if (isset($_SESSION["counter"])){
    $counter = $_SESSION["counter"];
  } else {
    $counter = 0;
  } // end if
  $counter++;
  print "<h2>Counter: $counter</h2> \n";


  //store new data in counter
  $_SESSION["counter"] = $counter;

  print <<< HERE
<form action = ""
    method = "post">
  <p>
    <button type = "submit">
      count
    </button>
  </p>
</form>
```

```
HERE;

?>
</body>
</html>
```

## Starting the Session

Session variables usually use cookies, and for technical reasons, cookie information must be sent to the client before any text is written to the page. (The cookie information must be sent in the document header, and PHP sends a document header automatically as soon as text is written, so you must explicitly set up the session first to prevent this.... Whew. Did you really want to know that?)

Any program that uses sessions should have a special PHP snippet at the very beginning that looks like this:

```
<?php session_start() ?>
```

**WARNING** The session_start() code should be the very first line of your PHP program. If there is any HTML or PHP in front of this code, the session will not work correctly. Even blank spaces have been known to cause problems. Be sure to place this line at the very top of your program if you want to use a session variable. If you see this error:

```
"Cannot modify header information - headers already sent"
```

You've probably got your session_start() code in the wrong place.

## Working with Session Data

Session data is stored in a special variable called $_SESSION. This variable acts like a suitcase, allowing you to store and retrieve information in the session. Even if you have hundreds of users simultaneously using your site, the session keeps track of the data for each particular user without you having to do anything beyond setting up the session.

Use a special syntax to create a regular variable from the session. This line does the work:

```
$counter = $_SESSION["counter"];
```

This code goes to the session variable, finds an element called "counter" (if it exists), and places the value into a new ordinary variable called $counter. This line essentially unpacks counter from the session suitcase and puts it in an ordinary variable. You can use $counter like any other variable.

When you're done manipulating your session variable, you'll usually want to pack it back into the session so the next pass of your program can use it. This code is pretty similar:

```
$_SESSION["counter"] = $counter;
```

You don't normally work with a session variable directly. It's more common to unload it into a regular variable, do work with the normal variable, then pack it back into the session when you're done with it. Don't forget to put the variable back in the session, or its value will be lost.

## Using Sessions Well

There are a few more tips for working with sessions. Sometimes you need to know if a session variable is already set. The isset() function can be used to tell you if the session already has a value, returning true if the session has a value, or false if it does not. Typically, you'll use this technique to initialize a session variable.

For example:

```
if (isset($_SESSION["counter"])){
  $counter = $_SESSION["counter"];
} else {
  $counter = 0;
} // end if
```

This code ensures the $counter variable has a value whether it was set in the session or not.

You can also explicitly destroy a session variable using the unset() function.

```
unset($_SESSION["counter"]);
```

Typically, this is unnecessary, as the cookie mechanism is already time-limited, and session variables will automatically be destroyed shortly after they are used. In practice, you might use the unset() function while testing your programs just so you can clear out a session.

Testing programs that use sessions can be tricky. The easiest way to do this is to use the web developer toolbar for Firefox. This wonderful tool has a feature for clearing all session cookies (Cookies – clear session cookies). The web developer toolbar has many other very useful features for cookie management, including the ability to easily view all cookies currently active, clear all cookies, and turn cookie management on and off. This free toolbar is definitely worth the download.

# WRITING THE POKER DICE PROGRAM

It's time to take another look at the Poker Dice program that made its debut at the beginning of this chapter. As usual, this program doesn't do anything you haven't already learned. It is a little more complex than the trivial sample programs I show you in this chapter, but it's surprisingly compact considering how much it does. It won't surprise you that arrays and loops are the secret to this program's success.

## Setting Up the XHTML

As always, a basic XHTML page serves as the foundation for the PHP program. Note that because this program will use a session variable to keep track of the player's cash, it begins with a special PHP segment to start the session.

Remember, if you're using sessions, the session_start() function needs to be the very first line, even before the XHTML begins.

The rest of the header loads up a CSS file and sets up the title.

```
<?php session_start() ?>

<!DOCTYPE html PUBLIC "-//W3C//DTD XHTML 1.0 Strict//EN"
"http://www.w3.org/TR/xhtml1/DTD/xhtml1-strict.dtd">
<html lang="EN" dir="ltr" xmlns="http://www.w3.org/1999/xhtml">
<head>
<title>poker dice</title>
<link rel = "stylesheet"
      type = "text/css"
      href = "pd.css" />
</head>

<body>

<h1>pokerDice.php</h1>
<?php
```

## Building the Main Code Body

The Poker Dice program is long enough to merit functions. I broke it into smaller segments here, but you may want to look at its entirety, which is on the CD that accompanies this book.

The main part of the code sets up the general program flow. Most of the work is done in other functions called from this main area.

```php
<?php
//set things up if it's the first time here, otherwise play
if (filter_has_var(INPUT_POST, "doNext")){
  play();
} else {
  startGame();
} // end if
```

The first order of business is to determine whether the user has been here before. If this is the first time here (which will be the case if the doNext variable does not exist), call the startGame() function to set up the game's initial values. Otherwise, go to the main gameplay function called play(). The doNext variable will be used to describe what the program should do next. For now, the important thing is whether the variable exists. Its actual purpose becomes clear in the discussion of the play() function below.

## Starting up the Game

The startGame() function gives the user an initial cash balance of $100. The $cash variable will need to be tracked over several runs of the program, so it is stored in a session variable.

```php
function startGame(){
  // if it's the first time here, set up initial cash,
  // and do firstPass
  $cash = 100;
  $_SESSION["cash"] = 100;
  firstPass();
} // end reset
```

Finally, the startGame() function kick-starts the gameplay by calling the firstPass() function (described below).

## Playing the Game

The central part of this game is controlled by the play() function:

```php
function play(){
  //alternate control between firstPass and secondPass
  //functions based on $doNext
  $doNext = filter_input(INPUT_POST, "doNext");

  if ($doNext == "firstPass"){
    firstPass();
```

```
    } else {
      secondPass();
      evaluate();
    } // end if
} // end play
```

If you look carefully at the program as it is running, you see it runs in two different modes. Each turn consists of two possible passes. On the first pass, the user is given the ability to save attractive dice. The second pass has slightly different behavior. The user can't save any dice on this pass, but the roll is scored, and money is added or subtracted from the user's cash.

The $doNext variable is used to describe what will be done next. Each form generated by the program will contain a hidden field called doNext, which will indicate what the program should do.

If $doNext contains the value "firstPass", the program runs the aptly named firstPass() function. Otherwise, the program runs the secondPass() function. After the second pass, the program evaluates the hand to determine how to change the player's score.

## Creating the First Pass Output

The firstPass() function creates the output used on the first pass. This version of the program prints out the dice, but it also adds a checkbox to each die so the user has the ability to keep a particular die.

```
function firstPass(){
  $cash = $_SESSION["cash"];
  print <<< HERE
      <h2>First Pass</h2>
        <form method = "post"
        action = "">
    <fieldset>

HERE;

  for ($i = 0; $i < 5; $i++){
    $die[$i] = rand(1, 6);
    //print "$i: $die[$i] ";
    print <<< HERE

      <div class = "dieImage">
```

```
            <img src = "die$die[$i].jpg"
                 alt = "$i" />
            <input type = "checkbox"
                   name = "keepIt[$i]"
                   value = "$die[$i]" />
        </div>

HERE;

  } // end for
  print <<< HERE
        <input type = "hidden"
               name = "doNext"
               value = "secondPass" />

        <button type = "submit">
           go
        </button>
        <p>Cash: $cash</p>
     </fieldset>
   </form>

HERE;
   $_SESSION["cash"] = $cash;
 } // end firstPass
```

The function begins by printing out a simple form. For each die, there is a random integer roll. The die images are printed using string interpolation. Note that under each die is a checkbox. The checkboxes are in an array called keepIt. The value of each checkbox is the value of the corresponding die.

```
        <input type = "checkbox"
               name = "keepIt[$i]"
               value = "$die[$i]" />
```

Remember that checkboxes have unique behavior in PHP. If the box is checked, it will be returned to the server. If the box is not checked, it will not be sent to the server at all.

Note that I kept everything tidy by putting each image and checkbox into a div that I could then format with some clever CSS.

I add a hidden field containing the `doNext` variable telling the program it should call `secondPass` next. I also add the Submit button.

Finally, the `$cash` variable is stored to the session variable.

---

**SESSIONS OR HIDDEN FIELDS?**

This program has several persistent elements. The `keepIt` array, the `doNext` variable, and the `cash` variable all need to be reused on multiple passes of the form. Any data that comes directly from user input (like `keepIt`) must be form data, but the `doNext` and `cash` variables could be stored either as a hidden field on the form or as a session variable. It's largely a matter of taste. Some programmers use session variables for everything, and some use hidden fields exclusively. Most use a combination. In this particular example, it seemed clearest to me that each form would indicate what should happen next, so I stored the `doNext` value in the forms. The `cash` variable seemed to be easier to work with as a session variable, so that's how I implemented it.

---

## Building the Second Pass Output

The second pass is similar to the first, but not identical. On the second pass, there will be a `keepIt` array. This array is formed by the checkboxes built in the first pass. Any die that was checked will result in a value in the `keepIt` array.

If the user elected to keep a die, the original value will be used again. If not, a new random value is rolled.

```
function secondPass(){
  global $die;
  //get cash from session variable
  $cash = $_SESSION["cash"];
  //print "cash: $cash <br />";

  print <<< HERE
  <h2>Second Pass</h2>
  <form method = "post"
        action = "">
```

```
        <fieldset>

HERE;
  //check to see if keepIt exists
  // (which happens if any of the checkboxes is checked)
  if (filter_has_var(INPUT_POST, "keepIt")){
    //pull all values from form
    $formVals = filter_input_array(INPUT_POST);
    //extract $keepIt array (easiest way to handle array input)
    $keepIt = $formVals["keepIt"];

    for ($i = 0; $i < 5; $i++){
      //if any values are empty, replace them with zero
      if (empty($keepIt[$i])){
        $keepIt[$i] = 0;
      } // end if
      //print "$i) $keepIt[$i] <br />";
    } // end for loop
  } else {
    //keepIt doesn't exist, so make it with
    //all zero values
    $keepIt = array(0, 0, 0, 0, 0);
  } // end if


  for ($i = 0; $i < 5; $i++){
    //replace the image if the current value
    //of keepIt is non-zero
    if ($keepIt[$i] == 0){
      $die[$i] = rand(1, 6);
    } else {
      $die[$i] = $keepIt[$i];
    } // end if

    print <<< HERE
      <div class = "dieImage">
        <img src = "die$die[$i].jpg"
             alt = "$i" />
```

```
      </div>

HERE;

  } // end for
  print <<< HERE
      <input type = "hidden"
            name = "doNext"
            value = "firstPass" />
      <button type = "submit">
        go
      </button>
    </fieldset>
  </form>

HERE;

} // end secondPass
```

Since `keepIt` is an array, I used the `filter_input_array()` technique to extract the data from the form. Remember that checkboxes create a variable only if they are checked. If the user chooses not to keep anything, `keepIt` will not exist. In that case, I just create a new `keepIt` array with all zeros.

If `keepIt` does exist, it will only contain elements for die that were checked. The `empty()` function can be used to determine if a particular variable has been created. If this is the case, I create the array entry and set it to zero.

```
    for ($i = 0; $i < 5; $i++){
      //if any values are empty, replace them with zero
      if (empty($keepIt[$i])){
        $keepIt[$i] = 0;
      } // end if
      //print "$i) $keepIt[$i] <br />";
    } // end for loop
```

By the time this analysis is finished, I'm guaranteed to have a `keepIt` array with five elements. It will contain zero if the user wanted to roll a new die in that position, or the value of the previous roll if the user chose to keep the roll.

The next step is to roll a new value if necessary or copy the previous value if desired. A simple if structure does the job:

```php
for ($i = 0; $i < 5; $i++){
  //replace the image if the current value
  //of keepIt is non-zero
  if ($keepIt[$i] == 0){
    $die[$i] = rand(1, 6);
  } else {
    $die[$i] = $keepIt[$i];
  } // end if

  print <<< HERE
    <div class = "dieImage">
      <img src = "die$die[$i].jpg"
           alt = "$i" />
    </div>

HERE;

} // end for
```

## Creating the evaluate() Function

The evaluate() function's purpose is to examine the $die array and see if the user has achieved patterns worthy of reward. Again, I print the entire function here and show some highlights after.

```php
function evaluate(){
  global $die;
  //set up payoff
  $payoff = 0;
  //create $numVals
  for($i = 1; $i <= 6; $i++){
    $numVals[$i] = 0;
  } // end for loop


  //count the dice
  for ($theVal = 1; $theVal <= 6; $theVal++){
```

```
  for ($dieNum = 0; $dieNum < 5; $dieNum++){
    if ($die[$dieNum] == $theVal){
      $numVals[$theVal]++;
    } // end if
  } // end dieNum for loop
} // end theVal for loop

//print out results
//   for ($i = 1; $i <= 6; $i++){
//    print "$i:  $numVals[$i]<br />\n";
//   } // end for loop

//count how many pairs, threes, fours, fives
$numPairs = 0;
$numThrees = 0;
$numFours = 0;
$numFives = 0;

for ($i = 1; $i <= 6; $i++){
  switch ($numVals[$i]){
    case 2:
      $numPairs++;
      break;
    case 3:
      $numThrees++;
      break;
    case 4:
      $numFours++;
      break;
    case 5:
      $numFives++;
      break;
  } // end switch
} // end for loop

print "<p> \n";

//check for two pairs
```

```php
if ($numPairs == 2){
  print "You have two pairs!<br />\n";
  $payoff = 1;
} // end if

//check for three of a kind and full house
if ($numThrees == 1){
  if ($numPairs == 1){
    //three of a kind and a pair is a full house
    print "You have a full house!<br />\n";
    $payoff = 5;
  } else {
    print "You have three of a kind!<br />\n";
    $payoff = 2;
  } // end 'pair' if
} // end 'three' if

//check for four of a kind
if ($numFours == 1){
  print "You have four of a kind!<br />\n";
  $payoff = 5;
} // end if

//check for five of a kind
if ($numFives == 1){
  print "You got five of a kind!<br />\n";
  $payoff = 10;
} // end if

//check for straights
if (($numVals[1] == 1)
  && ($numVals[2] == 1)
  && ($numVals[3] == 1)
  && ($numVals[4] == 1)
  && ($numVals[5] == 1)){
  print "You have a straight!<br />\n";
  $payoff = 10;
} // end if

if (($numVals[2] == 1)
```

```
      && ($numVals[3] == 1)
      && ($numVals[4] == 1)
      && ($numVals[5] == 1)
      && ($numVals[6] == 1)){
      print "You have a straight!<br />\n";
      $payoff = 10;

    } // end if

    $cash = $_SESSION["cash"];
    //print "Cash: $cash<br />\n";
    //subtract some money for this roll
    $cash -= 2;
    print "You bet 2<br />\n";
    print "Payoff is $payoff<br />\n";
    $cash += $payoff;
    print "Cash: $cash<br />\n";
print "</p> \n";

//store cash back to session:
$_SESSION["cash"] = $cash;
} // end evaluate
```

The evaluate() function's general strategy is to subtract $2 for the player's bet each time. (Change this to make the game easier or harder.) I create a new array called $numVals, which tracks how many times each possible value appears. Analyzing the $numVals array is an easier way to track the various scoring combinations than looking directly at the $die array. The rest of the function checks each of the possible scoring combinations and calculates an appropriate payoff.

## Counting the Dice Values

When you think about the various scoring combinations in this game, it's important to know how many of each value the user rolled. The user gets points for pairs, three-, four-, and five of a kind, and straights (five values in a row). I made a new array called $numVals, which has six elements. $numVals[1] contains the number of ones the user rolled. $numVals[2] shows how many twos, and so on.

```
//count the dice
for ($theVal = 1; $theVal <= 6; $theVal++){
  for ($dieNum = 0; $dieNum < 5; $dieNum++){
    if ($die[$dieNum] == $theVal){
```

```
        $numVals[$theVal]++;
      } // end if
    } // end dieNum for loop
  } // end theVal for loop

  //print out results
  //   for ($i = 1; $i <= 6; $i++){
  //     print "$i:  $numVals[$i]<br />\n";
  //   } // end for loop
```

To build the $numVals array, I stepped through each possible value (1 through 6) with a for loop. I used another for loop to look at each die and determine if it showed the appropriate value. (In other words, I checked for 1s the first time through the outer loop, then 2s, then 3s, and so on.) If I found the current value, I incremented $numVals[$theVal] appropriately.

Notice the lines at the end of this segment that are commented out. Moving on with the scorekeeping code if the $numVals array did not work as expected was moot, so I put in a quick loop that tells me how many of each value the program found. This ensures my program works properly before I add functionality.

It's smart to periodically check your work and make sure that things are working as you expected. When I determined things were working correctly, I placed comments in front of each line to temporarily turn the debugging code off. Doing this removes the code, but it remains if something goes wrong and I need to look at the $numVals array again.

## Counting Pairs, Twos, Threes, Fours, and Fives

The $numVals array has most of the information I need, but it's not quite in the right format. The user earns cash for pairs and for three-, four-, and five of a kind.

To check for these conditions, I use some other variables and another loop to look at $numVals.

```
  //count how many pairs, threes, fours, fives
  $numPairs = 0;
  $numThrees = 0;
  $numFours = 0;
  $numFives = 0;

  for ($i = 1; $i <= 6; $i++){
    switch ($numVals[$i]){
      case 2:
        $numPairs++;
```

```
      break;
    case 3:
      $numThrees++;
      break;
    case 4:
      $numFours++;
      break;
    case 5:
      $numFives++;
      break;
  } // end switch
} // end for loop
```

First, I created variables to track pairs, and three-, four-, and five of a kind. I initialized all these variables to 0. I then stepped through the $numVals array to see how many of each value occurred. If, for example, the user rolled 1, 1, 5, 5, 5, $numVals[1] equals 2 and $numVals[5] equals 3.

After the switch statement executes, $numPairs equals 1 and $numThrees equals 1. All the other $num variables still contain 0. Creating these variables makes it easy to determine which scoring situations (if any) have occurred.

## Looking for Two Pairs

All the work setting up the scoring variables pays off, because it's now very easy to determine when a scoring condition has occurred. I award the user $1 for two pairs (and nothing for one pair). If the value of $numPairs is 2, the user has gotten two pairs; the $payoff variable is given the value 1.

```
//check for two pairs
if ($numPairs == 2){
  print "You have two pairs!<br />\n";
  $payoff = 1;
} // end if
```

Of course, you're welcome to change the payoffs. As it stands, this game is somewhat generous, but that makes it fun for the user (and sadly, it isn't real money).

## Looking for Three of a Kind and a Full House

I combine the checks for three of a kind and full house (which is three of a kind and a pair). The code first checks for three of a kind by looking at $numThrees. If the user has three of a kind, it then checks for a pair. If both these conditions are true, it's a full house and the user is rewarded appropriately. If there isn't a pair, the user gets a meager reward for the three of a kind.

```
//check for three of a kind and full house
if ($numThrees == 1){
  if ($numPairs == 1){
    //three of a kind and a pair is a full house
    print "You have a full house!<br />\n";
    $payoff = 5;
  } else {
    print "You have three of a kind!<br />\n";
    $payoff = 2;
  } // end 'pair' if
} // end 'three' if
```

## Checking for Four of a Kind and Five of a Kind

Checking for four and five of a kind is trivial. Looking at the appropriate variables is the only necessity.

```
//check for four of a kind
if ($numFours == 1){
  print "You have four of a kind!<br />\n";
  $payoff = 5;
} // end if

//check for five of a kind
if ($numFives == 1){
  print "You got five of a kind!<br />\n";
  $payoff = 10;
} // end if
```

## Checking for Straights

Straights are a little trickier, because two are possible. The player could have the values 1-5 or 2-6. To check these situations, I used two compound conditions. A compound condition is made of a number of ordinary conditions combined with special logical operators. Look at the straight-checking code to see an example:

```
//check for straights
if (($numVals[1] == 1)
  && ($numVals[2] == 1)
  && ($numVals[3] == 1)
```

```
     && ($numVals[4] == 1)
     && ($numVals[5] == 1)){
     print "You have a straight!<br />\n";
     $payoff = 10;
   } // end if

   if (($numVals[2] == 1)
     && ($numVals[3] == 1)
     && ($numVals[4] == 1)
     && ($numVals[5] == 1)
     && ($numVals[6] == 1)){
     print "You have a straight!<br />\n";
     $payoff = 10;


   } // end if
```

Notice how each if statement has a condition made of several subconditions joined by the && operator? The && operator is called a Boolean and operator. You can read it as and. The condition is evaluated to TRUE only if all the subconditions are true.

## Cashing Out

The last part of the evaluate() code does some basic housekeeping:

```
   $cash = $_SESSION["cash"];
   //print "Cash: $cash<br />\n";
   //subtract some money for this roll
   $cash -= 2;
   print "You bet 2<br />\n";
   print "Payoff is $payoff<br />\n";
   $cash += $payoff;
   print "Cash: $cash<br />\n";
print "</p> \n";

//store cash back to session:
$_SESSION["cash"] = $cash;
} // end evaluate
```

The first task is to retrieve the $cash variable from the session. I then subtract two dollars for the current bet, then add the payoff calculated earlier in this function. I report the new balance to the user and store the new cash balance back to the session so it will be available in the next round.

# SUMMARY

You are rounding out your basic training as a programmer, adding rudimentary looping behavior to your bag of tricks. Your programs can repeat based on conditions you establish. You know how to build `for` loops that work forwards, backwards, and by skipping values. You also know how to create `while` loops. You know the guidelines for creating a well-behaved loop and how to form arrays manually and with the `array()` directive. Stepping through all elements of an array using a loop is possible, and your program can keep track of persistent variables by storing them in form fields in your output pages, as well as using session variables. You put all these skills together to build an interesting game. In Chapter 5, you extend your ability to work with arrays and loops by building more powerful arrays and using specialized looping structures.

## CHALLENGES

1. Modify the `Poker Dice` game in some way. Add your own graphics or background, modify the payoffs, or add a new rule.

2. Write the classic "I'm thinking of a number" game. Have the computer randomly generate a number and let the user guess its value. Tell the user if he is too high, too low, or correct. When he guesses correctly, tell how many turns it took. No arrays are necessary, but you will need to have persistent data with hidden fields or session variables.

3. Write "I'm thinking of a number" in reverse. This time the user generates a random integer between 1 and 100, and the computer guesses the number. Let the user pick from "too high," "too low," or "correct" each turn. Your algorithm should be able to guess in seven turns or fewer.

4. Write a program that deals a random poker hand. Use one of the many free card image sets available on the web. Your program does not need to score the hand. It simply needs to deal out a hand of five random cards. Use an array to handle the deck.

5. Enhance the program in number four so it ranks the card hand. Your ranking mechanism will be similar to the one used in the `Poker Dice` game, but you have to consider suits as well.

# BETTER ARRAYS AND STRING HANDLING

In this chapter you will learn some important skills that improve your work with data. You learn about some more sophisticated ways to work with arrays and how to manage text information with more flair. Specifically, you learn how to do these things:

- Manage arrays with the `foreach` loop
- Create and use associative arrays
- Extract useful information from some of PHP's built-in arrays
- Build basic two-dimensional arrays
- Build two-dimensional associative arrays
- Break a string into smaller segments
- Search for one string inside another

## INTRODUCING THE WORD SEARCH PROGRAM

By the end of this chapter, you will create a fun program that generates word search puzzles. The user enters a series of words into a list box, as shown in Figure 5.1.

**FIGURE 5.1**

The user enters a list of words and a size for the finished puzzle.

The program then tries to generate a word search based on the user's word list. (It isn't always possible, but the program can usually generate a puzzle.) One possible solution for the word list shown in Figure 5. 1 is demonstrated in Figure 5.2.

If desired, the program can also generate an answer key based on the puzzle. This capability is shown in Figure 5.3.

The secret to the Word Search game (and indeed most computer programs) is the way the data is handled. Once I determined a good scheme for working with the data in the program, the actual programming wasn't too tough.

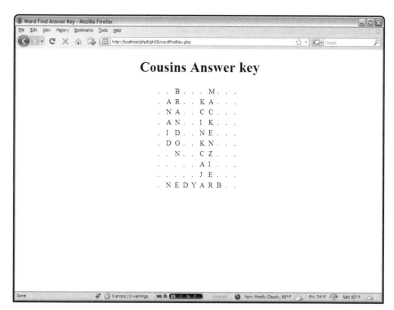

## Using the foreach Loop to Work with an Array

As I mentioned in Chapter 4, "Loops and Arrays," for loops and arrays are natural companions. In fact, PHP supplies a special kind of loop called the *foreach* loop that makes it even easier to step through each array element.

## Introducing the foreach.php Program

The program shown in Figure 5.4 illustrates how the `foreach` loop works.

**FIGURE 5.4**

Although it looks just like normal HTML, this page was created with an array and a `foreach` loop.

The HTML page is generated by surprisingly simple code:

```
<!DOCTYPE html PUBLIC "-//W3C//DTD XHTML 1.0 Strict//EN"
"http://www.w3.org/TR/xhtml1/DTD/xhtml1-strict.dtd">
<html lang="EN" dir="ltr" xmlns="http://www.w3.org/1999/xhtml">
<head>
<title>For Each</title>
</head>
<body>
<h1>Foreach Loop Demo</h1>
<?php

$list = array("alpha", "beta", "gamma", "delta", "epsilon");

print "<ul>\n";
foreach ($list as $value){
    print "  <li>$value</li>\n";
```

```
} // end foreach
print "</ul>\n";
?>
</body>
</html>
```

All the values in the list are created in the $list variable using the array() function.

The foreach loop works a lot like a for loop, except it is a bit simpler. The first parameter of the foreach construct is an array—in this case, $list. The keyword as indicates the name of a variable that holds each value in turn. In this case, the foreach loop steps through the $list array as many times as necessary. Each time through the loop, the function populates the $value variable with the current member of the $list array. In essence, this foreach loop works just like the following traditional for loop:

```
foreach ($list as $value){
    print " <li>$value</li>\n";
} // end foreach
```

Here's your traditional for loop:

```
for ($i = 0; $i < length($list); $i++);
  $value = $list[$i];
  print " <li>$value</li>\n";
} // end for loop
```

 **TRICK** The main difference between a foreach loop and a for loop is the presence of the index variable ($i in this example). If you're using a foreach loop and need to know the current element's index, use the key() function.

The foreach loop can be an extremely handy shortcut for stepping through each value of an array. Since this is a common task, knowing how to use the foreach loop is an important skill. As you learn some other kinds of arrays, you see how to modify the foreach loop to handle these other array styles.

## CREATING AN ASSOCIATIVE ARRAY

PHP is known for its extremely flexible arrays. You can easily generate a number of interesting and useful array types in addition to the ordinary arrays you've already made. One of the handiest types is called an *associative array*.

While it sounds complicated, an associative array (sometimes called a *dictionary*) is much like a normal array. While regular arrays rely on numeric indices, an associative array has a string index. Figure 5.5 shows a page created with two associative arrays.

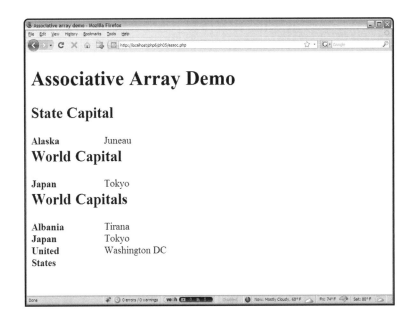

## Examining the assoc.php Program

Imagine that you want to store a list of capital cities. You could certainly store the cities in an array. However, if your main interest is in the relationship between a state and its capital, it could be difficult to maintain the relationship using arrays. In this particular instance, it would be nice if you could use the name of the state as the array index (the element's number, or position, within the array) rather than a number.

## Building an Associative Array

Here is the code from `assoc.php`, which generates the array of state capitals:

```
$stateCap["Alaska"] = "Juneau";
$stateCap["Indiana"] = "Indianapolis";
$stateCap["Michigan"] = "Lansing";
```

The associative array is just like a normal array, except the index values are strings. Note that the indices must be inside quotation marks. Once you have created an associative array, it is used much like a normal array.

```
$cap = $stateCap["Alaska"];
print <<<HERE

<h2>State Capital</h2>
<dl>
  <dt>Alaska</dt>
  <dd>$cap</dd>
</dl>
HERE;
```

Once again, the array's index is a quoted string. The associative form is terrific for data like this. In essence, it lets you "look up" the capital city if you know the state name.

## IN DIZZY-ARRAY

If all this associative array talk is making you dizzy, don't panic. It's just a new name for something you're very familiar with. Think about the way HTML attributes work. Each tag has a number of attributes that you can use in any order. For example, a standard button might look like this:

```
<input type = "button"
       value = "Save the world. ">
```

This button has two attributes. Each attribute is made up of a name/value pair. The keywords `type` and `value` are *names* (or indices, or keys, depending on how you want to think of it) and the terms `button` and `Save the world.` are the *values* associated with those names. Cascading style sheets (CSS) use a different syntax for exactly the same idea. The CSS element indicates a series of modifications to the paragraph tag:

```
p (background-color:red;
   color:yellow;
   font-size:14pt)
```

While the syntax is different, the same pattern applies. The critical part of a CSS definition is a list of name/value pairs.

Associative arrays naturally pop up in one more place. As information comes into your program from an HTML form, it comes in as an associative array. The name of each element becomes an index, and the value of that form element is translated to the value of the array element. Later in this chapter you see how to take advantage of this.

As associative array is simply a data structure used when the name/value relationship is the easiest way to work with some kind of data.

## Building an Associative Array with the array() Function

If you know the values you want in your array, you can use the array() function to build an associative array. However, building associative arrays requires a slightly different syntax than the garden variety arrays you encountered in Chapter 4.

I build the $worldCap array using the array() syntax:

```
$worldCap = array(
  "Albania"=>"Tirana",
  "Japan"=>"Tokyo",
  "United States"=>"Washington DC"
  );
```

The array() function requires the data when you are building an ordinary array, but doesn't require specified indices. The function automatically generates each element's index by grabbing the next available integer. In an associative array, you are responsible for providing both the data and the index.

The general format for this assignment uses a special kind of assignment operator. The => operator indicates that an element holds some kind of value. I generally read it as holds, so you can say "Japan holds Tokyo". In other words, "Japan" => "Tokyo" indicates that PHP should generate an array element with the index "Japan" and store the value "Tokyo" in that element. You can access the value of this array just like any other associative array:

```
$cap = $worldCap["Japan"];

print <<<HERE
<h2>World Capital</h2>
<dl>
  <dt>Japan</dt>
  <dd>$cap</dd>
</dl>
HERE;
```

## Using foreach with Associative Arrays

The `foreach` loop is just as useful with associative arrays as it is with vanilla arrays. However, it uses a slightly different syntax. Take a look at this code from the `assoc.php` page:

```
foreach ($worldCap as $country => $capital){
  print "$country: $capital<br>\n";} // end foreach
```

A `foreach` loop for a regular array uses only one variable because the index can be easily calculated. In an associative array, each element in the array has a unique index and value. The associative form of the `foreach` loop takes this into account by indicating two variables. The first variable holds the index. The second variable refers to the value associated with that index. Inside the loop, you can refer to the current index (`$country`) and value (`$capital`) using whatever variable names you designated in the `foreach` structure.

Each time through the loop, you are given a name/value pair. In this example, the name is stored in the variable `$country`, because all the indices in this array are names of countries. Each time through the loop, `$country` has a different value. In each iteration, the value of the `$capital` variable contains the array value corresponding to the current value of `$country`.

 Unlike traditional arrays, you cannot rely on associative arrays to return in any particular order when you use a `foreach` loop to access array elements. If you need elements to show up in a particular order, call them explicitly.

## Using Built-In Associative Arrays

Associative arrays are extremely handy because they reflect a kind of information storage very frequently used. In fact, you've been using associative arrays in disguise ever since Chapter 2, "Using Variables and Input." Whenever your PHP program receives data from a form, that data is actually stored in a number of associative arrays for you. The `filter_input()` function you've been using to extract information from web forms actually is extracting data from one of a number of associative arrays.

When you worked with session variables in Chapter 4, you were also working with an associative array.

Even when you use automated tools like `filter_input()`, it's useful to know how to use the built-in arrays because:

- Use of `filter_input` isn't yet widespread; you'll see lots of existing code that uses the associative array technique instead.
- As of PHP6, you can't use `filter_input()` for everything; for some types of input (like session variables) you still need to use associative arrays.

- Occasionally you'll find the built-in arrays easier to work with than the `filter_input()` technique.

## Introducing the formReader.php Program

The `formReader.php` program is actually one of the first PHP programs I ever wrote, and it's one I use frequently. It's very handy, because it can take the input from any HTML form and report the names and values of each of the form elements on the page. To illustrate, Figure 5.6 shows a typical web page with a form. (This one is called `sampleForm.html` but the `formReader` program works with any form.)

When the user clicks the Submit Query button, `formReader` responds with some basic diagnostics, as you can see from Figure 5.7.

## Reading the $_REQUEST Array

All the fields sent to your program are automatically stored in a special associative array called `$_REQUEST`. Each field name on the original form becomes a key, and the value of that field becomes the value associated with that key. If you have a form with a field called `userName`, you can get the value of the field by calling `$_REQUEST["userName"]`.

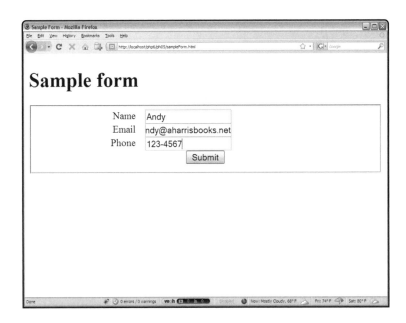

**FIGURE 5.6**

This form, which has three basic fields, calls the `formReader.php` program.

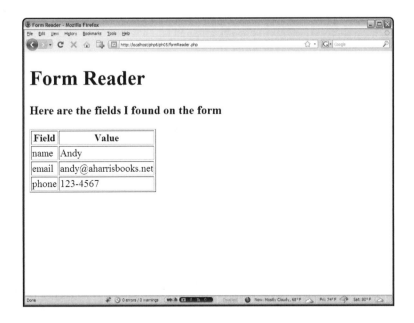

**FIGURE 5.7**

The
formReader.php
program
determines each
field and its value.

The $_REQUEST array is also useful because you can use a foreach loop to quickly determine the names and values of all form elements known to the program. The formReader.php program source code illustrates how this is done:

```
<!DOCTYPE html PUBLIC "-//W3C//DTD XHTML 1.0 Strict//EN"
"http://www.w3.org/TR/xhtml1/DTD/xhtml1-strict.dtd">
<html lang="EN" dir="ltr" xmlns="http://www.w3.org/1999/xhtml">
<head>
  <title>Form Reader</title>

</head>
<body>
<h1>Form Reader</h1>
<h3>Here are the fields I found on the form</h3>
<?php
print <<<HERE
<table border = "1">
<tr>
  <th>Field</th>
  <th>Value</th>
</tr>
HERE;
```

```
foreach ($_REQUEST as $field => $value){
  print <<<HERE
  <tr>
    <td>$field</td>
    <td>$value</td>
  </tr>
HERE;
} // end foreach
print "</table>\n";

?>

</body>
</html>
```

Note how I stepped through the $_REQUEST array. Each time through the foreach loop, the current field name is stored in the $field variable and the value of that field is stored in $value.

**TRICK** I use this script when I'm debugging my programs. If I'm not getting the form elements I expected from a form, I put a foreach $_REQUEST loop in at the top of my program to make sure I know exactly what's being sent to the program. Often this type of procedure can help you find misspellings or other bugs.

PHP supplies a number of other extremely useful associative arrays. If you want to see a list of all the variables sent through the get mechanism, you can use $_GET. The $_POST array contains only those variables sent through a post request. The $_SESSION array contains all the session variables. In fact, the $_REQUEST array is simply the union of $_POST, $_GET, $_SESSION, and $_COOKIE.

**TIP** It's possible that you'll see another variable shown on your form. If you've been experimenting with session variables, a sessionID variable may appear with a strange value. This is used to help the browser keep track of session variables. You can use the web developer toolbar (in Firefox) to clear session variables, or ignore them, as they will be automatically deleted when you close the browser.

There are a few other special variables you might investigate in the PHP documentation for special situations.

The $_SERVER variable contains information about the web server (especially $_SERVER ['REMOTE_ADDR']) that can be used to determine the IP address of the user. Finally, the $_FILES array contains a link to any files uploaded onto the server.

These variables are called *superglobals* because they are automatically set as global variables and can be used anywhere in the program (even in functions) without any special global declaration.

## IN THE REAL WORLD

The superglobals seem pretty great, and they are very popular tools. In fact, right now it is more common to use $_REQUEST to extract data from a form than to use the filter_input() technique described in the book. I recommend filter_input() because it uses the superglobals, but adds a layer of filtering to them. The default behavior of filter_input() makes the variables much more secure than they would be using straight $_REQUEST, and it gives you the ability to filter with much more detail, specifying that a particular input should only yield integer data, or should be pre-filtered to be an appropriate format for an e-mail address. See the extensive documentation for filter_input() on the PHP documentation site.

## CREATING A MULTIDIMENSIONAL ARRAY

Arrays are very useful structures for storing various kinds of data into the computer's memory. Normal arrays are much like lists. Associative arrays are like name/value pairs. A third special type, a *multidimensional array*, acts much like table data. For instance, imagine you were trying to write a program to help users determine the distance between major cities. You might start on paper with a table like Table 5.1.

| TABLE 5.1 DISTANCES BETWEEN MAJOR CITIES | | | | |
|---|---|---|---|---|
| | **Indianapolis** | **New York** | **Tokyo** | **London** |
| Indianapolis | 0 | 648 | 6476 | 4000 |
| New York | 648 | 0 | 6760 | 3470 |
| Tokyo | 6476 | 6760 | 0 | 5956 |
| London | 4000 | 3470 | 5956 | 0 |

It's reasonably common to work with this sort of tabular data in a computer program. PHP (and most languages) provides a special type of array to assist in working with this kind of information. The basicMultiArray program featured in Figures 5.8 and 5.9 illustrates how a program can encapsulate a table.

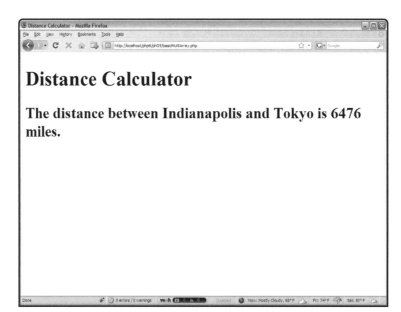

**FIGURE 5.8**

The user can choose origin and destination cities from select groups.

**FIGURE 5.9**

The program looks up the distance between the cities and returns an appropriate value.

## Building the HTML for the Basic Multidimensional Array

Using a two-dimensional array is pretty easy if you plan well. I first wrote out my table on paper. (Actually, I have a write-on, wipe-off board in my office for exactly this kind of situation.) I assigned a numeric value to each city:

Indianapolis = 0

New York = 1

Tokyo = 2

London = 3

This makes it easier to track the cities later on.

The HTML code builds the two select boxes and a Submit button in a form.

```
<!DOCTYPE html PUBLIC "-//W3C//DTD XHTML 1.0 Strict//EN"
"http://www.w3.org/TR/xhtml1/DTD/xhtml1-strict.dtd">
<html lang="EN" dir="ltr" xmlns="http://www.w3.org/1999/xhtml">
<head>
  <title>Basic multi-dimensional array</title>
</head>
<body>
<h1>Basic 2D Array</h1>

<form action = "basicMultiArray.php"
      method = "post">
<table>
<tr>
  <th>First city</th>
  <th>Second city</th>
</tr>

<!-- note each option value is numeric -->

<tr>
  <td>
    <select name = "cityA">
      <option value = "0">Indianapolis</option>
      <option value = "1">New York</option>
      <option value = "2">Tokyo</option>
```

```
      <option value = "3">London</option>
    </select>
  </td>

  <td>
    <select name = "cityB">
      <option value = "0">Indianapolis</option>
      <option value = "1">New York</option>
      <option value = "2">Tokyo</option>
      <option value = "3">London</option>
    </select>
  </td>
</tr>

<tr>
  <td colspan = "2">
    <input type = "submit"
           value = "calculate distance" />
  </td>
</tr>
</table>
</form>

</body>
</html>
```

Recall that when the user submits this form, it sends two variables. The cityA variable contains the value property associated with whatever city the user selected; cityB likewise contains the value of the currently selected destination city. I carefully set up the value properties so they coordinate with each city's numeric index. If the user chooses New York as the origin city, the value of $cityA is 1, because I decided that New York would be represented by the value 1. I'm giving numeric values because the information is all stored in arrays, and normal arrays take numeric indices. (In the next section I show you how to do the same thing with associative arrays.)

## Responding to the Distance Query

The PHP code that determines the distance between cities is actually quite simple once the arrays are in place:

```
<!DOCTYPE html PUBLIC "-//W3C//DTD XHTML 1.0 Strict//EN"
"http://www.w3.org/TR/xhtml1/DTD/xhtml1-strict.dtd">
<html lang="EN" dir="ltr" xmlns="http://www.w3.org/1999/xhtml">
<head>
<title>Distance Calculator</title>
</head>
<body>
<h1>Distance Calculator</h1>
<?php

$cityName = array("Indianapolis", "New York", "Tokyo", "London");

$distance = array(
  array(0, 648, 6476, 4000),
  array(648, 0, 6760, 3470),
  array(6476, 6760, 0, 5956),
  array(4000, 3470, 5956, 0)
);

$cityA = filter_input(INPUT_POST, "cityA");
$cityB = filter_input(INPUT_POST, "cityB");

$fromCity = $cityName[$cityA];
$toCity = $cityName[$cityB];

$result = $distance[$cityA][$cityB];

print "<h2>The distance between $fromCity and $toCity is $result miles.</h2>
\n";

?>

</body>
</html>
```

## Storing City Names in the $city Array

I have two arrays in this program, $city and $distance. The $city array is a completely normal array of string values. It contains a list of city names. I set up the array so the numeric values

I assigned to the city would correspond to the index in this array. Remember that array indices usually start with 0, so Indianapolis is 0, New York is 1, and so on.

The user won't care that Indianapolis is city 0, so the $city array assigns names to the various cities. If the user chose city 0 (Indianapolis) for the $cityA field, I can refer to the name of that city as $city[$cityA] because $cityA contains the value 0 and $city[0] is Indianapolis.

## Storing Distances in the $distance Array

The distances don't fit into a regular list, because it requires two values to determine a distance. You must know from which city you are coming and going to calculate a distance. These two values correspond to rows and columns in the original table. Look again at the code that generates the $distance array:

```
$distance = array(
  array(0, 648, 6476, 4000),
  array(648, 0, 6760, 3470),
  array(6476, 6760, 0, 5956),
  array(4000, 3470, 5956, 0)
);
```

The $distance array is actually an array full of other arrays! Each of the inner arrays corresponds to distance from a certain destination city. For example, since Indianapolis is city 0, the first (zeroth?) inner array refers to the distance between Indy and the other cities. If it helps, you can think of each inner array as a row of a table, and the table as an array of rows.

It might sound complicated to build a two-dimensional array, but it is more natural than you may think. If you compare the original data in Table 5.1 with the code that creates the two-dimensional array, you see that all the numbers are in the right place.

**TRICK**   No need to stop at two dimensions. It's possible to build arrays with three, four, or any other number of dimensions. However, it becomes difficult to visualize how the data works with these complex arrays. Generally, one and two dimensions are as complex as a beginner's arrays need to get. For more complex data types, look toward file-manipulation tools and relational data structures, which you learn throughout the rest of this book.

## Getting Data from the $distance Array

Once data is stored in a two-dimensional array, it is reasonably easy to retrieve. To look up information in a table, you need to know the row and column. A two-dimensional array requires two indices—one for the row and one for the column.

To find the distance from Tokyo (city number 2) to New York (city number 1), simply refer to $distance[2][1]. The code for the program gets the index values from the form:

```
$result = $distance[$cityA][$cityB];
```

This value is stored in the variable $result and then sent to the user.

## MAKING A TWO-DIMENSIONAL ASSOCIATIVE ARRAY

You can also create two-dimensional associative arrays. It takes a little more work to set it up, but the effort can be worthwhile because the name/value relationship in associative arrays eliminates the need to track numeric identifiers for each element. Another version of the multiArray program illustrates how to use associative arrays to generate the same city-distance program.

**TRICK** Since this program looks exactly like the basicMultiArray program to the user, I am not showing the screen shots. All of this program's interesting features are in the source code.

### Building the HTML for the Associative Array

The HTML page for this program's associative version is much like the indexed version, except for one major difference. See if you can spot the difference in the source code:

```
<!DOCTYPE html PUBLIC "-//W3C//DTD XHTML 1.0 Strict//EN"
"http://www.w3.org/TR/xhtml1/DTD/xhtml1-strict.dtd">
<html lang="EN" dir="ltr" xmlns="http://www.w3.org/1999/xhtml">
<head>
<title>2D Array</title>
</head>
<body>
<h1>2D Array</h1>

<form action = "multiArray.php"
      method = "post">
<table border = "1">

<tr>
  <th>First city</th>
  <th>Second city</th>
</tr>
```

```
<!-- note each option value is a string -->

<tr>
  <td>
    <select name = "cityA">
      <option value = "Indianapolis">Indianapolis</option>
      <option value = "New York">New York</option>
      <option value = "Tokyo">Tokyo</option>
      <option value = "London">London</option>
    </select>
  </td>

  <td>
    <select name = "cityB">
      <option value = "Indianapolis">Indianapolis</option>
      <option value = "New York">New York</option>
      <option value = "Tokyo">Tokyo</option>
      <option value = "London">London</option>
    </select>
  </td>
</tr>

<tr>
  <td colspan = "2">
    <input type = "submit"
            value = "calculate distance" />
  </td>
</tr>
</table>
</form>


</body>
</html>
```

The only difference between this HTML page and the last one is the `value` properties of the `select` objects. In this case, the `distance` array is an associative array, so it does not have numeric indices. Since the indices can be text values, I send the actual city name as the value for $cityA and $cityB.

## Responding to the Query

The code for the associative response is interesting, because it spends a lot of effort to build the fancy associative array. Once the array is created, it's very easy to work with.

```
<!DOCTYPE html PUBLIC "-//W3C//DTD XHTML 1.0 Strict//EN"
"http://www.w3.org/TR/xhtml1/DTD/xhtml1-strict.dtd">
<html lang="EN" dir="ltr" xmlns="http://www.w3.org/1999/xhtml">
<head>
<title>Distance Calculator</title>
</head>
<body>
<h1>Distance Calculator</h1>

<?php
//create arrays
$indy = array (
  "Indianapolis" => 0,
  "New York" => 648,
  "Tokyo" => 6476,
  "London" => 4000
  );
$ny = array (
  "Indianapolis" =>648,
  "New York" => 0,
  "Tokyo" => 6760,
  "London" => 3470
  );
$tokyo = array (
  "Indianapolis" => 6476,
  "New York" => 6760,
  "Tokyo" => 0,
  "London" => 5956
  );
$london = array (
  "Indianapolis" => 4000,
  "New York" => 3470,
  "Tokyo" => 5956,
  "London" => 0
  );
```

```
//set up master array
$distance = array (
  "Indianapolis" => $indy,
  "New York" => $ny,
  "Tokyo" => $tokyo,
  "London" => $london
  );

$cityA = filter_input(INPUT_POST, "cityA");
$cityB = filter_input(INPUT_POST, "cityB");

$result = $distance[$cityA][$cityB];
print "<h3>The distance between $cityA and $cityB is $result miles.</h3>";

?>

</body>
</html>
```

## Building the Two-Dimensional Associative Array

The basic approach to building a two-dimensional array is the same whether it's a normal array or uses associative indexing. Essentially, you create each row as an array and then build an array of the existing arrays. In the traditional array, the indices were automatically created. The development of an associative array is a little more complex, because you need to specify the key for each value. As an example, look at the code used to generate the $indy array:

```
$indy = array (
  "Indianapolis" => 0,
  "New York" => 648,
  "Tokyo" => 6476,
  "London" => 4000
  );
```

Inside the array, I used city names as indices. The value for each index refers to the distance from the current city (Indianapolis) to the particular destination. The distance from Indianapolis to Indianapolis is 0, and the distance from Indy to New York is 648, and so on.

I created an associative array for each city and put those associative arrays together in a kind of mega-associative array:

```
//set up master array
$distance = array (
  "Indianapolis" => $indy,
  "New York" => $ny,
  "Tokyo" => $tokyo,
  "London" => $london
  );
```

This new array is also an associative array, but each of its indices refers to an array of distances.

## Getting Data from the Two-Dimensional Associative Array

Once the two-dimensional array is constructed, it's extremely easy to use. The city names themselves are used as indices, so there's no need for a separate array to hold city names. Once the city names are extracted from the form, the data can be output in two lines of code:

```
$cityA = filter_input(INPUT_POST, "cityA");
$cityB = filter_input(INPUT_POST, "cityB");

$result = $distance[$cityA][$cityB];
print "<h3>The distance between $cityA and $cityB is $result miles.</h3>";
```

 **TRICK**  You can combine associative and normal arrays. It is possible to have a list of associative arrays and put them together in a normal array, or vice versa. PHP's array-handling capabilities allow for a phenomenal level of control over your data structures.

## MANIPULATING STRING VALUES

The Word Search program featured at the beginning of this chapter uses arrays to do some of its magic, but arrays alone are insufficient for handling the tasks needed for this program. The Word Search program takes advantage of a number of special string manipulation functions to work extensively with text values. PHP has a huge number of string functions that give you an incredible ability to fold, spindle, and manipulate string values.

## Demonstrating String Manipulation with the Pig Latin Translator

As a context for describing string manipulation functions, consider the program featured in Figures 5.10 and 5.11. This program allows the user to enter a phrase into a text box and converts the phrase into a bogus form of Latin.

**FIGURE 5.10**

The pigify
program lets the
user type some
text into a text
area.

**FIGURE 5.11**

The program
translates
immortal prose
into incredible
silliness.

If you're not familiar with Pig Latin, it's a silly kid's game. Essentially, you take the
first letter of each word, move it to the end of the word, and add *ay*. If the word
begins with a vowel, simply end the word with *way*.

The `pigify` program uses a number of string functions to manipulate the text:

```
<!DOCTYPE html PUBLIC "-//W3C//DTD XHTML 1.0 Strict//EN"
"http://www.w3.org/TR/xhtml1/DTD/xhtml1-strict.dtd">
<html lang="EN" dir="ltr" xmlns="http://www.w3.org/1999/xhtml">
<head>
      <title>Pig Latin Generator</title>
</head>
<body>
<h1>Pig Latin Generator</h1>
<?php

if (!filter_has_var(INPUT_POST, "inputString")){
  print <<<HERE
  <form action = ""
     method = "post">
   <fieldset>
    <textarea name = "inputString"
             rows = "20"
             cols = "40"></textarea>
     <input type = "submit"
           value = "pigify" />
   </fieldset>
  </form>

HERE;
} else {
  //there is a value, so we'll deal with it

  $inputString = filter_input(INPUT_POST, "inputString");
  $newPhrase = "";
  //break phrase into array
  $words = split(" ", $inputString);
  foreach ($words as $theWord){
    $theWord = rtrim($theWord);
    $firstLetter = substr($theWord, 0, 1);
    $restOfWord = substr($theWord, 1, strlen($theWord)-1);
    //print "$firstLetter) $restOfWord <br /> \n";
```

```
  if (strstr("aeiouAEIOU", $firstLetter)){
    //it's a vowel
    $newWord = $theWord . "way";
  } else {
    //it's a consonant
    $newWord = $restOfWord . $firstLetter . "ay";
  } // end if
  $newPhrase = $newPhrase . $newWord . " ";
} // end foreach
print "<p>$newPhrase</p> \n";


} // end if


?>
</body>
</html>
```

## Building the Form

This program uses a PHP page to create an input form and to respond directly to the input. It begins by looking for the existence of the $inputString variable. This variable does not exist the first time the user gets to the page. In this situation, the program builds the appropriate HTML page and awaits user input. The program runs again after the user hits the Submit button, but this time the $inputString variable has a value. The rest of the program uses string manipulation functions to create a Pig Latin version of the input string.

## Using the split() Function to Break a String into an Array

One of the first tasks for pigify is to break the entire string that comes from the user into individual words. PHP provides a couple of interesting functions for this purpose. The split() function takes a string and breaks it into an array based on some sort of delimiter, or separator character. The split() function takes two arguments. The first argument is a delimiter and the second is a string to break up.

I want each word to be a different element in the array, so I use space (" ") as a delimiter. The following line takes the $inputString variable and breaks it into an array called $words. Each word is a new array element.

```
  $words = split(" ", $inputString);
```

Once the $word array is constructed, I step through it with a foreach loop. I stored each word temporarily in $theWord inside the array.

## Trimming a String with rtrim()

Sometimes when you split a string into an array, each array element still has the split character at the end. In the pigify game, there is a space at the end of each word, which can cause some problems later. PHP provides a function called rtrim() which automatically removes spaces, tabs, newlines, and other whitespace from the end of a string. I used the rtrim() function to clean off any trailing spaces from the split() operation and returned the results to $theWord.

```
$theWord = rtrim($theWord);
```

 **TRICK** In addition to rtrim(), PHP has ltrim(), which trims excess whitespace from the beginning of a string and trim(), which cleans up both ends of a string. Also, there's a variation of the trim commands that allows you to specify exactly which characters are removed.

## Finding a Substring with substr()

The algorithm's behavior depends on the first character of each word. I need to know all the rest of the word without the first character. The substr() function is useful for getting part of a string. It requires three parameters.

- The string you want to get a piece from
- Which character you want to begin with (starting with 0 as usual)
- How many characters you want to extract

I got the first letter of the word with this line:

```
$firstLetter = substr($theWord, 0, 1);
```

It gets one letter from $theWord starting at the beginning of the word (position 0). I stored that value in the $firstLetter variable.

It's not much more complicated to get the rest of the word:

```
$restOfWord = substr($theWord, 1, strlen($theWord) -1);
```

Once again, I need to extract values from $theWord. This time I begin at character 1 (which humans would refer to as the second character). I don't know directly how many characters to get, but I can calculate it. I should grab one less character than the total number of characters in the word. The strlen() function is perfect for this operation, because it returns the number of characters in any string. I can calculate the number of letters I need with `strlen($theWord) - 1`. This new decapitated word is stored in the `$restOfWord` variable.

## Using strstr() to Search for One String Inside Another

The next task is to determine if the first character of the word is a vowel. You can take a number of approaches to this problem, but perhaps the easiest is a searching function. I created a string with all the vowels (`"aeiouAEIOU"`) and then I searched for the existence of the `$firstLetter` variable in the vowel string.

The `strstr()` function is perfect for this task. It takes two parameters: the string you are looking for (given the adorable name haystack in the online documentation) and the string you are searching in (the needle).

To search for the value of the `$firstLetter` variable in the string constant `"aeiouAEIOU"`, I used the following line:

```
if (strstr("aeiouAEIOU", $firstLetter)){
```

The `strstr()` function returns the value `FALSE` if the needle was not found in the haystack. If the needle was found, it returns the position of the needle in the haystack parameter. In this case, I'm really concerned only whether `$firstLetter` is found in the list of variables. If so, it's a vowel, which changes the way I modify the word.

## Using the Concatenation Operator

Most of the time in PHP you can use string interpolation to combine string values. However, sometimes you need a formal operation to combine strings. The process of combining two strings is called *concatenation*. (I love it when simple ideas have complicated names.) The period (.) is PHP's concatenation operator.

If a word in Pig Latin begins with a vowel, it should end with the string `"way"`. I used string concatenation to make this work:

```
$newWord = $theWord . "way";
```

When the word begins with a consonant, the formula for creating the new word is slightly more complicated, but is still performed with string concatenation:

```
$newWord = $restOfWord . $firstLetter . "ay";
```

**TRICK** Testing has shown that the concatenation method of building strings is dramatically faster than interpolation. If speed is an issue, you might want to use string concatenation rather than string interpolation.

## FINISHING THE PIGIFY PROGRAM

Once I created the new word, I added it and a trailing space to the $newPhrase variable. When the foreach loop has finished executing, $newPhrase contains the Pig Latin translation of the original phrase.

### Translating Between Characters and ASCII Values

Although it isn't necessary in the pigify program, the Word Search program requires the ability to randomly generate a character. I do this by randomly generating an ASCII value and translating that number to the appropriate character. (ASCII is the code used to store characters as binary numbers in the computer's memory.) The ord() function is useful in this situation. The uppercase letters are represented in ASCII by numbers between 65 and 90.

To get a random uppercase letter, I can use the following code:

```
$theNumber = random(65, 90);
$theLetter = ord($theNumber);
```

 One of the most important features of PHP6 is support for an enhancement of ASCII called *Unicode*. The Unicode standard allows for text to be created in a wide variety of world languages, and it's a welcome addition to PHP. For this introductory book, I'm sticking with the English UTF-8 form of Unicode, which is functionally equivalent to the old ASCII standard.

## RETURNING TO THE WORD SEARCH CREATOR

The Word Search program is stored in three files. First, the user enters a word list and puzzle information into an HTML page. This page calls the main wordFind.php program, which analyzes the word list, creates the puzzle, and prints it out. Finally, the user has the opportunity to print an answer key, which is created by a simple PHP program.

### Getting the Puzzle Data from the User

The wordFind.html page is the user's entry point into the word find system. This page is a standard XHTML form with a number of basic elements:

```
<!DOCTYPE html PUBLIC "-//W3C//DTD XHTML 1.0 Strict//EN"
"http://www.w3.org/TR/xhtml1/DTD/xhtml1-strict.dtd">
<html lang="EN" dir="ltr" xmlns="http://www.w3.org/1999/xhtml">
<head>
<title>Word Find Puzzle Maker</title>
<link rel = "stylesheet"
```

```
        type = "text/css"
        href = "wordFind.css" />

</head>
<body>
<h1>Word Puzzle Maker</h1>

<form action = "wordFind.php"
      method = "post">
<fieldset>
<label>puzzle name</label>
<input type = "text"
       name = "name"
       value = "My Word Find" />

<label>height</label>
<input type = "text"
       name = "height"
       value = "10"
       size = "5" />

<label>width</label>
<input type = "text"
       name = "width"
       value = "10"
       size = "5" />
<label>Word List</label>
<textarea rows="10" cols="60" name = "wordList"></textarea>

<p>Please enter one word per row, no spaces</p>

<button type="submit">
  make puzzle
</button>
</fieldset>
</form>
</body>
</html>
```

The form's `action` property points to the `wordFind.php` program, which is the primary program in the system. I used the `post` method to send data to the program because I expect to send large strings to the program. The `get` method allows only small amounts of data to be sent to the server, because that information is encoded into the URL.

The form features basic text boxes for the puzzle name, height, and width. This data determines how the puzzle is built. The `wordList text` area is expected to house a list of words, which create the puzzle.

## Setting Up the Response Page

The bulk of the work in the `wordFind` system happens in the `wordFind.php` page. This program has a small amount of HTML to set the stage, but the vast bulk of this file is made up of PHP code.

```php
<?php session_start() ?>

<!DOCTYPE html PUBLIC "-//W3C//DTD XHTML 1.0 Strict//EN"
"http://www.w3.org/TR/xhtml1/DTD/xhtml1-strict.dtd">
<html lang="EN" dir="ltr" xmlns="http://www.w3.org/1999/xhtml">
<head>
<title>Word Find Puzzle</title>
<link rel = "stylesheet"
      type = "text/css"
      href = "wordFind.css" />

</head>

<body>

<?php
// word Find
// by Andy Harris, 2008
// for PHP6/MySQL programming for the Absolute Beginner.
// Generates a word search puzzle based on a word list
// entered by user.  User can also specify the size of
// the puzzle and print out an answer key if desired
```

Notice the comments at the beginning of the code. Since this program's code is a little more involved than most of the programs you have seen in this book, I decided to comment it more carefully. My comments here basically lay out the plan for this program.

It's a really good idea to add comments to your programs so you can more easily determine what they do. You'll be amazed how little you understand your own code after you've been away from it for a couple of days. Good comments can make it much easier to maintain your code, and make it easier for others to fix and improve your programs later.

## Working with the Empty Data Set

In a production version of the program, I don't expect the PHP code to ever be called without an HTML page, so I put a link to the correct page. If you run the php page directly without the HTML, the user will see a link to the original page rather than an error message.

```
//check for a word list
if (!filter_has_var(INPUT_POST, "wordList")){
  print <<< HERE
    <p>
      This program is meant to be run from the
      <a href = "wordFind.html">wordFind</a>
      page.
    </p>
HERE;
} else {
```

## Building the Program's Main Logic

The main logic for the program begins by retrieving the word list and puzzle parameters from the user's form. Then it tries to convert the list into an array. This type of text analysis is sometimes called *parsing*.

The program then repeatedly tries to build the board until it succeeds. Once the program has successfully created the board, it creates an answer key and adds the random letters with the addFoils() function. Finally, the program prints the completed puzzle.

```
} else {
  //get puzzle data from HTML form
  $boardData = array(
    "width" => filter_input(INPUT_POST, "width"),
    "height" => filter_input(INPUT_POST, "height"),
    "name" => filter_input(INPUT_POST, "name")
  );

  //try to get a word list from user input
```

```
if (parseList() == TRUE){
  $legalBoard = FALSE;

  //keep trying to build a board until you get a legal result
  while ($legalBoard == FALSE){
    clearBoard();
    $legalBoard = fillBoard();
  } // end while

  //make the answer key
  $key = $board;
  $keyPuzzle = makeBoard($key);

  //make the final puzzle
  addFoils();
  $puzzle = makeBoard($board);

  //print out the result page
  printPuzzle();

} // end parsed list if
} // end word list exists if
```

The program begins by building a simple associative array to hold the board data. The board's width, height, and name are stored in an array so they will be easy to pass to functions.

```
//get puzzle data from HTML form
$boardData = array(
  "width" => filter_input(INPUT_POST, "width"),
  "height" => filter_input(INPUT_POST, "height"),
  "name" => filter_input(INPUT_POST, "name")
);
```

The word list is more complicated. A function will attempt to convert the text field into an array of words, or it will return the value FALSE if it cannot do so. (For example, one of the words might be too long to fit in the allotted space.)

```
//try to get a word list from user input
if (parseList() == TRUE){
```

The $legalBoard variable describes whether you currently have a legal board. Its value will begin as FALSE, and when we have a completed board, it will become TRUE. This mechanism allows the program to try several times until it gets a legal board.

```
$legalBoard = FALSE;
```

The main thrust of the program is a simple while loop:

```
//keep trying to build a board until you get a legal result
while ($legalBoard == FALSE){
  clearBoard();
  $legalBoard = fillBoard();
} // end while
```

The program will clear the board, and run the fillBoard() method. This method returns a Boolean value: TRUE if it was able to create a legal game board, or FALSE if there was some problem. This process is continued until there is a legal board.

Once there is a legal board in place, the rest of the code prints the board out and prepares an answer key:

```
//make the answer key
$key = $board;
$keyPuzzle = makeBoard($key);

//make the final puzzle
addFoils();
$puzzle = makeBoard($board);

//print out the result page
printPuzzle();

  } // end parsed list if
} // end word list exists if
```

You should be able to tell the general program flow even if you don't understand exactly how things happen. The main section of a well-defined program should give you a bird's eye view of the action. Most of the details are delegated to functions. Since the functions are reasonably well named, you can get an overview of the program first without worrying about functional details. That's a good design principle.

Most of the remaining chapter is devoted to explaining how these functions work. Try to make sure you've got the basic gist of the program's flow; then you see how all of it is done.

## Parsing the Word List

One important early task involves analyzing the word list that comes from the user. The word list comes as one long string separated by newline (\n) characters. The parseList() function converts this string into an array of words. It has some other important functions too, including converting each word to uppercase, checking for words that do not fit in the designated puzzle size, and removing unneeded carriage returns.

```
function parseList(){
  //gets word list, creates array of words from it
  //or return false if impossible

  global $word, $wordList, $boardData;

  $wordList = filter_input(INPUT_POST, "wordList");
  $itWorked = TRUE;

  //convert word list entirely to upper case
  $wordList = strtoupper($wordList);

  //split word list into array
  $word = split("\n", $wordList);

  foreach ($word as $currentWord){
    //take out trailing newline characters
    $currentWord = rtrim($currentWord);

    //stop if any words are too long to fit in puzzle
    if ((strLen($currentWord) > $boardData["width"]) &&
        (strLen($currentWord) > $boardData["height"])){
      print "$currentWord is too long for puzzle";
      $itWorked = FALSE;
    } // end if

  } // end foreach
  return $itWorked;
} // end parseList
```

The first thing I did was use the strtoupper() function to convert the entire word list into uppercase letters. Word search puzzles always seem to use capital letters, so I decided to convert everything to that format.

The long string of characters with newlines (which normally comes from a text area) is not a useful format here, so I converted the long string into an array called $word. The split() function works perfectly for this task. I split on the string "\n". This is the newline character, so it should convert each line of the text area into an element of the new $word array.

The next task was to analyze each word in the array with a foreach loop. When I tested this part of the program, it became clear that sometimes the trailing newline character was still there, so I used the rtrim() function to trim off any unnecessary trailing whitespace.

It is impossible to create the puzzle if the user enters a word larger than the height or width of the puzzle board, so I check for this situation by comparing the length of each word to the board's height and width. Note that if the word is too long, I simply set the value of the $itWorked variable to FALSE.

Earlier in this function, I initialized the value of $itWorked to TRUE. By the time the function is finished, $itWorked still contains the value TRUE if all the words were small enough to fit in the puzzle. If any of the words were too large, the value of $itWorked is FALSE and the program stops.

## Clearing the Board

Word Search uses a crude but effective technique to generate legal game boards (boards that contain all the words in the list). It creates random boards repeatedly until it finds one that is legal. While this may seem like a wasteful approach, it is much easier to program than many more sophisticated methods and produces remarkably good results for simple problems.

### IN THE REAL WORLD

Although this program does use a "brute force" approach to find a good solution, you see a number of ways the code is optimized to make a good solution more likely. One example of this is the way the program stops if one of the words is too long to fit in the puzzle. This prevents a long processing time while the program tries to fit a word in the puzzle when it cannot be done. A number of other places in the code do some work to steer the algorithm toward good solutions and away from pitfalls. Because of these efforts, you'll find that the program is actually pretty good at finding word search puzzles. There will be some puzzles the program will not be able to create (especially if there are a lot of large words on a small puzzle board), but the program is surprisingly good at building most puzzles.

The game board is often recreated several times during one program execution. I needed a function that could initialize the game board or reset it easily. The game board is stored in a two-dimensional array called $board. When the board is "empty," each cell contains the period (.) character. I chose this convention because it gives me something visible in each cell and provides a character that represents an empty cell. The clearBoard() function sets or resets the $board array so that every cell contains a period.

```
function clearBoard(){
  //initialize board with a . in each cell
  global $board, $boardData;

  for ($row = 0; $row < $boardData["height"]; $row++){
    for ($col = 0; $col < $boardData["width"]; $col++){
      $board[$row][$col] = ".";
    } // end col for loop
  } // end row for loop
} // end clearBoard
```

This code is the classic nested for loop so common to two-dimensional arrays. Note that I used for loops rather than foreach loops because I was interested in the loop indices. The outer for loop steps through the rows. Inside each row loop, another loop steps through each column. I assigned the value "." to the $board array at the current $row and $col locations. Eventually, "." is placed in every cell in the array.

**TRICK** I determined the size of the for loops by referring to the $boardData associative array. Although I could have done this a number of ways, I chose the associative array for several reasons. The most important is clarity. It's easy for me to see by this structure that I'm working with the height and width related to board data. Another advantage in this context is convenience. Since the height, width, and board name are stored in the $boardData array, I could make a global reference to the $boardData variable and all its values would come along. It's like having three variables for the price of one.

## Filling the Board

Of course, the purpose of clearing the board is to fill it in with the words from the word list. This happens in two stages: filling the board and adding the words. The fillBoard() function controls the entire process of filling up the whole board, but the details of adding each word to the board are relegated to the addWord() function (which you see next).

The board is only complete if each word is added correctly. Each word is added only if each of its letters is added without problems. The program calls `fillBoard()` as often as necessary to get a correct solution. Each time `fillBoard()` runs, it may call `addWord()` as many times as necessary until each word is added. The `addWord()` function in turn keeps track of whether it is able to successfully add each character to the board.

The general `fillBoard()` function plan is to generate a random direction for each word and then tell the `addWord()` function to place the specified word in the specified direction on the board.

The looping structure for the `fillBoard()` function is a little unique, because the loop could exit two ways. If any of the words cannot be placed in the requested manner, the puzzle generation stops immediately and the function returns the value FALSE. However, if the entire word list is successfully placed on the game board, the function should stop looping, but report the value TRUE.

You can achieve this effect a number of ways, but I prefer often to use a special Boolean variable for this purpose. Boolean variables are variables meant to contain only the values TRUE and FALSE. Of course, PHP is pretty easygoing about variable types, but you can make a variable act like a Boolean simply by assigning it only the values TRUE or FALSE. In the `fillBoard()` function, look at how the `$keepGoing` variable is used. It is initialized to TRUE, and the function's main loop keeps running as long as this is the case.

However, the two conditions that can cause the loop to exit—the `addWord()` function failed to place a word correctly, or the entire word list has been exhausted—cause the `$keepGoing` variable to become FALSE. When this happens, the loop stops and the function shortly exits.

```
function fillBoard(){
  //fill board with list by calling addWord() for each word
  //or return false if failed

  global $word;
  $direction = array("N", "S", "E", "W");
  $itWorked = TRUE;
  $counter = 0;
  $keepGoing = TRUE;
  while($keepGoing){
    $dir = rand(0, 3);
    $result = addWord($word[$counter], $direction[$dir]);
    if ($result == FALSE){
      //print "failed to place $word[$counter]";
```

```
        $keepGoing = FALSE;
        $itWorked = FALSE;
      } // end if
      $counter++;
      if ($counter >= count($word)){
        $keepGoing = FALSE;
      } // end if
    } // end while
    return $itWorked;

} // end fillBoard
```

The function begins by defining an array for directions. At this point, I decided only to support placing words in the four cardinal directions, although it would be easy enough to add diagonals. (Hey, that sounds like a dandy end-of-chapter exercise!) The $direction array holds the initials of the four directions I have decided to support at this time. The $itWorked variable is a Boolean which reports whether the board has been successfully filled. It is initialized to TRUE. If the addWord() function fails to place a word, the $itWorked value is changed to FALSE.

The $counter variable counts which word I'm currently trying to place. I increment the value of $counter each time through the loop. When $counter is larger than the $word array, the function has successfully added every word and can exit triumphantly.

To choose a direction, I simply created a random value between 0 and 3 and referred to the associated value of the $direction array.

The last line of the function returns the value of $itWorked. The fillBoard() function is called by the main program until it succeeds. This success or failure is reported to the main program by returning the value of $itWorked.

## Adding a Word

The fillBoard() function handles the global process of adding the word list to the game board, but addWord() adds each word to the board. This function expects two parameters: the word and a direction.

The function cleans up the word and renders slightly different service based on which direction the word is placed. It places each letter of the word in an appropriate cell while preventing it from being placed outside the game board's boundary. It also checks to make sure that the cell does not currently house some other letter from another word (unless that letter happens to be the one the function is already trying to place). The function may look long and complex at first, but when you look at it more closely you find it's extremely repetitive.

```php
function addWord($theWord, $dir){
  //attempt to add a word to the board or return false if failed
  global $board, $boardData;

  //remove trailing characters if necessary
  $theWord = rtrim($theWord);

  $itWorked = TRUE;

  switch ($dir){
   case "E":
     //col from 0 to board width - word width
     //row from 0 to board height
     $newCol = rand(0, $boardData["width"] - 1 - strlen($theWord));
    $newRow = rand(0, $boardData["height"]-1);

     for ($i = 0; $i < strlen($theWord); $i++){
       //new character same row, initial column + $i
       $boardLetter = $board[$newRow][$newCol + $i];
       $wordLetter = substr($theWord, $i, 1);

       //check for legal values in current space on board
       if (($boardLetter == $wordLetter) ||
          ($boardLetter == ".")){
         $board[$newRow][$newCol + $i] = $wordLetter;
       } else {
         $itWorked = FALSE;
       } // end if
     } // end for loop
     break;

    case "W":
      //col from word width to board width
      //row from 0 to board height
      $newCol = rand(strlen($theWord), $boardData["width"] -1);
      $newRow = rand(0, $boardData["height"]-1);
      //print "west:\tRow: $newRow\tCol: $newCol<br>\n";

      for ($i = 0; $i < strlen($theWord); $i++){
        //check for a legal move
```

```
        $boardLetter = $board[$newRow][$newCol - $i];
        $wordLetter = substr($theWord, $i, 1);
        if (($boardLetter == $wordLetter) ||
            ($boardLetter == ".")){
          $board[$newRow][$newCol - $i] = $wordLetter;
        } else {
          $itWorked = FALSE;
        } // end if
      } // end for loop
      break;

case "S":
 //col from 0 to board width
 //row from 0 to board height - word length
  $newCol = rand(0, $boardData["width"] -1);
  $newRow = rand(0, $boardData["height"]-1 - strlen($theWord));
  //print "south:\tRow: $newRow\tCol: $newCol<br>\n";

  for ($i = 0; $i < strlen($theWord); $i++){
    //check for a legal move
    $boardLetter = $board[$newRow + $i][$newCol];
    $wordLetter = substr($theWord, $i, 1);
    if (($boardLetter == $wordLetter) ||
        ($boardLetter == ".")){
      $board[$newRow + $i][$newCol] = $wordLetter;
    } else {
      $itWorked = FALSE;
    } // end if
  } // end for loop
  break;

case "N":
 //col from 0 to board width
 //row from word length to board height
  $newCol = rand(0, $boardData["width"] -1);
  $newRow = rand(strlen($theWord), $boardData["height"]-1);

  for ($i = 0; $i < strlen($theWord); $i++){
    //check for a legal move
```

```
    $boardLetter = $board[$newRow - $i][$newCol];
    $wordLetter = substr($theWord, $i, 1);
    if (($boardLetter == $wordLetter) ||
        ($boardLetter == ".")){
      $board[$newRow - $i][$newCol] = $wordLetter;
    } else {
      $itWorked = FALSE;
    } // end if
    } // end for loop
    break;

  } // end switch
  return $itWorked;
} // end addWord
```

The addWord() function's main focus is a switch structure based on the word direction. The code inside the switch branches are similar in their general approach.

## Closely Examining the East Code

It's customary in Western languages to write from left to right, so the code for E, which indicates write towards the East, is probably the most natural to understand. I explain how that code works and then show you how the other directions differ.

Here's the code fragment that attempts to write a word in the Easterly direction:

```
case "E":
    //col from 0 to board width - word width
    //row from 0 to board height
    $newCol = rand(0, $boardData["width"] - 1 - strlen($theWord));
    $newRow = rand(0, $boardData["height"]-1);

    for ($i = 0; $i < strlen($theWord); $i++){
      //new character same row, initial column + $i
      $boardLetter = $board[$newRow][$newCol + $i];
      $wordLetter = substr($theWord, $i, 1);

      //check for legal values in current space on board
      if (($boardLetter == $wordLetter) ||
          ($boardLetter == ".")){
        $board[$newRow][$newCol + $i] = $wordLetter;
      } else {
```

```
    $itWorked = FALSE;
  } // end if
} // end for loop
break;
```

## Determining Starting Values for the Characters

The code steps through the word one letter at a time, placing each letter in the next cell to the right of the previous one. I could have chosen any random cell and checked to see when the code got outside the board range, but this would have involved some complicated and clunky code.

A more elegant solution is to carefully determine what the range of appropriate starting cells are and choose cells within that range. For example, if I'm placing the word elephant (with eight letters) from left to right in a puzzle with a width of 10, zero and one are the only legal columns for the starting "e." (Remember, computers usually start counting at zero.) If I place elephant in the same puzzle but from right to left, the last two columns (eight and nine) are the only legal options for the "e" character. Once I recognized this fact, I had to figure out how to encode this idea so it could work with any size words in any size puzzle.

---

### IN THE REAL WORLD

By far the most critical part of this code is the comments at the beginning. Even though I'm a reasonably experienced programmer, it's easy to get confused when you start solving problems of any reasonable complexity. Just to remind myself, I placed these comments to explain exactly what the parameters of this chunk of code are.

I referred to these comments many times while I was writing and debugging the code. If I hadn't given myself clear guidance on what I was trying to do, I would have gotten so lost I probably wouldn't have been able to write the program.

---

I need a random value for the row and column to figure out where to place each word. However, that random value must be within an appropriate range based on the word length and board width. By trial and error and some sketches on a white board, I determined that `$boardData["width"] - 1` is the largest column in the game board and that `strlen($theWord)` is the length of the current word in characters.

If I subtract the word length from the board width, I get the largest legal starting value for a left-to-right placement. That's how I got this slightly scary formula:

```
$newCol = rand(0, $boardData["width"] - 1 - strlen($theWord));
```

The smallest legal starting value for this kind of placement is 0, because column zero always works when you're going right to left and the word is the same size or smaller than the puzzle (which has been established). Row number doesn't matter in an Eastward placement, because any row in the puzzle is legal—all letters are placed on the same row.

Once I know the word's largest and smallest legal starting places, I can randomly generate that starting point knowing that the entire word can be placed there legally as long as it doesn't overlap any other.

I used a for loop to pull one character at a time using the substr() function. The for loop counter ($i) is used to determine the starting character of the substring, which is always one character long. Each character is placed at the same row as the starting character, but at a column offset by the position in the word. Revisit the elephant example: If the starting position chosen is column one, the character E is placed in column one, because E is at the 0th position in the word elephant, and 1 + 0 = 1. When the counter ($i) gets to the letter L, it has the value 1, so it is placed in column two, and so on.

If the formula for choosing the starting place and the plan for placing subsequent letters in place work correctly, you cannot add a letter outside the puzzle board. However, another bad thing could happen if a character from a previously placed word is in a cell that the current word wants. The code checks the current cell on the game board to see its current status. If the cell contains the value ".", it is empty and the new character can be freely placed there. If the cell contains the value that the current word wants to place in the cell, the program can likewise continue without interruption. However, if the cell contains any other character, the loop must exit and the program must reset the board and try again. Do this by setting the $itWorked value to FALSE.

### Printing in the Other Directions

Once you understand how to print words when the direction is East, you see that the other directions are similar. However, I need to figure out each direction's appropriate starting values and what cell to place each letter in. Table 5.2 summarizes these values.

A little explanation of Table 5.2 is in order. Within the table, I identified the minimum and maximum column for each direction, as well as the minimum and maximum row. This was easiest to figure out by writing some examples on graph paper. The placement of each letter is based on the starting row and column, with i standing for the position of the current letter within the word. In direction W, I put the letter at position 2 of my word into the randomly chosen starting row, but at the starting column minus 2. This prints the letters from right to left. Work out the other examples on graph paper so you can see how they work.

| | E | W | S | N |
|---|---|---|---|---|
| **TABLE 5.2** | **SUMMARY OF PLACEMENT DATA** | | | |
| min Col | 0 | word width | 0 | 0 |
| max Col | board width – 1 –word width | board width – 1 | board width – 1 | board width – 1 |
| min Row | 0 | 0 | 0 | word width |
| max Row | board height – 1 | board height – 1 | board height – 1 –word width | board height – 1 |
| letter col | start + i | start –i | start | start |
| letter row | start | start | start + i | start –i |

## IN THE REAL WORLD

This is exactly where computer programming becomes mystical for most people. Up to now you've probably been following, but this business of placing the characters has a lot of math in it, and you didn't get to see me struggle with it. It might look to you as if I just knew what the right formulas were. I didn't. I had to think about it carefully *without* the computer turned on. I got out a white board (my favorite programming tool) and some graph paper and tried to figure out what I meant mathematically when I said *write the characters from bottom to top*.

This is hard, but you can do it. The main thing to remember? Turn off the computer. Get some paper and figure out what it is you're trying to tell the computer to do. Then you can start writing code. You may get it wrong (at least I did). But if you've written down your strategy, you can compare what you expected to happen with what did happen, and likely solve even this kind of somewhat mathematical problem.

## Making a Puzzle Board

By the time the `fillBoard()` function has finished calling `addWord()` to add all the words, the answer key is complete. Each word is in place and any cell that does not contain one of the words still has a period. The main program copies the current `$board` variable over to the `$key` array. The answer key is now ready to be formatted into a form the user can use.

However, rather than writing one function to print the answer key and another to print the finished puzzle, I wrote one function that takes the array as a parameter and creates a long string of HTML code placing that puzzle in a table.

```
function makeBoard($theBoard){
  //given a board array, return an HTML table based on the array
  global $boardData;
  $puzzle = "";
  $puzzle .= "<table>\n";
  //check logic here
  for ($row = 0; $row < $boardData["height"]; $row++){
  $puzzle .= "<tr>\n";
    for ($col = 0; $col < $boardData["width"]; $col++){
      $puzzle .= "  <td>{$theBoard[$row][$col]}</td>\n";
    } // end col for loop
    $puzzle .= "</tr>\n";
  } // end row for loop
  $puzzle .= "</table>\n";
  return $puzzle;
} // end printBoard;
```

Most of the function deals with creating an HTML table, which is stored in the variable $puzzle. Each puzzle row begins by building an HTML <tr> tag and creates a <td></td> pair for each table element. Although I'm not a big fan of using HTML tables for layout, it seems to me that a word search puzzle is a great example of tabular data, so the HTML table is a good formatting choice here.

TRAP Sometimes PHP has trouble correctly interpolating two-dimensional arrays. If you find an array is not being correctly interpolated, try two things:

- Surround the array reference in braces as I did in the code in makeBoard()
- Forego interpolation and use concatenation instead. For example, you could have built each cell with the following code:

```
$puzzle .= "  <td>{$theBoard[$row][$col]}</td>\n";
```

## Adding the Foil Letters

The puzzle itself can be easily derived from the answer key. Once the words in the list are in place, all it takes to generate a puzzle is replacing the periods with some other random letters. I call these other characters *foil letters* because it is their job to foil the user. This is actually quite easy compared to the process of adding the words.

```
function addFoils(){
  //add random dummy characters to board
  global $board, $boardData;
  for ($row = 0; $row < $boardData["height"]; $row++){
    for ($col = 0; $col < $boardData["width"]; $col++){
      if ($board[$row][$col] == "."){
        $newLetter = rand(65, 90);
        $board[$row][$col] = chr($newLetter);
      } // end if
    } // end col for loop
  } // end row for loop
} // end addFoils
```

The function uses the standard pair of nested loops to cycle through each cell in the array. For each cell that contains a period, the function generates a random number between 65 and 90. These numbers correspond to the ASCII numeric codes for the capital letters. I used the chr() function to retrieve the letter that corresponds to that number and stored the new random letter in the array.

## Printing the Puzzle

The last step in the main program is to print results to the user. So far, all the work has been done behind the scenes. Now it is necessary to produce an HTML page with the results. The printPuzzle() function performs this duty. The printBoard() function has already formatted the actual puzzle and answer key tables as HTML. The puzzle HTML is stored in the $puzzle variable, and the answer key is stored in $keyPuzzle.

```
function printPuzzle(){
  //print out page to user with puzzle on it

  global $puzzle, $word, $keyPuzzle, $boardData;
  //print puzzle itself

  print <<<HERE
  <h1>{$boardData["name"]}</h1>
  $puzzle
  <h3>Word List</h3>
  <ul>

HERE;
  //print word list
```

```php
foreach ($word as $theWord){
  $theWord = rtrim($theWord);
  print "<li>$theWord</li>\n";
} // end foreach
print "</ul>\n";
$puzzleName = $boardData["name"];

//print form for requesting answer key.
//save answer key as session var

$_SESSION["key"] = $keyPuzzle;
$_SESSION["puzzleName"] = $puzzleName;


print <<<HERE

<form action = "wordFindKey.php"
      method = "post"
      id = "keyForm">
<div>
<input type = "submit"
       value = "show answer key" />
</div>
</form>

HERE;

} // end printPuzzle
```

This function mainly deals with printing standard HTML from variables that have been created during the program's run. The name of the puzzle is stored in $boardData["name"]. The puzzle itself is simply the value of the $puzzle variable. I printed the word list by a foreach loop creating a list from the $word array.

The trickiest part of the code is working with the answer key. It is easy enough to print the answer key directly on the same HTML page. In fact, this is exactly what I did as I was testing the program. However, the puzzle won't be much fun if the answer is right there, so I allowed the user to press a button to get the answer key. The key is related only to the currently generated puzzle. If the same word list were sent to the Word Search program again, it would likely produce a different puzzle with a different answer.

The secret is to store the current answer key and puzzle name in session variables, and pass control to another program. I created a form with nothing but a Submit button. When the user presses the Submit button, wordFindKey is called, which will be able to extract the answer key from the session variable and print it for the reader.

## Printing the Answer Key

The wordFindKey program is very simplistic, because all the work of generating the answer key was done by the Word Search program. wordFindKey has only to retrieve the puzzle name and answer key from session variables and print them out. Since the key has already been formatted as a table, the wordFindKey program needn't do any heavy lifting.

```php
<?php session_start() ?>

<!DOCTYPE html PUBLIC "-//W3C//DTD XHTML 1.0 Strict//EN"
"http://www.w3.org/TR/xhtml1/DTD/xhtml1-strict.dtd">
<html lang="EN" dir="ltr" xmlns="http://www.w3.org/1999/xhtml">
<head>
<title>Word Find Answer Key</title>
<link rel = "stylesheet"
      type = "text/css"
      href = "wordFind.css" />

</head>
<body>

<?php
//answer key for word find
//called from session variable

$puzzleName = $_SESSION["puzzleName"];
$key = $_SESSION["key"];

print <<<HERE

<h1>$puzzleName Answer key</h1>
$key

HERE;
?>
</body>
</html>
```

## Summary

In this chapter you saw how important it is to put together data in meaningful ways. You looked at a number of more powerful arrays and tools to manipulate them. You learned how to use the foreach loop to look at each element of an array in turn. You can use string indices to generate associative arrays and make two-dimensional arrays using both numeric and string indices. You learned how to do several kinds of string-manipulation tricks, including searching for one string inside another, extracting substrings, and splitting a string into an array. You put all these skills together in an interesting and detailed application. You should be proud of your efforts.

## CHALLENGES

1. Add the ability to use diagonals in your puzzles. (Hint: You need only combine the formulas I established. You don't need any new ones.)

2. Make a more challenging version of the Word Search game. Create an array of all the letters used in the word list, and use only those letters for the foil letters.

3. Create a game of Battle Ship for two players on the same computer. The game prints a grid. (Preset the fleet locations to make it easier.) Let the user choose a location on the grid via a checkbox. Report the result of his firing back and then give the screen to the second user.

4. Write a version of Conway'sLife. This program simulates cellular life on a grid with three simple rules.

   a. Each cell with exactly three neighbors becomes or remains alive.

   b. Each cell currently alive with exactly two neighbors remains alive.

   c. All other cells die off.

   Randomly generate the first cell and let the user press a button to generate the next generation.

# WORKING WITH FILES

As your experience in programming grows, the relative importance of data becomes increasingly apparent. You began your understanding of data with simple variables, but learned how simple and more complex arrays can make your programs more flexible and more powerful. However, data stored in the computer's memory is transient, especially in the server environment. It is often necessary to store information in a form that is more persistent than the constructs you have learned so far. PHP provides a number of powerful functions for working with text files. With these skills, you create extremely useful programs. Specifically, you learn how to:

- Open files for read, write, and append access
- Use file handles to manipulate text files
- Write data to a text file
- Read data from a text file
- Open an entire file into an array
- Modify text data on the fly
- Get information about all the files in a particular directory
- Get a subset of files based on filenames

## PREVIEWING THE QUIZ MACHINE

This chapter's main program is a fun and powerful tool that you can use in many different ways. It is not simply one program, but a system of programs that work together to let you automatically create, administer, and grade multiple-choice quizzes.

---

### IN THE REAL WORLD

It is reasonably easy to build an HTML page that presents a quiz and a PHP program to grade only that quiz. However, if you want several quizzes, it might be worth the investment in time and energy to build a system that can automate the creation and administration of quizzes. The real power of programming comes into play not just when you solve one immediate problem, but when you can produce a solution that can be applied to an entire range of related problems. The quiz machine is an example of exactly such a system. It takes a little more effort to build, but the effort really pays off when you have a system to reuse.

---

### Entering the Quiz Machine System

Figure 6.1 shows the system's main page. The user needs a password to take a test and an administrative password to edit a test. In this case, I entered the administrative password (it's absolute—like in Absolute Beginner's Guide) into the appropriate password box, and I'm going to edit the Monty Python quiz.

 **TRICK** I refer to the quiz machine as a system rather than a program because it uses a number of programs intended to work together.

### Editing a Quiz

The screen shown in Figure 6.2 appears when the user enters the correct password. You can see the requested quiz in a special format on the screen.

The quiz administrator can edit the quiz. Each quiz has a name, instructor e-mail address, and password. Each question is stored in a single line with the question, four possible answers, and the correct answer separated by colon (:) characters.

**FIGURE 6.1**

The user is an administrator preparing to edit a quiz.

**FIGURE 6.2**

The user is editing a quiz.

## Taking a Quiz

Users with knowledge of the appropriate password can take any of the quizzes known to the system. If a user chooses to take the Monty Python quiz, the screen shown in Figure 6.3 appears.

**FIGURE 6.3**

The user is taking the Monty Python quiz. If you want to become a serious programmer, you should probably rent this movie. It's part of the culture.

## Seeing the Results

When the user takes a quiz, the user's responses are sent to a program that grades the quiz and provides immediate feedback, as shown in Figure 6.4.

**FIGURE 6.4**

The grading program provides immediate feedback and stores the information in a file so the administrator can see it later.

## Viewing the Quiz Log

The system keeps a log file for each quiz so the administrator can see each person's score. Figure 6.5 shows how people have done on the Monty Python quiz.

FIGURE 6.5

The log viewer allows you to see a summary of quiz responses.

Although the resulting log looks very simplistic, it is generated in a format that can easily be imported into most gradebook programs and spreadsheets. This is very handy if you use the quiz in a classroom setting.

## SAVING A FILE TO THE FILE SYSTEM

Your PHP programs can access the server's file system to store and retrieve information.

Your programs can create new files, add data to files, and read information from the files. You start by writing a program that creates a file and adds data to it.

## Introducing the saveSonnet.php Program

The saveSonnet.php program shown in the following code opens a file on the server and writes one of Shakespeare's sonnets to that file on the server.

Normally I show you a screen shot of every program, but that isn't useful since this particular program doesn't display anything on the screen. The next couple of programs read this file and display it onscreen. You see what they look like when the time comes.

```
<!DOCTYPE html PUBLIC "-//W3C//DTD XHTML 1.0 Strict//EN"
"http://www.w3.org/TR/xhtml1/DTD/xhtml1-strict.dtd">
<html lang="EN" dir="ltr" xmlns="http://www.w3.org/1999/xhtml">
<head>
<title>SaveSonnet</title>
</head>
<body>
<?php

$sonnet76 = <<<HERE
Sonnet # 76, William Shakespeare

Why is my verse so barren of new pride,
So far from variation or quick change?
Why with the time do I not glance aside
To new-found methods, and to compounds strange?
Why write I still all one, ever the same,
And keep invention in a noted weed,
That every word doth almost tell my name,
Showing their birth, and where they did proceed?
O! know sweet love I always write of you,
And you and love are still my argument;
So all my best is dressing old words new,
Spending again what is already spent:
For as the sun is daily new and old,
So is my love still telling what is told.

HERE;

$fp = fopen("sonnet76.txt", "w");
fputs($fp, $sonnet76);
fclose($fp);

?>
</body>
</html>
```

Most of the code stores the contents of Shakespeare's 76th sonnet to a variable called `$sonnet76`. The remaining three lines save the data in the variable to a text file.

## Opening a File with fopen()

The `fopen()` command opens a file. Note that you can create files on the web server only—you cannot directly create a file on the client machine, because you do not have access to that machine's file system. (If you did, any server-side program would be able to create viruses with extreme ease.) However, as a server-side programmer, you already have the ability to create files on the server. The programs you are writing are files. Your programs can write files as if they are you.

**TRAP** The ownership of files created by your PHP programs can be a little more complicated, depending on your operating system, server, and PHP configurations. Generally, any file that your program creates is owned by a special user called PHP or by the account you were in when you wrote the program. This makes a big difference in an operating system like UNIX, where file ownership is a major part of the security mechanism. The best way to discover how this works is to write a program that creates a file and then look at that file's properties.

The filename is the first parameter of the `fopen()` function. This filename can include directory information or it can be a relative reference starting from the current file's location.

**TRAP** Always test your programs, especially if they use a relative reference for a filename. It's possible that your current directory is not the default directory. Also, the filename is based on the actual file server system, rather than the file's URL.

**TRAP** Some servers are set up to require a full filename for `fopen()` and included files. If you have trouble opening a file, use the complete filename for the file rather than a relative reference to that file. On Windows systems, this should begin with the drive name (e.g., `c:\apache\htdocs\myfile.txt`); in UNIX and Linux, use the `pwd` command to find the complete path of the file (e.g., `/home/aharris/htdocs/myFile.txt`).

You can create a file anywhere on the server to which you have access. Your files can be in the parts of your directory system open to the web server. (If you don't specify otherwise, files will go into the `public_html` or `htdocs directory`.) Sometimes, though, you might not want your files to be directly accessible to users by typing a URL. You can control access to these files as follows:

- Place them outside the public HTML space.
- Set permissions so they can be read by you (and programs you create) but not by anyone else.

## Creating a File Handle

When you create a file with the fopen() command, the function returns an integer called a file handle (sometimes also called a file pointer). This special number refers to the file in subsequent commands. You aren't usually concerned about this handle's actual value, but need to store it in a variable (I usually use $fp) so your other file-access commands know which file to work with.

## Examining File Access Modifiers

The final parameter in the fopen() command is an access modifier. PHP supports a number of access modifiers, which determine how your program interacts with the file. Table 6.1 lists these modifiers. Files are usually opened for these modes: reading, writing, or appending. Read mode opens a file for input, so your program can read information from the file. You cannot write data to a file that is opened in read mode. Write mode allows you to open a file for output access. If the file does not exist, PHP automatically creates it for you. (If it does exist, it is wiped out and the new file goes in its place.) Append mode allows you to write to a file without destroying the current contents. When you write to a file in append mode, all new data is added to the end of the file.

You can use a file for random access, which allows a file to be open simultaneously for input and output, but such files are often not needed in PHP. The relational database techniques provide the same capability with more flexibility and a lot less work. However, the other forms of file access (read, write, and output) are extremely useful, because they provide easy access to the file information.

## TABLE 6.1 FILE ACCESS MODIFIERS

| Modifier | Type | Description |
| --- | --- | --- |
| "r" | Read-only | Program can read from the file |
| "w" | Write | Writes to the file, overwriting it if it already exists |
| "a" | Append | Writes to the end of the file |
| "r+" "w+" | Read and Write | Random access. Read or write to a specified part of the file |

Be very careful about opening a file in write mode. If you open an already existing file for write access, PHP creates a new file and overwrites and destroys the old file's contents.

---

## IN THE REAL WORLD

The "r+" and "w+" modifiers are used for another form of file access, called random access, which allows simultaneous reading and writing to the same file. While this is a very useful tool, I won't spend a lot of time on it in this book. The sequential-access methods in this chapter are fine for simple file storage problems; the XML and relational database techniques described in the remainder of this book aren't any more difficult than the random access model and provide far more power.

---

## Writing to a File

The saveSonnet program opens the sonnet76.txt file for write access. If there were already a file in the current directory, it is destroyed. The $fp variable stores the file pointer for the text file. Once this is done, you can use the fputs() function to actually write data to the file.

You might be noticing a trend here. Most of the file access functions begin with the letter f: fopen(), fclose(), fputs(), fgets(), feof(). This convention is inherited from the C language. It can help you remember that a particular function works with files. Of course, every statement in PHP that begins with f isn't necessarily a file function (foreach is a good example), but most function names in PHP that begin with f are file-handling commands.

The fputs() function requires two parameters. The first is a file pointer, which tells PHP where to write the data. The second parameter is the text to write out to the file.

## Closing a File

The fclose() function tells the system that your program is done working with the file and should close it.

Drive systems are much slower than computer memory and take a long time to spool up to speed. For that reason, when a program encounters an fputs() command, it doesn't always immediately save the data to a file on the disk. Instead, it adds the data to a special memory buffer and writes the data to the physical disk only when a sufficient amount is on the buffer or the program encounters an `fclose()` command. This is why it's important to close your files. If the program ends without encountering an `fclose()` statement, PHP is supposed to automatically close the file for you, but what's supposed to happen and what actually happens are often two very different things.

## LOADING A FILE FROM THE DRIVE SYSTEM

You can retrieve information from the file system. If you open a file with the `"r"` access modifier, you can read information from the file.

### Introducing the loadSonnet.php Program

The `loadSonnet.php` program, shown in Figure 6.6 loads the sonnet saved by `saveSonnet.php` and displays it as befits the work of the Bard.

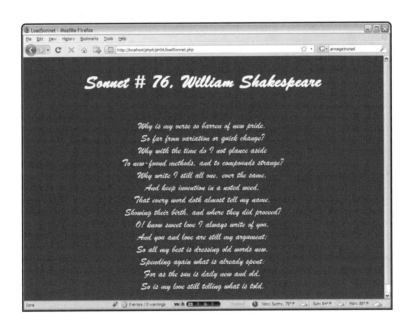

**FIGURE 6.6**

The file has been loaded from the drive system and prettied up a bit with some cascading style sheets (CSS) tricks.

The code for the `loadSonnet` program follows:

```
<!DOCTYPE html PUBLIC "-//W3C//DTD XHTML 1.0 Strict//EN"
"http://www.w3.org/TR/xhtml1/DTD/xhtml1-strict.dtd">
<html lang="EN" dir="ltr" xmlns="http://www.w3.org/1999/xhtml">
<head>
<title>LoadSonnet</title>
```

```
<style type = "text/css">
body{
  background-color: darkred;
  color: white;
  font-family: 'Brush Script MT', script;
  font-size: 1.5em;
  text-align: center;
}
</style>

</head>
<body>
<div>
<?php
$fp = fopen("sonnet76.txt", "r");

//first line is title
$line = fgets($fp);
print "<h1>$line</h1>\n";

//print rest of sonnet
while (!feof($fp)){
  $line = fgets($fp);
  print "$line <br />\n";
} // end while

fclose($fp);

?>
</div>
</body>
</html>
```

## Beautifying Output with CSS

CSS styles are the best way to improve text appearance. By setting up a simple style sheet, I very quickly improve the sonnet's appearance without changing the text. Notice especially how I indicated multiple fonts in case my preferred font was not installed on the user's system.

## Using the "r" Access Modifier

To read from a file, you must get a file pointer by opening that file for "r" access. If the file does not exist, you get the result FALSE rather than a file pointer.

 TRICK

You can open files anywhere on the Internet for read access. If you supply a URL as a filename, you can read the URL as if it were a local file. However, you cannot open URL files for output.

I opened sonnet76.txt with the fopen() command using the "r" access modifier and again copied the resulting integer to the $fp file pointer variable.

## Checking for the End of the File with feof()

When you are reading data from a file, your program doesn't generally know the file length. The fgets() command, which gets data from a file, reads one line of the file at a time. Since you can't be sure how many lines are in a file until you read it, PHP provides a special function called feof(), which stands for file end of file (apparently named by the Department of Redundancy Department).

This function returns the value FALSE if any more lines of data are left in the file. It returns TRUE when the program is at the end of the data file. Most of the time when you read file data, you use a while loop that continues as long as feof() is not true. The easiest way to set up this loop is with a statement like this:

```
while (!feof($fp)){
```

The feof() function requires a file pointer as its sole parameter.

## Reading Data from the File with fgets()

The fgets() function gets one line of data from the file, returns that value as a string, and moves a special pointer to the next line of the file. Usually this function is called inside a loop that continues until feof() is TRUE.

## READING A FILE INTO AN ARRAY

It is often useful to work with a file by loading it into an array in memory. Frequently you find yourself doing some operation on each array line. PHP provides a couple of features that simplify this type of operation. The cartoonifier.php program demonstrates one way of manipulating an entire file without using a file pointer.

## Introducing the cartoonifier.php Program

The `cartoonifier.php` program illustrated in Figure 6.7 is a truly serious and weighty use of advanced server technology.

This program loads the entire sonnet into an array, steps through each line, and converts it to a unique cartoon dialect by performing a search and replace operation.

**FIGURE 6.7**

This is how a cartoon character reads Shakespeare. Classy, huh?

```
<!DOCTYPE html PUBLIC "-//W3C//DTD XHTML 1.0 Strict//EN"
"http://www.w3.org/TR/xhtml1/DTD/xhtml1-strict.dtd">
<html lang="EN" dir="ltr" xmlns="http://www.w3.org/1999/xhtml">
<head>
<title>Cartoonify</title>
</head>
<body>
<div>
<?php
$fileName = "sonnet76.txt";

$sonnet = file($fileName);
$output = "";
```

```
foreach ($sonnet as $currentLine){
  $currentLine = str_replace("r", "w", $currentLine);
  $currentLine = str_replace("l", "w", $currentLine);
  $output .= rtrim($currentLine) . "<br />\n";
} // end foreach
  $output .= "You wascally wabbit!<br />\n";

print $output;

?>
</div>
</body>
</html>
```

## Loading the File into an Array with file()

Some shortcut file-handling tricks do not require you to create a file pointer. You might recall the readFile() command from Chapter 1, "Exploring the PHP Environment." That file simply reads a file and echoes it to the output. The file() command is similar, because it does not require a file pointer. It opens a file for input and returns an array, with each file line occupying one array element. This can make file work easy, because you can use a foreach loop to step through each line and perform modifications.

**TRAP** Reading a file into an array is attractive because it's easy; you can quickly work with the file once it's in memory. The problem comes when working with very large files. The computer's memory is finite and large files can cause problems. For larger data files, try a one-line-at-a-time approach using the fgets() function inside a loop.

## Using str_replace() to Modify File Contents

Inside the foreach loop, it's a simple matter to convert all occurrences of "r" and "l" to the letter "w" with the str_replace() function. The resulting string is added to the $output variable, which is ultimately printed to the screen.

---

### IN THE REAL WORLD

This particular application is silly and pointless, but the ability to replace all occurrences of one string with another in a text file is useful in a variety of circumstances. For example, you could replace every occurrence of the left brace (<) character in an HTML document with the &lt; sequence. This results in a source code listing that's directly viewable on the browser. You might use such technology for form letters, taking information in a text template and replacing it with values pulled from the user or another file.

---

## WORKING WITH DIRECTORY INFORMATION

When you are working with file systems, you often need to work with the directory structure that contains the files. PHP contains several commands that assist in directory manipulation.

### Introducing the imageIndex.php Program

The `imageIndex.php` program featured in Figure 6.8 is a simple utility that generates an index of all `jpg` and `gif` image files in a particular directory.

Anytime the user clicks a thumbnail, a full version of the image is displayed. The techniques that display the images can be used to get selected file sets from any directory. The `imageIndex.php` program automatically generates a thumbnail page based on all the image files in a particular directory.

```
<!DOCTYPE html PUBLIC "-//W3C//DTD XHTML 1.0 Strict//EN"
"http://www.w3.org/TR/xhtml1/DTD/xhtml1-strict.dtd">
<html lang="EN" dir="ltr" xmlns="http://www.w3.org/1999/xhtml">
<head>
<title>imageIndex</title>
</head>
<body>

<?php
// image index
// generates an index file containing all images in a particular directory

//point to whatever directory you wish to index.
```

```php
//index will be written to this directory as imageIndex.html
$dirName = "./pics";
$dp = opendir($dirName);
chdir($dirName);

//add all files in directory to $theFiles array
$currentFile = "";
while ($currentFile !== false){
  $currentFile = readDir($dp);
  $theFiles[] = $currentFile;
} // end while

//extract gif and jpg images
$imageFiles = preg_grep("/jpg$|gif$/", $theFiles);


$output = <<<HERE
<!DOCTYPE html PUBLIC "-//W3C//DTD XHTML 1.0 Strict//EN"
"http://www.w3.org/TR/xhtml1/DTD/xhtml1-strict.dtd">
<html lang="EN" dir="ltr" xmlns="http://www.w3.org/1999/xhtml">
<head>
<title>imageIndex</title>
</head>
<body>

<div>
HERE;

foreach ($imageFiles as $currentFile){
  $output .= <<<HERE
<a href = "$currentFile">
  <img src = "$currentFile"
      height = "50"
      width = "50"
      alt = "$currentFile" />
</a>

HERE;
```

```
} // end foreach

$output .= <<<HERE
</div>
</body>
</html>

HERE;


//save the index to the local file system
$fp = fopen("imageIndex.html", "w");
fputs ($fp, $output);
fclose($fp);
//readFile("imageIndex.html");

print <<<HERE
<p>
<a href = "$dirName/imageIndex.html">
   image index
</a>
</p>

HERE;
 ?>

</body>
</html>
```

FIGURE 6.8

This program creates a thumbnail index of all images in a given directory.

## Creating a Directory Handle with openDir()

Of course, directory operations focus on a particular directory. It's smart to store a directory name in a variable for easy changing, as directory conventions change when you migrate your programs to different systems. In the imageIndex program, I stored the target directory in a variable called $dirName. You can store the directory as a relative reference (in which case it is located in reference to the current program's directory) or as an absolute reference (in the current file system).

## Getting a List of Files with readdir()

The readdir() function reads a file from a valid directory pointer. Each time you call the readdir() function, it returns the name of the next file it finds, until no files are left. When the function has run out of files, it returns the value FALSE.

I find it useful to store all the directory files in an array, so I usually loop like this:

```
//add all files in directory to $theFiles array
$currentFile = "";
while ($currentFile !== false){
  $currentFile = readDir($dp);
  $theFiles[] = $currentFile;
} // end while
```

This loop keeps going until the $currentFile variable is FALSE, which happens when no files are left in the directory. Each time through the loop, it uses the readdir() function to load a new value into $currentFile, then adds the value of $currentFile to the $theFiles array. When I assign a value to an array without specifying the index, the item is simply placed at the next available index value. Loading an array in PHP is easy this way.

**TRICK** The special !== operator is a little different from the comparison operators you have seen before. Here it prevents a very specific type of error. It's possible that the user might have a file actually called "false" in the directory. If that's the case, the more normal condition $currentFile != false would give a strange result, because PHP could confuse a file named "false" with the actual literal value false. The !== operator specifies a comparison between actual objects rather than values, and it works correctly in this particular odd circumstance.

## Selecting Particular Files with preg_grep()

Once all the files from a particular directory are stored in an array, you often want to work with a subset of those files. In this particular case, I'm interested in graphic files, which end with the characters gif or jpg.

The oddly named preg_grep() function is perfect for this task. It borrows some clever ideas from UNIX shells and the Perl programming language. Grep (Generalized Regular Expression Parser) is the name of a UNIX command that filters files according to a pattern. preg indicates that this form of grep uses Perl-style regular expressions. Regardless of the funny name, the function is very handy.

If you look back at the code in imageIndex.php, you see this line:

```
$imageFiles = preg_grep("/jpg$|gif$/", $theFiles);
```

This code selects all the files that end with jpg or gif and copies them to another array called $imageFiles.

## Using Basic Regular Expressions

While it's possible to use string-manipulation functions to determine which files to copy to the new array, you might want to work with string data in a more detailed way. In this particular situation, I want all the files with gif or jpg in them. Comparing for two possible values with normal string manipulations isn't easy. Also, I didn't want any filename containing these two values, but only those filenames that end with gif or jpg. Regular expressions are a special convention often used to handle exactly this kind of situation, and much more.

Table 6.2 summarizes the main regular expression elements.

| TABLE 6.2 | SUMMARY OF BASIC REGULAR EXPRESSION OPERATORS | | | |
|---|---|---|---|---|
| **Operator** | **Description** | **Sample Pattern** | **Matches** | **Doesn't Match** |
| . | any character but newline | . | e | \n |
| ^ | beginning of string | ^a | apple | banana |
| $ | end of string | a$ | banana | apple |
| [characters] | any characters in braces | [abcABC] | a | d |
| [char range] | describe range of characters | [a-zA-z] | r | 9 |
| \d | any digit | \d\d\d-\d\d\d\d | 123-4567 | the-thing |
| \b | word boundary | \bthe\b | the | theater |
| + | one or more occurrences of preceding character | \d+ | 1234 | text |
| * | zero or more occurrences of preceding character | [a-zA-z]\d* | a5 | a |
| {digit} | repeat preceding character that many times | \d{3}-\d{4} | 123-4567 | 999-99-9999 |
| \| | or operator | apple\|banana | apple, banana | peach |
| (pattern segment) | store results in pattern memory returned with numeric code | (^.).*/1$ | gig, blab (any word that starts and ends with same letter) | |

**TRICK** Note that square braces can contain either characters or a range of characters as indicated in the examples.

To illustrate, I explain how the "/jpg$|gif$/" expression works. The expression "/jpg$|gif$/" matches on any string that ends with jpg or gif.

- Slashes usually mark the beginning and end of regular expressions. The first and last characters of the expression are these slashes.
- The pipe (|) character indicates *or*, so I'm looking for jpg *or* gif.
- The dollar sign ($) indicates the end of a string in the context of regular expressions, so jpg$ only matches on the value jpg if it's at the end of a string.
- Note that case is important here, so JPG won't be matched.

Regular expressions are extremely powerful if a bit cryptic. PHP supports a number of special functions that use regular expressions in addition to preg_grep. Look in the online Help under "Regular Expression Functions—Perl compatible" for a list of these functions as well as details on how regular expressions work in PHP. If you find regular expressions baffling, you can usually find a string-manipulation function (or two) that does the same general job.

## Storing the Output

Once the $imageFiles array is completed, the program uses the data to build an HTML index of all images and stores that data to a file. Since it's been a bit since you've seen that code, I reproduced a piece of it here:

```
foreach ($imageFiles as $currentFile){
  $output .= <<<HERE
<a href = "$currentFile">
  <img src = "$currentFile"
        height = "50"
        width = "50"
        alt = "$currentFile" />
</a>

HERE;

} // end foreach

$output .= <<<HERE
</div>
</body>
</html>
```

```
HERE;


//save the index to the local file system
$fp = fopen("imageIndex.html", "w");
fputs ($fp, $output);
fclose($fp);
//readFile("imageIndex.html");

print <<<HERE
<p>
<a href = "$dirName/imageIndex.html">
  image index
</a>
</p>

HERE;
```

I use a `foreach` loop to step through each `$imageFiles` array element. I add the HTML to generate a thumbnail version of each image to a variable called `$output`. Finally, I open a file called `imageIndex.html` in the current directory for writing, put the value of `$output` to the file, and close the file handle. Finally, I add a link to the file.

> You might be tempted to use a `readFile()` command to immediately view the contents of the file. I was. This may not work correctly, because the web browser assumes the `imageList.php` directory is the current directory. Inside the program, I changed to another directory within the local file system, but the web browser has no way of knowing that. The HTML was full of broken links when I did a `readFile()`, because all the relative links in the HTML page pointed towards files in another directory. When I add a link to the page instead, the web browser itself can find all the images, because the HTML files and the images are both in the same directory.

## WORKING WITH FORMATTED TEXT

Text files are easy to work with, but they are extremely unstructured. Sometimes you might want to impose a bit of formatting on a text file to work with data. You learn some more formal data management skills in the next couple of chapters, but with a few simple tricks, you can do quite a lot with plain text files.

## Introducing the mailMerge.php Program

To illustrate how to use text files for basic data storage, I created a simple mail-merge program. The results are shown in Figure 6.9.

You can see that the same letter was used repeatedly, each time with a different name and e-mail address. The name and e-mail information was pulled from a file.

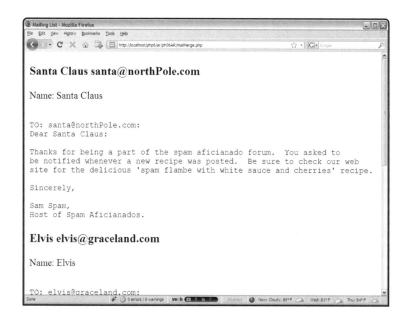

**FIGURE 6.9**

This program creates form letters from a simple data file.

## Determining a Data Format

The data file (shown in Figure 6.10) for this program is simply a file created in Notepad. Each line consists of a name and an e-mail address, separated by a tab character.

**TRICK**

This particular format (one line per record, tab-separated fields) is called a tab-delimited file. Because you can easily create a tab-delimited file in a text editor, spreadsheet, or any other kind of program, such files are popular. It's also quite easy to use another character as a separator. Spreadsheet programs often save in a comma-delimited format (CSV for comma-separated values) but string data does not work well in this format because it might already have embedded commas.

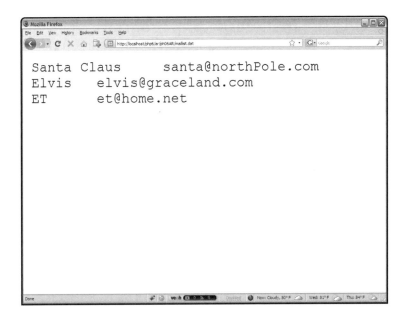

**FIGURE 6.10**

The data is stored in a simple text file.

## Examining the mailMerge.php Code

The basic strategy for the mailMerge.php program is very simple. Take a look at the code and you might be surprised at how easy it is:

```
<!DOCTYPE html PUBLIC "-//W3C//DTD XHTML 1.0 Strict//EN"
"http://www.w3.org/TR/xhtml1/DTD/xhtml1-strict.dtd">
<html lang="EN" dir="ltr" xmlns="http://www.w3.org/1999/xhtml">
<head>
<title>Mailing List</title>
</head>
<body>

<?php
//Simple Mail merge
//presumes tab-delimited file called maillist.dat

$theData = file("maillist.dat");



foreach($theData as $line){
```

```
$line = rtrim($line);
print "<h3>$line</h3>\n";
list($name, $email) = split("\t", $line);
print "<p>Name: $name</p> \n";

$message = <<<HERE

TO: $email:
Dear $name:

Thanks for being a part of the spam aficionado forum.  You asked to
be notified whenever a new recipe was posted.  Be sure to check our web
site for the delicious 'spam flambe with white sauce and cherries' recipe.

Sincerely,

Sam Spam,
Host of Spam Aficionados.

HERE;

  print "<pre>$message</pre> \n";

} // end foreach

?>
</body>
</html>
```

## Loading Data with the file() Command

The first step is loading the data into the form. Instead of using the file pointer technique, I use a special shortcut. The file() command takes a filename and automatically loads that file into an array. Each line of the file becomes an element of the array. This is especially useful when your text file contains data, because each line in my data file represents one individual's data.

The file() command is so easy you might be tempted to use it all the time. The command loads the entire file into memory, so you should only use it for relatively small files. When you use the fgets() technique, you only need one line from the file in memory at a time, so the fgets() method can be effectively used on any size file without affecting performance. Using file() on a very large file can be extremely slow and could potentially crash your server.

## Splitting a Line into an Array and to Scalar Values

You might recall the split() function from Chapter 5, "Better Arrays and String Handling." This function separates string elements based on some delimiter. I use the split() function inside a foreach loop to break each line into its constituent values. In this program I'm using the tab character (\t) as the delimiter.

However, I really don't want an array in this situation. Instead, I want the first value on the line to be read into the $name variable, and the second value stored in $email. The list() function allows you to take an array and distribute its contents into scalar (non- array) variables. In this particular situation, I never stored the results of the split() function in an array at all, but immediately listed the contents into the appropriate scalar variables. Once the data is in the variables, you can easily interpolate it into a mail-merge message.

The next obvious step for this program is to automatically send each message as an e-mail. PHP provides a function called mail(), which makes it quite easy to add this functionality. However, the function is dependent on how the server is set up and doesn't work with equal reliability on every server.

Also, there are good and not-so-good reasons to send e-mail through a program. It's completely legitimate to send e-mails to people when they request it or to have a program send you e-mails when certain things happen. For example, my own more secure version of the tester program sends an e-mail when conditions indicate potential cheating. A program that sends unsolicited e-mail to people is rude and causes bad feelings about your site.

## CREATING THE QUIZMACHINE.PHP PROGRAM

The quiz tool from the beginning of this chapter is an entire system of programs designed to work together—in this case, five different programs. Each quiz is stored in two separate files, which the programs automatically generate. Figure 6.11 illustrates how the various programs fit together.

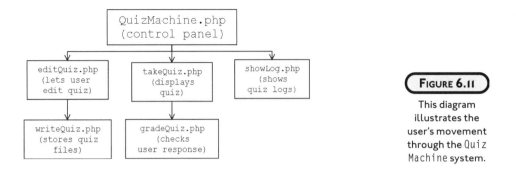

**FIGURE 6.11**

This diagram illustrates the user's movement through the Quiz Machine system.

The QuizMachine.php program is the entry point to the system for both the test administrator and the quiz taker. The program essentially consists of three forms that allow access to the other parts of the program. To ensure a minimal level of security, all other programs in the system require password access.

The QuizMachine.php program primarily serves as a gateway to the other parts of the system. If the user has administrative access (determined by a password), he can select an exam and call the editQuiz.php page. This page loads the quiz's actual master file (if it already exists) or sets up a prototype quiz and places the quiz data in a web page as a simple editor. The editQuiz program calls the writeQuiz.php program, which takes the results of the editQuiz form and writes it to a master test file and an HTML page.

If the user wants to take a quiz, the system moves to the takeQuiz.php page, which checks the user's password and presents the quiz if authorized. When the user indicates he is finished, the gradeQuiz.php program grades the quiz and stores the result in a text file.

Finally, the administrator can examine the log files resulting from any of the quizzes by indicating a quiz from the quizMachine page. The showLog.php program displays the appropriate log file.

## Building the QuizMachine.php Control Page

The heart of the quiz system is the QuizMachine.php page. The user directly enters this page only. All the other parts are called from this page or from one of the pages it calls. This page acts as a control panel. It consists of three parts, which correspond to the three primary jobs this system can do: writing or editing quizzes, taking quizzes, and analyzing quiz results. In each of these cases, the user has a particular quiz in mind, so the control panel automatically provides a list of appropriate files in each segment. Also, each of these tasks requires a password.

The main part of the `QuizMachine.php` program simply sets up the opening HTML and calls a series of functions, which do all the real work:

```
<!DOCTYPE html PUBLIC "-//W3C//DTD XHTML 1.0 Strict//EN"
"http://www.w3.org/TR/xhtml1/DTD/xhtml1-strict.dtd">
<html lang="EN" dir="ltr" xmlns="http://www.w3.org/1999/xhtml">
<head>
<title>Quiz Builder</title>

<link rel = "stylesheet"
      type = "text/css"
      href = "quiz.css" />

</head>
<body>
<h1>Quiz Machine</h1>

<?php

getFiles();
showTest();
showEdit();
showLog();
```

The program calls `getFiles()` first. This function examines a directory and gets a list of the files in that directory. This list of filenames is used in the other functions. The next three functions generate HTML forms. Each form contains a select list that is dynamically generated from the file list. The button corresponding to each form submits the form to the appropriate PHP page.

TRICK

Make another version of this main page for the people who will take your test. On the new page, you don't even show the administrative options. It's very easy to make such a page. Simply copy the `QuizMachine.php` program to another file and remove the calls to the `showEdit()` and `showLog()` functions.

## Getting the File List

Since most of the code in the `QuizMachine` program works with a list of files, the `getFiles()` function shown below is charged with that important task.

```
function getFiles(){
  //get list of all files for use in other routines

  global $dirPtr, $theFiles;

  chdir(".");
  $dirPtr = openDir(".");
  $currentFile = readDir($dirPtr);
  while ($currentFile !== false){
    $theFiles[] = $currentFile;
    $currentFile = readDir($dirPtr);
  } // end while

} // end getFiles
```

The first thing this function does is change the file system so it points at the current directory; then the program sets up a pointer variable to that directory.

**TRAP** The directory that holds the PHP programs is open for anybody to see. You might not want your test files to be so conspicuous. To simplify this example, I kept all the test files in the same directory as the program itself, but you can (and probably should) keep the data files in a different directory. You might store all the data files in a part of your directory that is unavailable to the web (away from your public_html structure, for instance) so that people can't see the answer key by browsing to it. If you do this, change each directory reference throughout the system.

I then created an array called theFiles, which holds every filename in the directory. The theFiles variable is global, so it is shared with the program and other functions that declare a reference to it.

### Showing the 'Take a Test' List

Most of your users don't create or edit quizzes. Instead, they take them. To take a test, the user must choose a test and enter the password associated with it. To simplify choosing a test, the showTest() function grabs all the HTML files in the quiz directory and places them in a select list. The password goes in an ordinary password field. The code in showTest() creates a form that calls the takeQuiz.php program when it is submitted:

```php
function showTest(){
  //print a list of tests for user to take

  global $theFiles;


  //select only quiz html files
  $testFiles = preg_grep("/mas$/", $theFiles);

  //generate the select box first
  $selQuiz = "    <select name = \"takeFile\"> \n";
  foreach ($testFiles as $myFile){
    $fileBase = substr($myFile, 0, strlen($myFile) - 4);
    $selQuiz .= <<<HERE
      <option value = "$fileBase">
        $fileBase
      </option>

HERE;
  } // end foreach
  $selQuiz .= "    </select> \n";

  print <<<HERE
<form action = "takeQuiz.php"
      method = "post">

  <fieldset>
    <h3>Take a quiz</h3>
    <label>quiz password</label>
    <input type = "password"
           name = "password" />

    <label>quiz</label>
    $selQuiz

    <button type = "submit">
      Take quiz
    </button>
```

```
  </fieldset>
</form>

HERE;
} // end showTest
```

Although the code is long, almost all of it is pure HTML. The PHP part selects HTML files and places them in the select group. This code fragment uses the preg_grep() to select filenames ending in mas and creates an option tag for that file.

Note that I stripped out the .mas part of the filename because I won't need it. It would complicate some of the code coming up in the takeQuiz program.

### Showing the Edit List

The showEdit() function works a lot like showTest(), listing the system's master files. It will generally return the same list as the editFiles() list, but I did the work separately, as I want to be able to use all three of these functions independently.

```
function showEdit(){
  // let user select a master file to edit

  global $theFiles;
  //get only quiz master files
  $testFiles = preg_grep("/mas$/", $theFiles);

  //generate the select box first
  $selEdit = "    <select name = \"editFile\"> \n";
  foreach ($testFiles as $myFile){
    $fileBase = substr($myFile, 0, strlen($myFile) - 4);
    $selEdit .= <<<HERE
      <option value = "$fileBase">
        $fileBase
      </option>

HERE;

  } // end foreach
  // add a 'new quiz' option
  $selEdit .= <<<HERE
      <option value = "new">
```

```
        new quiz
      </option>

HERE;

  $selEdit .= "    </select> \n";


  //edit a quiz
  print <<<HERE
<form action = "editQuiz.php"
     method = "post">

  <fieldset>
    <h3>Edit a quiz</h3>
    <label>admin password</label>
    <input type = "password"
           name = "password"
           value = "absolute"/>

    <label>quiz</label>
    $selEdit

    <button type = "submit">
      Edit quiz
    </button>
  </fieldset>
</form>

HERE;

} // end showEdit
```

The showEdit() function is just like showQuiz() but the form points to the editQuiz.php program and the file list is based on those files ending in mas.

There's one other subtle but important difference: Look at the code for the select element and you'll see a new quiz option. If the user chooses this option, the editQuiz() function won't try to load a quiz file into memory, but sets up for a new quiz instead.

I preloaded the password into the various password fields for testing purposes. This makes it easy to test your programs, because you don't have to type in the password every time you want to test the code. Of course, you'll want to remove the password before you release the code to the public, or everybody who runs your program will have administrative access.

### Showing the Log List

The last segment is meant for the quiz administrator. It allows the user with administrator access to view the log of any system quiz. This log shows who has taken the test, where and when she took it, and her score. When the user clicks the Submit button associated with this part of the page, the showLog.php program takes over.

```php
function showLog(){

  //let user choose from a list of log files
  global $theFiles;
  $testFiles = preg_grep("/log$/", $theFiles);

  //generate the select box first
  $selLog = "    <select name = \"logFile\"> \n";
  foreach ($testFiles as $myFile){
    $fileBase = substr($myFile, 0, strlen($myFile) - 4);
    $selLog .= <<<HERE
      <option value = "$fileBase">
        $fileBase
      </option>

HERE;

  } // end foreach
  $selLog .= "    </select> \n";

  //edit a quiz
  print <<<HERE
<form action = "showLog.php"
      method = "post">

  <fieldset>
    <h3>View a quiz log</h3>
    <label>admin password</label>
    <input type = "password"
```

```
          name = "password"
          value = "absolute" />

   <label>quiz</label>
   $selLog

   <button type = "submit">
     View log
   </button>
  </fieldset>
 </form>

HERE;

} // end showLog
```

I decided that all `log` files would end with .log, so the program can easily get a list of log files to place in the select group. Note that the list of log files isn't exactly the same as the list of master files, as there will only be a log file if somebody has taken one of the tests.

## Editing a Test

For simplicity's sake, I decided on a very simple test format. The first three lines of the test file contain the test's name, the instructor's e-mail address, and the test's password. The test data itself follows. Each problem takes up one line (although it can wrap freely—a line is defined by a carriage return character). The problem has a question followed by four possible answers and the correct answer. A colon separates each element.

---

### In the Real World

You think question formatting has too many rules? I agree. This is a limitation of the sequential-file access technique that's storing the data. In Chapters 8-12, you learn ways that aren't quite so picky. However, this is a relatively easy way to store your data, so I wrote the program to assist the process as much as is practical. You generally want to write your program so the user never has to know the underlying data structure. A better solution would be to create a form that automatically stores data in the right structure, but that can wait for an end-of-chapter exercise.

---

The `editQuiz.php` program assists the user in creating and editing quizzes. It's a simple program because the real work happens after the user edits and presses the Submit button.

## Getting Existing Test Data

The first chore of the `editQuiz` program is determining which quiz the user is requesting. Remember that the value `new` indicates that the user wants to build a new test; that value is treated specially. Any other value is the foundation of a test filename, so I open the appropriate master file and load its values into the appropriate form elements:

```
<!DOCTYPE html PUBLIC "-//W3C//DTD XHTML 1.0 Strict//EN"
"http://www.w3.org/TR/xhtml1/DTD/xhtml1-strict.dtd">
<html lang="EN" dir="ltr" xmlns="http://www.w3.org/1999/xhtml">
<head>
<title>Quiz Builder</title>

<link rel = "stylesheet"
      type = "text/css"
      href = "quiz.css" />

</head>
<body>
<h1>Edit a Quiz</h1>
<?php

//retrieve variables from form
$password = filter_input(INPUT_POST, "password");
$editFile = filter_input(INPUT_POST, "editFile");

if ($password != "absolute"){
  print <<<HERE

<p class = "error">
Incorrect Password.<br />
You must have a password in order to edit this quiz.
</p>
</body>
</html>

HERE;
```

```
} else {
  //check to see if user has chosen a form to edit
  if ($editFile == "new"){
    //if it's a new file, put in some dummy values
    $quizName = "sample test";
    $quizEmail = "root@localhost";
    $quizData = "q:a:b:c:d:correct";
    $quizPwd = "php";
  } else {
    //open up the file and get the data from it
    $editFile .= ".mas";
    $fp = fopen($editFile, "r");
    $quizName = fgets($fp);
    $quizEmail = fgets($fp);
    $quizPwd = fgets($fp);
    $quizData = "";
    while (!feof($fp)){
      $quizData .= fgets($fp);
    } // end while
  } // end 'new form' if
```

I decided to code the value `absolute` (from the name of this book series) as an administrative password. Each test has its own password and the administrative functions (like editing a quiz) have their own passwords. If the `password` field has any other value besides my chosen password, the program indicates a problem and refuses to move forward.

**TRAP** An administrative password keeps casual snoops out of your system, but it's nowhere near bullet-proof security. This system is not appropriate for situations where you must absolutely secure the tests.

Once you know the user is authorized to edit tests, determine if it's a new or existing quiz. If the quiz is new, I simply add sample data to the variables, which are used for the upcoming form. If the user wants to see an existing test, I open the file for read access and grab the first three lines, which correspond to the `$quizName`, `$quizEmail`, and `$quizPwd` fields. A `foreach` loop loads the rest of the file into the `$quizData` variable.

**TRICK** You might wonder why the quiz needs a password field if it took a password to get to this form. The quiz system has multiple levels of security. Anybody can get to the `quizBuilder.php` page. However, to move to one of the other pages, the user must have the right kind of password. Only an administrator should go to the editPage and showLog programs, so these programs require special administrative password access. Each quiz also has an associated password. The quiz master file stores the password so you can associate a different password for each quiz. In this way, the users authorized to take one test won't take other tests (and confuse your log files).

## Printing the Form

Once the variables are loaded with appropriate values, it's a simple matter to print an HTML form and let the user edit the quiz. The form is almost all pure HTML with the quiz variables interpolated into the appropriate places:

```
print <<<HERE

<form action = "writeQuiz.php"
      method = "post">

  <fieldset>
    <label>Quiz Name</label>
    <input type = "text"
           name = "quizName"
           value = "$quizName" />

    <label>Instructor Email</label>
    <input type = "text"
           name = "quizEmail"
           value = "$quizEmail" />

    <label>Password</label>
    <input type = "text"
           name = "quizPwd"
           value = "$quizPwd" />

    <textarea name = "quizData"
              rows = "20"
              cols = "60">
$quizData</textarea>

    <button type = "submit">
      save quiz
```

```
      </button>
    </fieldset>
  </form>
HERE;


} // end if


?>
</body>
</html>
```

## Writing the Test

The administrator has finished editing a quiz file. Now what? That quiz file must be stored to the file system and an HTML page generated for the quiz. The writeQuiz.php program performs these duties.

## Setting Up the Main Logic

Creating two files is your first job. The quiz name can be the filename's foundation, but many file systems choke at spaces within filenames. I use the str_replace() function to replace all spaces in $quizName to underscore characters (_). Then I create a filename ending in .mas for the master file and another filename ending in .html for the actual quiz.

To create the HTML file, I open it for write output. Then I use the buildHTML() function (described shortly) to build the HTML code, write that code to the HTML file, and close the file. The master file is built pretty much the same way, except it calls the buildMas() function to create the appropriate text for the file.

```
<!DOCTYPE html PUBLIC "-//W3C//DTD XHTML 1.0 Strict//EN"
"http://www.w3.org/TR/xhtml1/DTD/xhtml1-strict.dtd">
<html lang="EN" dir="ltr" xmlns="http://www.w3.org/1999/xhtml">
<head>
<title>Write Quiz</title>

<link rel = "stylesheet"
      type = "text/css"
      href = "quiz.css" />

</head>
<body>
```

```php
<?php
//given a quiz file from editQuiz,
//generates a master file and an HTML file for the quiz

//load variables from form
$quizName = filter_input(INPUT_POST, "quizName");
$quizEmail = filter_input(INPUT_POST, "quizEmail");
$quizPwd = filter_input(INPUT_POST, "quizPwd");
$quizData = filter_input(INPUT_POST, "quizData");

//open the output file
$fileBase = str_replace(" ", "_", $quizName);
$htmlFile = $fileBase . ".html";
$masFile = $fileBase . ".mas";


$htfp = fopen($htmlFile, "w");
$htData = buildHTML();
fputs($htfp, $htData);
fclose($htfp);


$msfp = fopen($masFile, "w");
$msData = buildMas();
fputs($msfp, $msData);
print <<<HERE
<pre>
$msData
</pre>

HERE;

fclose($msfp);
```

To make sure things are going well, I add a check to the end of the page that prints out the master file's actual contents. This program's output lets the administrator see that the test is working correctly. The administrator can take the test and submit it to the grading program from this page. If there is a problem, it's convenient to have the actual contents of the .mas file visible on the page.

## Building the Master File

The master file routine is very straightforward:

```
function buildMas(){
  //builds the master file
  global $quizName, $quizEmail, $quizPwd, $quizData;
  $msData = $quizName . "\n";
  $msData .= $quizEmail . "\n";
  $msData .= $quizPwd . "\n";
  $msData .=  $quizData;
  return $msData;
} // end buildMas
```

The critical part is remembering the file structure rules, so any program that reads this file doesn't get confused. The elements come in this order:

- Quiz name
- A newline character
- The $quizEmail variable
- The $quizPwd variable
- All $quizData (usually several lines)

Note that the function doesn't actually store the data to the file, but returns it to the main program. This allows me to write the data to both the file and to the page.

## Building the HTML File

The function that creates the HTML is a little more involved, but is manageable. The basic strategy is this: Build an HTML form containing all the questions. For each line of the master file, build a radio group. Place the question and all the possible answers in a set of nested <ol> elements. At the end of the page, there should be one Submit button. When the user clicks the Submit button, the system calls the gradeQuiz.php page, which evaluates the user's responses.

```
function buildHTML(){
  global $quizName, $quizData;
  $htData = <<<HERE

<!DOCTYPE html PUBLIC "-//W3C//DTD XHTML 1.0 Strict//EN"
"http://www.w3.org/TR/xhtml1/DTD/xhtml1-strict.dtd">
<html lang="EN" dir="ltr" xmlns="http://www.w3.org/1999/xhtml">
```

```
<head>
<title>$quizName</title>
<style type = "text/css">
ol ol {
  border-bottom: 1px solid black;
}

ol ol li {
  list-style-type: upperAlpha;
}
</style>
</head>
<body>

HERE;

  //get the quiz data
  $problems = split("\n", $quizData);
  $htData .= <<<HERE

<h1>$quizName</h1>

<form action = "gradeQuiz.php"
      method = "post">
  <fieldset>
    <label>Name</label>
    <input type = "text"
           name = "student" />

    <ol>

HERE;
  $questionNumber = 1;

  foreach ($problems as $currentProblem){
      list($question, $answerA, $answerB, $answerC, $answerD, $correct) =
      explode (":", $currentProblem);
      $htData .= <<<HERE
```

```
      <li>
        $question
        <ol>
          <li>
            <input type = "radio"
                   name = "quest[$questionNumber]"
                   value = "A" />
              $answerA
          </li>

      <li>
        <input type = "radio"
               name = "quest[$questionNumber]"
               value = "B" />
          $answerB
      </li>

      <li>
        <input type = "radio"
               name = "quest[$questionNumber]"
               value = "C" />
        $answerC
      </li>

      <li>
        <input type = "radio"
               name = "quest[$questionNumber]"
               value = "D" />
          $answerD
      </li>

    </ol>

  </li>

HERE;
    $questionNumber++;
```

```
  } // end foreach
  $htData .= <<<HERE
</ol>

<input type = "hidden"
       name = "quizName"
       value = "$quizName" />

<input type = "submit"
       value = "submit quiz" />
</fieldset>
</form>
</body>
</html>

HERE;

  //print $htData;
  return $htData;
} // end buildHTML
```

Most of the critical information this function needs is stored in $quizData. Each line of $quizData stores one question, so I use a split() function to break $quizData into an array called $problems. A foreach loop steps through each problem. Each problem contains a list of values, which is separated into a series of scalar variables with the combination of split() and list().

Within the foreach loop, I also add the HTML code necessary to print the current question's information. Take a careful look at the code for the radio buttons. Recall from your HTML experience that radio buttons that operate as a group should all have the same name. I did this by calling them all quest[$questionNumber]. The $questionNumber variable contains the current question number, and this value is interpolated before the HTML code is written. Question number 1 has four different radio buttons called quest[1]. The gradeQuiz program sees this as an array called $quest. Remember that radio buttons work by sending only the value associated with the button in the group that's currently selected, so you'll get an array called $quest with one value per question. Each value is the response that the user indicated.

At the end of the HTML, I add the quiz name (as a hidden field) and the Submit button.

## Taking a Quiz

The point of all this work is to have a set of quizzes your users can take, so it's good to have a program to present the quizzes. Actually, since the quizzes are saved as HTML pages, you could simply provide a link to a quiz and be done with it, but I wanted a little more security. I wanted the ability to store my quiz files outside the normal public_html file space and to have basic password protection so people don't take a quiz until I know it's ready. (I don't release the password until I'm ready for people to take the quiz.) Also, I can easily turn "off" a quiz by simply changing its password.

The takeQuiz page's only real job is to check the user's password against the indicated test's password and allow access to the quiz as appropriate.

```php
<?php
//takeQuiz.php
//given a quiz file, prints out that quiz
//no doctype, because that's embedded in HTML

//get password and filebase from form
$takeFile = filter_input(INPUT_POST, "takeFile");
$password = filter_input(INPUT_POST, "password");

//get the password from the file
$masterFile = $takeFile . ".mas";
$fp = fopen($masterFile, "r");
//the password is the third line, so get the first two lines, but ignore them
$dummy = fgets($fp);
$dummy = fgets($fp);
$magicWord = fgets($fp);
$magicWord = rtrim($magicWord);
fclose($fp);

if ($password == $magicWord){
  $htmlFile = $takeFile . ".html";
  //print out the page if the user got the password right
  readFile($htmlFile);
} else {
  print <<<HERE
<!DOCTYPE html PUBLIC "-//W3C//DTD XHTML 1.0 Strict//EN"
"http://www.w3.org/TR/xhtml1/DTD/xhtml1-strict.dtd">
```

```
<html lang="EN" dir="ltr" xmlns="http://www.w3.org/1999/xhtml">
<head>
<title>Quiz Builder</title>

<link rel = "stylesheet"
      type = "text/css"
      href = "quiz.css" />

</head>
<body>

<p class = "error">
Incorrect Password.<br />
You must have a password in order to take this quiz.
</p>
</body>
</html>

HERE;
} // end if
?>
```

The password associated with a test is stored in the test file, so once I know which test the user wants to take, I can open that file and extract the password. The password is stored in the file's third line. The only way to get to it with a sequential access file is to load the first two lines into a dummy variable and then load the password into a variable called $magicWord. If the user indicates a password that matches $magicWord, I use the readFile() function to send the contents of the quiz HTML page to the browser. If not, I send a message indicating the password was incorrect.

 **TRICK**  This is a dandy place to set up a little more security. I keep a log file of every access in a production version of this system, so I know if somebody has been trying to get at my system 1,000 times from the same machine within a second (a sure sign of some kind of automated attack) or other mischief. I can also check to see that later on when a page has been submitted, it comes from the same computer that requested the file in the first place. I can also check the request and submission times to reject quizzes that have been out longer than my time limit.

## Grading the Quiz

One advantage of this kind of system is the potential for instantaneous feedback for the user. As soon as the user clicks the Submit button, the gradeQuiz.php program automatically grades the quiz and stores a results log for the administrator.

### Opening the Files

The gradeQuiz program, like all the programs in this system, relies on files to do all its important work. In this case, the program uses the master file to get the answer key for the quiz and writes to a log file.

```php
<?php

//retrieve data from form
$student = filter_input(INPUT_POST, "student");
$quizName = filter_input(INPUT_POST, "quizName");
$quest = $_REQUEST["quest"];

print <<<HERE

<!DOCTYPE html PUBLIC "-//W3C//DTD XHTML 1.0 Strict//EN"
"http://www.w3.org/TR/xhtml1/DTD/xhtml1-strict.dtd">
<html lang="EN" dir="ltr" xmlns="http://www.w3.org/1999/xhtml">
<head>
<title>Grade for $quizName, $student</title>
<link rel = "stylesheet"
      type = "text/css"
      href = "quiz.css" />
</head>
<body>

<h1>Grade for $quizName, $student</h1>
HERE;


//open up the correct master file for reading
$fileBase = str_replace(" ", "_", $quizName);
$masFile = $fileBase . ".mas";
$msfp = fopen($masFile, "r");
```

```
$logFile = $fileBase . ".log";

//the first three lines are name, instructor's email, and password
$quizName = fgets($msfp);
$quizEmail = fgets($msfp);
$quizPwd = fgets($msfp);
```

The master file is opened with read access. The first three lines are unimportant, but I must read them to get to the quiz data.

## Creating an Answer Key

I start by generating an answer key from the master file, stepping through each question in the file and extracting all the normal variables from it (although I'm interested only in the $correct variable). I then store the $correct value in an array called $key. At the end of this loop, the $key array holds the correct answer for each quiz question.

```
//step through the questions building an answer key
$numCorrect = 0;
$questionNumber = 1;
while (!feof($msfp)){
  $currentProblem = fgets($msfp);

  list($question, $answerA, $answerB, $answerC, $answerD, $correct) =
  split (":", $currentProblem);
  $key[$questionNumber] = $correct;
  $questionNumber++;
} // end while
fclose($msfp);
```

### Checking the User's Response

The user's responses come from the HTML form as an array called $quest. The correct answers are in an array called $key. To grade the test, I step through both arrays at the same time, comparing the user's response with the correct response. Each time these values are the same, the user has gotten an answer correct. The user was incorrect when the values are different or there was a problem with the test itself; don't discount that as a possibility. Unfortunately, you can't do much about that, because the test author is responsible for making sure the test is correct. Still, you might be able to improve the situation somewhat by providing a better editor that ensures the test is in the right format and each question has an answer registered with it.

```php
//Check each answer from user
for ($questionNumber = 1; $questionNumber <= count($quest); $questionNumber++){
  $guess = $quest[$questionNumber];
  $correct = $key[$questionNumber];
  $correct = rtrim($correct);
  //print "$questionNumber, Guess = $guess, Correct = $correct.<br>\n";
  if ($guess == $correct){
    //user got it right
    $numCorrect++;
    print "<p>problem # $questionNumber was correct</p> \n";
  } else {
    print <<<HERE
    <p style = "color: red">
      problem # $questionNumber was incorrect
    </p>

HERE;
  } // end if
} // end for
```

I give a certain amount of feedback, telling whether the question was correct, but I decide not to display the right answer. You might give the user more or less information, depending on how you're using the quiz program.

## Reporting the Results to Screen and Log File

After checking each answer, the program reports the results to the user as a raw score and a percentage. The program also opens a log file for append access and adds the current data to it. Append access is just like write access, but rather than overwriting an existing file, it adds any new data to the end of it.

```php
$percentage = ($numCorrect /count($quest)) * 100;

print <<<HERE
<p>
  you got $numCorrect right
  for $percentage percent
</p>
HERE;
```

```
date_default_timezone_set("AMERICA/INDIANA/INDIANAPOLIS");
$today = date("F j, Y, g:i a");

//print "Date: $today<br>\n";
$location = getenv("REMOTE_ADDR");
//print "Location: $location<br>\n";

//add results to log file
$lgfp = fopen($logFile, "a");
$logLine = $student . "\t";
$logLine .= $today . "\t";
$logLine .= $location . "\t";
$logLine .= $numCorrect . "\t";
$logLine .= $percentage . "\n";

fputs($lgfp, $logLine);
fclose($lgfp);

?>
</body>
</html>
```

I add a few more elements to the log file that might be useful to a test administrator. Of course, I add the student's name and current date. I also added a location variable, which uses the $REMOTE_ADDR environment variable to indicate which machine the user was on when she submitted the exam. This can be useful because it can alert you to certain kinds of hacking. (A person taking the same quiz several times on the same machine but with a different name, for example.)

I also indicated the current time. Time manipulation is a little more complex in PHP 6 than it was in previous versions, but it is very powerful.

```
date_default_timezone_set("AMERICA/INDIANA/INDIANAPOLIS");
$today = date("F j, Y, g:i a");
```

The gradeQuiz program adds the number correct and the percentage to the log file as well, then closes the file.

Notice that the data in the log file is delimited with tab characters. This is done so an analysis program could easily work with the file using the split command. Also, most spreadsheet programs can read a tab-delimited file, so the log file is easily imported into a spreadsheet for further analysis.

**TRICK**

In PHP 6, all times are related to specific time zones, so whenever you work with time information, be sure to set the time zone of your web server. The date() function requires a special formatting string. The particular format I'm using specifies a full text date (F) containing the day of the month with no leading zeros (j), the year in four digits (Y), a comma, the hour in a 12-hour format (g), the minutes (i), and an AM/PM indicator (a).

If you are interested in some other format, check the PHP date format documentation for a dizzying array of options.

**TRICK**

You can really improve the logging functionality if you want to do some in-depth test analysis. For example, store each user's response to each question in the quiz. This gives you a database of performance on every question, so you could easily determine which questions are causing difficulty.

## Viewing the Log

The showLog.php program is actually very similar to the takeQuiz program. It checks the password to ensure the user has administrator access, then opens the log using the file() function. It prints the file results inside a <pre></pre> pair, so the tab characters are preserved.

```
<!DOCTYPE html PUBLIC "-//W3C//DTD XHTML 1.0 Strict//EN"
"http://www.w3.org/TR/xhtml1/DTD/xhtml1-strict.dtd">
<html lang="EN" dir="ltr" xmlns="http://www.w3.org/1999/xhtml">
<head>
<title>Quiz Builder</title>

<link rel = "stylesheet"
      type = "text/css"
      href = "quiz.css" />

</head>
<body>
<?php
//showLog.php
//shows a log file
//requires admin password

$password = filter_input(INPUT_POST, "password");
$logFile = filter_input(INPUT_POST, "logFile");
```

```
$logFile .= ".log";

if ($password == "absolute"){
  $lines = file($logFile);
  print "<pre>\n";
  foreach ($lines as $theLine){
    print $theLine;
  } // end foreach
  print "</pre>\n";

} else {
  print <<<HERE
  <p class = "error">
Incorrect Password.<br />
You must have a password in order to view this log.
</p>

HERE;
} // end if

?>
</body>
</html>
```

Improve this program by writing the data into an HTML table. However, not all spreadsheets can easily work with HTML table data, so I prefer the tab format. It isn't difficult to add data analysis to the log viewer, including mean scores, standard deviation, and suggested curve values.

## SUMMARY

This chapter explored the use of sequential files as a data storage and retrieval mechanism. You learned how to open files in read, write, and append modes and you know how file pointers refer to a file. You wrote data to a file and loaded data from a file with appropriate functions. You learned how to load an entire file into an array. You can examine a directory and determine which files are in the directory. You learned how to use basic regular expressions in the preg_grep() function to display a subset of files in the directory. Finally, you put all this together in a multi-program system that allows multiple levels of access to an interesting data set. You should be proud.

## CHALLENGES

1. Improve the quiz program in one of the ways I suggested throughout the chapter: Add the ability to e-mail test results, put in test score analysis, improve the quiz editing page, or try some improvement of your own design.

2. Some of the values in this system should be shared among the different programs (the root directory and administrative password come to mind). Store these values in a configuration file, and modify the quiz programs to read the data from this file when needed.

3. Create a source code viewer. Given a filename, the program should read the file into memory and convert each instance of < into the HTML attribute &lt;. Save this new file to another name, so you can show your source code to others.

4. Create a simple guest book. Let the user enter information into a form, and add her comment to the bottom of the page when she clicks the Submit button. You can use one or two files for this.

# WRITING PROGRAMS WITH OBJECTS

Object-oriented programming (sometimes abbreviated as OOP) is an important development in programming languages. Some languages such as Java are entirely object-oriented and require an intimate understanding of the object-oriented paradigm. PHP, in keeping with its easygoing nature, supports a form of object-oriented programming, but does not require it. In this chapter, you learn what objects are and how to build them in PHP. Specifically, you learn how to:

- Use a custom class to build enhanced web pages
- Design a basic class of your own
- Build an instance of a class
- Leverage inheritance, encapsulation, and polymorphism
- Create properties and methods in your classes

## INTRODUCING THE SUPERHTML OBJECT

Back when I used to program in Perl (before PHP existed), I really liked a feature called cgi.pm. This module simplified server-based programming. One of my favorite things about the module was the way it allowed you to quickly build web pages without writing HTML/XHTML. Once I understood how to use cgi.pm, I was creating web pages with unbelievable speed and ease. PHP doesn't have this feature built in, so I decided to make a similar object myself using the object-oriented paradigm. The SuperHTML object described in this chapter replicates that object and serves as an example of OOP methodology. Throughout this chapter, you see the object being used, then you'll learn how to build it and modify it for your own purposes.

As you look at the SuperHTML object, you should think of it at two levels:

- First, ignore the inner workings of the object and learn how to use it. There's a lot to this class, and it has a lot of potential to improve your PHP programming.

- Second, examine how it was built. This comes after you've played with the object for a while. There's no doubt you'll have some ideas on how to improve it. Once you understand how objects work in PHP, you'll be able to build even more-powerful objects on your own.

## Building a Simple Document with SuperHTML

The SuperHTML object is a special type of entity that allows you to automatically create and modify a web page. It can be tricky to understand what an object is, so I'll start by just showing you how this one works. Take a look at Figure 7.1 to see a simple XHTML page.

What makes this document interesting is the way it was built. The source code for BasicSuper.php is different from any other code you've seen so far. It's okay if it doesn't make sense yet. Just look over the code to see how simple it is, and I'll explain it all.

```php
<?php
include "SuperHTMLDef.php";
$s = new SuperHTML("Basic Super Page");
$s->buildTop();
$s->buildBottom();
print $s->getPage();
?>
```

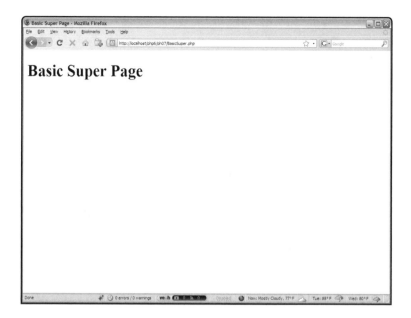

**FIGURE 7.1**

The basic
superHTML page
looks just like an
ordinary XHTML
page to the user.

## Including a File

The first thing this code does is import another file. The `include` statement retrieves data from another file and interprets it as HTML code. In this case, I'm including a file called `SuperHTMLDef.php`. That file contains the definition for the `SuperHTML` object.

One of the joys of OOP is using an object without understanding exactly how it works. Rest assured you'll see the code in the file soon enough. For now be sure you understand how to access code in another program.

**TRAP**

If you are having trouble with the `include` command, check the value of `open_basedir` in `php.ini`. (The easiest way to do this is to run a program with the `phpInfo()` command in it.) The `open_base` dir variable is set to `null` by default, which means PHP can load files from anywhere in the server's file system, but your administrator may have this access limited. You may need to reset this value on the server or bribe your server administrator to get this value changed. They (administrators, not servers) generally respond well to Twinkies.

## Creating an Instance of the SuperHTML Object

The next line creates a new variable called $s:

```
$s = new SuperHTML("Basic Super Page");
```

This variable contains an object. Objects are complex variable types that can contain both variables and code. (You learn how to build your own objects later in this chapter.) The SuperHTML object is a custom object I invented that describes a fancy kind of web page. Since it's an object, it has certain characteristics, called properties, and it has certain behaviors, called methods. By invoking the object's methods, you can do some really neat things without a lot of work. Most of the properties are hidden in this particular example, but they're still there. Notice that when I created $s, I indicated a name for the page: Basic Super Page. That name will be used to form the title of the page as well as a caption.

No doubt, you recall my advice to use descriptive names for things. You might be composing an angry e-mail to me now about the variable called $s: That's clearly not a descriptive name. However, I'm following a convention that's reasonably common among object-oriented programmers. When I have one particular object that I'm going to use a lot, I give it a one-character name to keep the typing simple. If that bothers you, the global search and replace feature of your favorite text editor is a reasonable option.

## Building the Web Page

The web page shown in Figure 7.1 has all the normal accoutrements, like <head> and <body> tags, a <title>, and even a headline in <h1> format. However, you can see that the code doesn't directly include any of these elements. Instead, it has two lines of PHP that both invoke the $s object.

```
$s->buildTop();
$s->buildBottom();
```

Both buildTop() and buildBottom() are considered methods, which are simply functions associated with a particular object type. In effect, because $s is a SuperHTML object, it knows how to build the top and bottom of the web page. The buildTop() method generates the following HTML code automatically:

```
<!DOCTYPE html PUBLIC "-//W3C//DTD XHTML 1.0 Strict//EN"
"http://www.w3.org/TR/xhtml1/DTD/xhtml1-strict.dtd">
<html lang="EN" dir="ltr" xmlns="http://www.w3.org/1999/xhtml">
<head>
  <meta http-equiv="content-type" content="text/xml; charset=utf-8" />
  <title>Basic Super Page</title>
  <link rel = "stylesheet"
        type = "text/css"
        href = "Basic_Super_Page.css" />
</head>
<body>
  <h1>Basic Super Page</h1>
```

The code isn't amazing, but it does a lot of work. It sets up an XHTML strict template, sets the title and headline according to the indicated page title, and makes a link to a stylesheet with the same name.

It's not that amazing that the function can generate all that HTML code; the code is fairly predictable. What's neat is the way the SuperHTML object knew what its title and headline should be. The phrase Basic Super Page is the string that initializes the SuperHTML object. The buildBottom() method is even easier than buildTop(), because it simply adds some boilerplate page-ending code:

```
</body>
</html>
```

## Writing Out the Page

The buildTop() and buildBottom() directives feel a lot like function calls, because they are very similar to the functions you've already created and used many times. However, these functions are designed to work within the context of a particular object. A function attached to an object is referred to as a method of the object. A cow object might have moo() and giveMilk() methods.

 The syntax for referring to properties and methods in PHP is the arrow syntax (->). There isn't one key to indicate this operator. It is the combination of the dash and the greater-than symbol.

Note that neither `buildTop()` nor `buildBottom()` actually write any code to the screen. Instead, they prepare the page as a long string property inside the object. `SuperHTML` has a method called `getPage()` that returns the actual HTML code for the page. The programmer can then save the code to a file, print it out, or whatever. In this case, the following line simply prints out the results of the `getPage()` method:

```
print $s->getPage();
```

## Working with the Title Property

It's possible to designate a title when you create a `SuperHTML` object, but what if you want to change the title later? Objects can store code in methods, and they can also store data in properties. A property is like a variable attached to a particular object. The `SuperHTML` object has a title property. The `cow` object might have a `breed` property and an `age` property. The `Properties.php` page featured in Figure 7.2 illustrates this feature.

The `Properties.php` program begins exactly like the `Basic Super Page` you saw earlier. I even created the `$s` variable with the same initial value (`Basic Super Page`).

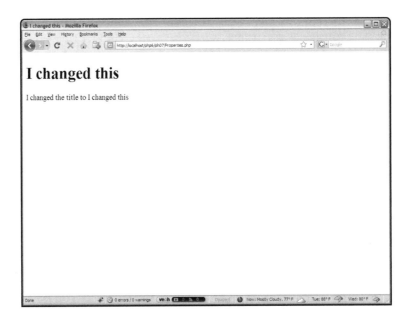

**FIGURE 7.2**

I created this page with one title and then changed the title with a method.

When I created the `SuperHTML` object, the title property was automatically set to `Basic Super Page`. It's possible to directly change the title, like this:

```
$s ->title = "new title";
```

As you see when you look at the SuperHTML code itself, this approach can cause some problems. It's generally better to use special methods to get information to and from properties. Take a look at the following code for Property.php and you'll see a better way to change a property value.

```php
<?php
include "SuperHTMLDef.php";
$s = new SuperHTML("Basic Super Page");
$s->setTitle("I changed this");
$s->buildTop();
$title = $s->getTitle();
$s->tag("p", "I changed the title to $title");
$s->buildBottom();
print $s->getPage();
?>
```

The $s->setTitle() method allows me to add a new value to a property. The $s->getTitle() method gets a value from a property. These special methods are usually called access methods because they allow access to properties. I'll explain more about access methods later in this chapter when you start building your own object.

---

### IN THE REAL WORLD

If you've programmed in languages like Visual Basic, C#, or Java, you might argue that you have directly accessed properties without using these access methods. The truth is, access methods in these languages are usually behind the scenes. When you assign a value to an object property, the appropriate access method is automatically implemented.

---

## Adding Text and Tags with SuperHTML

The SuperHTML object makes it easy to build a basic HTML framework, but you always need other kinds of tags. SuperHTML has some general methods for adding various kinds of tags and text to a document. Figure 7.3 illustrates a page (addingTags.php) using these features.

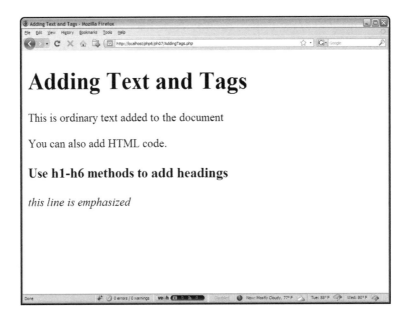

**FIGURE 7.3**

This page includes
some text and
HTML tags.

One of the primary features of SuperHTML is the way it separates the creation of a web page from its display. You want to be able to easily generate a page and then display it onscreen, write it to a file, or do whatever else you want with it. For that reason, you won't simply print things out. Instead, you'll keep adding stuff to the SuperHTML object and then print the whole thing out when you're done.

That means you need some mechanism for adding things to the page. The SuperHTML object contains more than 25 methods for adding various kinds of objects to the document. (Don't panic. Most of them are really very simple.) Two methods in particular are extremely useful. Look at the code for AddingTags.php and see what I mean.

```php
<?php
include "SuperHTMLDef.php";
$s = new SuperHTML("Adding Text and Tags");
$s->buildTop();

$s->addText("<p>This is ordinary text added to the document</p>");
$s->addText("<div>You can also add HTML code.</div>");

$s->h3("Use h1-h6 methods to add headings");
$s->addText("<div>");
$s->tag("em", "this line is emphasized");
```

```
$s->addText("</div>");
$s->buildBottom();
print $s->getPage();
?>
```

The addText() method expects a string as its only parameter. It then adds that text to the document in memory. As you can see, the text can even contain HTML data. You can also pass multi-line strings or text with interpolated variables.

The addText() method is really the only method you need to build the page in memory. However, the point of the SuperHTML object is to make page development faster and easier. I actually use the addText() method when I need to add actual text to a page or when I need a tag I haven't yet implemented in SuperHTML.

Look at the following line:

```
$s->h3("Use h1-h6 methods to add headings");
```

This code accepts a string as a parameter, then surrounds the text with <h3></h3> tags and writes it to the document in memory. Of course, there are similar methods for h1 through h6. You could expect similar methods for all the basic HTML tags.

I didn't create shortcuts for all the HTML tags, for two reasons. One reason is once you see the mechanism for creating a new tag method, you can modify SuperHTML very easily to have methods for all your favorite tags. The other reason I didn't make shortcuts for all the tags is the very special method described in the following line:

```
$s->tag("em", "this line is emphasized");
```

The tag() method is a workhorse. It expects two parameters. The first is the tag you want to implement (without the angle braces). In this case I want to italicize, so I'm implementing the i tag. The second parameter is the text you want sent to the document. After this function is completed, the document has the following text added to the end:

```
<em>this line is emphasized</em>
```

If you look at the HTML source code for AddText.php, you see that's exactly what happened.

The great thing about the tag() method is its flexibility. It can surround any text with any tag. Any tag can be implemented by calling the tag() method with the tag name as the first parameter and the tag's text as the second parameter.

## Creating Lists the SuperHTML Way

Even if you only use the addText() and tag() methods, you can create some really nice, flexible web pages. However, this object's real power comes with some specialized methods that solve specific display problems. When you think about it, a lot of PHP constructs have natural companions in the HTML world. For example, if you have an array of data in PHP, you frequently want to display it in some form of HTML list. Figure 7.4 demonstrates a page with a number of lists, all automatically generated from arrays.

You've probably already written code to generate an HTML list from an array. Although it's not difficult, it can be tedious. It'd be great if you could just hand off that functionality and not worry about it when you've got other problems to solve. The SuperHTML object has exactly that capability. The code Lists.php illustrates a number of ways to do this.

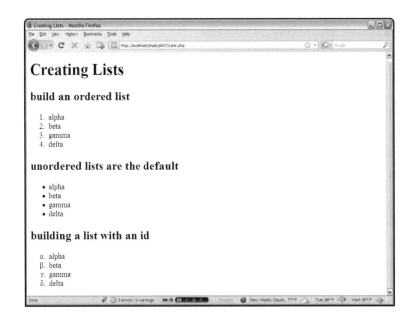

**FIGURE 7.4**

The superHTML object makes it easy to build lists from arrays.

```php
<?php
include "SuperHTMLDef.php";
$s = new SuperHTML("Creating Lists");
$s->buildTop();

$myArray =array( "alpha", "beta", "gamma", "delta");

$s->h2("build an ordered list");
```

```
$s->buildList($myArray, "ol");

$s->h2("unordered lists are the default");
$s->buildList(array("alpha", "beta", "gamma", "delta"));

$s->h2("building a list with an id");
$s->buildList($myArray, "ol id = 'fancy'");
$s->buildBottom();
print $s->getPage();
?>
```

## Building a Basic List

I started the list.php code by creating an array called (cleverly enough) $myArray. The buildList() method requires two parameters, an array, and a list type. Then I invoke the function:

```
$s->buildList($myArray, "ol");
```

The SuperHTML object responds by adding the following code to its internal representation of the page:

```
<ol>
 <li>alpha</li>
 <li>beta</li>
 <li>gamma</li>
 <li>delta</li>
</ol>
```

As you can see, each array item is enclosed in <li></li> tags, and the entire array is encased in an <ol></ol> set with appropriate indentation. You'll be much more willing to use arrays when you have an easy tool like this to display them.

## Building an Ad Hoc List

Of course, you don't always want an ordered list. The next call to the buildList() method is different from the first version in two ways:

```
$s->buildList(array("alpha", "beta", "gamma", "delta"));
```

- First, I built this one on the fly rather than using a predefined array. This is useful when you want to build a list quickly but don't already have an array. Just put the list values in an ad hoc array before sending the array to the buildList() method.

- Second, this call is different because of the lack of a list type. If I don't indicate what type of list I want, SuperHTML is smart enough to guess and put a legal value in for me. This behavior is a good example of a principle called *polymorphism*, where an object can act differently in different situations. (Of course, the formal definition is a little more profound than that, but this is good enough for now.) You can probably guess that the default list type is unordered.

## Building More Specialized Lists

The buildList() method has one more trick up its sleeve. If you look back at the third list on the HTML output, it obviously has a custom style attached (as it displays the list item numbers in lowercase Greek characters). You can specify a class or a title for your list, like this:

```
$s->buildList($myArray, "ol id = 'fancy'");
```

I then created a stylesheet called "Creating_Lists.css." Note the stylesheet is just like the title, but with all spaces replaced with underscores. Every SuperHTML page looks for a stylesheet with a name related to the page title in this way. (If no such page exists, the default styles are used.) I added a very simple style rule to the CSS page to get the Greek symbols:

```
#fancy {
  list-style-type: lower-greek;
}
```

Of course, the CSS style you create can be as detailed as you want. This mechanism allows you to continue using CSS as your primary markup mechanism; the SuperHTML class encourages the construction of valid XHTML and provides hooks for CSS styling.

## Making Tables with SuperHTML

All the SuperHTML features you've seen up to now are pretty handy, but the main thing I wanted was easy work with tables. I tend not to use tables as much as I once did, because modern CSS formatting discourages the use of tables for layout. Still, you'll often find yourself thinking about complex data that lends itself to table-based output. In particular, when you have a two-dimensional array, the natural display mechanism is an HTML table.

You'll frequently find yourself writing data in tables, and it can be confusing to switch from PHP to HTML syntax (especially when you add SQL to the mix, because at that point you're thinking in three very different languages at once). I wanted some features that easily let you build HTML tables from PHP data structures. Figure 7.5 shows a program with this capability.

The basic plan for building tables with SuperHTML is similar to the approach for making lists. However, tables are based on data structures more complex than lists, as you can see when you peruse the code for Tables.php shown in Figure 7.5.

**FIGURE 7.5**

These tables were made automatically by the SuperHTML object.

```php
<?php
include "SuperHTMLDef.php";
$s = new SuperHTML("Creating Tables");
$s->buildTop();

$s->h3("build table from 2d array");
$myArray = array(
  array("English", "Spanish", "Japanese"),
  array("One", "Uno", "Ichi"),
  array("Two", "Dos", "Nii"),
  array("Three", "Tres", "San")
);
$s->buildTable($myArray);

$s->h3("build table row-by-row");
$s->startTable();
$s->tRow(array("English", "Greek"), "th");
```

```
$s->tRow(array("a", "alpha"));
$s->tRow(array("b", "beta"));
$s->endTable();

$s->buildBottom();
print $s->getPage();
?>
```

## Creating a Basic Table

Early in this chapter, I mentioned that PHP arrays and HTML lists are natural companions. Each row of an HTML table can be seen as a PHP array, and a table can be seen as an array of rows. An array of arrays is a two-dimension array. It shouldn't surprise you that building a table from a two-dimension array is easy. After I created an array called $myArray, turning it into a table with one line of code was trivial:

```
$s->buildTable($myArray);
```

### Creating a More Complex Table

The buildTable() method is really easy, but it isn't flexible enough for all needs. Frequently (especially in database applications) I want to build the top of the table, a header row, a series of rows in a loop, and then close off the table. I decided to add a more powerful suite of table-creation methods. These make it possible to make more sophisticated tables, like the second one on Table.php.

The following code builds a table line-by-line:

```
$s->h3("build table row-by-row");
$s->startTable();
$s->tRow(array("English", "Greek"), "th");
$s->tRow(array("a", "alpha"));
$s->tRow(array("b", "beta"));
$s->endTable();
```

The startTable() method creates the code that begins the table definition. The parameter indicates the table's border width. If you don't indicate a border width, it defaults to 1. (Gosh, polymorphism is wonderful!) It won't surprise you that the end of the table is indicated by the endTable() method.

The cool part of this approach is the tRow() method, which makes up the table body. This method can accept one or two parameters. The first parameter is an array of values that populates the row. Of course, this can be an array variable or created on the fly (as in this example). The second `tRow()` parameter is cell type. The default type is `td`, but you can specify `th` if you want a header row. You can also designate a particular style, class, or id for a table row to enable more sophisticated style. For example, you could make a row red like this:

```
$s->tRow(array("b", "beta"), "th style = 'color: red'");
```

I explain fully how all this works in the `form.php` program coming up next. Call the `tRow()` method once for each table row. In an actual program, this frequently happens inside some sort of loop.

## Creating Super Forms

The `SuperHTML` object is useful, but if it is really going to be helpful, it must easily build form elements such as textboxes and Submit buttons. Most of these objects are reasonably easy to build, but I've always found drop-down menus (HTML select objects) tedious to program. The `SuperHTML` object has a powerful, flexible, and easy approach to building various form elements. The page featured in Figure 7.6 was produced using some special object features.

**FIGURE 7.6**

Forms are no problem for SuperHTML.

The form program code looks a little more involved than some other examples, but it's not any more difficult than anything you've already seen. First, I give you the code in full, and then I break it apart and show you the features.

```php
<?php
include "SuperHTMLDef.php";
$s = new SuperHTML("Working with Forms");
$s->buildTop();

$s->startForm();
$s->label("User Name");
$s->textbox("userName", "Joe");

$numbers = array(
  "1"=>"ichii",
  "2"=>"nii",
  "3"=>"san",
  "4"=>"shi"
);

$s->label("Favorite number");
$s->select("favNumber", $numbers);

$s->submit();
$s->endForm();

print $s->formResults();

$s->buildBottom();

print $s->getPage();

?>
```

## Building a Simple Form and Adding a Text Box

The following code snippet builds the most basic SuperHTML form:

```php
$s->startForm();
$s->label("User Name");
$s->textbox("userName", "Joe");
$s->submit();
$s->endForm();
```

Begin a form with the `startForm()` method. This method can take up to two parameters. The first is the action (the PHP program that will be called when this form is submitted). The default action is empty, which calls the current program again. The second parameter is the method, which defaults to "post."

SuperHTML has a number of shortcut methods for creating form elements, including `label()`, `textbox()`, `select()`, and `submit()`.

The `label()` method is used for creating labels. These optional elements are usually used to hold instructions. While the label itself has no formatting, it is a useful placeholder for CSS coding, so you can make the form look however you want. The `label()` method takes one parameter, which is the text of the label.

The `textbox()` method can take one or two parameters. The first parameter is the `id` of the resulting `<input>` element. The second (optional) parameter is the element's default value. If you do not specify a value, it is left blank.

Of course, the `submit()` method creates a Submit button, with the indicated caption. However, if you leave off the `submit` method's second parameter, your HTML code will show the typical `Submit Query` caption.

The `endForm()` method ends the form definition. You can see that building forms with SuperHTML is quite simple. Most of the details are taken care of by the library.

## Building Drop-Down Menus

There are a number of times you'll want the user to choose input from a limited number of options. Often, the value you want to send to the next program isn't exactly what the user sees. The appropriate HTML device for this situation is the `<select>` element with a bunch of `<option>` objects inside. If you try to map the `select` and `option` combination to a PHP structure, the most obvious comparison is an associative array as you used in Chapter 5, "Better Arrays and String Handling." Take a look at the following code fragment to see how this works.

```
$numbers = array(
  "1"=>"ichii",
  "2"=>"nii",
  "3"=>"san",
  "4"=>"shi"
);
$s->label("Favorite number");
$s->select("favNumber", $numbers);
```

I created an associative array using numbers as indices and the Japanese names for the numerals as the values.

Once I had created the array, it was easy to create a select object with the cleverly named `select()` method. The two parameters are the name of the resulting `select` object and the array. This code produces the following HTML:

```
<label>
  Favorite number
</label>

<select name = "favNumber" >
  <option value = "1">ichii</option>
  <option value = "2">nii</option>
  <option value = "3">san</option>
  <option value = "4">shi</option>
</select>
```

You can see the nice relationship between the associative array in PHP and the HTML `select` object. `SuperHTML` makes it easy to build a select object from an associative array.

---

### BUILDING FORMS WITH TABLES

The main reason I wrote the original version of `SuperHTML` was to simplify form creation. Before XHTML and CSS were accepted standards, you almost always had to use tables to build nice-looking forms. While it isn't difficult to build forms using tables for layout, the code got very messy and difficult to work with. Now that I use CSS for layout, I do not recommend formatting your forms with tables. Several of the methods of the `SuperHTML` object were designed with table- based form design in mind. I've kept those methods in this version of `SuperHTML`, but I no longer recommend their use.

---

### Viewing Form Results

Usually when I build a PHP page that responds to a form, I begin by retrieving the names and values of all the fields that come from the form. This is useful because often I make mistakes in my field names or forget exactly what I'm expecting the form to send. It would be nice to have a really easy way to do this. Of course, `SuperHTML` has this feature built in. If you fill in the form elements in `Forms.php` and click the Submit button, you get another version of `Forms.php`, but this one also includes form data, as shown in Figure 7.7.

**FIGURE 7.7**

SuperHTML has a great tool for quickly seeing the results of a form.

The code that produces these results is quite simple:

```
print $s->formResults();
```

If there was no previous form, `formResults()` returns an empty string. If the page has been called from a form, the resulting code looks something like this:

```
<dl>
  <dt>userName</dt>
  <dd>Joe</dd>

  <dt>favNumber</dt>
  <dd>1</dd>

</dl>
```

## UNDERSTANDING OOP

The SuperHTML project uses many OOP features to do its work. Before digging into the innards of SuperHTML itself, it makes sense to think more about what objects are and how to create them in PHP.

## Objects Overview

As you've seen, objects have properties, which are characteristics of the object, and methods, which are things the object can do.

In addition to supporting properties and methods, a properly designed object should reflect certain values of the object-oriented paradigm.

**TRICK** Many discussions of OOP indicate that objects also have events. An event is some sort of stimulus the object can respond to. Events are indeed important in OOP, but they are not often used in PHP programming, because events are meant to capture things that happen in real time. PHP programs rarely involve real-time interaction with the user, so events are not as critical in PHP objects as they are in other languages.

### Encapsulation

An object can be seen as some data (the properties) and some code (the methods) for working with that data. Alternatively, you could see an object as a series of methods and the data that supports these methods. Regardless, you can use an object without knowing exactly how it is constructed or how it works behind the scenes. This principle of encapsulation is well supported by PHP. You take advantage of encapsulation when you build ordinary functions. Objects take the notion of encapsulation one step further by grouping together code and data.

### Inheritance

Inheritance is the idea that an object can be inherited from another object. Imagine if you had to build a police car. You could build a factory that begins with sheet metal and other raw materials, or you could start with a more typical car and simply add the features that make it a police car. Inheritance involves taking an existing type of object and adding new features to create a new object type. PHP supports at least one kind of inheritance, as you see later in this chapter.

### Polymorphism

You've encountered polymorphism in the SuperHTML description. Polymorphism involves an object's ability to act somewhat differently under different circumstances. The form of inheritance in SuperHTML is used to handle unexpected or missing data. PHP supports some types of polymorphism, but to be honest this is more a factor of the permissive and loose variable typing of PHP than any particular object-oriented design consideration.

## Creating a Basic Object

One of the easiest ways to understand something is to look at an example. Begin by looking at the basic critter in Figure 7.8.

FIGURE 7.8

The critter is a very simple demonstration of objects.

Of course, you won't see anything special if you look at the HTML output or the simpleCritter.php HTML source code. The interesting work was done in the php code:

```
<!DOCTYPE html PUBLIC "-//W3C//DTD XHTML 1.0 Strict//EN"
"http://www.w3.org/TR/xhtml1/DTD/xhtml1-strict.dtd">
<html lang="EN" dir="ltr" xmlns="http://www.w3.org/1999/xhtml">
<head>
<title>Critter</title>
</head>
<body>
<?php
// BASIC OOP DEMO

//define the critter class
class Critter{
  var $name;
} // end Critter class
```

```
//make an instance of the critter
$theCritter = new Critter();

//assign a value to the name property
$theCritter->name = "Andrew";

//return the value of the name property
print "<p>";
print "My name is ";
print $theCritter->name;
print "</p> \n";
?>
</body>
</html>
```

## Defining the SimpleCritter Class

The `SimpleCritter` program works in classic object-oriented style. First, it defines what a critter is and then it creates an instance of that design. Consider this part of the code:

```
//define the critter class
class Critter{
    var $name;
} // end Critter class
```

The `class` keyword indicates that I am defining a class. A class is a design or template for something. A recipe is a good example of a class. You wouldn't actually eat the index card with the `cookie recipe` on it, but you use that recipe to create cookies, which you can eat. The recipe is the class and cookies are instances of that class. (Great. Now I'm hungry.)

When I defined the `Critter` class, I was defining what a critter would be like (the recipe), but I haven't made one yet (the cookie). My `Critter` class is extremely simple. Right now it only has one property, which is the variable `$name`. Class definitions get a lot more complicated, but this is a good start.

**TRAP** Note the use of the `var` keyword to specify an instance variable. This keyword indicates that you're explicitly creating a variable. You don't have to use the `var` keyword when you create ordinary variables in PHP (and almost nobody does). The `var` keyword (or the `private` keyword you'll learn later in this chapter) is necessary in a class definition, or the variable will not be interpreted correctly.

## Creating an Instance of the Critter Class

Once you've defined a class, you want to have an instance or two of that class. One of the great things about objects is how easily you can make multiple instances of some class. However, for this example you just make one instance. The code that creates an instance looks like this:

```
$theCritter = new Critter();
```

I created a new variable called $theCritter and used the new keyword to indicate I wanted to instantiate some sort of object. Of course, I made an instance of the Critter class.

 **TRICK** It's traditional to begin class names with uppercase letters and instances (like most other variables) in lowercase letters. I follow that convention through this book, so $theCritter is an instance and Critter is a class. In PHP, it's also easy to see that Critter isn't a variable because it doesn't begin with a dollar sign.

## Working with an Object's Properties

Once you have an instance of an object, you can manipulate the properties of that instance. The $theCritter variable is an instance of the Critter class, so I can assign a value to the name property of $theCritter.

```
//assign a value to the name property
$theCritter->name = "Andrew";
```

Notice a couple of things about this:

- You can attach values to instances of a class, not to the class itself. Each instance of a class has a different set of properties, and affecting one does not affect all the others.

- Look carefully at the syntax for assigning a value to the name property. The variable you are dealing with is $theCritter. The name property is kind of like a subvariable of $the-Critter. Use the instance->property syntax to refer to an object's property.

 **TRAP** It's actually considered dangerous to directly access a property as I'm doing in this example. However, I do it here for the sake of clarity. As soon as I show you how to create a method, you'll build access methods. That way you don't have to directly access properties.

## Retrieving Properties from a Class

The basic syntax for retrieving a property value from a class is much like adding a property.

```
//return the value of the name property
print "<p>";
print "My name is ";
```

```
print $theCritter->name;
print "</p> \n";
```

Again, note the syntax: $theCritter is the variable and name is its property.

## Adding Methods to a Class

To make a class really interesting, it needs to have some sort of behavior as well as data. This is where methods come in. I'll improve on the simple Critter class so it has methods with which to manipulate the name property. Here's the new code, found in methods.php:

```
<!DOCTYPE html PUBLIC "-//W3C//DTD XHTML 1.0 Strict//EN"
"http://www.w3.org/TR/xhtml1/DTD/xhtml1-strict.dtd">
<html lang="EN" dir="ltr" xmlns="http://www.w3.org/1999/xhtml">
<head>
<title>Critter</title>
</head>
<body>
<?php
// Adding methods

//define the critter class
class Critter{

  private $name;

  function __construct($handle = "anonymous"){
    $this->name = $handle;
  } // end constructor

  function setName($newName){
    $this->name = $newName;
  } // end setName

  function getName(){
    return $this->name;
  } // end getName

} // end Critter class
```

```
//make an instance of the critter
$theCritter = new Critter();

//print original name
print "<p>Initial name: " . $theCritter->getName() . "</p>\n";

print "<p>Changing name...</p>\n";
$theCritter->setName("Melville");
print "<p>New name: " . $theCritter->getName() . "</p>\n";

?>
</body>
</html>
```

This code produces the output indicated in Figure 7.9.

**FIGURE 7.9**

This critter can change his name on the fly.

The basic technique for creating methods is to build a function within the context of a class definition. That function then becomes a method of the class.

## Protecting Your Data

Object-oriented programmers prefer to protect key variables and control access to these variables. This can prevent errors and encourage code re-use. Note how the $name variable was created in this program. It's a subtle but critical difference:

```
private $name;
```

The private keyword is a special modifier only used in object definitions. It indicates that the specified variable can only be referred to inside the object. That is, once you make an instance of the object called myCritter, you can no longer directly access the name property directly. Instead, you'll use special methods to modify and retrieve the name. The methods will assure name has a legal value.

## Building a Constructor

The first function defined in most classes is called the constructor. Constructors are special methods used to build an object. Any code you want to occur when the object first appears should go in the constructor. Most often you use the constructor to initialize your properties, so I do that for the Critter class:

```
function __construct($handle = "anonymous"){
  $this->name = $handle;
} // end constructor
```

To specify that a function is a class constructor, it should be called __construct. (That's construct preceded by two underscores.)

**TRAP** The __construct name for constructors was added in PHP 5. If you have an earlier version of PHP, the constructor will have the same name as the class, but is still a function defined within the class.

The constructor is often used to initialize properties—in this case the name property. Whenever you use the new() keyword to create an instance of a class, that class' constructor is called. Notice that the constructor accepts a parameter. If you want to make a parameter optional in any PHP function, assign a default value to the parameter, as I have done here. This is a sneaky way that PHP achieves polymorphism.

The other great thing about the constructor is how it guarantees that the name property will have a value. You can't have an object without a name. Even if the user creates an instance without a name, the name will be automatically set to "anonymous."

The $this keyword refers to the current instance, so $this->name means "the name property of the current object." Typically you refer to an object's properties and methods using the

$this variable when you're inside the object definition, and with the instance variable name when you're outside the object definition.

## Creating a Property Setter

The setName() method is an example of a property access method that allows you to change a property through a method. The code for setName() is pretty clean:

```
function setName($newName){
  $this->name = $newName;
} // end setName
```

Setter methods usually begin with set and they always accept a parameter. The parameter is the value the user wants to change. Inside the method, I modify the actual instance variable associated with the name property. Access methods are useful because I can do a number of things to test the information before I make any property changes. For example, if I decided that all my critter names should be fewer than five characters, I could modify setName() to enforce that rule.

```
function setName($newName){
  if (strlen($newName) > 5{
    $newName = substr($newName, 0, 5);
  } // end if
  $this->name = $newName;
} // end setName
```

This is a trivial example, but access methods can do a lot to prevent certain kinds of problems. For example, if your program is expecting numeric input and gets a string instead, your access method can quietly (or not so quietly, if you want) change the value to something legal without the program crashing. Use of access methods can be a splendid way to add polymorphism to your classes. If you are using a class that has access methods, you should always use them rather than directly modifying a property. If you directly modify a property, you are circumventing the safety net provided by the access method.

## Building a Getter Method to Retrieve Property Values

It's also good to have methods that return property values. These methods are called getter methods, and they are usually very straightforward, such as this one:

```
function getName(){
  return $this->name;
} // end getName
```

The `getName()` method simply returns the value of the appropriate property. This is useful because you might have different ways of returning the same value. Sometimes you might have a getter for a property that doesn't actually exist! For example, if you were creating a `circle` class, it might have `setRadius()`, `getRadius()`, `getArea()`, and `getCircumference()` methods. The user should be able to read and write the circle's radius and should be able to read the circumference and area. These values aren't actually stored in the class, because they are derived from the radius. The programmer using the class doesn't have to know or care about this, but simply knows that some properties are read/write and some are read only.

## Using Access Methods to Manipulate Properties

With `getter` and `setter` methods in place, it's easy to manipulate an object's properties.

```
//make an instance of the critter
$theCritter = new Critter();

//print original name
print "<p>Initial name: " . $theCritter->getName() . "</p>\n";

print "<p>Changing name...</p>\n";
$theCritter->setName("Melville");
print "<p>New name: " . $theCritter->getName() . "</p>\n";

?>
</body>
</html>
```

Anytime I want to change the name, I invoke the `setName()` method. To retrieve the name, I use the `getName()` method.

**TRICK**

Note that the terms "get" and "set" make sense in the context of the programmer using the class, not the programmer designing the class. The target audience for most objects is programmers rather than the general public. When you build an object, you're writing code to make a programmer's job easier.

## Reusing Class Files

Object-oriented programming is used to save programmers time. The basic idea is to build a useful class or two, and put them in their own PHP file. Then all your other programs that want to use that class can import the file.

As an example, I'll take the `Critter` definition and put it in its own file, like this:

```php
<?php
// Critter definition

//define the critter class
class Critter{

  var $name;

  function __construct($handle = "anonymous"){
    $this->setName($handle);
  } // end constructor

  function setName($newName){
    $this->name = $newName;
  } // end setName

  function getName(){
    return $this->name;
  } // end getName

} // end Critter class
?>
```

Notice there's no HTML and no code that uses the class. This file simply contains the definition for the class inside the normal php tags. Once I've got the class definition safely stored in a file, I can reuse it easily. I made one minor but useful change in the Critter class definition: Notice that the constructor no longer sets the name property directly, but uses the setName method instead. Just to see how this works, take a quick look at includeCritter.php:

```php
<!DOCTYPE html PUBLIC "-//W3C//DTD XHTML 1.0 Strict//EN"
"http://www.w3.org/TR/xhtml1/DTD/xhtml1-strict.dtd">
<html lang="EN" dir="ltr" xmlns="http://www.w3.org/1999/xhtml">
<head>
<title>Include Critter</title>
</head>
<body>
<?php
include "critter.php";
$myCritter = new Critter("Jonathan");
```

```
print $myCritter->getName();
?>
</body>
</html>
```

The one new feature of this program is how it includes the `Critter` class definition from another file. Since objects are meant to be re-used, it makes a lot of sense to put a class in its own file. Then any program that wants to use the class can simply import the php file containing the original class definition.

## Inheriting from a Parent Class

You've seen encapsulation and polymorphism. The third pillar of OOP is a concept called inheritance.

Inheritance is used to build on previous work and add new features to it. It is used to build common functionality and at the same time allow variation. In writing a game using `Critters`, for example, I define all the characteristics common to everything in the base `Critter` class and then add a bunch of subclasses for the various types. These subclasses incorporate additions or deviations from the basic behavior. Think again of the police car I mentioned earlier in this chapter. The car is a base class while a police car is an extension of the base class.

The `Inherit.php` program adds some new features to the basic `Critter` class:

```
<!DOCTYPE html PUBLIC "-//W3C//DTD XHTML 1.0 Strict//EN"
"http://www.w3.org/TR/xhtml1/DTD/xhtml1-strict.dtd">
<html lang="EN" dir="ltr" xmlns="http://www.w3.org/1999/xhtml">
<head>
<title>Glitter Critter</title>
</head>
<body>
<?php

// Incorporating Inheritance

//pull up the Critter class
include "critter.php";

//create new Glitter Critter based on Critter
```

```
class GlitterCritter extends Critter{
  //add one method
  function glow(){
    print "<p>" . $this->name . " gently shimmers...</p> \n";
  } // end glow


  //over-ride the setName method
  function setName($newName){
    $this->name = "Glittery " . $newName;
  } // end setName


} // end GC class def

//make an instance of the new critter
$theCritter = new GlitterCritter("Gloria");

//GC has no constructor, so it 'borrows' from its parent

print "<p>Critter name: " . $theCritter->getName() . "</p> \n";

//invoke new glow method
$theCritter->glow();
?>
</body>
</html>
```

The program begins by including the previously designed Critter class. I could now make instances of that class, but I have something sneakier in mind. I want to make a new type of Critter that knows how to glow. I'll call it the GlitterCritter. (I also wrote prototypes for the HitterCritter, BitterCritter, and SpitterCritter, but I decided not to include them in the book.)

I defined the GlitterCritter just like any other class, except for the extends keyword:

```
class GlitterCritter extends Critter{
```

Unless I indicate otherwise, the GlitterCritter will act just like an ordinary Critter. It automatically inherits all properties, methods, and even the constructor from the parent class. The extends keyword indicates that the GlitterCritter is an extension or improvement of the Critter class. I added two methods to the class. One brand new method is called glow(). The original `Critter` class doesn't have a `glow()` method. The other method is called `setName()`. The original `Critter` class has a `setName()` method as well.

When you run the program, you see a page like Figure 7.10.

**FIGURE 7.10**

The `GlitterCritter` has some new tricks and borrows others from the ordinary `Critter`.

Since `GlitterCritter` is based on `Critter` and I'm making an instance of `GlitterCritter`, the default behavior of `$theCritter` is just like an ordinary `Critter`. `GlitterCritter` doesn't have a constructor, so it uses the constructor from `Critter`. When I added the `glow()` method, the `GlitterCritter` was able to do something its parent could not. When I created a new method that had the same name as a method in the parent class, the new method overrode the original method, changing the behavior. Note that I didn't change the constructor at all, but since the constructor calls the `addName()` method, `GlitterCritter` names all begin with `Glitter`.

---

## IN THE REAL WORLD

Entire books have been written about OOP. This chapter means to whet your appetite for the power and flexibility this programming style offers. I encourage you to read more about OOP and to investigate languages that support the paradigm more completely than does PHP.

## BUILDING THE SUPERHTML CLASS

Now that you understand something about object-oriented methodology, you can look at the innards of the SuperHTML. Although the class has a lot of code, everything is made up of very simple code elements. The object-oriented nature of the class is what gives it its real power. As you look through the code, I give suggestions on areas you could improve the code or ways to extend the class.

## Overall Strategy

The SuperHTML object is a class about building a complete XHTML page. One instance of the class represents a page under construction. A few methods are used to define the general structure (buildTop(), buildBottom(), startForm(), and so on). Most of the methods are used to add a particular XHTML element to the page. There are methods for most of the common HTML structures. For example, you can use h1("my headline"); to create a level one headline containing the text "my headline." There are similar functions for easily creating lists, tables, form elements, and more.

In addition to the functions that immediately add these elements to the page, there are variations that build the construct and return it as a string. These are useful if you want to see what code the function will create, but you don't want it added directly to the page under construction. All these functions begin with g (for "get") so in addition to a textbox() method that automatically adds a text box to the page, there's a gTextBox() method that returns the code used to build the text box.

The g functions are useful if you want to nest elements, like this:

```
$s->tag("div", $s->gTag("p", "hi there"));
```

This code will produce a paragraph tag inside a div.

Finally, the getPage() method returns a big string containing the entire page. Generally you'll call this method last, and use it to display your page or save it to a file.

The class file is meant to be included in other programs, so I stripped it of all unnecessary HTML and PHP code. The only thing in the file is the class definition.

```php
<?php

// SuperHTML Class Def
// Andy Harris
// PHP / MySQL Programming for the Absolute Beginner
// 3rd Ed. (Now XHTML strict compliant)
```

```
class SuperHTML{

  //properties
  var $title;
  var $thePage;
```

You might be surprised that the entire SuperHTML class has only two properties. It could have a lot more, but I didn't need them to get the basic functionality I wanted. The title property holds the page title, which appears as both the title and a level-one headline. The thePage property is special, because it is a string variable that contains all the code for the resulting HTML output.

## Creating the Constructor

You might expect a complex object to have an involved constructor, but it isn't necessarily so.

```
function __construct($tTitle = "Super HTML"){
  //constructor
  $this->setTitle($tTitle);
} // end constructor
```

The constructor copies a temporary title value over to the title property using the currently undefined setTitle() method.

### Manipulating Properties

You would expect to find access methods for the properties, and SuperHTML has a few. There is a setTitle(), a getTitle(), and a getPage() method. However, there's no explicit setPage() method because I intend for the programmer to build the page incrementally through all the other methods.

```
function getTitle(){
  return $this->title;
} // end getTitle

function setTitle($tTitle){
  $this->title = $tTitle;
} // end setTitle

function getPage(){
```

```
    return $this->thePage;
  } // end getPage
```

Each of these methods is simplistic. You could improve them by checking for possible illegal values or adding default values.

## Adding Text

The SuperHTML program doesn't print anything. All it ever does is create a big string (thePage) and allow a programmer to retrieve that page.

The addText() function adds to the end of $thePage whatever input is fed it, along with a trailing newline character. Like most of the functions in the class, a g version returns the value with a newline but doesn't write anything to $thePage.

The gAddText() method isn't necessary, but I included it for completeness.

```
function addText($content){
  //given any text (including HTML markup)
  //adds the text to the page
  $this->thePage .= $content;
  $this->thePage .= "\n";
} // end addText


function gAddText($content){
  //given any text (including HTML markup)
  //returns the text
  $temp= $content;
  $temp .= "\n";
  return $temp;
} // end addText
```

## Building the Top of the Page

The top of almost every web page I make is nearly identical, so I wanted a function to automatically build that stuff for me. The buildTop() method takes a multi-line string of all my favorite page-beginning code and adds it to the page using the addText() method.

```
function buildTop(){
  $cssFile = str_replace(" ", "_", $this->title);
  $temp = <<<HERE
<!DOCTYPE html PUBLIC "-//W3C//DTD XHTML 1.0 Strict//EN"
"http://www.w3.org/TR/xhtml1/DTD/xhtml1-strict.dtd">
```

```
<html lang="EN" dir="ltr" xmlns="http://www.w3.org/1999/xhtml">
<head>
  <meta http-equiv="content-type" content="text/xml; charset=utf-8" />
  <title>$this->title</title>
  <link rel = "stylesheet"
        type = "text/css"
        href = "$cssFile.css" />
</head>
<body>
  <h1>$this->title</h1>

HERE;
    $this->addText($temp);
  } // end buildTop;
```

If you want a different beginning code (a particular CSS style, for example), you can override my buildTop() with one that includes your own code. If you do not call the buildTop and buildBottom functions, you could then use the result as a page fragment within some other page.

## Creating the Bottom of the Page

The bottom of the page is very easy. I just built some standard page-ending HTML and added it to thePage.

```
  function buildBottom(){
    //builds the bottom of a generic web page
    $temp = <<<HERE
</body>
</html>

HERE;
    $this->addText($temp);
  } // end buildBottom;
```

## Adding Headers and Generic Tags

The tag() method is very useful, because it allows you to surround any text with any XHTML tag (or even an XML tag) you want. The gTag function is similar, but doesn't store anything to $thePage. To simplify my coding, I wrote gTag() first. This method creates a temporary variable containing the tag name and contents, nicely formatted. (One of the things I didn't like about cgi.pm is how horrible the resulting HTML code looked. I want code produced by my programs to look as good as code produced directly by me.)

The tag() method calls gTag() and adds the results with addText(). If I make a change to the gTag() function, I won't have to remember to make the same change in tag(). It's good to avoid rewriting code when you can.

```
//general tag function
function tag($tagName, $contents){
  //given any tag, surrounds contents with tag
  //improve so tag can have attributes
  $this->addText($this->gTag($tagName, $contents));
} // end tag

function gTag($tagName, $contents){
  //given any tag, surrounds contents with tag
  //improve so tag can have attributes
  //returns tag but does not add it to page
  $temp = "<$tagName>\n";
  $temp .= "   " . $contents . "\n";
  $temp .= "</$tagName>\n";
  return $temp;
} // end tag

//header functions
function h1($stuff){
  $this->tag("h1", $stuff);
} // end h1

function h2($stuff){
  $this->tag("h2", $stuff);
} // end h2

function h3($stuff){
  $this->tag("h3", $stuff);
} // end h3

function h4($stuff){
  $this->tag("h4", $stuff);
```

```
} // end h4

function h5($stuff){
  $this->tag("h5", $stuff);
} // end h5

function h6($stuff){
  $this->tag("h6", $stuff);
} // end h6
```

The h1() through h6() methods are all wrappers around the tag() method that simply provide shortcuts for these very common HTML tags. Of course, you could add shortcuts for all your other favorite tags.

## Creating Lists from Arrays

I like the list methods because they really clean up my code. The buildList() methods require two parameters. The first is an array, which contains all the elements in the eventual list. The second parameter is the list type, without the angle braces. The list type defaults to ul, but it could also be ol.

The method uses a foreach() loop to step through each element in the array and then adds an <li></li> pair around the element. As usual, the function's g version returns this value to the programmer, and the other version adds it to $thePage.

```
function gBuildList($theArray, $type = "ul"){
  //given an array of values, builds a list based on that array
  $temp= "<$type> \n";
  foreach ($theArray as $value){
    $temp .= " <li>$value</li> \n";
  } // end foreach
  //shorten type if it included style information
  $type = substr($type, 0, 2);
  $temp .= "</$type> \n";
  return $temp;
} // end gBuildList

function buildList($theArray, $type = "ul"){
  $temp = $this->gBuildList($theArray, $type);
```

```
      $this->addText($temp);
    } // end buildList
```

## Building Definition Lists

Definition lists are special lists with name-value pairs. They are especially useful for displaying the contents of associative arrays.

```
  function gDl ($listVals){
    //Create a definition list from an associative array
    $temp = "";
    $temp .= "<dl>\n";
    foreach ($listVals as $term => $def){
      $temp .= "  <dt>$term</dt> \n";
      $temp .= "  <dd>$def</dd> \n";
    } // end foreach
    $temp .= "</dl> \n";
    return $temp;
  }


  function dl($listVals){
    $this->addText($this->gDl($listVals));
  } // end dl
```

The dl functions expect an associative array parameter. The key of each pair is placed in a dt pair, and the value is placed in dd tags. You can then use CSS to style the data however you want. This is an attractive alternative to two-column tables.

## Creating Tables from Two-Dimension Arrays

The buildTable() methods work much like the buildList() methods, but they expect two-dimension arrays. The gBuildTable() code begins by printing the table header. It then creates a foreach loop to handle the rows. Inside the loop, it adds the <tr> tag and then opens a second loop to handle the data array representing each of the row's cells. This data is encased in <td></td> tags and added to the temporary variable. At the end of the cell loop it is the end of a table row, so the </tr> tag is added to the temporary variable. By the time both loops are finished, the function has provided an HTML table with decent formatting.

```
  function gBuildTable($theArray){
    //given a 2D array, builds an HTML table based on that array
    $table = "<table> \n";
    foreach ($theArray as $row){
```

```
    $table .= "<tr> \n";
    foreach ($row as $cell){
      $table .= "  <td>$cell</td> \n";
    } // end foreach
    $table .= "</tr> \n";
  } // end foreach
  $table .= "</table> \n";

  return $table;
} // end gBuildTable

function buildTable($theArray){
  $temp = $this->gBuildTable($theArray);
  $this->addText($temp);
} // end buildTable
```

You might improve this code to allow variables including a table caption, border size, style sheet, and whether the first row or column should be treated as table headers.

## Creating Tables One Row at a Time

The other set of table functions allows you to build a table one row at a time. The startTable() method begins the table. The $tRow() method builds a table row from an array and accepts a rowType parameter. EndTable() builds the end-of-table code.

```
function startTable(){
  $this->thePage .= "<table>\n";
} // end startTable

function tRow ($rowData, $rowType = "td"){
  //expects an array in rowdata, prints a row of th values
  $this->thePage .= "<tr> \n";
  foreach ($rowData as $cell){
    $this->thePage .= "  <$rowType>$cell</$rowType> \n";
  } // end foreach
  $this->thePage .= "</tr> \n";
} // end tRow

function endTable(){
```

```
  $this->thePage .= "</table> \n";
} // end endTable
```

To be honest, I find the 2D array approach in `buildTable()` a lot more flexible and powerful than this technique, but I kept it in so you could see an alternative.

## Creating Forms

Simplifying form creation is one of the design goals of the `SuperHTML` class, so it's no surprise that the class contains several useful methods for creating forms. The `startForm()` and `endForm()` methods make the general form setup easy.

```
function startForm($action = "", $method = "post"){
  //begins form creation with fieldset
  $temp = <<<HERE
  <form action = "$action"
        method = "$method">
    <fieldset>

HERE;
  $this->thePage .= $temp;
} // end startForm

function endForm(){
  //adds form end tag
  $this->thePage .= <<<HERE
    </fieldset>
  </form>

HERE;

}// end endForm
```

The `startForm()` method expects up to two parameters. The `action` parameter specifies the action of the form (that is, which PHP program it will call when the form is submitted) and the `method` parameter determines the submission method (usually "get" or "post"). Both parameters have default arguments, so the user doesn't have to specify either. Note that my form always contains a fieldset. This makes the page standards-compliant, and gives me a nice element to modify with CSS styles if I want.

## Building Basic Form Objects

The basic form-element methods involve no fancy programming. I added the text that should be printed and allowed appropriate parameters so the user could customize the form objects as needed.

```php
function label($value) {
  $this->tag("label", $value);
} // end label

function gTextbox($name, $value = ""){
  // returns but does not print
  // an input type = text element
  // used if you want to place form elements in a table
  $temp = <<<HERE
     <input type = "text"
            name = "$name"
            value = "$value" />

HERE;

  return $temp;
} // end textBox

function textbox($name, $value = ""){
  $this->addText($this->gTextbox($name, $value));
} // end textBox

function gSubmit($value = "Submit Query"){
  // returns but does not print
  // an input type = submit element
  // used if you want to place form elements in a table
  $temp = <<<HERE
    <button type = "submit">
     $value
    </button>

HERE;
```

```
    return $temp;
} // end submit

function submit($value = "Submit Query"){
  $this->addText($this->gSubmit($value));
} // end submit
```

The `label()` method creates a quick label (using the `tag()` function). Labels are great for forms, because they can be easily styled.

Text boxes expect a name (which will become the `name` property of the resulting text box) and an optional value (which will become the default text in the textbox).

You might want to add some similar functions for creating passwords, hidden fields, and text areas.

The `submit()` function works very much like the other form functions. It creates a simple XHTML Submit button.

 **WARNING** The `SuperHTML` program doesn't check for valid names or other potential errors. You might add this feature to your own version.

## Building Select Objects

The `select` object is derived from an associative array. It expects a name for the entire structure and an associative array. For each element in the associative array, the index is translated to the value property of an `option` object. Also, the value of the array element becomes the text visible to the user.

```
function gSelect($name, $listVals){
  //given an associative array,
  //prints an HTML select object
  //Each element has the appropriate
  //value and displays the associated name
  $temp = "";
  $temp .= "<select name = \"$name\" >\n";
  foreach ($listVals as $val => $desc){
    $temp .= "  <option value = \"$val\">$desc</option> \n";
  } // end foreach
  $temp .= "</select> \n";
```

```
    return $temp;

} // end gSelect

function select($name, $listVals){
    $this->addText($this->gSelect($name, $listVals));
} // end select
```

## Responding to Form Input

One more SuperHTML object method quickly produces a name/value pair for each element in the $_REQUEST array. In effect, this returns any form variables and their associated values.

```
function formResults(){
    //returns the names and values of all form elements
    //in an HTML definition list
  if (!empty($_REQUEST)){
     $this->dl($_REQUEST);
  } // end isset
} // end formResults
```

The method checks $_REQUEST to see if it's empty. If not, the user has previously entered data in a form, so the contents of the $_REQUEST associative array are formatted with the very handy dl() method.

## SUMMARY

This chapter introduced the basic concepts of object-oriented programming. You saw that objects incorporate properties and methods. You learned how objects implement inheritance, polymorphism, and encapsulation. You experimented with the SuperHTML class and learned how to expand it when creating your own useful and powerful object classes.

## CHALLENGES

1. Rewrite one of your earlier programs using the SuperHTML object.

2. Add support for more HTML tags in the SuperHTML class.

3. Create an extension of SuperHTML that has a custom header reflecting the way you begin your web pages.

4. Add support for checkboxes and radio buttons.

5. Improve the buildTable() method so it automatically makes the first row or column a parameter-based header.

6. Rewrite an earlier program with custom objects.

CHAPTER

# XML AND CONTENT MANAGEMENT SYSTEMS

T he web has been changing since its inception. Two particular advances are especially important for PHP programmers to understand. The first is the concept of a content management system (CMS). This is a type of application that simplifies the creation and manipulation of complex websites. XML is a data management technique often used in CMS applications as well as other kinds of programming. PHP is an ideal language for implementing XML and CMS solutions. In this chapter, you explore these exciting topics. You also do these things:

- Build a basic CMS system using only one PHP program
- Examine XML as a data storage scheme
- Implement the `simpleXML` Application Programming Interface (API) for working with XML
- Create a more sophisticated CMS using XML

## UNDERSTANDING CONTENT MANAGEMENT SYSTEMS

When the web began, it was conceived as a web of interconnected documents. The ability to link any document to any other was powerful. However, as developers began utilizing the web, the freeform nature of the Internet sometimes caused headaches. In particular, it became somewhat challenging to manage a large system of related pages, to customize content for individual users, and to maintain consistency in a website that might contain hundreds or thousands of documents. Also, the nature of the web began to change. Instead of simply being a repository of documents, the web has become a series of interconnected applications. Much of the web's content is no longer stored in HTML pages, but is created dynamically by programs such as PHP.

CMS has become a popular solution for creating a dynamic website that connects many HTML pages and serves them up in a flexible, efficient manner. (Flexibility in this context means the site owner has many options for determining the layout and content of the page.) A number of very popular free and commercial CMSs are based on PHP. CMSs frequently include such features like these:

- **User management.** Users can log into the system. A CMS often has multiple user-access levels so some can add content and others can view content.

- **Separation of content into blocks.** Content can be grouped into semantic blocks based on its meaning. For example, rather than having arbitrary web pages as the basic unit, you can organize news stories, web links, and other elements into HTML pages.

- **Isolation of layout from content.** A CMS usually separates the system content from the layout. This is done for a number of reasons:

  - The appearance of the entire site should be uniform, even if many people contribute content.

  - Content developers shouldn't have to worry about formatting or how to write HTML code.

  - The layout should be adaptable to handle new designs or technologies.

- **User-contributed content.** Many CMSs include the ability to support online forums and message boards. In addition, you can often grant write access so users can add content to your site. For example, if you're running a site for a church, you might allow the children's pastor to directly add content to appropriate parts. You could control access, so people cannot access parts they should not change. You can even allow public access through message forums or automated content management based on individual user preferences.

- **Date Sensitivity.** Many CMS systems allow you to date your data so things only show up when you want them to.

## Examining Existing Content Management Systems

There are dozens of freely available CMS programs. Take a look at `http://www.opensourcecms.com` to try out existing CMS systems. These systems generally require database access to run, but in this chapter, you learn how to build your own CMS even before you've learned to work with relational data.

Still, it's good to see how CMS systems work before you try to build your own from scratch. Here are a few examples...

## Moodle

Moodle (`http://moodle.org/`) is designed for educators who want to build an online classroom. Figure 8.1 shows Moodle in action.

**FIGURE 8.1**

Moodle is designed for teachers and students.

Even teachers who don't know much about the web can use Moodle to run sophisticated online courses.

## WordPress

WordPress (`http://wordpress.org/`) is a popular blogging platform. It's a special-purpose CMS meant to help you easily set up a blog site. You can see a copy of WordPress running in Figure 8.2.

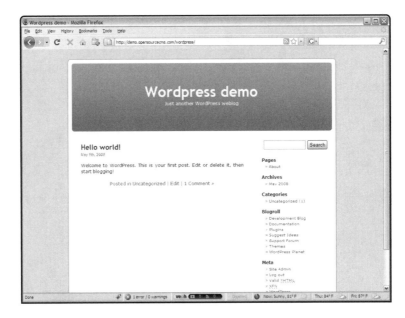

WordPress is a
popular blogging
CMS.

## Drupal

Drupal (http://drupal.org/) is a third popular CMS. It is often used to form the basis of community sites, with features like forums and blogging. Drupal is currently one of the most popular CMS systems in use. Figure 8.3 shows a Drupal site.

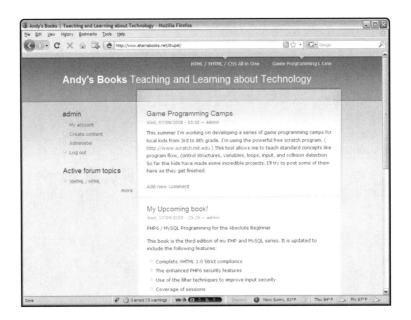

Drupal is one of
the most popular
CMS packages.

Regardless of the particular CMS, the general concepts are the same. A CMS system is nothing more than a data structure of some sort controlled by a series of PHP programs. All the content is stored in a database or other format, and the job of the PHP programs is to generate custom pages on the fly from the data sources.

Most CMS systems have multiple levels of access, so the administrator can make changes that the ordinary users cannot.

Any user with appropriate access (determined by the administrator) can alter content by adding news items, surveys, links, and other elements. Additionally, authorized users can change the site's overall appearance by choosing a new theme, which could include new colors, fonts, icons, and layout.

The simple CMS systems you'll build in this chapter aren't quite as sophisticated as the big boys, but they do have all the same key features, especially the ability to separate and re-use content.

As of this writing, none of the major CMS systems have been completely tested in PHP 6 (because I'm writing this book before the official release of PHP 6). For that reason, my screenshots were taken on an older system. The open-source scene tends to react very quickly to new releases, so you can expect to see new versions of all the CMS packages shortly after the final release.

## Introducing simpleCMS

The CMS programs already described are powerful, but they can be overkill for many personal websites. Also, many of the CMS systems still cling to outmoded practices like table-based layout.

I wanted to create a lightweight content management system that provided many of the core features a more complex system provides, but be easier to build and maintain. I actually created two related CMSs, which I describe in the rest of this chapter.

The `simpleCMS` system is easy to use and modify and adds tremendous flexibility.

### Viewing Pages from a User's Perspective

A CMS system is designed to be changed, so although I can show an example of a site using the system, the actual possibilities are much larger than a particular figure will show. Still, Figure 8.4 illustrates how my web page looks using simpleCMS.

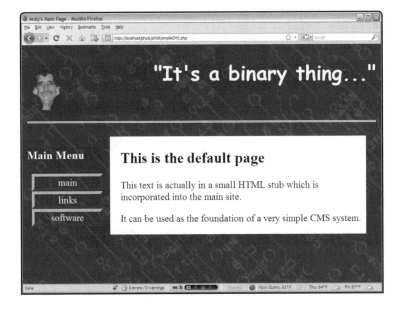

**FIGURE 8.4**

While this looks like an ordinary page, it was created with a CMS.

This page has a couple of interesting features. It follows a fairly standard design, with three primary segments of the page. A standard banner goes across the top of the page. This banner remains the same even when other parts of the page change. A list of links, which acts as a menu, occupies the left side. You can use multiple menus to support a complex web hierarchy. The page's main section contains dynamic content. This part of the page will change frequently. When it changes, however, the other parts of the page will not. The HTML code for the page is combined from three different HTML pages and one CSS style. One (surprisingly simple) PHP script controls all the action.

## COULDN'T I GET THE SAME EFFECT WITH FRAMES?

HTML frames were originally designed to allow the same sort of functionality, but frames have proven to be extremely frustrating for both users and developers. It's reasonably easy to create a frame-based website, but much harder to build such a site that behaves well. If you've traversed the web for any time, you've bumped into those frames within frames that eventually eat your entire screen away. The Back button acts unpredictably inside a frame context, and it's difficult to maintain a consistent style across multiple frames. While `simpleCMS` looks like a frameset, it's actually all one XHTML file generated from a number of smaller files.

## Examining the PHP Code

Look at the source code for simpleCMS, which is extraordinarily simple:

```php
<?php
  //Simple CMS
  //Extremely Simple CMS system
  //Andy Harris for PHP/MySQL 3rd Ed.


  //retrieve variables
  if (filter_has_var(INPUT_GET, "menu")){
    $menu = filter_input(INPUT_GET, "menu");
  } else {
    $menu = "menu.html";
  } // end if

  if (filter_has_var(INPUT_GET, "content")){
    $content = filter_input(INPUT_GET, "content");
  } else {
    $content = "default.html";
  } // end if

  include ("top.html");

  print "<div class = \"menuPanel\"> \n";
  include ($menu);
  print "</div> \n";

  print "<div class = \"item\"> \n";
  include ($content);
  print "</div> \n";

?>
</body>
</html>
```

The code expects two parameters. These parameters are both URLs for HTML files that are displayed by the system. A default value is supplied if either parameter is blank. The core of the program is a series of include statements, which loads and displays a file. Note that there's no actual content in this page! All the PHP program does is retrieve values for menu and item and use them to generate the page on the fly.

 **TRICK** The simpleCMS system relies heavily on CSS features including positionable elements and style classes. If you're rusty on these techniques, look through the tutorials on my website.

- The next include loads a page called Top.html. This page (if it exists) appears as a banner across the top of the screen. It is shown for every page in the system.
- The other include statements load and display the requested files inside special CSS span elements. If the CSS defines a span class called menuPanel, the $menu page contents are shown according to that style.
- Likewise, the $content variable displays according to an item style, if one is defined.

 **TRAP** Recall that the div and span tags are special HTML tags that are extremely useful for CSS applications. If you need a refresher on these tags or on CSS, refer to my website: www.aharrisbooks.net.

## Looking at the Header

The simpleCMS program always calls in a page called top.html. This page contains all the XHTML code necessary for starting the standards-compliant page:

```
<!DOCTYPE html PUBLIC "-//W3C//DTD XHTML 1.0 Strict//EN"
"http://www.w3.org/TR/xhtml1/DTD/xhtml1-strict.dtd">
<html lang="EN" dir="ltr" xmlns="http://www.w3.org/1999/xhtml">
<head>
  <meta http-equiv="content-type" content="text/xml; charset=utf-8" />
  <title>Andy's Main Page</title>
  <link rel = "stylesheet"
       type = "text/css"
       href = "menuLeft.css" />
</head>

<body>
  <h1>"It's a binary thing..."</h1>
```

This code contains only the top of the page. It holds that data that will be consistent regardless of your site. If you want to change the heading, for example, you can change it in this one file, and it automatically changes in all pages, because you create the headline in only one place and re-use it then. Note that the heading also loads in the stylesheet.

## Viewing the CSS

In a CMS, it's critical that content and layout remain separate. I'm using CSS as my primary layout management tool. At a minimum, I need to define styles for the menu and content area, because the PHP code is placing text in these elements. You can add any other CSS elements you want.

Here's the basic CSS I used:

```
/*
    this style places a menu on the left and an item section in
    the center.  Intended for use with CMS demos for
    PHP/MySql for the Abs. Beg, Andy Harris
*/

body {
  background-image: url("backgroundRed.png");
}

h1 {
  color: #FFFFFF;
  font-family: "Comic Sans MS";
  text-align: right;
  background-image: url("andyGoofy.gif");
  background-position: left;
  background-repeat: no-repeat;
  height: 100px;
  border-bottom: 3px double white;
}

.menuPanel {
  float: left;
  width: 22%;
  color: white;
}

.menuPanel li {
```

```
  list-style-type: none;
  margin-left: -2em;
  text-align: center;
}

.menuPanel a {
  color: white;
  border: 5px red outset;
  text-decoration: none;
  display: block;
}

.menuPanel a:hover {
  border: 5px red inset;
}

.item {
  float: left;
  width: 70%;
  padding-left: 3%;
  margin-left: 2%;
  background-color: white;
}
```

I defined the background style for all pages created by this system. I defined h1 with a custom graphic, and I set text colors to work well with the dark red background color.

Most of the work in the CSS style defines the two primary display elements in the page: the menu class and the item class. The menu is floated to the left, and the lists and links inside the menu are styled to look like buttons. The item element is also floated, but set with a background color so it will be easier to read.

The CSS file isn't directly loaded by the PHP program. Instead, I decided to have the CSS imported by the head.html so the CSS import statement can be automated. This also gives the potential for complex CSS (like conditional comments to handle problems in IE browsers).

**TRICK** It's important that I used percentage measurements in the CSS elements, because I don't know the user's screen resolution. By indicating position and width in percentages, I have a style that works well regardless of the browser size.

---

### IN THE REAL WORLD

**What about browsers that don't support CSS? Some would argue that a table-based approach to layout (as PHP-Nuke and many other CMS tools use) would work across more browsers than this CSS-centric approach. While it's true some older browsers support tables but not CSS, tables have their own problems as page layout tools.**

**Tables were never really designed for that purpose, so to get a layout exactly like you want, you often have to build a Byzantine complex of tables nested within tables, with all sorts of odd colspan tricks and invisible borders.**

**The positionable CSS elements were invented partially to provide a simpler, more uniform solution to page layout headaches. It's rare now to encounter a browser that can't handle CSS, and CSS is by all measures a better way to handle layout than tables.**

---

Of course, this CSS code is just a sample, and you can modify it to your own purposes. The key is to see how CSS can be integrated into your design from the beginning.

## Inspecting the Menu System

The real key to the `simpleCMS` is the way it's used. Each page that the user sees is a combination of three different HTML pages: a banner, menu, and content page. The `simpleCMS.php` program puts these three elements together according to a specific style sheet. For this example, presume that the CSS style and banner remain the same for every system-displayed page. (This is usually the behavior you want.) In other words, each page is derived from a template, much like objects are derived from classes.

You never directly link to any of the pages in your system. Instead, you link to the `simpleCMS.php` program and pass the content file (and menu file, if you want) you want displayed. Recall that `simpleCMS` requires two parameters. Most PHP programs get their parameters from HTML forms, but you may remember from Chapter 2, "Using Variables and Input," that parameters can be sent through the URL via the `GET` protocol. You can make any page display as an element of your CMS by calling it as a parameter.

To clarify, take a look at the `menu.html` code:

```
<h3>Main Menu</h3>
<ul>
  <li><a href = "simpleCMS.php?content=default.html">
```

```
        main</a>
  </li>
  <li><a href = "simpleCMS.php?content=links.html">
      links</a>
  </li>
  <li><a href = "simpleCMS.php?content=software.html">
      software</a>
  </li>
</ul>
```

Notice the trick? The first link refers to a page called default.html. Rather than directly linking to default.html, I linked to simpleCMS and passed the value default.html as the content parameter. When simpleCMS runs, it places the default banner (top.html) and the default menu (menu.html), but places the contents of default.html in the new page's item area. I didn't send a menu parameter, but I could have, and it would have placed some other page in the menu area.

In short, you can place any page in the menu area by assigning its URL to the menu parameter; you can assign any page to the item area by assigning its value to the content parameter. Any page you want displayed using the CMS must be called through a link to the CMS program, which pastes together all the other pages. You can place any HTML into any of the segments, but your menu usually goes in the menu area and is usually written only with links running back through the CMS.

You can create a reasonably sophisticated multilevel CMS with only this very basic program by experimenting with different menus, CSS styles, and banners.

## Looking at Content Blocks

Each of the content blocks is a small snippet of XHTML code without a header. For example, here's my code for software.html.

```
<!-- software.html -->
<h2>Software</h2>
<p>
  Here are some links to great software tools:
</p>

<ul>
  <li><a href = "http://www.aptana.com">aptana</a>
      A really great web and PHP editor</li>
```

```
<li><a href = "http://www.apachefriends.org/en/xampp.html">xampp</a>
    Wonderful installer for apache, PHP, and mySQL</li>
<li><a href = "http://www.mozilla.com/en-US/firefox/">Firefox</a>
    The web developer's browser</li>
</ul>
```

The great thing about this code is its simplicity. Since this code is meant to be embedded into another page, it doesn't need a header or CSS. This page is easy to edit, because it contains nothing extraneous. (And, of course, the `SuperHTML` object could be used to generate all of this from some sort of a template file.)

## IMPROVING THE CMS WITH XML

Although the `simpleCMS` presented earlier is extremely powerful, it is limited to only two parameters. It would be great if you could control even more information on every pass through the CMS. It also would be nice to determine the page title, CSS style, top area, menu page, and body on every pass through the system. However, the `get` method approach used in `simpleCMS` quickly becomes cumbersome when you're sending more than one or two parameters.

The `get` method allows limited amounts of data to be passed. The URLs get tedious when you have that much information to send. Most CMSs use an alternative method of storing the information about intended page values. A lot of CMSs (like PHP-Nuke) use the full power of relational databases. This is a wonderful way to go, but it can be somewhat involved for a basic demonstration. There is a more-powerful alternative than basic parameter passing, although it's not quite as intimidating as a relational data structure.

### Introducing XML

eXtensible Markup Language, or XML, has become a major topic of conversation in the software industry in the last few years. It isn't just a language, but a flexible and sensible alternative for manipulating data. It's really a language for describing data.

XML feels a lot like HTML (because they're related) but XML is quite a bit more flexible. In a nutshell, XML allows you to use HTML-style syntax to describe anything. XHTML is simply HTML that also follows the stricter standards of XML.

For example, if you want to talk about pets, you could use the following code:

```
<?xml version="1.0" encoding="utf-8" ?>
<pets>

  <cat>
    <name>Lucy</name>
    <color>tabby</color>
    <breed>shorthair</breed>
  </cat>
  <dog name = "Muchacha"
       color = "brown"
       breed = "mutt" />
</pets>
```

As you look at this fragment of (entirely fictional) XML code, you see an unmistakable resemblance to HTML. XML uses many conventions that are familiar to HTML developers, including nested and closing tags and attributes. The most significant difference is the tags themselves. HTML tags are specifically about web page markup, but XML tags can describe anything. As long as you have (or can write) a program to interpret the XML code, you can use HTML-like code to describe the information. XML, like XHTML allows you to encode data in two different ways. In the `cat` example, I stored a number of small nodes inside the major (cat) node. For the `dog`, I stored data as a series of attributes, each with a name – value pair.

## Working with XML

XML has a number of data-management tool advantages. XML files can be stored and manipulated as string data and ordinary text files. This makes it easy to duplicate data and move it around the Internet. XML data is somewhat self-documenting. You can look at XML data in a text editor and have a good idea what it means. This would be impossible if the data were stored in a database table or proprietary format. Most languages have features that allow you to easily extract data from an XML document even if you don't know exactly how the document is formatted. Many data packages allow you to export a database as XML data.

## Understanding XML Rules

XML is very similar to HTML, but it is not quite as forgiving on syntax. Remember these rules when creating an XML document:

- XML is case sensitive. Most tags use lowercase or camelCase (just like PHP). `<pet>` and `<PET>` are two different tags.

- All attributes must be encased in quotation marks. In HTML, quotation marks are always optional. In XML, almost all attribute values should be quoted. For example, `<dog name = muchacha>` is not legal in XML. The appropriate expression is `<dog name = "muchacha">`.

- All tags require an ending tag. HTML is pretty forgiving about whether you include ending tags. XML is much stricter. Every tag must have an ending tag or indicate with a trailing slash that it doesn't have an end. In the earlier example, `<cat>` has an ending `</cat>` tag. I defined `dog` to encase all its data in attributes rather than subtags, so it doesn't have an explicit ending tag. Notice how the `dog` tag ends with a slash (`/>`) to indicate it has no end tag.

## Examining main.xml

The second CMS system in this chapter uses XML files to store page information. To see why this could be useful, take a look at the XML file that describes my main page in the new XML-based content management system (XCMS):

```
<?xml version="1.0" encoding="utf-8"?>
<cpage>
  <title>Andy's main Page</title>
  <css>menuLeft.css</css>
  <top>top.html</top>
  <menu>menuX.html</menu>
  <content>default.html</content>
</cpage>
```

The entire document is stored in a `<cpage></cpage>` element. `cpage` represents a CMS page. Inside the page are five parameters. Each page has a title as well as URLs to a CSS style, top page, menu page, and content page. The XML succinctly describes all the data necessary to build a page in my CMS. I build such an XML page for every page I want displayed in my system. It is actually pretty easy because most of the pages are the same except for the content.

**TRICK**    It would be even easier in a real-world application, because I would probably build an editor to create the XML pages automatically. That way the user would never have to know he was building XML. Sounds like another great end-of-chapter project!

## Simplifying the Menu Pages

The menu page isn't as complicated when all the data is stored in the XML pages. Each call to the system requires only one parameter: the name of the XML file containing all the layout instructions. Here's the menu page after changing it to work with the XML files:

```
<h3>Main Menu</h3>
<!-- menu page modified for XML version of CMS -->
<ul>
  <li><a href = "XCMS.php?theXML=main.xml">
      main</a>
  </li>
  <li><a href = "XCMS.php?theXML=links.xml">
      links</a>
  </li>
  <li><a href = "XCMS.php?theXML=software.xml">
      software</a>
  </li>
</ul>
```

This menu calls the XML version of the CMS code (XCMS.php) and sends to it the XML filename that describes each page to be created. Of course, you must examine how the XML data is manipulated in that program. Start, though, with a simpler program that looks at XML data.

## INTRODUCING XML PARSERS

A program that reads and interprets XML data is usually called an XML parser. PHP 6 actually ships with three different XML parsers. I focus on the one that's easiest to use. It's called the simpleXML API and comes standard with PHP 5 and later. An API is an application programming interface—an extension that adds functionality to a language.

**TRICK** If you're using another version of PHP, you can either try loading the simpleXML API as an add-on or work with another XML parser. The DOM (Document Object Model) parser, if it's enabled, works much like simpleXML. Older versions of PHP include a parser based on SAX (Simple API for XML). This is also relatively easy to use, but uses a completely different model for file manipulation. Still, with careful reading of the online Help, you can figure it out: The concepts remain the same. If you can use simpleXML, it's a great place to start, because it's a very easy entry into the world of XML programming.

## Working with Simple XML

The `simpleXML` model is well named, because it's remarkably simple to use once you understand how it sees data. XML data can be thought of as a hierarchy tree (much like the directory structure on your hard drive). Each element (except the root) has exactly one parent, and each element has the capacity to have a number of children. The `simpleXML` model treats the entire XML document as a special object called an XML node. Table 8.1 illustrates the main methods of the `simplexml_element` object.

### TABLE 8.1   METHODS OF THE SIMPLEXML OBJECT

| Method | Returns |
| --- | --- |
| `->asXML()` | An XML string containing the contents of the node |
| `->attributes()` | An associative array of the node's attributes |
| `->children()` | An array of `simplexml_element` nodes |
| `->xpath()` | An array of `simplexml_elements` addressed by the path |

These various elements manipulate an XML file to maneuver the various file elements.

## Working with the simpleXML API

Take a look at the `XMLDemo` program featured in Figure 8.8, which illustrates the `simpleXML` API.

The HTML output isn't remarkable, but the source code that generates the page is interesting in a number of ways.

**FIGURE 8.5**

This page extracts
all its data from an
XML file.

```
<!DOCTYPE html PUBLIC "-//W3C//DTD XHTML 1.0 Strict//EN"
"http://www.w3.org/TR/xhtml1/DTD/xhtml1-strict.dtd">
<html lang="EN" dir="ltr" xmlns="http://www.w3.org/1999/xhtml">
<head>
<title>XML Demo</title>
<link rel = "stylesheet"
      type = "text/css"
      href = "XMLDemo.css" />
</head>
<body>

<h1>XML Demo</h1>

<?php

//load up main.xml and examine it

$xml = simplexml_load_file("main.xml");

print "<h3>original XML</h3> \n";
$xmlText = $xml->asXML();
```

```
$xmlText = htmlentities($xmlText);
print "<pre>$xmlText</pre> \n";

print "<h3>extract a named element</h3> \n";
print "<p>$xml->title</p> \n";

print "<h3>Extract as an array</h3> \n";
print "<dl> \n";
foreach ($xml->children() as $name => $value){
  print "  <dt>$name:</dt>   <dd>$value</dd> \n";
} // end foreach

print "</dl> \n";
?>
</body>
</html>
```

## Creating a simpleXML Object

The first significant line of code uses the `simplexml_load_file()` command to load an XML document into memory. This command loads a document and creates an instance of the `simpleXML` object. All your other work with `simpleXML` involves using the `simpleXML` object's methods.

**TRICK** You can also create an XML object from a string using `simplexml_load_string()`. This might be useful if you want to build an XML file from within your code.

The XML object is stored in the aptly named `$xml` variable. I can then extract data easily from XML.

## Viewing the XML Code

It might be useful to look at the actual XML code as you explore the code, so I reproduced it on the page. `simpleXML` does not keep the data in its plain text format, but converts it into a special data structure so it is easier to use. If you do want to see it as text-based XML, you can use the `asXML()` method to produce the XML code used to show part of the document. Note that you can use `asXML()` on the entire XML object or on specific subsets of it. This can be handy when you need to debug XML code. XML code does not display well in an HTML page, so I used PHP's built-in `htmlentities()` function to convert all HTML/XML characters to their appropriate HTML entity tags, then displayed the entire XML document inside a `<pre></pre>` set.

## Accessing XML Nodes Directly

simpleXML sees your XML as a series of nested objects. (See Chapter 7 for a review of object-oriented Programming in PHP.) The main XML node is an object, and each of its subnodes is a property of the main node. Each of these objects is also an XML node, which can have its own objects.

If you know the names of various tags in your document, you can access elements directly using object-oriented syntax. For example, the following line pulls the title element from the main page:

```
print $xml->title;
```

Note that the top-level tag set in my document (<cpage></cpage>) is automatically copied over to the $xml variable. Since title is a cpage subtag, the value of title is returned.

The great thing about simpleXML is how it lets you convert XML data to PHP objects, like this:

```
<dog>
    <paws>4</paws>
    <color>brown</color>
<dog>
```

When loaded into a simpleXML object, it becomes:

```
$dog->paws
$dog->color
```

**TRAP**    The node of an XML element could be interpreted as a string or an object. This can cause confusion, because PHP won't always treat a value extracted from XML exactly like you expect.

The title element is actually not a string variable, but another simpleXML object. You can use all the simpleXML methods on this object just as you do the main one. In this case, I simply wanted to print the text associated with title. simpleXML usually (but not always) correctly converts simpleXML elements to strings. In some cases (particularly when you want to use the results of a simpleXML query as part of an assignment or condition), you may need to force PHP to treat the element as string data.

For example, the following condition does not work as expected:

```
if ($xml->title == "main"){
```

It won't work because "main" is a string value and $xml->title is an object. They may appear to human readers to have the same value, but since they have different internal representations, PHP won't always recognize them as the same thing without minor coercion. You can use a technique called type casting to resolve this problem.

```
if ((string)$xml->title == "main"){
```

This version of the code forces the value from $xml->title into a string representation so it can be compared correctly.

## Using a foreach Loop on a Node

Much of the time you work with XML through various looping structures. Since XML code consists of name-value structures, it won't surprise you to find associative arrays especially helpful. The following code steps through a simple XML file and extracts the name and value of every tag evident from the top layer.

```
print "<h3>Extract as an array</h3> \n";
foreach ($xml->children() as $name => $value){
print "<b>$name:</b> $value<br /> \n";


} // end foreach
```

The reference to $xml->children() is a call to the $xmlsimpleXML object's children() method. This method returns an array of all the nodes belonging to $xml. Each of the elements in the array is a new simpleXML object with all the same methods as $xml. Since the children() method returns an array of values, I can use the foreach loop to conveniently step through each element of the array. Using the foreach loop's associative variant (described in Chapter 5) allows access to the document's name/value pairs.

Each time through the loop, the current tag is stored in $name and its associated value is stored in $value. This allows me to rapidly print all the data in the XML element according to whatever format I want.

## Manipulating More Complex XML with the simpleXML API

The features demonstrated in the XMLdemo are enough for working with the extremely simple XML variant used in the XCMS system, but you will want to work with more complex XML files with multiple tags. As an example, consider the following code, which could be used in an XML-enabled form of the quiz program featured in Chapter 6, "Working with Files."

```
<?xml version="1.0" encoding="utf-8"?>
<test>
  <problem type="mc">
    <question>What is your name?</question>
```

```
    <answerA>Roger the Shrubber</answerA>
    <answerB>Galahad the pure</answerB>
    <answerC>Arthur, King of the Britons</answerC>
    <answerD>Brave Sir Robin</answerD>
    <correct>C</correct>
  </problem>
  <problem type="mc">
    <question>What is your quest?</question>
    <answerA>I seek the holy grail</answerA>
    <answerB>I'm looking for a swallow</answerB>
    <answerC>I'm pining for the Fjords</answerC>
    <answerD>I want to be a lumberjack!</answerD>
    <correct>A</correct>
  </problem>
  <problem type="mc">
    <question>What is your favorite color?</question>
    <answerA>Red</answerA>
    <answerB>Green</answerB>
    <answerC>Orange</answerC>
    <answerD>Yellow.  No, Blue!</answerD>
    <correct>D</correct>
  </problem>
  <problem type="mc">
    <question>What is your command?</question>
    <answerA>I'm not to leave the room until you come and get him</answerA>
    <answerB>I'm going with you</answerB>
    <answerC>I'm not to let him enter the room</answerC>
    <answerD>It seems daft to be guarding a guard!</answerD>
    <correct>A</correct>
  </problem>
</test>
```

This code is a little more typical of most XML data because it has multiple levels of encoding. The entire document can be seen as an array of problem nodes, and each problem node can be viewed as a set of answers and the correct answer. The simpleXML API can handle these more complex documents with ease, as shown in the quizReader.php program displayed in Figure 8.6.

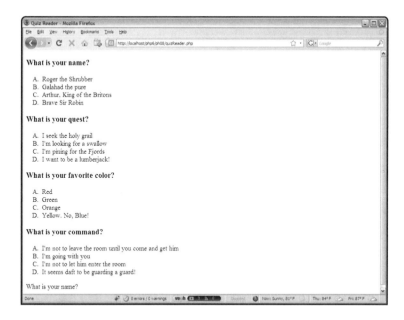

FIGURE 8.6

You can use simpleXML to parse more complex XML documents.

When the XML code is a little more complex, you may need to carefully examine the raw XML code to best interpret it. Once I recognized that the document is essentially an array of problems, the XML interpretation became relatively easy:

```
<!DOCTYPE html PUBLIC "-//W3C//DTD XHTML 1.0 Strict//EN"
"http://www.w3.org/TR/xhtml1/DTD/xhtml1-strict.dtd">
<html lang="EN" dir="ltr" xmlns="http://www.w3.org/1999/xhtml">
<head>
<title>Quiz Reader</title>
<style type = "text/css">
li {
  list-style-type: upper-alpha;
}
</style>
</head>
<body>
<?php
//quiz reader
//demonstrates working with more complex XML files

//load up a quiz file
```

```
$xml = simplexml_load_file("python.xml");

//step through quiz as associative array
foreach ($xml->children() as $problem){

  //print each question as an ordered list.
  print <<<HERE
  <h3>$problem->question</h3>
  <ol>
    <li>$problem->answerA</li>
    <li>$problem->answerB</li>
    <li>$problem->answerC</li>
    <li>$problem->answerD</li>
  </ol>

HERE;
} // end foreach

//directly accessing a node:
print "<p> \n";
print $xml->problem[0]->question;
print "</p> \n";

?>
</body>
</html>
```

This procedure can be done in a number of steps:

1. Load the quiz as XML data.
2. Use a foreach loop to examine each element of the xml's children() array as an individual problem. In this example, the $problem variable doesn't contain simple string data, but another node with its own elements.
3. Inside the loop, use tag references to indicate the elements of the problem you want to display. (Note that I chose not to display each question's answer, but I could have if I wanted.)

If you want to display a particular element's value, do so using array-style syntax. This line refers to problem number 0:

```
print $xml->problem[0]->question;
```

It then looks for a subelement of a problem called `question` and displays that value. If you are working with an extremely complicated XML document, you can use structures like this to map directly to a particular element. Essentially, the `simpleXML` system lets you think of an XML document as a set of nested arrays. This allows you access to a potentially complex document in whatever detail you want.

---

## In the Real World

**You might want to use XML data in these main instances:**

- **You want a better organizational scheme for your information but don't want to deal with a formal database system.** In this case, you can create your own XML language and build programs that work with the data. This is the use of XML described in this chapter.

- **You have XML data formatted in a predefined XML structure that you want to manipulate.** There are XML standards published for describing everything from virtual reality scenes and molecular models to multimedia slideshows. You can use the features of `simpleXML` (or one of PHP's other XML parsers) to manipulate this existing data and create your own program for interpreting it. Of course, HTML is rapidly becoming a subset of XML (in fact, the XHTML standard is simply HTML following stricter XML standards), so you can use XML tricks to load and manage an XHTML file. This might be useful for extracting a web page's links or examining a web page's images.

- **You need a stand-in for relational data.** Most database management systems allow you to import and export data in XML format. XML can be a terrific way to send complex data, such as database query results or complete data tables, to remote programs. Often programmers write client-side code in a language such as JavaScript or Flash and use a server-side program to send query results to the client as XML data.

---

## Returning to XCMS

With all this XML knowledge, you're ready to refit the CMS introduced earlier in this chapter with an XML structure. My basic plan for the XCMS is to allow more parameters for each page. The original CMS (without XML) allows two parameters. The parameters are added directly to URLs with the `post` method. This quickly becomes unwieldy. By switching to an XML format,

I can place all the parameters necessary for displaying a page into an XML document, then have my CMS program extract that data from the document.

## Extracting Data from the XML File

The XCMS program relies on repeated calls to the same program to generate the page data. The XCMS program is much like `simpleCMS` except—rather than pulling parameters directly from the URL—XCMS takes an XML filename as its single parameter and extracts all the necessary information from that file.

```php
<?php

//XCMS
//XML-Based Simple CMS system
//Andy Harris for PHP/MySQL Adv. Beg 2nd Ed.
// NOTE:  Requires simpleXML extensions in PHP 5.0!

//get an XML file or load a default

if (filter_has_var(INPUT_GET, "theXML")){
  $theXML = filter_input(INPUT_GET, "theXML");
} else {
  $theXML = "main.xml";
} // end if

//Open up XML file
$xml = simplexml_load_file($theXML);

if ( !$xml){
  print ("there was a problem opening the XML");

} else {

  //include ($xml->css);
  include($xml->top);

  print "<div class = \"menuPanel\"> \n";
  include ($xml->menu);
  print "</div> \n";
```

```
print "<div class = \"item\"> \n";
include ($xml->content);
print "</div> \n";

} // end if

?>
</body>
</html>
```

The first step is determining if an XML file has been sent through the $theXML parameter. If not, a default value of main.xml is defined. This, of course, presumes that a copy of main.xml is available and properly formatted. If the program is called with some other XML file as its parameter, that file is interpreted instead.

I then attempt to open the XML file. If the simplexml_load_file command is unsuccessful, it returns the value FALSE. The program reports this failure if it occurs. If it does not fail, the program creates a page based on the parameters indicated in this file. I expect a page with five parameters (top, css, title, menu, and content), but I could easily modify the program to accept as many parameters as you want. I ignored the title parameter in this particular program version because I have the page title already stored in top.html.

The program includes all the files indicated in the XML code, incorporating them in CSS styles when appropriate.

## Summary

Content management systems can help automate your website's creation. CMS tools allow you to build powerful multipart web documents, combining pages with a single style and layout. You learned how to install and customize the popular PHP-Nuke CMS. You also learned how to build a very basic CMS of your own using GET parameters to customize your page. You learned about XML and how to use the simpleXML tools to parse any XML files you encounter. Finally, you learned how to combine your newfound XML skills with CMS to build an XML-aware CMS.

## CHALLENGES

1. Install and configure PHP-Nuke or another CMS on your system.

2. Create a custom theme by analyzing and modifying an existing theme.

3. Modify simpleCMS with your own layout, images, and banner files.

4. Create an editor that allows the user to build XML pages for XCMS.

5. Write an XCMS module that allows authorized users to add new content (a news or guest book, for example).

# Using MySQL to Create Databases

hen you began programming in PHP, you started with very simple variables. Soon you learned how to do more interesting things with arrays and associative arrays. You added the power of files to gain tremendous new skills.

Now you learn how relational databases can be used to manage data. In this chapter, you discover how to build a basic database and how to hook it up to your PHP programs. Specifically, you learn:

- How to start the MySQL executable
- How to build basic databases
- The essential data definition SQL statements
- How to return a basic SQL query
- How to use phpMyAdmin to manage your databases
- How to incorporate databases into PHP programs

## Introducing the Adventure Generator Program

Databases are a serious tool but they can be fun, too. The program shown in Figures 9.1 through 9.4 shows how a database can be used to fuel an adventure game generator. The adventure generator is a system that allows users to create and play simple multiple-choice adventures. This style of game consists of several nodes. Each node describes some sort of decision. In each case, the user can choose from up to three options. The user's choice leads to a new decision. If the user makes a sequence of correct choices, he wins the game.

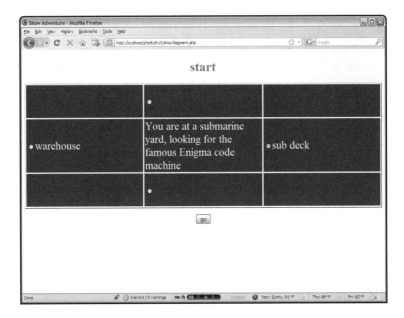

**FIGURE 9.1**

The user can choose an option. I'm hopping onto that sub...

This program is interesting as a game, but the really exciting part is how the user can modify this game. A user can use the same system to create and modify adventures. Figure 9.3 shows the data behind the Enigma game. Note that you can edit any node by clicking the appropriate button from this screen.

If the user chooses to edit a segment, the page shown in Figure 9.4 appears.

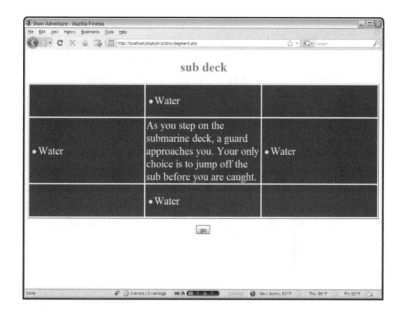

FIGURE 9.2

Maybe the warehouse would have been a better choice after all.

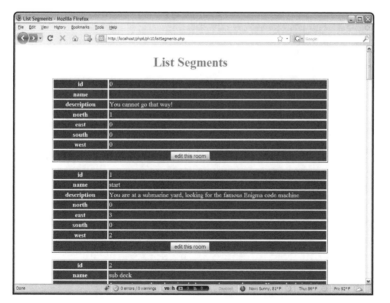

FIGURE 9.3

This page provides information about each segment in the game, including links to directly edit each segment.

As you can see, the data structure is the most important element of this game. You already know some ways to work with data, but this chapter introduces the notion of relational database management systems (RDBMS). An RDBMS is a system that helps programmers work with data. The adventure generator program uses a database to store and manipulate all the data.

**FIGURE 9.4**

From this screen, it
is possible to
change everything
about a node. All
the nodes that
have been created
so far are available
as new locations.

# USING A DATABASE MANAGEMENT SYSTEM

Data is such an important part of modern programming that entire programming languages
are devoted to manipulating databases. The primary standard for database languages is
Structured Query Language (SQL). SQL is a standardized language for creating databases,
storing information in databases, and retrieving information from databases. Special applications and programming environments specialize in interpreting SQL data and acting on it.

Often a programmer begins by creating a data structure in SQL, and then writes a program
in some other language (such as PHP) to allow access to that data. The PHP program can then
formulate data requests or updates, which are passed on to the SQL interpreter. This approach
has a couple of advantages:

- Once you learn SQL, you can apply it easily to a new programming language.
- You can easily add multiple interfaces to an existing data set because many programming languages have ways to access an SQL interpreter. Many relational database
  management systems are available, but the MySQL environment is especially well suited
  to working with PHP.

The basic concepts of SQL remain the same no matter what type of database you
are working on. Most of the SQL commands described in this chapter work without modification in Microsoft Access, Microsoft SQL Server, and Oracle, as well
as a number of other RDBMS packages.

I begin this chapter by explaining how to create a simple database in MySQL. You can work with this package a number of ways, but start by writing a script that builds a database in a text file. I use the SQL language, which is different in syntax and style from PHP. I show you how to use some visual tools to help you work with databases and how to use the SQLite data library built into PHP 5. In Chapter 10, "Connecting to Databases within PHP," I show you how to contact and manipulate your MySQL database from within PHP.

## WORKING WITH MYSQL

There are a number of RDBMS packages available. These programs vary in power, flexibility, and price. However, they all work in essentially the same way. Most examples in this book use the MySQL database.

- It is a very powerful program in its own right. It handles a large subset of the functionality of the most expensive and powerful database packages.

- It uses a standard form of the well-known SQL data language.

- It is released under an open-source license.

- It works on many operating systems and with many languages.

- It works very quickly and works well even with large data sets.

- PHP ships with a number of functions designed to support MySQL databases.

## Installing MySQL 6.0

If PHP is already on your web server, chances are that MySQL is there as well. Many installation packages install both MySQL and PHP on your system. If you do not control the web server directly, you might need to convince your server administrator to install MySQL. A version of the MySQL binary is available on the CD that accompanies this book.

**TRAP** Earlier versions of PHP had built-in MySQL support. The beta version of PHP 6 that I used for this book requires some minor configuration before it will use the MySQL functions. Run the phpInfo() command you learned in Chapter 1, "Exploring the PHP Environment," to see how your server is configured. If phpInfo() does not indicate support for MySQL, modify your PHP.INI file. Add or uncomment the following line in the Dynamic Extensions section of PHP.INI to enable MySQL support if it is not currently turned on:

```
extension=php_mysql.dll
```

## Using the MySQL Executable

MySQL is actually a number of programs. It has a server component that is always running, as well as a number of utility programs. The MySQL command line console shown in

Figure 9.5 is a basic program run from the command line. It isn't a very pretty program, but it provides powerful access to the database engine.

**FIGURE 9.5**

The MySQL
program connects
to a database.

You can use MySQL a number of ways, but the basic procedure involves connecting to a MySQL server, choosing a database, and then using the SQL language to control the database by creating tables, viewing data, and so on.

> **HINT**
> You must run `mysql.exe` from the command line. In Windows, choose run from the Start menu, then type in `cmd` and press the Enter key. At this text window, move to the appropriate window with the `cd` command (e.g., `cd\apache\mysql\bin`) and finally type `mysql` to begin the console.

The `MySQL.exe` console shipped with MySQL is the most basic way to work with the `MySQL` database. Although it won't win any user interface awards, the program offers low-level access to the database. This interface is important to learn, however, because it is very much like the way your programs will interface with the database system.

> **TRAP**
> If you're running your own web server, you must run the MySQL server before you can run the client. Under Windows, run the WinMySQLAdmin tool to start the MySQL server. This automatically starts the MySQL server and sets up your system so that MySQL is run as a service when your computer is booted (much like Apache). Turn off the MySQL server in the XAMPP Control Panel's Services section or with the MySQL tool menu that appears in the system tray.

## CREATING A DATABASE

Databases are described by a very specific organization scheme. To illustrate database concepts, I create and view a simple phone list. The data that will go in the phone list looks like Table 9.1.

| TABLE 9.1 PHONE LIST SUMMARY | | | | |
|---|---|---|---|---|
| **Id** | **firstName** | **lastName** | **e-mail** | **phone** |
| 0 | Andy | Harris | aharris@cs.iupui.edu | 123-4567 |
| 1 | Joe | Slow | jslow@myPlace.net | 987-6543 |

The phone list shows a very typical data table. Database people like to give special names to the parts of the database.

- Each row of the table is called a record. Records describe discrete (individually defined) entities.
- The list of records is called a table.
- Each record in a table has the same elements, which are called fields or columns.

Every record in the table has the same field definitions, but records can have different values in the fields. The fields in a table are defined in specific ways. Because of the way database tables are stored in files, the computer must always know how much room to allocate for each field. Therefore, each field's size and type is important. This particular database is defined with five fields. The id field is an integer. All the other fields contain string (text) data.

## Creating a Table

Of course, to use a database system, you need to learn how to build a table.

RDBMS programs use a language called SQL to create and manipulate databases. SQL is pretty easy to understand, compared to full-blown programming languages. You can usually guess what's going on even without a lot of knowledge. As an example, look at the following SQL code:

```
## build phone list
## for mySQL
USE chapter9;
DROP TABLE IF EXISTS phoneList;
```

```
CREATE TABLE phoneList (
  id int PRIMARY KEY,
  firstName VARCHAR(15),
  lastName VARCHAR (15),
  email VARCHAR(20),
  phone VARCHAR(15)
);

INSERT INTO phoneList
VALUES (
  0, 'Andy', 'Harris', 'aharris@cs.iupui.edu', '123-4567'
);

SELECT * FROM phoneList;
```

This code is an SQL script. It's like a PHP program in that it is a set of instructions for the computer. However, the PHP interpreter doesn't directly interact with the SQL language. Instead, these commands are sent to another program. As a PHP programmer, you will write code that sends commands to a database language. Just as your PHP code often writes code in HTML format for the browser to interpret, you'll write SQL code for the MySQL interpreter to use. Each line of SQL is terminated with a semicolon.

When this code is sent to an SQL-compliant database program (such as MySQL), it creates the database structure shown in Table 9.1.

### Using a Database

A data project can consist of several tables. The tables can be organized in a database.

You may have several database projects working in the same relational database system. In my case, I've put all the examples for this book in a database called "ph6." Sometimes your system administrator will assign a database to you. In any case, you will probably need to invoke that database with the USE command.

## SQL ADVANTAGES

Databases have been an important part of programming since the beginning, but the process of working with data has evolved. The advent of a common language that can be used in many applications was a very important step. SQL is a fourth-generation language. In general, these languages are designed to solve a particular type of problem. Some fourth-generation languages (like SQL) aren't full-blown programming languages, because they don't support data structures like branches and loops.

Still, these languages can serve a purpose. SQL is handy because it's widely supported. The SQL commands you learn in this chapter apply to most modern database programs with little to no modification. You can take the script in MySQL and send the same code to an Oracle or MS SQL Server database (two other very common choices), and all three data programs build the same database. If you upgrade to a more powerful data package, you can use your existing scripts to manipulate the data. If you're working with SQLite, your SQL commands will be almost identical to the commands used in MySQL.

Programming in traditional languages is perhaps the most powerful reason to have a scripting language with which to control databases. You can write a program in any language (like PHP, for example) that generates SQL code. You can then use that code to manipulate the database. This allows you to have complete flexibility, and lets your program act as the database interface.

SQL syntax is not exactly like that of PHP. SQL has a different culture, and it makes sense to respect the way SQL code has historically been written. SQL is generally not case-sensitive, but most SQL coders put all SQL commands in all uppercase letters. Also, you usually end each line with a semicolon when a bunch of SQL commands are placed in a file (as this code is).

If you don't already have a database to USE, you can make one with the CREATE command. For example, use these commands to create a database called myStuff:

```
CREATE DATABASE myStuff;
USE myStuff;
```

## Creating a Table

To create a table, you must indicate the table name as well as each field. For each field, list what type of data is held in the field, and (for text data) the field's characters length. As an example, the following code creates the phoneList table:

```
CREATE TABLE phoneList (
id INT PRIMARY KEY,
firstName VARCHAR(15),
lastName VARCHAR (15),
email VARCHAR(20),
phone VARCHAR(15)
);
```

You can think of fields as being much like variables, but while PHP is easygoing about what type of data is in a variable, SQL is very picky about the type of data in fields. In order to create an efficient database, MySQL needs to know exactly how many bytes of memory to set aside for every single field in the database. It does this primarily by requiring the database designer to specify the type and size of every field in each table. Table 9.2 lists a few of the primary data types supported by MySQL.

## TABLE 9.2    COMMON DATA TYPES IN MYSQL

| Data Type | Description |
| --- | --- |
| INT | Standard integer +/-2billion (roughly) |
| BIGINT | Big integer +/-9 X $10^{18th}$ |
| FLOAT | Floating-point decimal number 38 digits |
| DOUBLE | Double-precision floating-point 308 digits |
| CHAR(n) | Text with $n$ digits; if actual value is less than $n$, field is padded with trailing spaces |
| VARCHAR(n) | Text with $n$ digits; trailing spaces are automatically culled |
| TEXT | Larger text field |
| DATE | Date in YYYY-MM-DD format |
| TIME | Time in HH:MM:SS format |
| YEAR | Year in YYYY format |

TRICK

While the data types listed in Table 9.2 are by far the most commonly used, MySQL supports many others. Look in the online Help that ships with MySQL if you need a more specific data type. Other databases have a very similar list of data types.

You might notice that it is unnecessary to specify the length of numeric types (although you can determine a maximum size for numeric types as well as the number of digits you want stored in float and double fields). The storage requirements for numeric fields are based on the field type itself.

## Working with String Data in MySQL

Text values are usually stored in VARCHAR fields. These fields must include the number of characters allocated for the field. Both CHAR and VARCHAR fields have fixed lengths. The primary difference between them is what happens when the field contains a value shorter than the specified length.

Assume you declared a CHAR field to have a length of 10 with the following SQL segment:

```
firstName CHAR(10);
```

Later you store the value 'Andy' into the field. The field actually contains 'Andy '. (That is, Andy followed by six spaces.) CHAR fields pad any remaining characters with spaces. The VARCHAR field stores the number of characters needed up to a limit, and adds length data describing how long the data is. The VARCHAR field type is the one you use most often to store string data. CHAR is slightly more efficient if you know the exact length of the data and it won't change.

---

### DETERMINING THE LENGTH OF A VARCHAR FIELD

Data design is both a science and an art. Determining the appropriate length for your text fields is one of the oldest problems in data.

If you don't allocate enough room for your text data, you can cause a lot of problems for your users. I once taught a course called CLT SD WEB PRG because the database that held the course names didn't have enough room for the actual course name (Client-Side Web Programming). My students renamed it the Buy a Vowel course.

However, you can't make every text field a thousand characters long, either, because it would waste system resources. If you have a field that will usually contain only five characters and you allocate 100 characters, the drive still requires room for the extra 95 characters. If your database has thousands of entries, this can be a substantial cost in drive space. In a distributed environment, you have to wait for those unnecessary spaces to come across limited bandwidth.

It takes experimentation and practice to determine the appropriate width for your string fields. Test your application with real users so you can be sure you've made the right decision.

### Finishing the CREATE TABLE Statement

Once you understand field data types, the CREATE TABLE syntax makes a lot of sense. Only a few more details to understand:

- Use a pair of parentheses to indicate the field list once you specify CREATE TABLE.
- Name each field and follow it with its type (and length, if it's a CHAR or VARCHAR).
- Separate the fields with commas.
- Put each field on its own line and indent the field definitions. You don't have to, but I prefer to, because these practices make the code much easier to read and debug.

## Creating a Primary Key

You might be curious about the very first field in the phone list database. Just to refresh your memory, the line that defines that field looks like this:

```
id INT PRIMARY KEY,
```

Most database tables have some sort of field that holds a numeric value. This special field is called the primary key.

You can enter the code presented so far directly into the MySQL program. You can see the code and its results in Figure 9.6.

---

### IN THE REAL WORLD

A simple database could theoretically go without a primary key, but such fields are so important to more sophisticated databases that you might as well start putting them in. It's traditional to put a primary key in every table.

In Chapter 11, "Data Normalization," you learn more about the relational data model. In that discussion you learn how keys build powerful databases and more about creating proper primary keys. In fact, the adventure program you've already seen heavily relies on a key field even though there's only one table in the database.

---

## Using the DESCRIBE Command to Check a Table's Structure

Checking the structure of a table can be helpful, especially if somebody else created it or you don't remember exactly its field types or sizes. The DESCRIBE command lets you view a table structure.

FIGURE 9.6

Describing a table.

## Inserting Values

Once you've created a table, you can begin adding data to it. The INSERT command is the primary tool for adding records.

```
INSERT INTO phoneList VALUES (
0, 'Andy', 'Harris', 'aharris@aharrisbooks.net.', '123-4567' );
```

The INSERT statement allows you to add a record into a database. The values must be listed in exactly the same order the fields were defined. Each value is separated by a comma, and all VARCHAR and CHAR values must be enclosed in single quotation marks.

If you have a large amount of data to load, you can use the LOAD DATA command. This command accepts a tab-delimited text file with one row per record and fields separated by tabs. It then loads that entire file into the database. This is often the fastest way to load a database with test data. The following line loads data from a file called addresses.txt into the phoneList table:

```
LOAD DATA LOCAL INFILE "addresses.txt" INTO TABLE phoneList;
```

Figure 9.7 shows the MySQL tool after I have added one record to the table.

```
C:\WINDOWS\system32\cmd.exe - mysql -u root -p

| Field     | Type        | Null | Key | Default | Extra |
+-----------+-------------+------+-----+---------+-------+
| id        | int(11)     | NO   | PRI |         |       |
| firstName | varchar(15) | YES  |     | NULL    |       |
| lastName  | varchar(15) | YES  |     | NULL    |       |
| email     | varchar(20) | YES  |     | NULL    |       |
| phone     | varchar(15) | YES  |     | NULL    |       |
+-----------+-------------+------+-----+---------+-------+
5 rows in set (0.00 sec)

mysql> INSERT INTO phoneList
    -> VALUES (
    ->  0, 'Andy', 'Harris', 'andy@aharrisbooks.net', '123-4567'
    -> );
Query OK, 1 row affected, 1 warning (0.00 sec)

mysql>
```

**FIGURE 9.7**

MySQL tells you the operation succeeded, but you don't get a lot more information.

## IN THE REAL WORLD

As you are building a database, populate the database with test values. Don't use actual data at this point, because your database will not work correctly until you've messed with it for some time. However, your test values should be reflective of the kinds of data your database will house. This helps you spot certain problems like fields that are too small or missing.

## Selecting Results

Of course, you want to see the results of all your table-building activities. If you want to see the data in a table, you can use the SELECT command. This is perhaps the most powerful command in SQL, but its basic use is quite simple. Use this command to see all of the data in the phoneList table:

```
SELECT * FROM phoneList
```

This command grabs all fields of all records of the phoneList database and displays them in table format.

Figure 9.8 shows what happens after I add a SELECT statement to get the results.

FIGURE 9.8

Displaying the
contents of a table
with SELECT.

## Writing a Script to Build a Table

It is very important to understand how to create tables by hand in SQL, because your programs have to do this same work. However, it's very tedious to write your SQL code in the MySQL window directly. When you create real data applications, you often have to build and rebuild your data tables several times before you are satisfied with them, and this would be awkward in the command-line interface. Also, as you are writing programs that work with your database, you will likely make mistakes that corrupt the original data.

It's good to have a script ready for easily rebuilding the database with test data. Most programmers create a script of SQL commands with a text editor (use the same editor in which you write your PHP code) and use the SOURCE command to load that code. Here is an SQL script for creating the phoneList database:

```
## build phone list
## for mySQL

USE ph_6;
DROP TABLE IF EXISTS phoneList;

CREATE TABLE phoneList ( id INT PRIMARY KEY, firstName VARCHAR(15), lastName
VARCHAR (15),
email VARCHAR(20),
phone VARCHAR(15)

);
```

```
INSERT INTO phoneList
VALUES (
0, 'Andy', 'Harris', 'aharris@cs.iupui.edu', '123-4567'

);
SELECT * FROM phoneList;
```

This code isn't exactly like what I used in the interactive session, because the new code shows a few more features that are especially handy when you create SQL code in a script.

## Creating Comments in SQL

SQL is actually a language. Although it isn't technically a programming language, it has many of the same features. Like PHP and other languages, SQL supports several types of comment characters. The # sign is often used to signify a comment in SQL. Comments are especially important when you save a group of SQL commands in a file for later reuse. These comments can help you remember what type of database you were trying to build. It's critical to put basic comments in your scripts.

## Dropping a Table

It may seem strange to talk about deleting a table from a database before you've built one, but often (as in this case) a database is created using a script. Before you create a new table, you should check to see if it already exists. If it does exist, delete it with the DROP command. The following command does exactly that:

```
DROP TABLE IF EXISTS phoneList;
```

If the phoneList table currently exists, it is deleted to avoid confusion.

## Running a Script with SOURCE

You can create an SQL script with any text editor. It is common to save SQL scripts with the .sql extension. Inside MySQL, you can use the SOURCE command to load and execute a script file. Figure 9.9 shows MySQL after I run the buildPhonelist.sql script.

**TRAP** In Windows, I often drag a file from a directory view into a command-line program like MySQL. Windows copies the entire filename over, but it includes double quotation marks, which causes problems for the MySQL interpreter. If you drag a filename into MySQL, edit out the quotation marks.

```
C:\WINDOWS\system32\cmd.exe - mysql -u root -p
mysql>
mysql> SOURCE C:\Program Files\xampp\htdocs\php6\ph09\buildPhoneList.sql
Database changed
Query OK, 0 rows affected (0.00 sec)

Query OK, 0 rows affected (0.08 sec)

Query OK, 1 row affected (0.00 sec)

+----+-----------+----------+-----------------------+-----------+
| id | firstName | lastName | email                 | phone     |
+----+-----------+----------+-----------------------+-----------+
|  0 | Andy      | Harris   | aharris@cs.iupui.edu  | 123-4567  |
+----+-----------+----------+-----------------------+-----------+
1 row in set (0.00 sec)

mysql>
mysql>
mysql>
mysql>
mysql>
mysql>
mysql>
mysql>
mysql>
```

**FIGURE 9.9**

The SOURCE command allows you to read in SQL instructions from a file.

## WORKING WITH A DATABASE VIA PHPMYADMIN

It's critical to understand the SQL language, but sometimes you may want an alternative way to build and view your databases. The command line is functional, but it can be tedious to use. If you are running a web server, you can use an excellent front end called phpMyAdmin. This freeware program makes it much easier to create, modify, and manipulate databases.

### IN THE REAL WORLD

The phpMyAdmin interface is so cool that you'll be tempted to use it all the time. That's fine, but be sure you understand the underlying SQL code—your PHP programs have to work with plain-text SQL commands. It's fine to use a front-end tool while building and manipulating your data, but your users won't use this program. Your application is the user's interface to your database, so you must be able to do all commands in plain text from within PHP. I use phpMyAdmin, but I also make sure I always look at the code it produces so I can write it myself.

phpMyAdmin basically adds the visual editing tools of a program like Microsoft Access to the MySQL environment. It also adds some wonderful tools for adding records, viewing your data structure, exporting data to useful formats, and experimenting with data structures. The program is written in PHP, so install it to your server's HTML document path (usually htdocs if you're using the Apache server). If you used XAMPP to install your system, you already have phpMyAdmin, or you can download it for free at http://www.phpmyadmin.net/home_page/index.php.

 Some of the more advanced phpMyAdmin features—including the ability to automate relationships and create PDF diagrams of your data structures—require table installation and some other special configuration. If your server administrator has not enabled these features, consult an excellent tutorial at http://garv.in/tops/texte/mimetutorial.

## Connecting to a Server

MySQL is a client/server application. The MySQL server usually runs on the web server where your PHP programs reside. You can connect a MySQL client such as phpMyAdmin to any MySQL server. Figure 9.10 shows a connection to the local MySQL connection.

**FIGURE 9.10**

The main phpMyAdmin screen lets you choose a database in the left frame or perform administrative tasks in the main frame.

It's important to recognize that you can connect to any data server you have permission to use. This data server doesn't need to be on the same physical machine you are using. This is useful if you want to use phpMyAdmin to view data on a remote web server you are maintaining, for example. However, many remote web servers are not configured to accept this kind of access, so you should know how to work with the plain MySQL console.

The first time you run phpMyAdmin, it will probably ask for some login information. This data is stored so you don't have to remember it every time. However, if you want to change your login or experiment with some other phpMyAdmin features, edit the `config.inc.php` file installed in the main phpMyAdmin folder.

## CREATING AND MODIFYING A TABLE

phpMyAdmin provides visual tools to help you create and modify your tables. The phone list is way too mundane for my tastes, so I'll build a new table to illustrate phpMyAdmin features. This new table contains a number of randomly generated super heroes. Select a table from the left frame and use the Create New Table section of the resulting page to build a new table. Figure 9.11 shows the dialog box used to create a table or alter its structure.

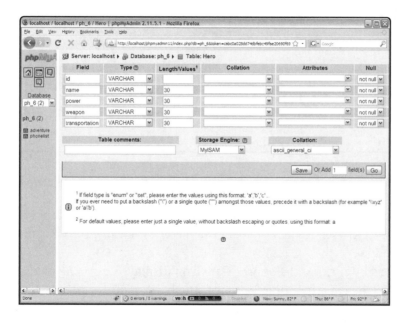

**FIGURE 9.11**

Creating a table in phpMyAdmin.

With phpMyAdmin you can choose variable types from a drop-down list; many field properties are available as checkboxes. It's critical that you choose a variable type (and a field length in case of character fields). When you finish creating or modifying the table, the proper SQL code is generated and executed for you.

**TRICK** Check this site out sometime when you're bored: http://home.hiwaay.net/ ~lkseitz/ comics/herogen/. Special thanks to Lee Seitz and his hysterical Super-Hero generator.

## Editing Table Data

You can use phpMyAdmin to browse your table in a format much like a spreadsheet. Figure 9.12 illustrates this capability.

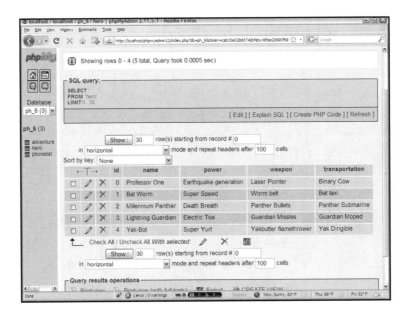

**FIGURE 9.12**

Use the Browse tab to view table data.

Follow these steps to edit a table in phpMyAdmin:

1. Select the table from the table list on the left side of the SQL screen. The table appears in a spreadsheet-like format in the main part of the screen. You can edit the contents of the table in this window.
2. Edit or delete a record by clicking the appropriate icon displayed near the record.
3. Add a row by clicking the corresponding link near the bottom of the table.
4. Leave the cell you edited or press the Enter key. Any changes you make on the table data are automatically converted into the appropriate SQL code.

## Exporting a Table

Some of phpMyAdmin's most interesting features involve exporting table information. You can generate a number of data formats. The Export tab looks like the page in Figure 9.13.

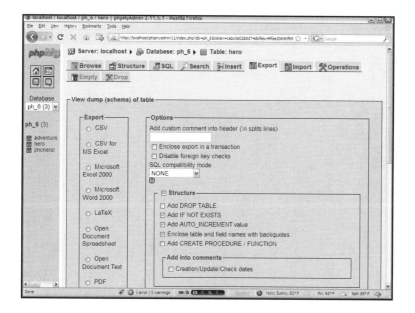

**FIGURE 9.13**

The Export Result Set dialog box allows you to save table data in a number of formats.

You might prefer to have your results saved in some sort of delimited format such as those discussed in Chapter 6, "Working with Files." You can easily generate such a format by choosing the Comma-Separated Value (CSV) option and selecting your delimiters. This is a good choice in these situations:

- You want your data to be readable by a spreadsheet.
- You are writing a program that can handle such a format but cannot directly access databases.

The Excel CSV format configures the data so an Excel spreadsheet can read it easily. The ordinary CSV format allows you to modify your output with a number of options. Figure 9.14 illustrates the CSV version of the hero data set.

Once you've created your data file, either save it using the appropriate link or copy and paste it to a spreadsheet. Most spreadsheet programs can read various forms of CSV data with minimal configuration. Figure 9.15 demonstrates the file as seen by Microsoft Excel.

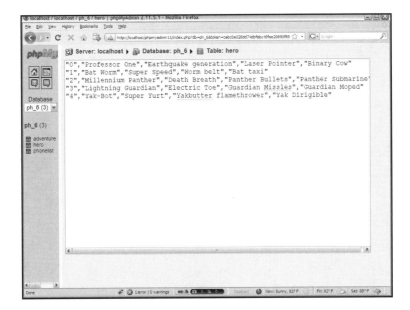

**FIGURE 9.14**

You can print CSV summaries of your data results.

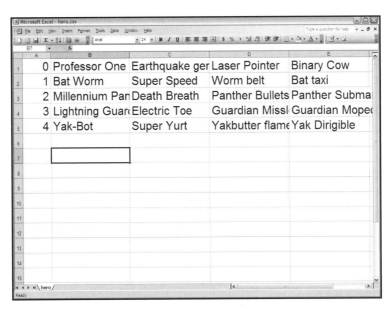

**FIGURE 9.15**

I set up the data as a tab-delimited file and read it into Excel.

You can also set up an XML file to hold the data. As you recall from Chapter 8, "XML and Content Management Systems," XML is much like HTML and describes the information in a self-documenting form, as shown in Figure 9.16.

**TRICK** You might use the XML feature to store a database as an XML file and then have a program read that file using XML techniques. This is a good way to work with a database even when the program can't directly deal with the database server.

**FIGURE 9.16**

Now the data is formatted as an XML file.

One last very useful export option: the SQL format. You can use this tool to automatically generate an SQL script for creating and populating a table. The SQL formatting utility is useful if you use the visual tools for creating and editing a table, but then want to re-create the table through a script. The dialog box shown in Figure 9.17 illustrates this tool's various options.

You can specify whether the resulting script generates the table structure alone or adds the data. You can also specify whether the resulting script contains various kinds of maintenance code such as commands to select a database and drop the specified table if it already exists. You can also specify the filename of the resulting script. Figure 9.18 shows the code that might result from an SQL export of the hero table.

**TRAP** The ability to automatically generate SQL scripts is incredibly powerful. It can be a great timesaver and you can learn a lot by examining the scripts written with such a feature. However, you are still the programmer and are responsible for code in your projects—even if you didn't write it directly. You must understand what the generated code does. Most of the code so far is stuff I've already described, but you may have to look up advanced features. As I've said: Know how to do this stuff by hand.

**FIGURE 9.17**

From this screen you can generate code that manufactures replicas of any database created or viewed with phpMyAdmin.

**FIGURE 9.18**

This code can be run on any MySQL server to make a copy of the hero database.

## CREATING MORE POWERFUL QUERIES

So far, the tables you've created haven't been any more powerful than HTML tables, and they're a lot more trouble. The excitement of databases comes when you use the information to solve problems. Ironically, the most important part of database work isn't usually getting the data, but filtering the data in order to solve some sort of problem.

You might want to get a listing of all heroes in your database whose last name begins with an E, or perhaps somebody parked a Yak Dirigible in your parking space and you need to know whom the driver is. You may also want your list sorted by special power or list only vehicles. All these (admittedly contrived) examples involve grabbing a subset of the original data. The SELECT statement is the SQL workhorse.

1. Click the SQL tab to get a query screen in phpMyAdmin.
2. Type in a query.
3. Click the Go button to see the query results.

You've seen the simplest form of this command getting all the data in a table, like this:

```
SELECT * FROM hero;
```

Figure 9.19 shows this form of the SELECT statement operating on the hero table.

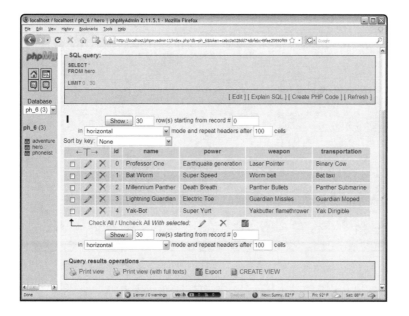

**FIGURE 9.19**

The result of the SELECT statement.

TRICK     phpMyAdmin is a wonderful tool for experimenting with SELECT statements because you can write the actual SQL by hand and see immediate results in a very clean format. If you don't want to (or cannot) use phpMyAdmin, do the same experiments directly in MySQL. It will work, but the results are formatted as text and not always as easy to see.

The `SELECT` statement is extremely powerful because it can grab a subset of data that can return only the requested fields and records. This process of asking questions of the database is commonly called a query. Note that phpMyAdmin sometimes adds elements to the query (notably the `limit` information). This increases the query's efficiency, but doesn't substantially change the query.

## Limiting Columns

You might not want all of the fields in a table. For example, you might just want a list of the name and weapon of everyone on your list. You can specify this by using the following `SELECT` statement, which is illustrated in Figure 9.20:

```
SELECT name, weapon
FROM hero;
```

**FIGURE 9.20**

Selecting a limited number of fields from a table.

This may seem like a silly capability for such a simple database as the `hero` list. However, you often run into extremely complicated tables with many fields and need to filter only a few fields. For example, I use a database to track student advisees. Each student's information contains lots of data, but I might just want a list of names and e-mail addresses. The ability to isolate the fields I need is one way to get useful information from a database.

The results of a query look a lot like a new table. You can think of a query result as a temporary table.

## Limiting Rows with the WHERE Clause

In addition to limiting the columns returned in a query, you may be interested in limiting the number of rows. For example, you might run across an evil villain who can only be defeated by a laser pointer. The query shown in Figure 9.21 illustrates a query that solves exactly this dilemma.

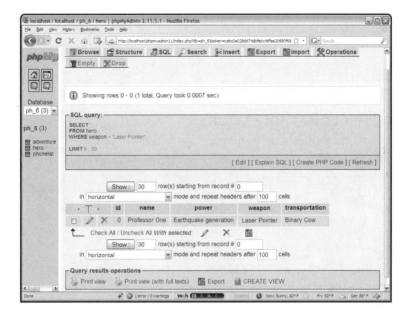

**FIGURE 9.21**

If you know how to set up the query, you can get very specific results. In this case, the query selects only those heroes with a laser pointer.

This code returns only the rows matching a specific condition:

```
SELECT *
FROM hero
WHERE weapon = 'Laser Pointer';
```

## Adding a Condition with a WHERE Clause

A WHERE statement in a query specifies which row(s) you want to see. This clause allows you to specify a condition. The database manager checks every record in the table. If the condition is TRUE for that record, it is included in the result set. The conditions in a WHERE clause are similar to those in PHP code, but they are not exactly the same. Use these symbols in SQL:

- For equality use the single equal sign (=).
- Encase text elements in single quotation marks (').
- Use ⟨, ⟩, and ⟨= or ⟩= and != conditions to limit your search.

Comparison operators are easy to understand for numeric data, such as integers and real numbers. It's not quite so obvious how a language will treat text comparisons. SQL has developed some standard rules, but each implementation might be somewhat different. SQL generally works in a case-insensitive way, so `Yak-Bot` would match `yak-bot` or `yAK-bOT`. Also, the < and > operators refer to alphabetic order, so the following selects all the records where the hero's name starts with A, B, or C.

```
SELECT *
FROM hero
WHERE name < 'D';
```

## Using the LIKE Clause for Partial Matches

Often you do not know the exact value of a field you are trying to match. The `LIKE` clause allows you to specify partial matches. For example, which heroes have some sort of super power? This query returns each hero whose power begins with the value `Super`:

```
SELECT *
FROM hero
WHERE power LIKE 'Super%';
```

The percent sign (%) can be a wild card, which indicates any character, any number of times. You can use a variation of the `LIKE` clause to find information about all heroes with a transportation scheme that starts with the letter B:

```
SELECT name, transportation
FROM hero
WHERE transportation LIKE 'B%';
```

You can also use the underscore character (_) to specify one character.

The simple wildcard character support in SQL is sufficient for many purposes. If you like regular expressions, you can use the `REGEXP` clause to specify whether a field matches a regular expression. This is a very powerful tool, but it is an extension to the SQL standard. It works fine in MySQL, but it is not supported in all SQL databases.

## Generating Multiple Conditions

You can combine conditions with `AND`, `OR`, and `NOT` keywords for more complex expressions. For example, the following code selects those heroes whose transportation starts with B and who have a power with `super` in its name.

```
SELECT *
FROM hero
WHERE transportation LIKE 'B%'
AND power LIKE '%super%';
```

Creating compound expressions is very useful as you build more complex databases with multiple tables.

## Sorting Results with the ORDER BY Clause

One more nifty SELECT statement feature is the ability to sort results by any field. Figures 9.22 and 9.23 illustrate how the ORDER BY clause can determine how tables are sorted.

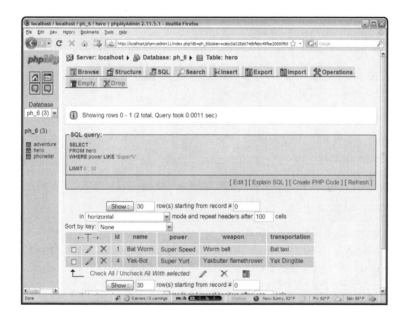

**FIGURE 9.22**

This query shows records with super-powers.

The ORDER BY clause allows you to determine how the data is sorted. You can specify any field you want as the sorting field, as you can see in Figure 9.23. Add the DESC clause to specify that data should be sorted in descending order.

**FIGURE 9.23**

Showing results
ordered by a
specific column.

## Changing Data with the UPDATE Statement

You can use SQL to modify the data in a database. The key to this behavior is the UPDATE statement. An example helps it make sense:

```
UPDATE hero
SET power = 'Super Electric Toe'
WHERE name = 'Lightning Guardian';
```

This code upgrades Lightning Guardian's power to the Super Electric Toe (which is presumably a lot better than the ordinary Electric Toe).

Generally, you should update only one record at a time. You can use a WHERE clause to select which record in the table is updated.

## RETURNING TO THE ADVENTURE GAME

The adventure game featured at the beginning of this chapter uses a combination of MySQL and PHP code. You learn more about the PHP part in Chapter 10, "Connecting to Databases within PHP." For now, you have enough information to start building the data structure that forms the core of the game.

## Designing the Data Structure

The adventure game is entirely about data and has an incredibly repetitive structure. The same code operates over and over, but on different parts of the database. I started the program by sketching out the primary play screen and thinking about what data elements I needed for each screen.

You can see that I simplified the game so that each choice boils down to seven elements. Each node (or decision point) consists of an id (or room number), a room name, and a description of the current circumstances. Each node also has pointers that describe what happens when the user chooses to go in various directions from that node. For example, if the user is in the warehouse (node 3) and chooses to go east, he goes to node 4, which represents the doorway. Going south from node 3 takes the user to node 5, which is the box. The data structure represents all the places the user can go in this game. I chose to think of winning and losing as nodes, so everything in the game can be encapsulated in the table.

It's critical to understand that creating the table on paper is the first step. Once you've decided what kind of data your program needs, you can think about how to put that data together. Choosing a database gives me an incredible amount of control and makes it pretty easy to work with the data. Perhaps the most amazing thing is that this program can handle an entirely different game simply by changing the database. I don't have to change a single line of code to make the game entirely different. All I have to do is point to a different database or change the database.

Once I decided on the data structure, I built an SQL script to create the first draft of the database. That script is shown here:

```
## build Adventure SQL File ## for MySQL ## Andy Harris DROP TABLE IF EXISTS
adventure;
CREATE TABLE ADVENTURE ( id int PRIMARY KEY, name varchar(20), description
varchar(200), north int, east int, south int, west int
);
INSERT INTO adventure values( 0, 'lost', 'You cannot go that way!', 1, 0, 0, 0
);
INSERT INTO adventure values( 1, 'start', 'You are at a submarine yard, looking
for the famous Enigma code machine', 0, 3, 0, 2 );
INSERT INTO adventure values( 2, 'sub deck', 'As you step on the submarine deck,
a guard approaches you. Your only choice is to jump off the sub before you are
caught.', 15, 15, 15, 15 );
INSERT INTO adventure values( 3, 'warehouse', 'You wait inside the warehouse.
You see a doorway to the east and a box to the south.', 0, 4, 5, 0 );
```

```
INSERT INTO adventure values(
4, 'doorway', 'You walked right into a group of guards. It does not look
good...', 0, 19, 0, 15 );
INSERT INTO adventure values(
5, 'box', 'You crawl inside the box and wait. Suddenly, you feel the box being
picked up and carried across the wharf!', 6, 0, 0, 7 );
INSERT INTO adventure values(
6, 'wait', '..You wait until the box settles in a dark space. You can move
forward or aft...', 8, 0, 9, 0 );
INSERT INTO adventure values(
7, 'jump out', 'You decide to jump out of the box, but you are cornered at the
end of the wharf.', 15, 19, 15, 15 );
INSERT INTO adventure values(
8, 'forward', 'As you move forward, two rough sailors grab you and hurl you out
of the conning tower.', 15, 15, 15, 15 );
INSERT INTO adventure values(
9, 'aft', 'In a darkened room, you see the Enigma device. How will you get it
out of the sub?', 13, 11, 10, 12 );
INSERT INTO adventure values(
10, 'signal on Enigma', 'You use the Enigma device to send a signal. Allied
forces recognize your signal and surround the ship when it surfaces', 14, 0, 0,
0 );
INSERT INTO adventure values(
11, 'shoot your way out', 'A gunfight on a submerged sub is a bad idea...', 19,
0, 0, 0 );
INSERT INTO adventure values(
12, 'wait with Enigma', 'You wait, but the sailors discover that Enigma is
missing and scour the sub for it. You are discovered and cast out in the torpedo
tube.', 15, 0, 0, 0 ); INSERT INTO adventure values(

13, 'replace Enigma and wait','You put the Enigma back in place and wait
patiently, but you never get another chance. You are discovered when the sub
pulls in to harbor.', 19, 0, 0, 0 );
INSERT INTO adventure values(
14, 'Win', 'Congratulations! You have captured the device and shortened the
war!', 1, 0, 0, 0 );
INSERT INTO adventure values(
15, 'Water', 'You are in the water. The sub moves away. It looks bad...', 19, 0,
```

```
0, 0 );
INSERT INTO adventure values( 16,'','', 0, 0, 0, 0 );
INSERT INTO adventure values( 17,'','', 0, 0, 0, 0 );
INSERT INTO adventure values( 18,'','', 0, 0, 0, 0 );
INSERT INTO adventure values( 19, 'Game Over' ,'The game is over. You lose.', 1,
0, 0, 0 );
SELECT id, name, north, east, south, west FROM adventure; SELECT id, description
FROM adventure;
```

I wrote this code by hand, but I could have designed it with phpMyAdmin just as easily. Note that I created the table, inserted values, and wrote a couple of SELECT statements to check the values. I like to have a script for creating a database even if I built it in a tool like phpMyAdmin, because I managed to mess up this database several times as I was writing the code for this chapter. It is very handy to have a script that instantly rebuilds the database without any tears.

## SUMMARY

Although you didn't write any PHP in this chapter, you did learn how to create a basic data structure using the SQL language. You learned how to work with the MySQL console to create and use databases and how to return data from your database using the SELECT statement. You know how to modify the SELECT statement to get more specific results. You know how phpMyAdmin can simplify the creation and manipulation of MySQL databases. You built a data structure for an adventure game.

---

### CHALLENGES

1. Design a database. Start with something simple like a phone list.
2. Create your database in SQL.
3. Write a batch program to create and populate your database.
4. Use phpMyAdmin to manipulate your database and view its results in other formats.

# CONNECTING TO DATABASES
# WITHIN PHP

After all this talk of databases, you might be eager to connect a database to your PHP programs. PHP is well known for its seamless database integration, especially with MySQL. It's actually quite easy to connect to a MySQL database from within PHP. Once you've established the connection, you can send SQL commands to the database and receive the results as data you can use in your PHP program.

By the end of this chapter, you will have built the adventure game featured at the beginning of Chapter 9, "Using MySQL to Create Databases." As you see, the programming isn't very hard if the data is designed well. Specifically, you learn how to:

- Get a connection to a MySQL database from within PHP
- Use a particular database
- Send a query to the database
- Parse the query results
- Check for data errors
- Build HTML output from data results

## CONNECTING TO THE HERO DATABASE

To show how database connections work, I built a simple PHP program that returns all the values in the hero database you created in Chapter 9. Figure 10.1 illustrates the showHero PHP program.

I decided to go back to this simpler database rather than the more complex adventure game. When you're learning new concepts, it's best to work with the simplest environment at first and then move to more complex situations. The adventure database has a lot of information in it, and the way the records point to each other is complicated. With a simpler database I was sure I understood the basics of data connection before working with a production database that is bound to have complexities of its own.

**FIGURE 10.1**

This program retrieves hero data from the database.

This is the code that generates this page:

```
<!DOCTYPE html PUBLIC "-//W3C//DTD XHTML 1.0 Strict//EN"
"http://www.w3.org/TR/xhtml1/DTD/xhtml1-strict.dtd">
<html lang="EN" dir="ltr" xmlns="http://www.w3.org/1999/xhtml">
<head>
<title>Show Heroes</title>
</head>
<body>
```

```
<h1>Show Heroes</h1>
<p>
<?php
//make the database connection
$conn = mysql_connect("localhost", "user", "password") or die (mysql_error());
mysql_select_db("ph_6", $conn);
$sql = "SELECT * FROM hero";
$result = mysql_query($sql, $conn) or die(mysql_error());

while($row = mysql_fetch_assoc($result)){
  foreach ($row as $name => $value){
    print "$name: $value <br />\n";
  } // end foreach
  print "<br /> \n";
} // end while
?>
</p>

</body>
</html>
```

Glance over the code and you see it's mostly familiar except for a few new functions that begin with mysql_. These functions allow access to MySQL databases. If you look through the PHP documentation, you see very similar functions for several other types of databases, including Oracle, Informix, mSQL, and ODBC. You'll find the process for connecting to and using other databases is pretty much the same no matter which database you're using.

This chapter details the process of connecting to a MySQL database. If you're using SQLite instead, please see the documentation on my website: www. aharrisbooks.net for how to modify this chapter's code to work with that alternate database. The concepts remain exactly the same, but some details change.

## Getting a Connection

The first job is to get a connection between your PHP program and your MySQL server. You can connect to any server you have permission to use. The mysql_connect function arranges the communication link between MySQL and PHP. Here's the connect statement from the showHero program:

```
$conn = mysql_connect("localhost", "user", "password") or die (mysql_error());
```

The `mysql_connect()` function requires three parameters:

- **Server name.** The server name is the name or URL of the MySQL server you want to connect to. (This is `localhost` if your PHP and MySQL servers reside on the same machine, which is frequently the case.) The server name may also incorporate a port number, like "localhost:3306". You may need to check with your server administrator to determine the exact server and port name to use with your programs.

- **Username.** The username in MySQL. Most database packages have user accounts.

- **Password.** The password associated with the MySQL user, identified by username.

 You will probably have to change the username and password fields if you are running this code on a server somewhere. I used default values to help you see the various parts of the connection, but you must change to your username and password if you try this code on a production server. These values are set when you initially set up a database server. Check Chapter 1 for details on setting up XAMPP.

You can use the same username and password you use to log into MySQL, and your program will have all the same access you do. Of course, you may want more restricted access for your programs. Create a special account, which has only the appropriate permissions, for program users.

The `mysql_connect()` function returns an integer referring to the database connection. You can think of this identifier much like the file pointers you learned in Chapter 6, "Working with Files." The data connection should be stored in a variable—I usually use something like `$conn`—because many of the other database functions need to access the connection.

The `or die()` portion of the statement is a special function that ends the program with a specific error if something went wrong. MySQL has a different set of error messages than PHP, so if something went wrong, you need to ask MySQL what went wrong. The `mysql_error()` function reports the last `mysql` error. If there was a problem with the connection, the code will explain what went wrong. It's a great idea to use the `die` mechanism whenever you connect to a database, so you'll have some useful information in case of errors.

## IN THE REAL WORLD

Database security is an important and challenging issue. You can do a few easy things to protect your data from most hackers. The first thing is to obscure your username and password information whenever you publish your code. I removed my username and password information from the code shown here. In a practice environment, you can leave these values blank, but ensure you don't have wide-open code that allows access to your data. If you need to post your code (for example, in a class situation), be sure to change the password to something besides your real password.

## Choosing a Database

A data connection can have a number of databases connected to it. The mysql_set_db() function lets you choose a database. The mysql_set_db() function works just like the USE command inside SQL. The mysql_set_db() function requires the database name and a data connection. This function returns the value FALSE if it is unable to connect to the specified database.

## Creating a Query

Creating a query is very easy. The relevant code from showHero.php is reproduced here:

```
//create a query
$sql = "SELECT * FROM hero";
$result = mysql_query($sql, $conn) or die(mysql_error());
```

Begin by placing SQL code inside a variable.

**TRAP** SQL commands entered into the SQL console or phpMyAdmin require a semicolon. When your PHP program sends a command to the DBMS, the semicolon is added automatically, so you should not end your SQL commands with semicolons. Of course, you assign these commands within a line of PHP code, which has its own semicolon. (Sheesh!)

The mysql_query() function allows you to pass an SQL command through a connection to a database. You can send any SQL command to the database with mysql_query(), including table creation statements, updates, and queries. The database returns a special element called a result set. If the SQL command was a query, the result variable holds a pointer to the data, which is taken apart in the next step. If it's a data definition command (the commands used to create and modify tables), the result object usually contains the string related to the operation's success or failure.

Like connection statements, mysql_query() has a lot of potential for error. Use the or die mechanism to get accurate information about what might have gone wrong if the program fails.

## Retrieving the Data

There are many ways to extract the data from the $result variable. The easiest is to treat the data in the form like an associative array.

```php
while($row = mysql_fetch_assoc($result)){
  foreach ($row as $name => $value){
    print "$name: $value <br />\n";
  } // end foreach
  print "<br /> \n";
} // end while
```

The mysql_fetch_assoc() command retrieves the next record from the result and stores it in an associative array. In this case, I pass the record to an array variable called $row. If there are no more rows to fetch, $row will be false and the loop will end.

Inside the while loop, set up a foreach loop to handle all the fields in the current record. It's easy to print the name and value in a list, so that's what I do for this simple example.

## RETRIEVING DATA IN AN HTML TABLE

HTML tables are perfect for displaying data. You can make a variant of the program to print out the data in a nice table, like Figure 10.2.

**FIGURE 10.2**

This version formats query results in an XHTML table.

The showHeroTable.php program featured in Figure 10.2 is very much like the simpler showHero.php, except it (obviously) creates a table.

Here's the overview of the code:

```
<!DOCTYPE html PUBLIC "-//W3C//DTD XHTML 1.0 Strict//EN"
"http://www.w3.org/TR/xhtml1/DTD/xhtml1-strict.dtd">
<html lang="EN" dir="ltr" xmlns="http://www.w3.org/1999/xhtml">
<head>
<title>Show Heroes</title>
</head>
<body>
<h1>Show Heroes</h1>
<?php
//make the database connection
$conn  = mysql_connect("localhost", "user", "password") or die (mysql_error());
mysql_select_db("ph_6", $conn);

//create a query
$sql = "SELECT * FROM hero";
$result = mysql_query($sql, $conn) or die(mysql_error);

print "<table border = \"1\">\n";

//get field names
print "<tr>\n";
while ($field = mysql_fetch_field($result)){
  print "  <th>$field->name</th>\n";
} // end while
print "</tr>\n\n";

//get row data as an associative array
while ($row = mysql_fetch_assoc($result)){
  print "<tr>\n";
  //look at each field
  foreach ($row as $col=>$val){
    print "  <td>$val</td>\n";
  } // end foreach
  print "</tr>\n\n";
```

```
}// end while

print "</table>\n";
?>
</body>
</html>
```

## Getting Field Names

I am printing the data in an HTML table. I could create the table headings by hand, because I know what all the fields are, but it's better to get the field information directly from the query. You won't always know which fields are being returned by a particular query. The next chunk of code manages this task:

```
print "<table border = \"1\">\n";

//get field names
print "<tr>\n";
while ($field = mysql_fetch_field($result)){
  print "  <th>$field->name</th>\n";
} // end while
print "</tr>\n\n";
```

The `mysql_fetch_field()` function expects a query result as its one parameter. It then fetches the next field and stores it in the `$field` variable. If no fields are left in the result, the function returns the value `FALSE`. This allows the field function to also be used as a conditional statement.

The `$field` variable is actually an object. You built a custom object in Chapter 7, "Writing Programs with Objects." The `$field` object in this case is much like an associative array. It has a number of properties (which can be thought of as field attributes). The field object has a number of attributes, listed in Table 10.1.

By far the most common use of the field object is determining the names of all the fields in a query. The other attributes can be useful in certain situations. You can see the complete list of attributes in MySQL Help that shipped with your copy of MySQL or online at `http://www.mysql.com`.

You use object-oriented syntax to refer to an object's properties. Notice that I printed `$field->name` to the HTML table. This syntax simply refers to the `name` property of the `field` object. For now, it's reasonably accurate to think of it as a fancy associative array.

| TABLE 10.1 | COMMONLY USED FIELD OBJECT PROPERTIES |
|---|---|
| **Property** | **Attribute** |
| max_length | Field length; especially important in VARCHAR fields |
| name | The field name |
| primary_key | TRUE if the field is a primary key |
| table | Name of table this field belongs to |
| type | This field's datatype |

## Parsing the Result Set

The rest of the code examines the result set. Refresh your memory:

```
//get row data as an associative array
while ($row = mysql_fetch_assoc($result)){
  print "<tr>\n";
  //look at each field
  foreach ($row as $col=>$val){
    print "  <td>$val</td>\n";
  } // end foreach
  print "</tr>\n\n";
}// end while


print "</table>\n";
```

The mysql_fetch_assoc() function fetches the next row from a result set. It requires a result pointer as its parameter, and it returns an associative array.

> A number of related functions are available for pulling a row from a result set. mysql_fetch_object() stores a row as an object, much like the mysql_fetch_fields() function does. The mysql_fetch_array() function fetches an array that can be treated as a normal array, an associative array, or both. I tend to use mysql_fetch_assoc() because I think it's the most straightforward approach for those unfamiliar with object-oriented syntax. Of course, you should feel free to investigate these other functions and use them if they make more sense to you.

If no rows are left in the result set, mysql_fetch_assoc() returns the value FALSE. The mysql_fetch_assoc() function call is often used as a condition in a while loop (as I did here to fetch each row in a result set). Each row represents a row of the eventual HTML table, so I print the HTML code to start a new row inside the `while` loop.

Once you've gotten a row, it's stored as an associative array. You can manipulate this array using a standard `foreach` loop. I assigned each element to `$col` and `$val` variables. I actually don't need `$col` in this case, but it can be handy to have. Inside the `foreach` loop, I placed code to print the current field in a table cell.

## Returning to the AdventureGame Program

At the end of Chapter 9, you created a database for an adventure game. Now that you know how to connect a PHP program to a MySQL database, you're ready to begin writing the game itself.

## Connecting to the Adventure Database

Once I built the database, the first PHP program I wrote was the simplest possible connection to the database. I wanted to ensure I got all the data correct.

The output simple program is shown in Figure 10.3.

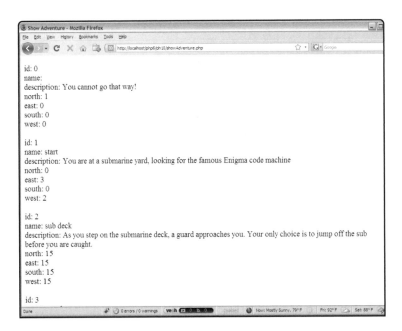

**FIGURE 10.3**

Start with a quick view of the data to ensure your connections are working.

Here's the code for that program:

```
<!DOCTYPE html PUBLIC "-//W3C//DTD XHTML 1.0 Strict//EN"
"http://www.w3.org/TR/xhtml1/DTD/xhtml1-strict.dtd">
<html lang="EN" dir="ltr" xmlns="http://www.w3.org/1999/xhtml">
<head>
<title>Show Adventure</title>
</head>
<body>
<p>
<?php
$conn  = mysql_connect("localhost", "user", "password") or die(mysql_error());
$select = mysql_select_db("ph_6", $conn);
$sql = "SELECT * FROM adventure";
$result = mysql_query($sql) or die(mysql_error());
while ($row = mysql_fetch_assoc($result)){

  foreach($row as $key=>$value){
    print "$key: $value<br />\n";
  } // end foreach
  print "<br />\n";

} // end while
?>
</p>
</body>
</html>
```

This simple program established the connection and ensured that everything was stored as I expected. Whenever I write a data program, I usually write something like this that quickly steps through my data to ensure everything is working correctly. There's no point in moving on until you know you have the basic connection.

## Displaying One Segment

The actual gameplay consists of repeated calls to the showSegment.php program, shown in Figure 10.4.

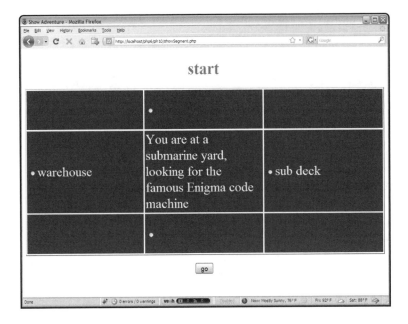

**FIGURE 10.4**

showSegment.ph
p displays a single
segment at a time
and lets the user
choose the next
step.

This program takes a segment ID as its one input and then uses that data to build a page based on that database's record. The only surprise is how simple the code is for this program.

```
<!DOCTYPE html PUBLIC "-//W3C//DTD XHTML 1.0 Strict//EN"
"http://www.w3.org/TR/xhtml1/DTD/xhtml1-strict.dtd">
<html lang="EN" dir="ltr" xmlns="http://www.w3.org/1999/xhtml">
<head>
<title>Show Adventure</title>
<link rel = "stylesheet"
      type = "text/css"
      href = "showSegment.css" />

</head>
<body>

//connect to database
$conn  = mysql_connect("localhost", "user", "password") or die(mysql_connect());

//get input
$room = filter_input(INPUT_POST, "room");
$room = mysql_real_escape_string($room);
```

```php
if (empty($room)){
  $room = 1;
} // end if

//prepare the query
$select = mysql_select_db("ph_6", $conn);
$sql = "SELECT * FROM adventure WHERE id = '$room'";
$result = mysql_query($sql)or die(mysql_connect());
$mainRow = mysql_fetch_assoc($result);
$theText = $mainRow["description"];

$mainRow = mysql_fetch_assoc($result);
$theText = $mainRow["description"];

$northButton = buildButton("north");
$eastButton = buildButton("east");
$westButton = buildButton("west");
$southButton = buildButton("south");
$roomName = $mainRow["name"];

print <<<HERE
<h1>$roomName</h1>
<form method = "post"
     action = "">
<table border = "1">
<tr>
  <td></td>
  <td>$northButton</td>
  <td></td>
</tr>

<tr>
  <td>$eastButton</td>
  <td>$theText</td>
  <td>$westButton</td>
</tr>

<tr>
```

```
  <td></td>
  <td>$southButton</td>
  <td></td>
</tr>

</table>
<p>
<input type = "submit"
       value = "go"
       id = "btnSubmit" />
</p>
</form>

HERE;

function buildButton($dir){
  //builds a button for the specified direction
  global $mainRow, $conn;
  $newID = $mainRow[$dir];
  $query = "SELECT name FROM adventure WHERE id = $newID";
  $result = mysql_query($query, $conn);
  $row = mysql_fetch_assoc($result);
  $roomName = $row["name"];

  $buttonText = <<< HERE
  <input type = "radio"
         name = "room"
         value = "$newID" />$roomName

HERE;

  return $buttonText;

} // end build button
?>
</body>
</html>
```

## Retrieving the Room Number from the Form

This program is meant to show all the information for one "room" of the adventure. The room number comes from a previous version of the form. It's very common to use data from an HTML form to create a query. However, there's a big potential for trouble here. An unscrupulous user can send garbage instructions to the form, potentially sending commands to the database under your permission. This type of mischief is called an *SQL Injection Attack*. Obviously, you don't want the mafia messing around with your databases, so you need to have a security measure or two in place. There are two main ways to protect yourself from this kind of nastiness:

- **Use the** `post` **mechanism.** It's very easy for a bad guy to change the parameters when your program uses the `get` mechanism. (Good guys use this trick too; I did in the last chapter.) However, if your program requires data to be sent via the post mechanism, the bad guy has to do more work (essentially writing a form that acts like yours) to do bad stuff. You can't always prevent malicious behavior, but you can make it harder to cause you trouble, and that's a good start.

- **Escape all strings that will be used in queries**. SQL Injection is a big enough problem that PHP has a built-in defense mechanism. The `mysql_real_escape_string()` function takes a string that has come from user input and sanitizes it, ensuring none of the sneaky tricks used in SQL injection get through.

My code retrieves data from the form using the `post` mechanism. It then uses the `mysql_real_escape_string()` function to clean the input. If there was no input (because it's the first time here) the value of `$room` is set to 1.

```
//connect to database
$conn  = mysql_connect("localhost", "user", "password") or die(mysql_connect());
$room = filter_input(INPUT_POST, "room");
$room = mysql_real_escape_string($room);
if (empty($room)){
  $room = 1;
} // end if
```

In any case, by the time this code snippet is done, `$room` will contain a clean, safe value that can be used as part of a query without worry of injection. (That even sounds nasty, doesn't it?) The `mysql_real_escape_string()` function requires a valid connection, so make sure you call this function after you've made your data connection.

## Making the Data Connection

The data connection is done in the typical way.

```
//prepare the query
$select = mysql_select_db("ph_6", $conn);
$sql = "SELECT * FROM adventure WHERE id = '$room'";
$result = mysql_query($sql) or die (mysql_error());
```

I then make an ordinary connection to the database and choose the record pertaining to the current room number. That query will be stored in the $mainRow variable as an associative array.

 **TRAP**     Do not interpolate variables from user input into sql queries unless you have run the string through the mysql_real_escape_string() function first. Running unchecked values sets you up for SQL injection attacks.

## Generating Variables for the Code

Most of the program writes the HTML for the current record to the screen. To make things simple, I created some variables for anything that might be tricky.

```
$mainRow = mysql_fetch_assoc($result);
$theText = $mainRow["description"];
$northButton = buildButton("north");
$eastButton = buildButton("east");
$westButton = buildButton("west");
$southButton = buildButton("south");
$roomName = $mainRow["name"];
```

I stored the description field of the current row into a variable named $theText. I made a similar variable for the room name.

---

### IN THE REAL WORLD

It isn't strictly necessary to store the description field in a variable. I've found that interpolating associative array values can be a little tricky. In general, I like to copy an associative value to some temporary variable if I'm going to interpolate it. It's just a lot easier that way.

---

The button variables are a little different. I decided to create an HTML option button to represent each of the places the user could go. I use a custom function called `buildButton()` to make each button.

## Writing the buildButton() Function

The procedure for building the buttons is repetitive enough to warrant a function. Each button is a radio button corresponding to a direction. The radio button will have a value that comes from the corresponding direction value from the current record. If the `north` field of the current record is 12 (meaning if the user goes North, load the data in record 12), the radio button's value should be 12.

The trickier thing is getting the appropriate label. The next room's ID is all that's stored in the current record. If you want to display the room's name, you must make another query to the database. That's exactly what the `buildButton()` function does:

```
function buildButton($dir){
  //builds a button for the specified direction
  global $mainRow, $conn;
  $newID = $mainRow[$dir];
  //print "newID is $newID";
  $query = "SELECT name FROM adventure WHERE id = $newID";
  $result = mysql_query($query, $conn);
  $row = mysql_fetch_assoc($result);
  $roomName = $row["name"];

  $buttonText = <<< HERE
<input type = "radio"
       name = "room"
       value = "$newID" />$roomName

HERE;

  return $buttonText;

} // end build button
```

The function follows these steps:

1. Borrows the $mainRow array (which holds the value of the main record this page is about) and the data connection in $conn.
2. Pulls the ID for this button from the $mainRow array and stores it in a local variable. The buildButton() function requires a direction name sent as a parameter. This direction should be the field name for one of the direction fields.
3. Repeats the query creation process, building a query that requests only the row associated with the new ID.
4. Pulls the room name from that array. Once that's done, it's easy to build the radio button text. The radio button is called room, so the next time this program is called, the $room variable corresponds to the user-selected radio button.

Of course, all this assumes that the data in the database is correct. If there is an incorrect value in the database, the program will not act properly. It might crash, it might send the user to the wrong room, or it could end up with a blank screen. Be sure to thoroughly test your data.

## Finishing the HTML

All that's left is adding a Submit button to the form and closing the form and HTML. The amazing thing is, that's all you need. This code alone is enough to let the user play this game. It takes some effort to set up the data structure, but then all you do is provide a link to the first record (by calling showSegment.php without any parameters). The program will keep calling itself.

## VIEWING AND SELECTING RECORDS

I suppose you could stop there, because the game is working, but the really great thing about this structure is how flexible it is. It doesn't take much more work to create an editor that lets you add and modify records.

This actually requires three different PHP programs. The first, shown in Figure 10.5, prints out a summary of the entire game and allows the user to edit any node.

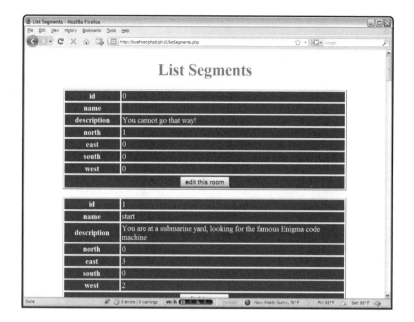

FIGURE 10.5

The
listSegments.php
program lists all
the data and
allows the user to
choose a record
for editing.

The code for the listSegments.php program is actually quite similar to the showAdventure.php program you saw before. It's simply cleaned up a bit to put the data in tables and has a form to call an editor when the user selects a record to modify.

```
<!DOCTYPE html PUBLIC "-//W3C//DTD XHTML 1.0 Strict//EN"
"http://www.w3.org/TR/xhtml1/DTD/xhtml1-strict.dtd">
<html lang="EN" dir="ltr" xmlns="http://www.w3.org/1999/xhtml">
<head>
<link rel = "stylesheet"
      type = "text/css"
      href = "listSegments.css" />

<title>List Segments</title>
</head>
<body>
<h1>List Segments</h1>
<?php

connect();

$sql = "SELECT * FROM adventure";
```

```php
$result = mysql_query($sql) or die(mysql_error());

while ($row = mysql_fetch_assoc($result)){
  print <<<HERE
<form action = "editSegment.php"
      method = "post">
<table border = "1">

HERE;
//  print "<table border = \"1\">\n";

  foreach($row as $key=>$value){
    //print "$key: $value<br>\n";
    $roomNum = $row["id"];
    print <<<HERE
  <tr>
    <th>$key</th>
    <td>$value</td>
  </tr>

HERE;

  } // end foreach
  print <<<HERE
  <tr>
    <td colspan = "2">
      <input type = "hidden"
             name = "room"
             value = "$roomNum" />
      <button type = "submit">
        edit this room
      </button>
    </td>
  </tr>
</table>

</form>
HERE;
```

```
} // end while

function connect(){
  global $conn, $select;
  $conn  = mysql_connect("localhost", "root", "xfdaio") or die(mysql_error());
  $select = mysql_select_db("ph_6", $conn);
} // end function


?>


</body>
</html>
```

The entire program is contained in a form, which calls editSegment.php when activated. The program opens a data connection and pulls all elements from the database. It builds a form for each record inside an HTML table. Each form has a hidden field with the room number, and a Submit button.

**TRICK** This is a really sneaky trick, but a good one. One web page can have any number of forms on it. Only the one that's submitted counts. So, even though my forms don't really have a lot of information (just the room number), the room number of only the form that was activated will get to the next program.

## Editing the Record

When the user has chosen a record from listSegments.php, the editSegment.php program (shown in Figure 10.6) swings into action.

It's important to understand that the editSegment program doesn't actually change the record in the database. Instead, it pulls up a form containing the requested record's current values and allows the user to determine the new values. The editSegment page is another form. When the user submits this form, control is passed to one more program, which actually modifies the database. The code for editSegment is very similar to the code that displays a segment in play mode. The primary difference is that all the record data goes into editable fields.

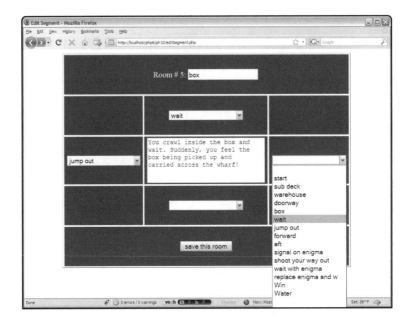

Take a careful look at how the game developer can select a room to go into for each position.
A drop-down menu shows all the existing room names. This device allows the game developer
to work directly with room names even though the database will be much more concerned
with room numbers.

```
<!DOCTYPE html PUBLIC "-//W3C//DTD XHTML 1.0 Strict//EN"
"http://www.w3.org/TR/xhtml1/DTD/xhtml1-strict.dtd">
<html lang="EN" dir="ltr" xmlns="http://www.w3.org/1999/xhtml">
<head>
<link rel = "stylesheet"
      type = "text/css"
      href = "listSegments.css" />

<title>Edit Segment</title>
<style type = "text/css">
body {
  color:red
}
td {
 color: white;
 background-color: blue;
 width: 20%;
```

```
 height: 5em;
 text-align: center;
}
</style>
</head>
<body>
<?php
$room = filter_input(INPUT_POST, "room");
$room = mysql_escape_string($room);
if (empty($room)){
  $room = 0;
} // end if

//connect to database
connect();


$sql = "SELECT * FROM adventure WHERE id = '$room'";
$result = mysql_query($sql) or die(mysql_error());
$mainRow = mysql_fetch_assoc($result);
$theText = $mainRow["description"];
$roomName = $mainRow["name"];
$northList = makeList("north", $mainRow["north"]);
$westList = makeList("west", $mainRow["west"]);
$eastList = makeList("east", $mainRow["east"]);
$southList = makeList("south", $mainRow["south"]);
$roomNum = $mainRow["id"];

print <<<HERE

<form action = "saveRoom.php"
      method = "post">

<table border = "1">
<tr>
  <td colspan = "3">
Room # $roomNum:
    <input type = "text"
           name = "name"
           value = "$roomName" />
```

```
    <input type = "hidden"
           name = "id"
           value = "$roomNum" />
  </td>
</tr>

<tr>
  <td></td>
  <td>$northList</td>
  <td></td>
</tr>

<tr>
  <td>$westList</td>
  <td>
    <textarea rows = "5"
              cols = "30"
              name = "description">$theText</textarea>
  </td>
  <td>$eastList</td>
</tr>

<tr>
  <td></td>
  <td>$southList</td>
  <td></td>
</tr>

<tr>
  <td colspan = "3">
    <input type = "submit"
           value = "save this room" />
  </td>
</tr>
</table>


</form>
```

```
HERE;

function makeList($dir, $current){
  //make a list of all the places in the system

  //how do I indicate the currently selected item?

  global $conn;
  $listCode = "<select name = \"$dir\">\n";
  $sql = "SELECT id, name FROM adventure";
  $result = mysql_query($sql);
  $rowNum = 0;
  while ($row = mysql_fetch_assoc($result)){
    $id = $row["id"];
    $placeName = $row["name"];
    $listCode .= "  <option value = \"$id\"";

    //select this option if it's the one indicated
    if ($rowNum == $current){
      $listCode .= "selected = \"selected\" \n ";
    } // end if
    if ($placeName == ""){
      $placeName = " ";
    } // end if
    $listCode .= ">$placeName</option>\n";
    $rowNum++;
  } // end while
  $listCode .= "</select> \n";
  return $listCode;
} // end makeList


function connect(){
  $conn   = mysql_connect("localhost", "root", "xfdaio") or die(mysql_error());
  $select = mysql_select_db("ph_6", $conn);
} // end function
?>
</body>
</html>
```

## Generating Variables

After the standard database connection, the code creates a number of variables. Some of these variables (`$theText`, `$roomName`, and `$roomNum`) are simplifications of the associative array. Another set of variables is the result of the `makeList()` function. This function's job is to return an HTML list box containing the room names of every segment in the database. The list box is set up so that whatever room number is associated with the indicated field is the default.

## Printing the HTML Code

The central part of the program consists of a large `print` statement that develops the HTML code. The code in this case is a large table enclosed in a form. Every field in the record has a form element associated with it. When the user submits this form, it should have all the data necessary to update a record in the database.

The one element the user should not be able to directly edit is the room number. This is stored in a hidden field. The directional room numbers are encoded in the list boxes. All other data is in appropriately named text boxes.

## Creating the List Boxes

The list boxes require a little bit of thought to construct.

The `makeList()` function expects two parameters. The `$dir` parameter holds the direction field name of the current list box. The `$current` parameter holds information about which room is currently selected for this particular field of the current record. The data connection handler `$conn` is the only global variable. The variable `$listCode` holds the actual HTML code of the list box returned to the main program.

The function makes a query to the database to request all the room names. Each name is added to the list box code at the appropriate time with the corresponding numeric value. Whenever the record number corresponds to the current value of the record, HTML code specifies that this should be the selected item in the list box.

Note that if the `$placeName` variable is empty, I replace it with the special value `" "` to prevent a warning about empty option tags.

## COMMITTING CHANGES TO THE DATABASE

One more program is necessary. The `editSegment.php` program allows the user to edit the data. When finished, the user submits the form, which calls the `saveRoom.php` program, shown in Figure 10.7.

```
<!DOCTYPE html PUBLIC "-//W3C//DTD XHTML 1.0 Strict//EN"
"http://www.w3.org/TR/xhtml1/DTD/xhtml1-strict.dtd">
<html lang="EN" dir="ltr" xmlns="http://www.w3.org/1999/xhtml">
<head>
<title>SaveRoom.php</title>
</head>
<body>

<?php
//Once a room has been edited by editSegment, this program
//updates the database accordingly.

//connect to database
$conn  = mysql_connect("localhost", "root", "xfdaio") or die(mysql_error());
$select = mysql_select_db("ph_6", $conn);

//pull data from form
$name = filter_input(INPUT_POST, "name");
$description = filter_input(INPUT_POST, "description");
$north = filter_input(INPUT_POST, "north");
$east = filter_input(INPUT_POST, "east");
```

```php
$south = filter_input(INPUT_POST, "south");
$west = filter_input(INPUT_POST, "west");
$id = filter_input(INPUT_POST, "id");

//clean up all data
$name = mysql_real_escape_string($name);
$description = mysql_real_escape_string($description);
$north = mysql_real_escape_string($north);
$east = mysql_real_escape_string($east);
$south = mysql_real_escape_string($south);
$west = mysql_real_escape_string($west);
$id = mysql_real_escape_string($id);


$sql = <<< END

UPDATE adventure
SET
  name = '$name',
  description = '$description',
  north = $north,
  east = $east,
  south = $south,
  west = $west
WHERE
  id = $id;

END;

print "<pre>$sql</pre> \n";


$result = mysql_query($sql) or die(mysql_error());
if ($result){
  print "<h3>$name room updated successfully</h3>\n";
  print "<p><a href = \"listSegments.php\">view the rooms</a></p>\n";
} else {
  print "<h3>There was a problem with the database</h3>\n";
} // end if
```

```
?>
</body>
</html>
```

This program begins with standard data connections.

It also pulls all the data from the previous form, and cleans it with `mysql_real_escape_string()`.

It then constructs an `UPDATE SQL` statement. The statement is quite simple, because all the work is done in the previous program. I then simply applied the query to the database and checked the result. An `UPDATE` statement won't return a record set like a `SELECT` statement. Instead, it will return the value `FALSE` if it was unable to process the command. If the update request was successful, I let the user know and provide a link to the `listSegments` program. If there was a problem, I provide some (not very helpful) feedback to the user. Note that I displayed the query for my own sake, but in a final version of the program I would hide this information from the user.

## SUMMARY

In this chapter you learned how to connect to a MySQL database from your PHP programs. You learned how to make a database connection, build a query, and pass that query to the database. You discovered how to retrieve the data into records, how to parse these records in to field–value pairs, and multiple ways of displaying data to the user.

You combined these skills to create an interesting and expandable game.

---

### CHALLENGES

1. **Add a** new room **command to the** adventure generator. **Hint: Think about how I created a new test in the** quiz machine **program from Chapter 6.**
2. **Write PHP programs to view, add, and edit records in the phone list.**
3. **Write a program that asks a user's name and searches the database for that user.**
4. **Create a front end for another simple database.**

# CHAPTER 11

# DATA NORMALIZATION

In Chapters 9 and 10, you learned how to create a basic database and connect it to a PHP program. PHP and MySQL are wonderful for working with basic databases. However, most real-world problems involve data that is too complex to fit in one table. Database designers have developed some standard techniques for handling complex data that reduce redundancy, improve efficiency, and provide flexibility. In this chapter, you learn how to use the relational model to build complex databases involving multiple entities. Specifically, you learn:

- How the relational model works
- How to build use-case models for predicting data usage
- How to construct entity-relationship diagrams to model your data
- How to build multi-table databases
- How joins are used to connect tables
- How to build a link table to model many-to-many relationships
- How to optimize your table design for later programming

## INTRODUCING THE SPY DATABASE

In this chapter, you build a database to manage your international spy ring. (You do have an international spy ring, don't you?) Saving the world is a complicated task, so you'll need a database to keep track of all your agents. Secret agents are assigned to various operations around the globe, and certain agents have certain skills. The examples in this chapter will take you through the construction of such a database. You'll see how to construct the database in MySQL. In Chapter 12, "Building a Three-Tiered Data Application," you use this database to make a really powerful spymaster application in PHP.

The spy database reflects a few facts about my spy organization (called the Pantheon of Humanitarian Performance, or PHP).

- Each agent has a code name.
- Each agent can have any number of skills.
- More than one agent can have the same skill.
- Each agent is assigned to one operation at a time.
- More than one agent can be assigned to one operation.
- A spy's location is determined by the operation.
- Each spy has an age (so I know when they should be claiming senior discounts).
- Each operation has only one location.

This list of rules helps explain some characteristics of the data. In database parlance, they are called *business rules*. I need to design the database so these rules are enforced.

---

### IN THE REAL WORLD

I set up this particular set of rules in a somewhat arbitrary way because they help make my database as simple as possible while still illustrating most of the main problems encountered in data design. Usually you don't get to make up business rules. Instead, you learn them by talking to those who use the data every day.

---

## THE badSpy DATABASE

As you learned in Chapter 9, "Using MySQL to Create Databases," it isn't difficult to build a data table, especially if you have a tool like phpMyAdmin. Table 11.1 illustrates the schema of my first pass at the spy database.

| TABLE 11.1 | BAD SPY SCHEMA |
| --- | --- |
| **Field** | **Type** |
| agentID | int(11) |
| name | varchar(30) |
| specialty | varchar(40) |
| assignment | varchar(40) |
| description | varchar(40) |
| location | varchar(20) |
| age | int(11) |

At first glance, the badSpy database design seems like it ought to work, but problems crop up as soon as you begin adding data to the table. Table 11.2 shows the results of the badSpy data after I started entering information about some of my field agents.

| TABLE 11.2 | | BAD SPY SAMPLE DATA | | | | |
| --- | --- | --- | --- | --- | --- | --- |
| agentID | name | specialty | assignment | description | location | age |
| 1 | Rahab | Electronics, Counterintelligence | Raging Dandelion | Plant Crabgrass | Sudan | 27 |
| 2 | Gold Elbow | Sabatoge, Doily design | Dancing Elephant | Infiltrate suspicious zoo | London | 47 |
| 3 | Falcon | Counterintelligence | Dancing Elephant | Infiltrate suspicious circus | London | 33 |
| 4 | Cardinal | Sabatoge | Enduring Angst | Make bad guys feel really guilty | Lower Volta | 29 |
| 5 | Blackford | Explosives, Flower arranging | Enduring Angst | Make bad guys feel really guilty | Lower Votla | 52 |

## Inconsistent Data Problems

Gold Elbow's record indicates that Operation Dancing Elephant is about infiltrating a suspicious zoo. Falcon's record indicates that the same operation is about infiltrating a suspicious circus. For the purpose of this example, I'm expecting that an assignment has only one description, so one of these descriptions is wrong. There's no way to know whether it's a zoo or a circus by looking at the data in the table, so both records are suspect. Likewise, it's hard to tell if Operation Enduring Angst takes place in Lower Volta or Lower Votla, because the two records that describe this mission have different spellings.

The circus/zoo inconsistency and the Volta/Votla problem share a common cause. In both cases the data-entry person (probably a low-ranking civil servant, because international spymasters are far too busy to do their own data entry) had to type the same data into the database multiple times. This kind of inconsistency causes all kinds of problems. Different people choose different abbreviations. You may see multiple spellings of the same term. Some people simply do not enter data if it's too difficult. When this happens, you cannot rely on the data. (Is it a zoo or a circus?) You also can't search the data with confidence. (I'll miss Blackford if I look for all operatives in Lower Volta, because he's listed as being in Lower Votla.) If you look carefully, you notice that I misspelled "sabotage." It will be very difficult to find everywhere this word is misspelled and fix them all.

## Problem with the Operation Information

There's another problem with this database. If for some reason Agent Rahab were dropped from the database (maybe she was a double agent all along), the information regarding Operation Raging Dandelion would be deleted along with her record, because the only place it is stored is as a part of her record. The operation's data somehow needs to be stored separately from the agent data.

## Problems with Listed Fields

The specialty field brings its own troubles to the database. This field can contain more than one entity, because spies should be able to do more than one thing. (My favorite combination is explosives and flower arranging.) Fields with lists in them can be problematic.

- It's much harder to figure out what size to make a field that may contain several entities. If your most talented spy has 10 different skills, you need enough room to store all 10 skills in every spy's record.
- Searching on fields that contain lists of data can be difficult.

You might be tempted to insert several different skill fields (maybe a `skill1`, `skill2`, and `skill3` field, for example), but this doesn't completely solve the problem. It is better to have a more flexible system that can accommodate any number of skills. The flat file system in this `badSpy` database is not capable of that kind of versatility.

## Age Issues

The `age` field sounds like a good idea, but in real life it's very difficult to use. People age every year, so how do I keep the ages up to date? I could update each spy's age on his or her birthday, but I'd need to have the birthday stored for each spy, and I'd need to run a script every day to check for any spy birthdays and increase the age. The other solution would be to simply age everyone once a year, but that doesn't seem very satisfying.

## DESIGNING A BETTER DATA STRUCTURE

The spy master database isn't complicated, but the badSpy database shows a number of ways even a simple database can go wrong. This database is being used to save the free world, so it deserves a little more thought. Fortunately, data developers have come up with a number of ways to think about data structure.

It is usually best to back away from the computer and think carefully about how data is used before you write a single line of code.

### Defining Rules for a Good Data Design

Data developers have come up with a list of rules for creating well-behaved databases:

- Break your data into multiple tables.
- Make no field with a list of entries.
- Do not duplicate data.
- Make each table describe only one entity.
- Don't store information that should be calculated instead.
- Create a single primary key field for each table.

A database that follows all these rules will avoid most of the problems evident in the badSpy database. Fortunately, there are some well-known procedures for improving a database so it can follow all these rules.

### Normalizing Your Data

Data programmers try to prevent the problems evident in the badSpy database through a process called *data normalization*. The basic concept of normalization is to break down a database into a series of tables. If each of these tables is designed correctly, the database is less likely to have the sorts of problems described so far. Entire books have been written about data normalization, but the process breaks down into three major steps, called normal forms.

### First Normal Form: Eliminate Listed Fields

The normal forms are officially listed in terms that would put a lawyer or mathematician to sleep. One "official" description of the first normal form looks like this:

A table is in first normal form if and only if it represents a relation. It does not allow nulls or duplicate rows.

Yea, that's catchy. It's really a lot simpler than it sounds: Eliminate listed fields (like the `specialty` field in this example).

The goal of the first normal form (sometimes abbreviated 1NF) is to eliminate repetition in the database. The primary culprit in the `badSpy` database is the `specialty` field. Having two different tables, one for agents and another for specialties, is one solution.

**TRICK**    Data designers seem to play a one-string banjo. The solution to almost every data design problem is to create another table. As you see, there is quite an art form to what should be in that new table.

The two tables would look somewhat like those shown in Tables 11.3 and 11.4.

### TABLE 11.3   AGENT TABLE IN 1NF

| Agent ID | Name | Assignment | Description | Location |
| --- | --- | --- | --- | --- |
| 1 | Rahab | Raging Dandelion | Plant Crabgrass | Sudan |
| 2 | Gold Elbow | Dancing Elephant | Infiltrate suspicious zoo | London |
| 3 | Falcon | Dancing Elephant | Infiltrate suspicious circus | London |

### TABLE 11.4   SPECIALTY TABLE IN 1NF

| Specialty ID | Name |
| --- | --- |
| 1 | electronics |
| 2 | counterintelligence |
| 3 | sabotage |

Note that I did not include all data in these example tables, but just enough to give you a sense of how these tables would be organized. Also, you learn later in this chapter a good way to reconnect these tables and assert the proper relationship between the agents and their specialties.

## Second Normal Form: Eliminate Redundancies

The official form of the second normal form is just as inspiring as the first normal form:

```
A table is in second normal form (2NF) only if it is in 1NF and all nonkey fields are
dependant entirely on the candidate key, not just part of it.
```

I bet the guy who wrote *that* is a lot of fun at parties...

Once all your tables are in the first normal form, the next step is to deal with all the potential redundancy issues. These mainly occur because data is entered more than one time. To fix this, you need to (you guessed it) build new tables. The agent table could be further improved by moving all data about operations to another table. Figure 11.1 shows a special diagram called an Entity Relationship diagram, which illustrates the relationships between these tables.

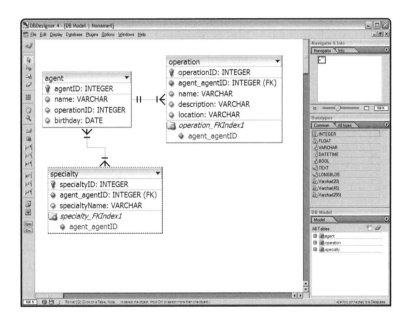

**FIGURE 11.1**

A basic Entity Relationship Diagram for the spy data.

An Entity Relationship diagram (ER diagram) reveals the relationships between data elements. In this situation, I thought carefully about the data in the spy database. As I thought about the data, three distinct entities emerged. By separating the operation data from the agent data, I have removed redundancy: The user enters operational data only one time. This eliminates several of the problems in the original database. It also fixes the situation where an operation's data was lost because a spy turned out to be a double agent. (I'm still bitter about that defection.)

The boxes in this diagram represent the *entities* (agents, operations, and specialties) and the lines between them represent the *relationships* between the entities. The reverse arrow (crow's feet) symbols on the relationship lines describe the types of relationships between the various entities. Read on about the third normal form, and then I explain how the various relationship types work.

## Third Normal Form: Ensure Functional Dependency

The third normal form concentrates on the elements associated with each entity.

The official description has the wit and charm you've come to expect:

```
A table is in 3NF if it is in 2NF and has no transitive dependencies on the candidate key.
```

For a table to be in the third normal form, that table must have a single primary key and every field in the table must relate only to that key. For example, the description field is a description of the operation, not the agent, so it belongs in the operation table.

In the third phase of normalization, you look through each piece of table data and ensure that it directly relates to the table in which it's placed. If not, either move it to a more appropriate table or build a new table for it.

This diagram illustrates the three entities in the spy database (at least up to now) and the relationships between them. Each entity is enclosed in a rectangle, and the lines between each represent the relationships between the entities. Take a careful look at the relationship lines. They have crow's feet on them to indicate some special relationship characteristics. There are essentially three kinds of relationships (at least in this overview of data modeling).

## Defining Relationship Types

The easiest way to normalize your databases is with a stylized view of them such as the ER diagram. ER diagrams are commonly used as a data-design tool. Take another look at the ER diagram for the spy database in Figure 11.2.

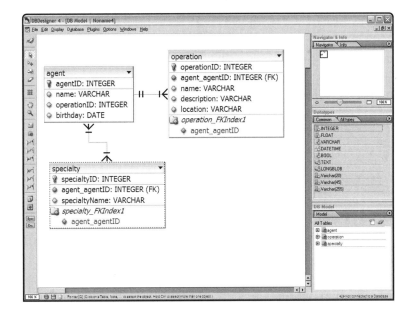

**FIGURE 11.2**

The ER diagram illustrates the relationships between data entities.

## Recognizing One-to-One Relationships

One-to-one relationships happen when each instance of entity A has exactly one instance of entity B. A one-to-one entity is described as a simple line between two entities with no special symbols on either end.

**TRICK** One-to-one relationships are rare, because if the two entities are that closely related, usually they can be combined into one table without any penalty. The spy ER diagram in Figure 11.2 has no one-to-one relationships.

## Describing Many-to-One Relationships

One-to-many (and many-to-one) relationships happen when one entity can contain more than one instance of the other. For example, each operation can have many spies, but in this example, each agent can only be assigned to one mission at a time. Thus, the agent-to-operation relationship is considered a many-to-one relationship, because a spy can have only one operation, but one operation can relate to many agents. In this version of ER notation, I'm using crow's feet to indicate the many sides of the relationship.

**TRICK** There are actually several different kinds of one-to-many relationships, each with a different use and symbol. For this overview, I treat them all the same and use the generic crow's feet symbol. When you start writing more-involved databases, investigate data diagramming more closely by looking into books on data normalization and software engineering. Likewise, data normalization is a far more involved topic than the brief discussion in this introductory book.

## Recognizing Many-to-Many Relationships

The final type of relationship shown in the spy ER diagram is a many-to-many relationship. This type of relationship occurs when each entity can have many instances of the other. Agents and skills have this type of relationship, because one agent can have any number of skills, and each skill can be used by any number of agents. A many-to-many relationship is usually shown by crow's feet on each end of the connecting line.

It's important to generate an ER diagram of your data including the relationship types, because different strategies for each type of relationship creation exist. These strategies emerge as I build the SQL for the improved spy database.

# Building Your Data Tables

After designing the data according to the rules of normalization, you are ready to build sample data tables in SQL. It pays to build your tables carefully to avoid problems. I prefer to build all my tables in an SQL script so I can easily rebuild my database if (okay, when) my programs mess up the data structure. Besides, enemy agents are always lurking about preparing to sabotage my operations.

I also add plenty of sample data in the script. You don't want to work with actual data early on, because you are guaranteed to mess up somewhere during the process. However, it is a good idea to work with sample data that is a copied subset of the actual data. Your sample data should anticipate some of the anomalies that might occur in actual data. (For example, what if a person doesn't have a middle name?)

My entire script for the spy database is available on the book's CD as buildSpy.sql. All SQL code fragments shown in the rest of this chapter come from that file and use the MySQL syntax.

## Setting Up the System

I began my SQL script with some comments that describe the database and a few design decisions I made when building the database:

```
########################################
# buildSpy.sql
# builds and populates all databases for spy examples
# uses mysql - should adapt easily to other rdbms
# by Andy Harris for PHP/MySQL for Abs. Beg
########################################

########################################
# conventions
```

```
###########################################
# primary key = table name . ID
# primary key always first fields
# all primary keys autonumbered
# all field names camel-cased
# only link tables use underscore
# foreign keys indicated although mySQL does not always enforce
# every table used as foreign reference has a name field
###########################################

###########################################
#housekeeping
###########################################

use ph_6;
DROP TABLE IF EXISTS badSpy;
DROP TABLE IF EXISTS agent;
DROP TABLE IF EXISTS operation;
DROP TABLE IF EXISTS specialty;
DROP TABLE IF EXISTS agent_specialty;
DROP TABLE IF EXISTS spyFirst;
```

Notice that I specified a series of conventions. These self-imposed rules help make my database easier to manage. Some of the rules might not make sense yet (because I haven't identified what a foreign key is, for instance), but the important thing is that I have clearly identified some rules that help later on.

The code then specifies the database and deletes all tables if they already existed. This behavior ensures that I start with a fresh version of the data. This is also ideal for testing, since you can begin each test with a database in a known state.

## Creating the agent Table

The normalized agent table is quite simple. The actual table is shown in Table 11.5.

The only data remaining in the agent table is the agent's name and a numerical field for the operation. The operationID field is used as the glue that holds together the agent and operation tables.

I've added a few things to improve the SQL code that creates the agent table.

| | | | |
|---|---|---|---|
| **TABLE 11.5** | | **THE AGENT TABLE** | |
| agentID | name | operationID | birthday |
| 1 | Bond | 1 | 1961-08-30 |
| 2 | Falcon | 1 | 1975-05-23 |
| 3 | Cardinal | 2 | 1979-01-27 |
| 4 | Blackford | 2 | 1956-10-16 |
| 5 | Rahab | 3 | 1981-09-14 |

These improvements enhance the behavior of the agent table, and simplify the table tremendously.

```
###########################################
# build agent table
###########################################

CREATE TABLE agent (
  agentID int(11) NOT NULL AUTO_INCREMENT,
  name varchar(50) default NULL,
  operationID int(11) default NULL,
  birthday date,
  PRIMARY KEY (agentID),
  FOREIGN KEY (operationID) REFERENCES operation (operationID)
);
```

Recall that the first field in a table is usually called the primary key. Primary keys must be unique and each record must have one.

- I named each primary key according to a special convention. Primary key names always begin with the table name and end with ID. I added this convention because it makes things easier when I write programs to work with this data.

- The NOT NULL modifier requires you to put a value in the field. In practice, this ensures that all records of this table must have a primary key.

- The AUTO_INCREMENT identifier is a special tool that allows MySQL to pick a new value for this field if no value is specified. This will ensure that all entries are unique. In fact, when AUTO_INCREMENT is set, you cannot manually add a value to the field.

- I added an indicator at the end of the CREATE TABLE statement to indicate that agentID is the primary key of the agent table.

**TRAP**  Not all databases use the `AUTO_INCREMENT` feature the same way as MySQL, but most offer an alternative. You might need to look up some other way to automatically generate key fields if you aren't using MySQL. Check the Help system for whatever DBMS you're using to learn any specific quirks.

- The `FOREIGN KEY` reference indicates that the `operationID` field acts as a reference to the operation table. Some databases use this information to reinforce relationships. Even if the database does not use this information, it can be useful documentation for the purpose of the field.

## Inserting a Value into the agent Table

The `INSERT` statements for the `agent` table have one new trick made possible by the primary key's `AUTO_INCREMENT` designation.

```
INSERT INTO agent VALUES(
  null, 'Bond', 1, '1961-08-30'
);
```

The primary key is initialized with the value `null`. This might be surprising because primary keys are explicitly designed to never contain a `null` value. Since the `agentID` field is set to `AUTO_INCREMENT`, the `null` value is automatically replaced with an unused integer. This trick ensures that each primary key value is unique.

## CONVERTING BIRTHDAY TO AGE

One obvious change in the agent data is the inclusion of the `birthday` rather than the agent's `age`. This reflects another important idea in data design: don't store data that should be calculated. The age of an agent is dynamic, which leads to problems. However, you can store the agent's birthdate (which doesn't change) and calculate the agent's age (and other potentially useful details) from this basic information.

## Introducing SQL Functions

SQL has a number of functions built in, which allow you to manipulate the data in various ways. Table 11.6 illustrates a few commonly used SQL functions.

Many of these functions are used to work with dates and times, which (as you see in a moment) can be extremely useful.

The `birthday` value is stored in the `agent` table, but you need to determine the age of the agent, perhaps in years and months.

| TABLE 11.6 | COMMON SQL FUNCTIONS |
|---|---|
| **Function** | **Description** |
| CONCAT(A, B) | Concatenates two string values to create a single string output. Often used to combine two or more fields into one |
| FORMAT(X, D) | Formats the number X to D significant digits |
| CURRDATE(), CURRTIME() | Returns the current date or time |
| NOW() | Returns the current date and time as one value |
| MONTH(), DAY(), YEAR(), WEEK(), WEEKDAY() | Extracts the given data from a date value |
| HOUR(), MINUTE(), SECOND() | Extracts the given data from a time value |
| DATEDIFF(A, B) | Determines the difference between two dates—commonly used to calculate ages |
| SUBTIMES(A, B) | Determines the difference between two times |
| FROMDAYS(INT) | Converts an integer number of days into a date value |

## Finding the Current Date

Begin by using the NOW() function to retrieve the current date and time.

```
SELECT NOW()
NOW()
2008-07-11 21:55:51
```

## Determining Age with DATEDIFF()

These values on their own aren't that useful, but you can compare the date returned by NOW() to the agent's birthday to determine how old the agent is.

```
SELECT
  name,
  NOW(),
  birthday,
  DATEDIFF(NOW(),birthday)
FROM agent;
```

The DATEDIFF() function takes two date values and returns the difference between them as a number of days. (See Table 11.7.)

| | | | TABLE 11.7 DETERMINING AGE WITH **DATEDIFF** |
|---|---|---|---|

| name | NOW() | birthday | DATEDIFF(NOW(),birthday) |
|---|---|---|---|
| Bond | 2008-07-11 21:53:42 | 1961-08-30 | 17117 |
| Falcon | 2008-07-11 21:53:42 | 1975-05-23 | 12103 |
| Cardinal | 2008-07-11 21:53:42 | 1979-01-27 | 10758 |
| Blackford | 2008-07-11 21:53:42 | 1956-10-16 | 18896 |
| Rahab | 2008-07-11 21:53:42 | 1981-09-14 | 9797 |

## Performing Math on Function Results

Of course, this is only mildly interesting. You can do some math on the results to get the age in years as shown in Table 11.8:

```
SELECT
  name,
  NOW(),
  birthday,
  DATEDIFF(NOW(),birthday) / 365 AS age
FROM agent;
```

| | TABLE 11.8 CALCULATING AGE IN YEARS | | |
|---|---|---|---|

| name | NOW() | birthday | age |
|---|---|---|---|
| Bond | 2008-07-11 21:59:27 | 1961-08-30 | 46.8959 |
| Falcon | 2008-07-11 21:59:27 | 1975-05-23 | 33.1589 |
| Cardinal | 2008-07-11 21:59:27 | 1979-01-27 | 29.4740 |
| Blackford | 2008-07-11 21:59:27 | 1956-10-16 | 51.7699 |
| Rahab | 2008-07-11 21:59:27 | 1981-09-14 | 26.8411 |

TRAP

Be aware that sometimes leap years can confuse the DATEDIFF function, which may cause calculations to be off by a few days.

## Converting Number of Days to a Date

Most of the standard math operations work in SQL, but there's a better way. You can convert the number of days back to a date with the FROM_DAYS() function as in Table 11.9.

```
SELECT
  name,
  NOW(),
  birthday,
  DATEDIFF(NOW(), birthday) as daysOld,
  FROM_DAYS(DATEDIFF(NOW(), birthday))
FROM agent;
```

### TABLE 11.9   USING FROM_DAYS()

| name | NOW() | birthday | daysOld | FROM_DAYS(DATEDIFF(NOW(), birthday)) |
|------|-------|----------|---------|--------------------------------------|
| Bond | 2008-07-11 22:02:01 | 1961-08-30 | 17117 | 0046-11-12 |
| Falcon | 2008-07-11 22:02:01 | 1975-05-23 | 12103 | 0033-02-19 |
| Cardinal | 2008-07-11 22:02:01 | 1979-01-27 | 10758 | 0029-06-15 |
| Blackford | 2008-07-11 22:02:01 | 1956-10-16 | 18896 | 0051-09-26 |
| Rahab | 2008-07-11 22:02:01 | 1981-09-14 | 9797 | 0026-10-28 |

## Extracting Years and Months from the Date

The FROM_DAYS() calculation will return the age as if it were a date in the ancient world, but now you can extract the year and days with appropriate functions as Table 11.10 illustrates:

```
SELECT
  name,
  NOW(),
  birthday,
  FROM_DAYS(DATEDIFF(NOW(), birthday)) as age,
  YEAR(FROM_DAYS(DATEDIFF(NOW(), birthday))) as years,
  MONTH(FROM_DAYS(DATEDIFF(NOW(), birthday))) as months
FROM agent;
```

| TABLE 11.10 | WORKING WITH YEAR() AND MONTH() FUNCTIONS | | | | |
|---|---|---|---|---|---|
| name | NOW() | birthday | age | years | months |
| Bond | 2008-07-11 22:03:09 | 1961-08-30 | 0046-11-12 | 46 | 11 |
| Falcon | 2008-07-11 22:03:09 | 1975-05-23 | 0033-02-19 | 33 | 2 |
| Cardinal | 2008-07-11 22:03:09 | 1979-01-27 | 0029-06-15 | 29 | 6 |
| Blackford | 2008-07-11 22:03:09 | 1956-10-16 | 0051-09-26 | 51 | 9 |
| Rahab | 2008-07-11 22:03:09 | 1981-09-14 | 0026-10-28 | 26 | 10 |

## Concatenating to Build the age Field

Finally, you can concatenate these values back to one field (See Table 11.11.):

```
SELECT
  name,
  birthday,
  CONCAT(
    YEAR(FROM_DAYS(DATEDIFF(NOW(), birthday))), ' years, ',
    MONTH(FROM_DAYS(DATEDIFF(NOW(), birthday))), ' months') as age
Bond
FROM agent;
```

| TABLE 11.11 | CREATING THE AGE FROM YEAR AND MONTH | |
|---|---|---|
| name | birthday | age |
| Bond | 1961-08-30 | 46 years, 11 months |
| Falcon | 1975-05-23 | 33 years, 2 months |
| Cardinal | 1979-01-27 | 29 years, 6 months |
| Blackford | 1956-10-16 | 51 years, 9 months |
| Rahab | 1981-09-14 | 26 years, 10 months |

## BUILDING A VIEW

While there's nothing terribly difficult about all this function gymnastics, it's way too much work to do all this every time you want to convert a birthday to a date. Well, that's true. MySQL 5.0 and later includes a wonderful tool called the *View*, which allows you to take complex information like all these date calculations and store it in the database itself. Take a look at the following code:

```
DROP VIEW IF EXISTS agentAgeView;
CREATE VIEW agentAgeView AS
SELECT
  name,
  birthday,
  operationID,
  CONCAT(
    YEAR(FROM_DAYS(DATEDIFF(NOW(), birthday))), ' years, ',
    MONTH(FROM_DAYS(DATEDIFF(NOW(), birthday))), ' months') as age
FROM agent;
```

If you look closely, it's almost the same query used to generate the age from the birthday, but I added a new CREATE VIEW statement (and I included the operationID value, which might be useful later on). When you run this code, nothing overt happens, but the database creates a new structure called agentView. The cool part happens when you run the following query:

```
SELECT * FROM agentView;
```

This extremely simple query yields a marvelous result, shown in Table 11.12.

| TABLE 11.12 | USING THE AGENTVIEW VIEW | | |
|---|---|---|---|
| name | birthday | operationID | age |
| Bond | 1961-08-30 | 1 | 46 years, 11 months |
| Falcon | 1975-05-23 | 1 | 33 years, 2 months |
| Cardinal | 1979-01-27 | 2 | 29 years, 6 months |
| Blackford | 1956-10-16 | 2 | 51 years, 9 months |
| Rahab | 1981-09-14 | 3 | 26 years, 10 months |

All the details of the age manipulation are buried. Now the agentView view can be treated just like a table (at least for SELECT queries) and it automatically creates an age from the birthday field. You can also do all the SELECT tricks on the view, and it still operates as expected:

```
SELECT
  name,
  age
FROM agentView
WHERE
  age < 30;
```

**TABLE 11.13    BUILDING QUERIES WITH agentVIEW**

| name | age |
|------|-----|
| Cardinal | 29 years, 6 months |
| Rahab | 26 years, 10 months |

A view isn't exactly like a table. You can't UPDATE or INSERT view data in a view. Views are meant to simplify SELECT queries. Also, the view data isn't really stored in the database as such. The data is all stored in the tables, and the view is just a formatted way of looking at the data that's actually stored in the tables. (See Table 11.13.)

## Creating a Reference to the operation Table

Take a careful look at the operationID field of the agent table. This field contains an integer, which refers to a particular operation. I also added an indicator specifying operationID as a foreign key reference to the operation table. The operationID field in the agent table contains a reference to the primary key of the operation table. This type of field is referred to as a foreign key.

**TRICK**  Some DBMS systems require you to specify primary and foreign keys. MySQL currently does not require this, but it's a good idea to do so anyway for two reasons. First, it's likely that future versions of MySQL will require these statements, because they improve a database's reliability. Second, it's good to specify in the code when you want a field to have a special purpose, even if the DBMS doesn't do anything with that information.

## Building the operation Table

The new operation table (Table 11.14) contains information referring to an operation.

**TABLE 11.14    THE operation TABLE**

| operation ID | name | description | location |
|--------------|------|-------------|----------|
| 1 | Dancing Elephant | Infiltrate suspicious zoo | London |
| 2 | Enduring Angst | Make bad guys feel really guilty | Lower Volta |
| 3 | Furious Dandelion | Plant crabgrass in enemy lawns | East Java |

Each operation gets its own record in the operation table. All the data corresponding to an operation is stored in the operation record. Each operation's data is stored only one time.

This has a number of positive effects:

- It's necessary to enter operation data only once per operation, saving time on data entry.
- Since there's no repeated data, you won't have data inconsistency problems (like the circus/zoo problem).
- The new database requires less space, because there's no repeated data.
- The operation is not necessarily tied to an agent, so you won't accidentally delete all references to an operation by deleting the only agent assigned to that mission. (Remember, this could happen with the original data design.)
- If you need to update operation data, you don't need to go through every agent to figure out who was assigned to that operation. (Again, you would have had to do this with the old database design.)

The SQL used to create the operation table is much like that used for the agent table:

```
###########################################
# build operation table
###########################################

CREATE TABLE operation (
  operationID int(11) NOT NULL AUTO_INCREMENT,
  name varchar(50) default NULL,
  description varchar(50) default NULL,
  location varchar(50) default NULL,
  PRIMARY KEY (`OperationID`)
);

INSERT INTO operation VALUES(
  null, 'Dancing Elephant',
  'Infiltrate suspicious zoo', 'London'
);
```

As you can see, the operation table conforms to the rules of normalization, and it also is much like the agent table. Notice that I'm being very careful about how I name things. SQL is (theoretically) case-insensitive, but I've found that this is not always true. (I have found this especially in MySQL, where the Windows versions appear unconcerned about case, but Unix versions treat operationID and OperationID as different field names.) I specified that all field names will use camel case (just like you've been doing with your PHP variables). I also named the key field according to my own formula (table name followed by ID).

## Using a Join to Connect Tables

The only downside to disconnecting the data tables is the necessity to rejoin the data when needed. The user doesn't care that the operation and the agent are in different tables, but he will want the data to look as if they were on the same table. The secret to reattaching tables is a tool called the inner join. Take a look at the following SELECT statement in SQL:

```
SELECT
  agent.name AS 'agent',
  operation.name AS 'operation',
FROM
  agent, operation
WHERE
  agent.operationID = operation.operationID
ORDER BY agent.name;
```

At first glance, this looks like an ordinary query, but it is a little different. It joins data from two different tables. Table 11.15 illustrates the results of this query.

### TABLE 11.15 COMBINING TWO TABLES

| agent | operation |
|-------|-----------|
| Blackford | Enduring Angst |
| Bond | Dancing Elephant |
| Cardinal | Enduring Angst |
| Falcon | Dancing Elephant |
| Rahab | Furious Dandelion |

## Creating Useful Joins

An SQL query can pull data from more than one table. To do this, follow a few basic rules.

- Specify the field names more formally if necessary. Notice that the SELECT statement specifies agent.name rather than simply name. This is necessary because both tables contain a field called name. Using the table.field syntax is much like using a person's first and last name. It's not necessary if there's no chance of confusion, but in a larger environment, the more complete naming scheme can avoid confusion.

- Use the AS clause to clarify your output. This provides an alias for the column and provides a nicer output. The 'as' component will show up as the column heading on the output table.

- Modify the FROM clause so it indicates both of the tables you're pulling data from. The FROM clause up to now has only specified one table. In this example, it's necessary to specify that data will be coming from two different tables.

- Indicate how the tables will be connected using a modification of the WHERE clause.

- The order of the table names in the WHERE clause does not matter, but getting the case incorrect can cause problems in some versions of MySQL.

## Examining a Join without a WHERE Clause

The WHERE clause helps clarify the relationship between two tables. As an explanation, consider the following query:

```
SELECT
  agent.name AS 'agent',
  operation.name AS 'operation',
FROM
  agent, operation
ORDER BY agent.name;
```

This query is much like the earlier query, except it includes the operationID field from each table and it omits the WHERE clause. You might be surprised by the results, which are shown in Table 11.16.

The results of this query are called a *Cartesian join*, which shows all possible combinations of agent and operation. Of course, you don't really want all the combinations—only those combinations where the two tables indicate the same operation ID.

## Adding a WHERE Clause to Make a Proper Join

Without a WHERE clause, all possible combinations are returned. The only concern-worthy records are those where the operationID fields in the agent and operation tables have the same value. The WHERE clause returns only these values joined by a common operation ID.

The secret to making this work is the operationID fields in the two tables. You've already learned that each table should have a primary key. The primary key field is used to uniquely identify each database record. In the agents table, agentID is the primary key. In operations, operationID is the primary key. (You might note my unimaginative but very useful naming convention here.)

| TABLE 11.16 | CARTESIAN JOIN BETWEEN AGENT AND OPERATION TABLES | | |
| --- | --- | --- | --- |
| **agent** | **agent Op ID** | **Op Op ID** | **operation** |
| Blackford | 1 | 1 | Dancing Elephant |
| Blackford | 1 | 2 | Enduring Angst |
| Blackford | 1 | 3 | Furious Dandelion |
| Bond | 1 | 1 | Dancing Elephant |
| Bond | 1 | 2 | Enduring Angst |
| Bond | 1 | 3 | Furious Dandelion |
| Cardinal | 2 | 2 | Enduring Angst |
| Cardinal | 2 | 1 | Dancing Elephant |
| Falcon | 1 | 1 | Dancing Elephant |
| Falcon | 1 | 2 | Enduring Angst |
| Falcon | 1 | 3 | Furious Dandelion |
| Rahab | 3 | 1 | Dancing Elephant |
| Rahab | 3 | 2 | Enduring Angst |
| Rahab | 3 | 3 | Furious Dandelion |

------

Op = operation

I was able to take all data that refers to the operation out of the agent table by replacing those fields with a field that points to the operations table's primary key. A field that references the primary key of another table is called a foreign key. Primary and foreign keys cement the relationships between tables.

## Adding a Condition to a Joined Query

Of course, you can still use the WHERE clause to limit which records are shown. Use the AND structure to build compound conditions. For example, this code returns the code name and operation name of every agent whose code name begins with B:

```
SELECT
  agent.name AS 'agent',
  operation.name AS 'operation',
FROM
  agent, operation
WHERE
  agent.operationID = operation.operationID
AND agent.name LIKE 'B%';
```

## THE TRUTH ABOUT INNER JOINS

**You should know that the syntax I provided here is a convenient shortcut supported by most DBMS systems. The inner join's formal syntax looks like this:**

```
SELECT agent.name, operation.name
FROM
agent INNER JOIN operation
ON agent.OperationID = operation.OperationID ORDER BY agent.name;
```

**Many data programmers prefer to think of the join as part of the WHERE clause and use the WHERE syntax. A few SQL databases (notably many offerings from Microsoft) do not allow the WHERE syntax for inner joins and require the INNER JOIN to be specified as part of the FROM clause. When you use this INNER JOIN syntax, the ON clause indicates how the tables will be joined.**

## Creating a View to Store a Join

Very often, you'll use a query to link up two (or more) tables that have been broken up by the normalization process. The VIEW statement that simplifies SQL functions can also be used to encode joins and make them easier to work with:

```
#######################################
# build agent operation view
#######################################
CREATE VIEW agentOpView AS
SELECT
  agent.name AS 'agent',
  operation.name AS 'operation',
  operation.description AS 'task',
  operation.location AS 'location'
FROM
  agent, operation
WHERE
  agent.operationID = operation.operationID;
```

This code is just an SQL SELECT statement linking together the agent and operation tables. I embedded the query in a CREATE VIEW structure, naming the view agentOpView. Notice that all the data fields (but none of the keys) are available in the views, and I gave names to each field that hide the original table relationship. When you run this code, your database will show a 'view', which looks a lot like a table. You can run a query on it, as shown in Table 11.17.

```
SELECT * FROM agentOpView
```

| | TABLE 11.17 | RUNNING THE AGENTOPVIEW | | |
|---|---|---|---|---|
| agent | age | operation | task | location |
| Bond | 46 years, 11 months | Dancing Elephant | Infiltrate suspicious zoo | London |
| Falcon | 33 years, 2 months | Dancing Elephant | Infiltrate suspicious zoo | London |
| Cardinal | 29 years, 6 months | Enduring Angst | Make bad guys feel really guilty | Lower Volta |
| Blackford | 51 years, 9 months | Enduring Angst | Make bad guys feel really guilty | Lower Volta |
| Rahab | 26 years, 10 months | Furious Dandelion | Plant crabgrass in enemy lawns | East Java |

With `agentOpView` in place, I can run queries against `agentOpView` as if it were a real table. The view doesn't really hold any data at all. It's just a placeholder for the query that joins up the two tables. But it's as easy to use as a real table, so you can do `SELECT` queries on the view as if it were a real table:

```
SELECT agent, location FROM agentOpView WHERE operation LIKE 'E%';
```

Views hide the join to make the data easier to use. Of course, you can't do `INSERT` or `UPDATE` queries on a view, because it doesn't really hold any data. Still, views make normalized data a lot easier to use than it used to be.

It's interesting that the outcome of this view is looking very much like the original `badSpy` database (at least to the end user) but the data underneath is much safer and better organized than it was in the original data structure.

## BUILDING A LINK TABLE FOR MANY-TO-MANY RELATIONSHIPS

Once you've created an ER diagram, you can create new tables to handle all the one-to-many relationships. It's a little less obvious what to do with many-to-many relationships, such as the link between agents and skills. Recall that each agent can have many skills, and several agents can use each skill. The best way to handle this kind of situation is to build a special kind of table.

## Enhancing the ER Diagram

Figure 11.3 shows a new version of the ER diagram that eliminates all many-to-many relationships.

**FIGURE 11.3**

This improved ER diagram uses a link table.

The ER diagram in Figure 11.3 improves on the earlier version shown in Figure 11.2 in a number of ways.

- I added (PK) to the end of every primary key.
- I added (FK) to the end of every foreign key.
- The placements of the lines in the diagram are now much more important. I now draw a line only between a foreign key reference and the corresponding primary key in the other table. Every relationship should go between a foreign key reference in one table and a primary key in the other.
- The other main improvement is the addition of the agent_specialty table. This table is interesting because it contains nothing but primary and foreign keys. Each entry in this table represents one link between the agent and specialty tables. All the actual data

referring to the agent or specialty are encoded in other tables. This arrangement provides a great deal of flexibility.

 **TRICK** Most tables in a relational database are about entities in the data set, but link tables are about relationships between entities.

## Creating the specialty Table

The `specialty` table is simple, as shown in Table 11.18.

| specialtyID | name |
|---|---|
| 1 | Electronics |
| 2 | Counterintelligence |
| 3 | Sabatoge |
| 4 | Doily Design |
| 5 | Explosives |
| 6 | Flower Arranging |

TABLE 11.18 THE SPECIALTY TABLE

As you can see, there is nothing in the `specialty` table that connects it directly with any particular agent. Likewise, you find no references to specialties in the `agent` table. The complex relationship between these two tables is handled by the new `agent_specialty` table.

```
CREATE TABLE agent_specialty (
  agent_specialtyID int(11) NOT NULL AUTO_INCREMENT,
  agentID int(11) default NULL,
  specialtyID int(11) default NULL,
  PRIMARY KEY (agent_specialtyID),
  FOREIGN KEY (agentID) REFERENCES agent (agentID),
  FOREIGN KEY (specialtyID) REFERENCES specialty (specialtyID)
);
```

This is called a link table because it manages relationships between other tables. Table 11.19 shows a sample set of data in the `agent_specialty` table.

| agent specialty ID | agent ID | specialty ID |
|---|---|---|
| TABLE 11.19 THE AGENT SPECIALTY TABLE | | |
| 1 | 1 | 2 |
| 2 | 1 | 3 |
| 3 | 2 | 1 |
| 4 | 2 | 6 |
| 5 | 3 | 2 |
| 6 | 4 | 4 |
| 7 | 4 | 5 |

## Interpreting the agent_specialty Table with a Query

Of course, the agent_specialty table is not directly useful to the user, because it contains nothing but foreign key references. You can translate the data to something more meaningful with an SQL statement:

```
SELECT
  agent.name as 'Agent',
  specialty.name as 'Specialty'
FROM
  agent, specialty, agent_specialty
WHERE agent.agentID = agent_specialty.agentID
  AND specialty.specialtyID = agent_specialty.specialtyID;
```

It requires two comparisons to join the three tables. It is necessary to forge the relationship between agent and agent_specialty by common agentID values. It's also necessary to secure the bond between specialty and agent_specialty by comparing the specialtyID fields. The results of such a query show that the correct relationships have indeed been joined, as you can see in Table 11.20.

The link table provides the linkage between tables that have many-to-many relationships. Each time you want a new relationship between an agent and a specialty, you add a new record to the agent_specialty table.

| TABLE 11.20 | QUERY INTERPRETATION OF AGENT_SPECIALTY TABLE |
|---|---|
| **Agent** | **Specialty** |
| Bond | Counterintelligence |
| Bond | Sabatoge |
| Falcon | Electronics |
| Falcon | Flower Arranging |
| Cardinal | Counterintelligence |
| Blackford | Doily Design |
| Blackford | Explosives |

## Building a View for the Link Table

Many-to-many joins are complex enough that they deserve their own view as well.

```
###########################################
# build agentSpecialty view
###########################################
DROP VIEW IF EXISTS agentSpecialtyView;

CREATE VIEW agentSpecialtyView as
SELECT
  agent.name,
  specialty.name
FROM
  agent, specialty, agent_specialty
WHERE agent.agentID = agent_specialty.agentID
  AND specialty.specialtyID = agent_specialty.specialtyID;
```

You can then use the view to simplify queries. For example, you can determine which agents know flower arrangement with this query:

```
SELECT
  *
FROM
  agentSpecialtyView
WHERE
  specialty LIKE 'FLOWER%';
```

(You know, flower arrangement can be a deadly art in the hands of a skilled practitioner.)

## SUMMARY

In this chapter you moved beyond programming to an understanding of data, the real fuel of modern applications. You learned how to take a poorly designed table and convert it into a series of well-organized tables that can avoid many data problems. You learned about three stages of normalization and how to build an Entity Relationship diagram. You can now recognize three kinds of relationships between entities and build normalized tables in SQL, including pointers for primary and foreign keys. You can connect normalized tables with INNER JOIN SQL statements. You know how to simulate a many-to-many relationship by building a link table. You learned how to build views to simplify working with functions and joins. The civilized world is safer for your efforts.

### CHALLENGES

1. Locate ER diagrams for data you commonly work with. Examine these documents and see if you can make sense of them.
2. Examine a database you use regularly. Determine if it follows the requirements stated in this chapter for a well-designed data structure. If not, explain what might be wrong with the data structure and how it might be corrected.
3. Design an improved data structure for the database you examined in question 2. Create the required tables in SQL and populate them with sample data.
4. Design a database to describe data for a programming problem. (Be warned, most data problems are a lot more complex than they first appear.) Create a data diagram, then build the tables and populate them with sample data.

# BUILDING A THREE-TIERED DATA APPLICATION

This book begins by looking at HTML pages, which are essentially static documents. It then reveals how to generate dynamic pages with the powerful PHP language. The last few chapters showed how to use a database management system such as MySQL to build powerful data structures. This chapter ties together the PHP programming and data programming aspects to build a full-blown data-management system for any database. The system you learn can easily be expanded to any kind of data project you can think of, including e-commerce applications. Specifically, you learn how to:

- Design a moderate-to-large data application
- Build a library of reusable data functions
- Optimize functions for use across data sets
- Include library files in your programs

There isn't really much new PHP or MySQL code to learn in this chapter. The focus is on building a larger project with minimum effort.

## INTRODUCING THE dbMASTER PROGRAM

The dbMaster program is a suite of PHP programs that allows access to the spy database created in Chapter 11, "Data Normalization." While the database created in that chapter is flexible and powerful, it is not easy to use unless you know

SQL. Even if your users do understand SQL, you don't want them to have direct control of a database, because too many things can go wrong.

You need to build some sort of front-end application to the database. In essence, this system has three levels.

- The client computer handles communication with the user.
- The database server (MySQL) manages the data.
- The PHP program acts as interpreter between the client and database. PHP provides the bridge between the client's HTML language and the database's SQL language.

This kind of arrangement is frequently called a three-tier architecture. As you examine the dbMaster program throughout this chapter, you learn some of the advantages of this particular approach.

One of the most important ideas in the dbMaster system is the complete separation of programming from data. You can use exactly the same system of programs to manage any database you want, just by changing a few variables. The system tries hard to extract everything it needs from the database itself. dbMaster can be the foundation of any data application you might want to begin.

## Viewing the Main Screen

Start by looking at the program from the user's point of view, as shown in Figure 12.1.

**FIGURE 12.1**

Select a query for quick access to data results.

Databases often have two or more very distinct levels of users. You might allow anyone to view data in the database, but you'll generally want to restrict access to manipulating the data: adding values, updating records, and deleting data.

The main page has two sections: an open section for viewing queries and a password-protected section for managing the data directly.

The first part of the form is a list of data requests. Each of these requests maps to a query.

## Viewing the Results of a Query

When the user selects a query and presses the Submit button, a screen like the one in Figure 12.2 appears.

**FIGURE 12.2**

You can quickly get the results of any query from the first page.

The queries are all prebuilt, which means the user cannot make a mistake by typing in inappropriate SQL code. This feature protects the data integrity and eliminates problems like SQL injection, but it limits access to a preset number of queries. Fortunately, the database administrator can add new queries easily. It's up to the administrator to create queries to solve particular problems. Fortunately, this is usually done quite easily.

## Viewing Table Data

The other part of the main screen (shown again in Figure 12.3) allows the user to directly manipulate data in the tables. Since this is a more powerful (and thus dangerous) enterprise, access to this part of the system is controlled by a password.

As an example, by selecting the agent table I see a screen like Figure 12.4.

From this screen, the user can see all the data in the chosen table. The page also gives the user links to add, edit, or delete records from the table. This page is automatically created for every table in the database.

## Editing a Record

If the user chooses to edit a record, a screen similar to Figure 12.5 appears.

The Edit Record page has some important features. First, the user cannot directly change the primary key. If she could do so, it would have profound destabilizing consequences on the database. Also note the way the `operationID` field is presented. The field itself is a primary key with an integer value, but it would be very difficult for a user to directly manipulate the integer values. Instead, the program provides a drop-down list of operations. When the user chooses from this list, the appropriate numerical index is sent to the next page.

**FIGURE 12.5**

The user can edit a record easily.

## Confirming the Record Update

When the user clicks the button, a new screen appears and announces the successful update as in Figure 12.6.

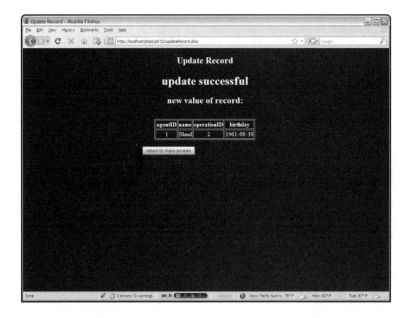

FIGURE 12.6

The update is
confirmed.

## Adding a Record

Adding a record to the table is a multistep process, much like editing a record. The first page
(shown in Figure 12.7) allows you to enter data in all the appropriate fields.

FIGURE 12.7

The Add Record
page includes a list
box for foreign key
references.

Like the Edit Record screen, the Add Record page does not allow the user to directly enter a primary key. This page also automatically generates drop-down SELECT boxes for foreign key fields like operationID.

## Processing the Add

When the user chooses to process the add, another page confirms the add (or describes the failure, if it cannot add the record). This confirmation page is shown in Figure 12.8.

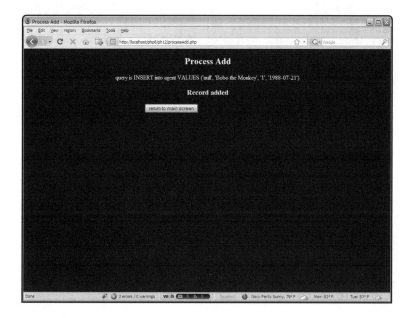

FIGURE 12.8

The user has successfully added an agent.

## Deleting a Record

The user can also choose to delete a record from the Edit Table page. This action results in the basic screen shown in Figure 12.9.

**TRICK**  You can tell from this example why it's so important to have a script for generating sample data. I had to delete and modify records several times when I was testing the system. After each test I easily restored the database to a stable condition by reloading the buildSpy.sql file with the MySQL SOURCE command.

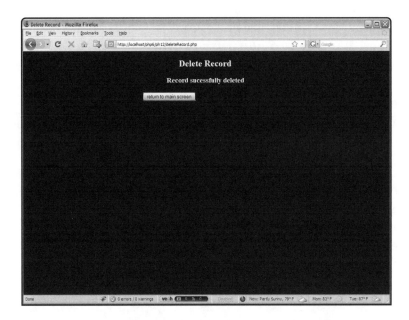

**FIGURE 12.9**

Deleting a record
is also very simple.

## BUILDING THE DESIGN OF THE SPYMASTER SYSTEM

It can be intimidating to think of all the operations in the SpyMaster system. The program has a lot of functionality. It could be overwhelming to start coding this system without some sort of strategic plan.

### Creating a State Diagram

Complex programming problems have many approaches. For this particular problem, I decided to concentrate on the flow of data through a series of modules. Figure 12.10 shows my overall strategy.

**FIGURE 12.10**

Simple state
diagram of the
dbMaster system.

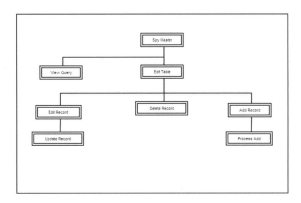

The illustration in Figure 12.10 is sometimes called a *state diagram*. This kind of illustration identifies what particular problems need to be solved and indicates modules that might be able to solve these problems.

I began the process by thinking about everything that a data-management system should be able to do. Each major idea is broken into a module. A module often represents a single functional entity, related to solving a specific problem. A PHP program often (although not always) supports each PHP page.

## The View Query Module

Obviously, users should be able to get queries from the database. This is one of the most common tasks of the system. I decided that the View Query module should be able to view any query sent to it and display an appropriate result.

## The Edit Table Module

The other primary task in a data system is data definition, which includes adding new records, deleting records, and updating information. This kind of activity can be destructive, so it should be controlled using some kind of access system. All data definition is based on the database's underlying table structure, so it is important to allow the three main kinds of data manipulation (editing, deletion, and updating) on each table.

The Edit Table module provides the interface to these behaviors. It shows all the current records in a table and lets the user edit or delete any particular record. It also has a button that allows the user to add a new record to this table. It's important to see that Edit Table doesn't actually cause anything to change in the database. Instead, it serves as a gateway to several other editing modules.

## The Edit Record and Update Record Modules

If you look back at the state diagram, you see the Edit Table module leading to three other modules. The Edit Record module shows one record and allows the user to edit the data in the record. However, the database isn't actually updated until the user submits changes, so editing a record is a two-step process. After the user determines changes in the Edit Record module, program control moves on to the Update Record module, which actually processes the request and makes the change to the database.

## The Add Record and Process Add Modules

Adding a record is similar to editing, as it requires two passes. The first module (Add Record) generates a form that allows the user to input the new record details. Once the user has determined the record data, the Process Add module creates and implements the SQL necessary to incorporate the new record in the table.

## The Delete Record Module

Deleting a record is a simple process. There's no need for any other user input, so it requires only one module to process a deletion request.

## DESIGNING THE SYSTEM

The state diagram is very helpful, because it allows you to see an overview of the entire process. More planning is still necessary, however, because the basic state diagram leaves a lot of questions unanswered. For example:

- Will the Edit Table module have to be repeated for each table?
- If so, will I also need copies of all other editing modules?
- Can I automate the process?
- What if the underlying data structure is changed?
- What if I want to apply a similar structure to another database?
- How can I allow queries to be added to the system?

## Why Make It so Complicated?

It is tempting to write a system specifically to manage the spy database. The advantage of such a system is that it will know exactly how to handle issues relevant to the spy system. For example, operationID is a foreign key reference in the agent table, so it should be selected by a drop-down list whenever possible. If you build a specific module to handle editing the agent table, you can make this happen.

However, this process quickly becomes unwieldy if you have several tables. Essentially, you'd need add, update, and delete modules for each table, which will really add up.

It is better to have a smart procedure that can build an edit screen for any table in the database. It would be even better if your program could automatically detect foreign key fields and produce the appropriate user-interface element (an HTML SELECT clause) when needed. In fact, you could build an entire library of generic routines that could work with any database. That's exactly the approach I chose. It's a little more work to prepare the generic functions, but that effort pays off when you can create a system for a new database in just a few minutes.

## Building a Library of Functions

Although the dbMaster system is the largest example in this book, most of it is surprisingly simple. The system's centerpiece is a file called dbLib.php. This file is not meant to run in the user's browser at all. Instead, it contains a library of functions that simplify coding of any database. I stored as much of the PHP code as I could in this library. All the other PHP programs in the system make use of the various functions in the library. This approach has a number of advantages:

- The overall code size is smaller since code does not need to be repeated.
- If I want to improve a module, I do it once in the library rather than in several places.
- It is extremely simple to modify the code library so it works with another database.
- The details of each particular module are hidden in a separate library so I can focus on the bigger picture when writing each PHP page.
- The routines can be reused to work with any table in the database.
- The routines can automatically adjust to changes in the data structure.
- I included all the PHP pages needed for basic operation.
- The functions can be easily reused for more project-specific PHP pages.
- The library can be readily reused for another project.

Figure 12.11 shows a more detailed state diagram.

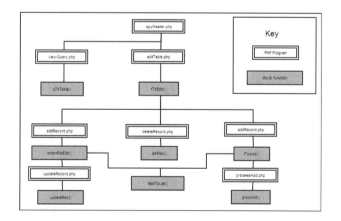

**FIGURE 12.11**

Detailed view of the state diagram.

When you begin looking at actual code, you'll see most of the PHP programs are extremely simple. They usually just collect data for a library function, send program control off to that function, and then print any output produced by the function.

## WRITING THE NON-LIBRARY CODE

I begin here by describing all the parts of this project except the library. The library module is driven by the needs of the other PHP programs, so it makes sense to look at the other programs first.

### Preparing the Database

The database for this segment is almost the same as the one used in Chapter 11. I added one table to store queries. All other tables are the same as those in Chapter 11. The SQL script that creates this new version of the spy database is available on the CD as buildSpy.sql.

Note I have modified the database slightly from Chapter 11, because the new version includes several queries as part of the data! In order to make the program reasonably secure, I don't want typical users to be able to make queries. I also don't want users to be limited to the few queries I thought of when building this system. One solution is to store a set of queries in the database and let appropriate users (those with the special password) modify the queries. I called my new table the storedQuery table. It can be manipulated in the system just like the other tables, so a user with password access can add, edit, and delete queries. If you don't have the admin password, you're limited to using the queries that have already been defined. Here is the additional code used to build the storedQuery table:

```
##########################################
# build storedQuery table
##########################################
DROP TABLE if exists storedQuery;
CREATE TABLE storedQuery (
  storedQueryID int(11) NOT NULL AUTO_INCREMENT,
  description varchar(30),
  text TEXT,
  PRIMARY KEY (storedQueryID)
);

INSERT INTO storedQuery VALUES (
  null,
  'agent info',
  'SELECT * FROM agent'
);
```

The storedQuery table has three fields. The description field holds a short English description of each query. The text field holds the query's actual SQL code. Note that the text field is of the special `TEXT` data type. I did this because queries are sometimes longer than the 255 character maximum of `varchar` fields.

## Examining the spyMaster.php Program

The `dbMaster.php` program is the entry point into the system. All access to the system comes from this page. It has two main parts. One handles queries from ordinary users, and the other allows more sophisticated access by authorized users. Each segment encapsulates an HTML form that sends a request to a particular PHP program. The first segment has a small amount of PHP code that sets up the query list box.

**TRAP**    Proper SQL syntax is extremely important when you store SQL syntax inside an SQL database as I'm doing here. It's especially important to keep track of single and double quotation marks. To include the single quotation marks that some queries require, precede the mark with a backslash character. For example, assume I want to store the following query:

```
SELECT * FROM agent WHERE agent.name = 'Bond';
```

I would actually store this text instead:

```
SELECT * FROM agent WHERE agent.name = \'Bond\'
```

## Creating the Query Form

```
<!DOCTYPE html PUBLIC "-//W3C//DTD XHTML 1.0 Strict//EN"
"http://www.w3.org/TR/xhtml1/DTD/xhtml1-strict.dtd">
<html lang="EN" dir="ltr" xmlns="http://www.w3.org/1999/xhtml">
<head>
<title>Spy Master Main Page</title>
<?php include "dbLib.php"; ?>

</head>
<body>
  <h1>Spy Master</h1>
<form action = "viewQuery.php"
      method = "post">
  <fieldset>
    <h2>View Data</h2>
    <select name = "queryID" size = "10">
    <?php
//get queries from storedQuery table
```

```
$dbConn = connectToDb();
$query = "SELECT * from storedQuery";
$result = mysql_query($query, $dbConn);
while($row = mysql_fetch_assoc($result)){
  $currentQuery = $row['storedQueryID'];
  $theDescription = $row['description'];
  print <<<HERE
      <option value = "$currentQuery">$theDescription</option>

HERE;
  } // end while
?>
    </select>
    <button type = "submit">
       execute request
    </button>
  </fieldset>
</form>
```

Most of the code is ordinary HTML. The HTML code establishes a form that calls viewQuery.php when the user presses the Submit button. I added some PHP code that generates a special input box based on the entries in the storedQuery table. That form comprises the top part of Figure 12.1.

## Including the dbLib Library

The first thing to notice is the include() statement. This command allows you to import another file. PHP reads that file and interprets it as HTML. An included file can contain HTML, cascading style sheets (CSS), or PHP code. Most of the functionality for the spy data program is stored in the dbLib.php library program.

 **TIP** I placed the include statement in its own php segment, so the library files are loaded into the HTML header. I did this so I could incorporate the CSS file in the library, and not have to include the CSS in each individual PHP program.

All the other PHP programs in the system begin by including dbLib.php. Once this is done, every function in the library can be accessed as if it were a locally defined function. This provides tremendous power and flexibility to a programming system.

I put all the files in the same directory for this example program, but in actual deployment, it's best to move your library files off of the server path. Your PHP code with passwords isn't available for bad guys to see. Just change your `include` statement to reflect the local path to your library file. For example: `include "/usr/aharris/libraries/dbLib.php"` grabs the file from a directory called `libraries` that is outside of my normal `htdocs` path.

## Connecting to the spy Database

The utility of the `dbLib` library becomes immediately apparent as I connect to the spy database. Rather than worrying about exactly what database I'm connecting to, I simply defer to the `connectToDb()` function in `dbLib()`. In the current code I don't need to worry about the details of connecting to the database. With a library I can write the connecting code one time and reuse that function as needed.

Look back at the `spymaster.php` code shown above. Notice the `connectToSpy()` function returns a data connection pointer I can use for other database activities.

 There's another advantage to using a library when connecting to a database. It's likely that if you move this code to another system you'll have a different way to log in to the data server. If the code for connecting to the server is centralized, it only needs to be changed in one place when you want to update the code. This is far more efficient than searching through dozens of programs to find every reference to the `mysql_connect()` function. Also, if you want to convert the MySQL-based code in this book to SQLite or another database system, you only have to change the `connectToSpy()` function. That's pretty cool, huh?

## Retrieving the Queries

I decided to encode a series of prepackaged queries into a table. (I explain more about my reasons for this in the section on the `viewQuery` program.) The main form must present a list of query descriptions and let the user select one of these queries. I use an SQL `SELECT` statement to extract everything from the `storedQuery` table. I then use the description and text fields from `storedQuery` to build a multiline list box. Each item shows a description of a query and presents a primary key to the next program so the program can look up the query in the database and execute it.

## Creating the Edit Table Form

The second half of the `spyMaster` program presents all the tables in the database and allows the user to choose a table for later editing. Most of the functionality in the system comes through this section. Surprisingly, there is no PHP code at all in this particular part of the page. An HTML form sends the user to the editTable.php program.

```
<form action = "editTable.php"
      method = "post">
  <fieldset>
    <h2>Edit / Delete table data</h2>
    <label>Password</label>
    <input type = "password"
           name = "pwd"
           value = "absolute" />

    <select name = "tableName"
            size = "5">
      <option value = "agent">agents</option>
      <option value = "specialty">specialties</option>
      <option value = "operation">operations</option>
      <option value = "agent_specialty">agent_specialty</option>
      <option value = "storedQuery">storedQuery</option>
    </select>

    <button type = "submit">
      edit table
    </button>
  </fieldset>

</form>

</body>
</html>
```

TRICK

To make debugging easier, I preloaded the password field with the appropriate password. In a production environment, you should, of course, leave the password field blank so the user cannot get into the system without the password.

## Building the viewQuery.php Program

When the user chooses a query, program control is sent to the viewQuery.php program. This program does surprisingly little on its own:

```
<!DOCTYPE html PUBLIC "-//W3C//DTD XHTML 1.0 Strict//EN"
"http://www.w3.org/TR/xhtml1/DTD/xhtml1-strict.dtd">
<html lang="EN" dir="ltr" xmlns="http://www.w3.org/1999/xhtml">
<head>
<title>View Query</title>
<?php include "dbLib.php"; ?>

</head>
<body>

<h1>Query Results</h1>

<?php

$dbConn = connectToDb();

//get $queryID from previous form
$queryID = filter_input(INPUT_POST, "queryID");
$queryID = mysql_real_escape_string($queryID);

//use the queryID to get the requested query from the database
$sql = "SELECT * FROM storedQuery WHERE storedQuery.storedQueryID = $queryID";
$result = mysql_query($sql) or die (mysql_error());
$row = mysql_fetch_assoc($result);

$theQuery = $row["text"];
//print "Query: $theQuery";

print qToTable($theQuery);

print mainButton();

?>

</body>
</html>
```

Once `viewQuery.php` connects to the library, it uses functions in the library to connect to the database. It then extracts the `$queryID` value from the preceding form, and uses that value to get the actual query from the database (remember, the queries are just text stored in the database). The query is then passed to the `qToTable()` function, which does most of the actual work. It takes whatever query is passed to it and returns the result of that query as XHTML output.

---

## WHY STORE QUERIES IN THE DATABASE?

You might wonder why I chose to store queries in the database. After all, I could have let the user type in a query directly or provided some form that allows the user to search for certain values. Either of these approaches has advantages, but they also pose some risks. It's very dangerous to allow direct access to your data from a web form. Malicious users can introduce Trojan horse commands that snoop on your data, change data, or even delete information from the database.

I sometimes build a form that has enough information to create an SQL query and then build that query in a client-side form. (Sounds like a good end-of-chapter exercise, right?) In this case, I stored queries in another table. People with administrative access can add new queries to the database, but ordinary users do not. I preloaded the `storedQuery` database with a number of useful queries, then added the capacity to add new queries whenever the situation demands it. Drawbacks remain (primarily that ordinary users cannot build custom queries), but it is far more secure than a system that builds a query based on user input.

This technique is also useful for older versions of MySQL that didn't have views. No matter how complex the queries become, I only have to write them one time and then store them in the database. The query becomes part of the data. Of course, if you're using a recent version of MySQL, your queries can incorporate views as well as tables, but they're still stored with the data.

---

The `str_replace()` function is necessary because SQL queries contain single quotation mark (') characters. When I store a query as a VARCHAR entity, the single quotation marks embedded in the query cause problems. The normal solution to this problem is to use a backslash, which indicates that the mark should not be immediately interpreted, but should be considered a part of the data. The problem with this is the backslash is still in the string when I try to execute the query. The `str_replace()` function replaces all instances of \' with a simple single quote ('). Note that the `qToTable()` function doesn't actually print anything to the screen. All it does is build a complex string of HTML code. The `viewQuery.php` program prints the code to the screen.

**TRICK** As a general rule, library code should not print anything directly to the screen. Instead, it should return a value to whatever program called it. This allows multiple uses for the data. For example, if the `qToTable()` function printed directly to the screen, you could not use it to generate a file. Since the library code returns a value but doesn't actually do anything with that value, the code that calls the function has the freedom to use the results in multiple ways.

The `mainButton()` function produces a simple XHTML form that directs the user back to the `spyMaster.php` page. Even though the code for this is relatively simple, it is repeated so often that it makes sense to store it in a function rather than copying and pasting it in every page of the system.

## Viewing the editTable.php Program

The `editTable.php` follows a familiar pattern. It has a small amount of PHP code, but most of the real work is sent off to a library function. This module's main job is to check for an administrative password. If the user does not have the appropriate password, further access to the system is blocked. If the user does have the correct password, the very powerful `tToEdit()` function provides access to the add, edit, and delete functions.

```
<!DOCTYPE html PUBLIC "-//W3C//DTD XHTML 1.0 Strict//EN"
"http://www.w3.org/TR/xhtml1/DTD/xhtml1-strict.dtd">
<html lang="EN" dir="ltr" xmlns="http://www.w3.org/1999/xhtml">
<head>
<title>Edit table</title>
<?php include("dbLib.php"); ?>
</head>

<body>
<h1>Edit Table</h1>

<?php

//check password
```

```
$pwd = filter_input(INPUT_POST, "pwd");
$tableName = filter_input(INPUT_POST, "tableName");

if ($pwd == $adminPassword){
  $dbConn = connectToDb();

  //sanitize $tableName before using it in SQL
  $tableName = mysql_real_escape_string($tableName);

  print tToEdit("$tableName");
} else {
  print "<h2>You must have administrative access to proceed</h2>\n";
} // end if
print mainButton();

?>
</body>
</html>
```

The $pwd value comes from a field in the spyMaster.php page. The $adminPassword value is stored in dbLibrary.php. (The default admin password is absolute, but you can change it to whatever you want by editing dbLib.php.) Remember that since $tableName will be used in an SQL query, it should be sanitized with the mysql_real_escape_string() function.

## Viewing the editRecord.php Program

The editTable.php program creates a complex form which can be used to edit or delete records, or add a new record to a particular table.

When the user chooses to edit a record (by pressing the Edit button in the record's row), the editRecord.php program is called. This program expects parameters called $tableName, $keyName, and $keyVal. These variables, automatically provided by tToEdit(), help editRecord build a query that returns whatever record the user selects. (You can read ahead to the description of tToEdit() for details on how this works.)

```
<!DOCTYPE html PUBLIC "-//W3C//DTD XHTML 1.0 Strict//EN"
"http://www.w3.org/TR/xhtml1/DTD/xhtml1-strict.dtd">
<html lang="EN" dir="ltr" xmlns="http://www.w3.org/1999/xhtml">
<head>
<title>Edit Record</title>
```

```php
<?php include "dbLib.php"; ?>
</head>
<body>
<h1>Edit Record</h1>
<?php

$dbConn = connectToDb();

// expects $tableName, $keyName, $keyVal
$tableName = filter_input(INPUT_POST, "tableName");
$keyName = filter_input(INPUT_POST, "keyName");
$keyVal = filter_input(INPUT_POST, "keyVal");


$tableName = mysql_real_escape_string($tableName);
$keyName = mysql_real_escape_string($keyName);
$keyVal = mysql_real_escape_string($keyVal);


$query = "SELECT * FROM $tableName WHERE $keyName = $keyVal";

//print rToEdit($query);
print smartRToEdit($query);
print mainButton();

?>
</body>
</html>
```

The editRecord.php program retrieves values from the previous form and uses them to build a query. This query is then passed to the smartRToEdit() library function. This function takes the single-record query and returns HTML code that lets the user appropriately update the record.

## Viewing the updateRecord.php Program

The smartRToEdit() function calls another PHP program called updateRecord.php. This program calls a library function that actually commits the user's changes to the database.

```
<!DOCTYPE html PUBLIC "-//W3C//DTD XHTML 1.0 Strict//EN"
"http://www.w3.org/TR/xhtml1/DTD/xhtml1-strict.dtd">
```

```
<html lang="EN" dir="ltr" xmlns="http://www.w3.org/1999/xhtml">
<head>
<title>Update Record</title>
<?php include "dbLib.php"; ?>
</head>

<body>

<h2>Update Record</h2>
<?php
$dbConn = connectToDb();

$fieldNames = "";
$fieldValues = "";

foreach ($_REQUEST as $fieldName => $value){
  if ($fieldName == "tableName"){
    $theTable = $value;
  } else {

    $fieldName = mysql_real_escape_string($fieldName);
    $value = mysql_real_escape_string($value);

    $fields[] = $fieldName;
    $values[] = $value;
  } // end if
} // end foreach

print updateRec($theTable, $fields, $values);

print mainButton();

?>
</body>
</html>
```

It is more convenient for the updateRec() function if the field names and values are sent as arrays. Therefore, the PHP code in updateRecord.php converts the $_REQUEST array to an array of fields and another array of values. These two arrays are passed to the updateRec() function, which processes them. Of course, any variables coming from a form that will be used in SQL statements are passed through mysql_real_escape_string() to protect against attack.

## Viewing the deleteRecord.php Program

The deleteRecord.php program acts in a now-familiar manner. It mainly serves as a wrapper for a function in the dbLib library. In this particular case, the program simply retrieves variables from the previous form, cleans them up, and sends these values (the name of the current table, the name of the key field, and the value of the current record's key) to the delRec() function. That function deletes the record and returns a message regarding the success or failure of the operation.

```
<!DOCTYPE html PUBLIC "-//W3C//DTD XHTML 1.0 Strict//EN"
"http://www.w3.org/TR/xhtml1/DTD/xhtml1-strict.dtd">
<html lang="EN" dir="ltr" xmlns="http://www.w3.org/1999/xhtml">
<head>
<title>Delete Record</title>
<?php include("dbLib.php"); ?>
</head>
<body>
<h2>Delete Record</h2>
<?php
$dbConn = connectToDb();

//retrieve data
$tableName = filter_input(INPUT_POST, "tableName");
$keyName = filter_input(INPUT_POST, "keyName");
$keyVal = filter_input(INPUT_POST, "keyVal");


$tableName = mysql_real_escape_string($tableName);
$keyName = mysql_real_escape_string($keyName);
$keyVal = mysql_real_escape_string($keyVal);



print delRec($tableName, $keyName, $keyVal);
print mainButton();
?>
```

```
</body>
</html>
```

## Viewing the addRecord.php Program

Adding a record, which requires two distinctive steps, is actually much like editing a record. The addRecord.php program calls the tToAdd() function, which builds a form allowing the user to add data to whichever table is currently selected. It isn't necessary to send any information except the name of the table to this function, because tToAdd() automatically generates the key value.

```
<!DOCTYPE html PUBLIC "-//W3C//DTD XHTML 1.0 Strict//EN"
"http://www.w3.org/TR/xhtml1/DTD/xhtml1-strict.dtd">
<html lang="EN" dir="ltr" xmlns="http://www.w3.org/1999/xhtml">
<head>
<?php include "dbLib.php"; ?>
<title>Add a Record</title>
</head>
<body>
<h2>Add Record</h2>
<?php

$dbConn = connectToDb();

$tableName = filter_input(INPUT_POST, "tableName");
$tableName = mysql_real_escape_string($tableName);

print tToAdd($tableName);
print mainButton();

?>

</body>
</html>
```

## Viewing the processAdd.php Program

The tToAdd() function called by the addRecord.php program doesn't actually add a record. Instead, it places an HTML form on the screen that allows the user to enter the data for a new record. When the user submits this form, he is passed to the processAdd.php program, which calls procAdd() in the library code. The procAdd() function generates the appropriate SQL code to add the new record to the table. In order to do this, procAdd() needs to know the field names and values. The names and values are passed to the function in arrays just like in updateRecord.php.

```
<!DOCTYPE html PUBLIC "-//W3C//DTD XHTML 1.0 Strict//EN"
"http://www.w3.org/TR/xhtml1/DTD/xhtml1-strict.dtd">
<html lang="EN" dir="ltr" xmlns="http://www.w3.org/1999/xhtml">
<head>
<?php include "dbLib.php"; ?>
<title>Process Add</title>
</head>
<body>
<h2>Process Add</h2>
<?php

$dbConn = connectToDb();

$fieldNames = "";
$fieldValues = "";

foreach ($_REQUEST as $fieldName => $value){
  if ($fieldName == "tableName"){
    $theTable = $value;
  } else {

    $fieldName = mysql_real_escape_string($fieldName);
    $value = mysql_real_escape_string($value);

    $fields[] = $fieldName;
    $values[] = $value;
  } // end if
} // end foreach

print procAdd($theTable, $fields, $values);

print mainButton();
```

```
?>
</body>
</html>
```

## CREATING THE dbLib LIBRARY MODULE

Although I have described several PHP programs in this chapter, most of them are simple. The dbLib library code does most of the heavy lifting. Having a library like dbLib makes data programming pretty easy, because you don't have to know all the dbLib details to make it work. All you need is a basic understanding of the functions in the library, what each function expects as input, and what it will produce as output.

Although this library has a good amount of code (over 500 lines, in fact), there are no new concepts in the library code. It's worth looking carefully at this code because it can give you a good idea of how to create your own libraries. You also find there's no better way to understand the library than to dig around under the hood.

### Setting a CSS Style

Some of the simplest elements can have profound effects. One example of this maxim is the storage of a CSS style in the library code. Each program in the system operates using the style specified in the library. This means you can easily change the look and feel of the entire system by manipulating one CSS file, included in the PHP file as ordinary HTML.

```
<link rel = "stylesheet"
      type = "text/css"
      href = "dbLib.css" />
```

**HINT** When you include a file, it is interpreted as HTML, not PHP. This means you can place any HTML code in an include file and it is automatically inserted in your output wherever the include function occurred. I took advantage of this fact to include a CSS block in the library. If you want PHP code in your library file, surround your code with PHP tags (<?php?>) in the library file. I didn't print the CSS code in the book, but be sure to look it over on the CD-ROM if you want to see how I got the visual layout to work.

### Setting Systemwide Variables

Another huge advantage of a library file is the ability to set and use variables that have meaning throughout the entire system. Since each PHP program in the system includes the library, all have access to any variables declared in the library file's main section. Of course, you need to use the global keyword to access a global variable from within a function.

```php
<?php

//variables
$userName = "root";
$dbPass = "xfdaio";
$serverName = "localhost";
$adminPassword = "absolute";
$dbName = "ph_6";
$dbConn = "";
$mainProgram = "spyMaster.php";
```

I stored a few key data points in the system-wide variables. The $userName, $dbPass, and $serverName variables set up the data connection. I did this because I expect people to reuse my library for their own databases. They definitely need to change this information to connect to their own copy of MySQL. It's much safer for them to change this data in variables than in actual program code. If you're writing code for reuse, consider moving anything the code adopter might change into variables.

The $adminPassword variable holds the password used to edit data in the system. Again, I want anybody reusing this library (including me) to change this value without having to dig through the code.

The $mainProgram variable holds the URL of the "control pad" program of the system. In the spy system, I want to provide access to spyMaster.php in every screen. The mainButton() function will use this information to provide a link back to the main page in every screen of the system.

As long as your data is organized according to the guidelines posted later in this chapter (in the section called "Optimizing Your Data"), you can build an entirely new data application from the dbLib program by changing just these variables so the library points to your data on your server. There's no need to edit the PHP at all!

## Connecting to the Database

The connectToDb() function is fundamental to the spy system. It uses system-level variables to generate a database connection. It prints an error message if it is unable to connect to the database. The mysql_error() function prints an SQL error message if the data connection was unsuccessful. This information may not be helpful to the end user, but it might give you some insight as you are debugging the system.

```php
function connectToDb(){
  //connects to the DB
```

```
global $serverName, $userName, $dbPass, $dbName;
$dbConn = mysql_connect($serverName, $userName, $dbPass);
if (!$dbConn){
  print "<h3>problem connecting to database...</h3>\n";
  print "<h3>" . mysql_error() . "</h3> \n";
} // end if

$select = mysql_select_db("$dbName");
if (!$select){
  print "<h3>problem selecting database...</h3>\n";
  print "<h3>" . mysql_error() . "</h3> \n";
} // end if
return $dbConn;
} // end connectToDb
```

The `connectToDb()` function returns a connection to the database that is subsequently used in the many queries passed to the database throughout the system's life span. Since all the details are in variables, you don't need to modify this program at all when you connect to a new database; simply change the access variables.

## Creating a Quick List from a Query

I created a few functions in the `spyMaster` library that didn't get used in the project's final version. The `qToList()` function is a good example. This program takes any SQL query and returns a simply formatted HTML segment describing the data. I find this format useful when debugging because no complex formatting gets in the way.

```
function qToList($query){
  //given a query, makes a quick list of data
  global $dbConn;
  $output = "<p> \n";
  $result = mysql_query($query, $dbConn);

  while ($row = mysql_fetch_assoc($result)){
    foreach ($row as $col=>$val){
      $output .= "$col: $val<br />\n";
    } // end foreach
    $output .= "</p> \n" ;
```

```
  } // end while
  return $output;
} // end qToList
```

Notice that I don't have to worry about sanitizing the data within the library. The various PHP programs will take care of that. By the time a variable gets passed to the library, I can safely assume that it has already been cleaned for SQL use.

## Building an HTML Table from a Query

The `qToTable()` function is a little more powerful than `qToList()`. It can build an HTML table from any valid SQL SELECT statement. The code uses the `mysql_fetch_field()` function to determine field names from the query result. It also steps through each row of the result, printing an HTML row corresponding to the record.

```
function qToTable($query){
  //given a query, automatically creates an HTML table output
  global $dbConn;
  $output = "";
  $result = mysql_query($query, $dbConn);

  $output .= "<table border = '1'>\n";
  //get column headings

  //get field names
  $output .= "<tr>\n";
  while ($field = mysql_fetch_field($result)){
    $output .= "  <th>$field->name</th>\n";
  } // end while
  $output .= "</tr>\n\n";

  //get row data as an associative array
  while ($row = mysql_fetch_assoc($result)){
    $output .= "<tr>\n";
    //look at each field
    foreach ($row as $col=>$val){
      $output .= "  <td>$val</td>\n";
    } // end foreach
    $output .= "</tr>\n\n";
  }// end while
```

```
  $output .= "</table>\n";
  return $output;
} // end qToTable
```

The viewQuery.php program calls the qToTable() function, but it could be used anytime you want an SQL query formatted as an HTML table (which turns out to be quite often).

 If you're following modern web development trends, you might notice that tables are rarely used for layout any more (I've avoided that practice in this book, for example). However, tables aren't evil. They're simply not meant to be general-purpose page layout tools. HTML tables are useful for displaying tabular data, and the results of an SQL query are about as tabular as you can get.

## Building an HTML Table for Editing an SQL Table

If the user has appropriate access, she should be allowed to add, edit, or delete records in any table of the database. While qToTable() is suitable for viewing the results of any SQL query, it does not provide these features. The tToEdit() function is based on qToTable() with a few differences:

- tToEdit() does not accept a query, but the name of a table. You cannot edit joined queries (or views) directly, only tables, so this limitation is sensible. tToEdit() creates a query that returns all records in the specified table.

- In addition to printing the table data, tToEdit() adds two miniature forms to each record.

- One form contains all the data needed by the editRecord.php program to begin the record-editing process.

- The other form added to each record sends all data necessary for deleting a record and calls the deleteRecord.php program.

One more form at the bottom of the HTML table allows the user to add a record to this table. This form contains information that the addRecord.php program needs. The tToEdit() function is really the core of the dbLib toolkit, and it's worth some study.

```
function tToEdit($tableName){
  //given a table name, generates HTML table including
  //add, delete and edit buttons

  $tableName = filter_input(INPUT_POST, "tableName");
  $tableName = mysql_real_escape_string($tableName);
```

```php
global $dbConn;
$output = "";
$query = "SELECT * FROM $tableName";

$result = mysql_query($query, $dbConn);

$output .= "<table border = '1'>\n";
//get column headings

//get field names
$output .= "<tr>\n";
while ($field = mysql_fetch_field($result)){
  $output .= "  <th>$field->name</th>\n";
} // end while

//get name of index field (presuming it's first field)
$keyField = mysql_fetch_field($result, 0);
$keyName = $keyField->name;

//add empty columns for add, edit, and delete
$output .= "<th></th><th></th>\n";
$output .= "</tr>\n\n";

//get row data as an associative array
while ($row = mysql_fetch_assoc($result)){
  $output .= "<tr>\n";
  //look at each field
  foreach ($row as $col=>$val){
    $output .= "  <td>$val</td>\n";
  } // end foreach
  //build little forms for add, delete and edit

  //delete = DELETE FROM <table> WHERE <key> = <keyval>
  $keyVal = $row["$keyName"];
  $output .= <<< HERE

<td>
  <form action = "deleteRecord.php"
```

```
      method = "post">
  <fieldset class = "tiny">
  <input type = "hidden"
       name = "tableName"
       value = "$tableName" />
  <input type= "hidden"
       name = "keyName"
       value = "$keyName" />
  <input type = "hidden"
       name = "keyVal"
       value = "$keyVal" />
  <input type = "submit"
       value = "delete" />
  </fieldset>
  </form>
  </td>

HERE;
    //update: won't update yet, but set up edit form
    $output .= <<< HERE
  <td>
    <form action = "editRecord.php"
        method = "post">
    <fieldset class = "tiny">
    <input type = "hidden"
        name = "tableName"
        value = "$tableName" />
    <input type= "hidden"
        name = "keyName"
        value = "$keyName" />
    <input type = "hidden"
        name = "keyVal"
        value = "$keyVal" />
    <input type = "submit"
        value = "edit" />
  </fieldset>
  </form>
  </td>
```

```
HERE;

    $output .= "</tr>\n\n";

  }// end while

    //add = INSERT INTO <table> {values}
    //set up insert form send table name
    $keyVal = $row["$keyName"];
    $output .= <<< HERE
<tr>
  <td colspan = "6">
    <form action = "addRecord.php"
          method = "post">
    <fieldset class = "tiny">
    <input type = "hidden"
           name = "tableName"
           value = "$tableName" />
    <button type = "submit">
       add a record
    </button>
    </fieldset>
    </form>
  </td>
</tr>
</table>

HERE;


  return $output;
} // end tToEdit
```

Look carefully at the forms for editing and deleting records. These forms contain hidden fields with the table name, key field name, and record number. This information will be used by subsequent functions to build a query specific to the record associated with that particular table row. You may have to look at the XHTML source code that tToEdit() produces to truly understand this function.

This program produces a page with dozens of small forms. The CSS I used for managing larger forms didn't look right with the forms embedded in tables (as most of these are) so I added a tiny class to the fieldset attribute. This allowed me to set up a new CSS rule for displaying tiny forms inside tables. Note also that I used hidden fields to pass data, as I found it more convenient than session variables in this particular instance.

## Creating a Generic Form to Edit a Record

The table created in tToEdit() calls a program called editRecord.php. This program accepts a one-record query. It prints out an HTML table based on the results of that query. The output of rToEdit() is shown in Figure 12.12.

**FIGURE 12.12**

The rToEdit() function is easy to write, but very dangerous.

The rToEdit function produces a very simple HTML form. Every field has a corresponding textbox. The advantage of this approach is that it works with any table. However, the use of this form is quite risky.

- The user should not be allowed to change the primary key, because that would edit some other record, which could have disastrous results.

- The operationID field is a foreign key reference. The only valid entries to this field are integers corresponding to records in the operation table. There's no way for the user to know what operation a particular integer is related to. Worse, she could enter any number (or any text) into the field. The results would be unpredictable, but almost certainly bad.

I fix these defects in the smartRToEdit() function coming up next, but begin by studying this simpler function, because smartRToEdit() is based on rToEdit().

```
function rToEdit ($query){
  //given a one-record query, creates a form to edit that record
  //works on any table, but allows direct editing of keys
  //use smartRToEdit instead if you can

  global $dbConn;
  $output = "";
  $result = mysql_query($query, $dbConn);
  $row = mysql_fetch_assoc($result);

  //get table name from field object
  $fieldObj = mysql_fetch_field($result, 0);
  $tableName = $fieldObj->table;

  $output .= <<< HERE
<form action = "updateRecord.php"
     method = "post">

<fieldset>

  <input type = "hidden"
       name = "tableName"
       value = "$tableName" />

HERE;

  foreach ($row as $col=>$val){
    $output .= <<<HERE
<label>$col</label>
<input type = "text"
       name = "$col"
       value = "$val" />

HERE;
  } // end foreach
```

```
$output .= <<< HERE
<button type = "submit">
  update this record
</button>
</fieldset>
</form>

HERE;
  return $output;
} // end rToEdit
```

> If the ordinary rToEdit() function is so dangerous, you might wonder why I included it at all. The answer is simple. rToEdit will work on absolutely any table in the database. The fancier smartRToEdit() coming up next is safer, but it relies on some assumptions about the design of the data. If you need to build your own data access functions, you can begin with the simpler rToEdit() as a base, and put your own security features in place based on the design of your data.

## Building a Smarter Edit Form

The smartRToEdit() function builds on the basic design of rToEdit() but compensates for a couple of major flaws in the rToEdit() design. Take a look at the smarter code:

```
function smartRToEdit ($query){
  //given a one-record query, creates a form to edit that record
  //Doesn't let user edit first (primary key) field
  //generates dropdown list for foreign keys
  //MUCH safer than ordinary rToEdit function

  // --restrictions on table design--
  //foreign keys MUST be named tableID where 'table' is table name
  //  (because mySQL doesn't recognize foreign key indicators)
  // I also expect a 'name' field in any table used as a foreign key
  //  (for same reason)

  global $dbConn;
  $output = "";
  $result = mysql_query($query, $dbConn);
  $row = mysql_fetch_assoc($result);
```

```
  //get table name from field object
  $fieldObj = mysql_fetch_field($result, 0);
  $tableName = $fieldObj->table;


  $output .= <<< HERE
<form action = "updateRecord.php"
      method = "post">
<fieldset>
  <input type = "hidden"
         name = "tableName"
         value = "$tableName" />
<dl>
HERE;
  $fieldNum = 0;
  foreach ($row as $col=>$val){
    if ($fieldNum == 0){
      //it's primary key.  don't make textbox,
      //but store value in hidden field instead
      //user shouldn't be able to edit primary keys
      $output .= <<<HERE

    <dt>$col</dt>
    <dd>$val
    <input type = "hidden"
           name = "$col"
             value = "$val" /></dd>


HERE;
    } else if (preg_match("/(.*)ID$/", $col, $match)) {
      //it's a foreign key reference
      // get table name (match[1])
      //create a listbox based on table name and its name field
      $valList = fieldToList($match[1],$col, $fieldNum, "name");

      $output .= <<<HERE
    <dt>$col</dt>
```

```
       <dd>$valList</dd>

HERE;

   } else {
     $output .= <<<HERE
   <dt>$col</dt>
   <dd>
   <input type = "text"
          name = "$col"
          value = "$val" /></dd>

HERE;
   } // end if
   $fieldNum++;
 } // end foreach
 $output .= <<< HERE
 </dl>
     <button type = "submit">
         update this record
     </button>
</fieldset>
</form>

HERE;
 return $output;
} // end smartRToEdit
```

What makes this function smart is its ability to examine each field in the record and make a guess about what sort of field it is. Figure 12.13 shows the result of the smartRToEdit() program so you can compare it to the not-so-clever function in Figure 12.12.

## Determining the Field Type

As far as this function is concerned, three field types in a record need to be handled differently.

- **Primary key.** If a field is the primary key, its value needs to be passed on to the next program, but the user should not be able to edit it.

**FIGURE 12.13**

The
smartRtoEdit
function prevents
a lot of possible
mistakes.

- **Foreign key.** If a field is a foreign key reference to another table, the user should only be able to indirectly edit the value. The best approach is to have a drop-down list box that shows values the user will recognize. Each of these values corresponds to a key in that secondary record. For example, in Figure 12.13 there is a list box for the operationID field. The operationID field is a foreign key reference in the agent table. The ordinary rToEdit() function allows the user to type any index number into the textbox without any real indication what data correlates to that index. This version builds a drop-down list showing operation names. The key value associated with those names is stored in the value attribute of each option. (Details to follow in the fieldToList() function.) The user doesn't have to know anything about foreign key references or relational structures—he simply chooses an operation from a list. That list is dynamically generated each time the user chooses to add a record, so it always reflects all the operations in the agency.
- **Neither a primary nor secondary key.** In this case, I print a simple textbox so the user can input the value of the field. In all cases, the output will reflect the current value of the field.

## Working with the Primary Key

The primary key value is much more important to the program than it is to the user. I decided to display it, but not to make it editable in any way. Primary keys should not be edited, but changed only by adding or deleting records.

I relied upon some conventions to determine whether a field is a primary key. I assumed that the first field of the record (field number 0) is the primary key. This is a very common convention, but not universal. Since I created the data design in this case, I can be sure that the number 0 field in every table is the primary key. For that field, I simply printed the field name and value in an ordinary HTML table row. I added the key's value in a hidden field so the next program has access to it.

**TIP**

You can use the `mysql_fetch_field()` function described in Chapter 9 to determine whether a field is a primary key or not. Each field has a "primary_key" identifier which is 1 if the field is a primary key or 0 if not. I have had trouble with this technique working on all databases, so I use the technique described here instead.

## Recognizing Foreign Keys

Unfortunately, there is no reliable way (at least in MySQL) to determine if a field is a foreign key reference. I had to rely on a naming convention to make sure my program recognizes a field as a foreign key reference. I decided that all foreign key fields in my database will have the foreign table's name followed by the value ID. For example, a foreign key reference to the `operation` table will always be called `operationID` in my database.

This is a smart convention to follow anyway, as it makes your field names easy to remember. It becomes critical in `smartRToEdit()` because it's the only way to tell whether a field is a foreign key reference. I used an `else if` clause to check the name of any field that is not the primary key (which was checked in the `if` clause). The `preg_match()` function lets me use a powerful regular expression match to determine the field's name.

**TRICK**

I used this statement to determine whether a field is a foreign key:

```
} else if (preg_match("/(.*)ID$/", $col, $match)) {
```

It uses a simple but powerful regular expression: `/(.*)ID$/`. This expression looks for any line that ends with ID. (Recall that the $ indicates the end of a string.) The .*indicates any number of characters. The parentheses around .* tell PHP to store all the characters before ID into a special array, called $match. Since there's only one pattern to match in this expression, all the characters before ID contain the table name. So, this regular expression takes the name of a field and determines if it ends with ID. If so, the beginning part of the field name (everything but ID) is stored to $match[1]. If $col contains operationID, this line returns TRUE (because operationID ends with ID) and the table name (operation) is stored in $match[1].

## Building the Foreign Key List Box

If a field is a foreign key reference, it is necessary to build a list box containing some sort of meaningful value the user can read. Since I need this capability in a couple of places (and smartRToEdit() is already pretty complex), I build a new function called fieldToList(). This function (explained in detail later in the "Building a List Box from a Field" section of this chapter) builds a drop-down HTML list based on a table and field name. Rather than worrying about the details of the fieldToList() function here, I simply figured out what parameters it would need and printed that function's results.

## Working with Regular Fields

Any field that is not a primary or foreign key is handled by the else clause, which prints out an rToEdit()-style textbox for user input. This textbox handles all fields that allow ordinary user input, but will not trap for certain errors (such as string data being placed in numeric fields or data longer than the underlying field accepts). These would be good code improvement. If the data designer did not name foreign key references according to my convention, those fields are still editable with a textbox, but the errors that could happen with rToEdit() are worth concern.

 **TIP** These special fields would also be terrific places to use the advanced filtering techniques of filter_input, which can help you verify that an input is a valid e-mail address, integer, or other format.

## Committing a Record Update

The end result of either rToEdit() or smartRToEdit() is an HTML form containing a table name and a bunch of field names and values. The updateRecord.php takes these values and converts them into arrays before calling the updateRec() function. It's much easier to work with the fields and values as arrays than in the somewhat amorphous context they embody after smartRToEdit() or rToEdit().

```
function updateRec($tableName, $fields, $vals){
  //expects name of a record, fields array values array
  //updates database with new values

  global $dbConn;

  $output = "";
  $keyName = $fields[0];
  $keyVal = $vals[0];
```

```php
$query = "";

$query .= "UPDATE $tableName SET \n";
for ($i = 1; $i < count($fields); $i++){
  $query .= $fields[$i];
  $query .= " = '";
  $query .= $vals[$i];
  $query .= "',\n";
} // end for loop

//remove last comma from output
$query = substr($query, 0, strlen($query) - 2);


$query .= "\nWHERE $keyName = '$keyVal'";


$result = mysql_query($query, $dbConn);
if ($result){
  $query = "SELECT * FROM $tableName WHERE $keyName = '$keyVal'";
  $output .= "<h1>update successful</h1>\n";
  $output .= "<h2>new value of record:</h2>";
  $output .= qToTable($query);
} else {
  $output .= "<h3>there was a problem...</h3><pre>$query</pre>\n";
} // end if
return $output;
} // end updateRec
```

The primary job of updateRec() is to build an SQL UPDATE statement based on the parameters passed to it. It is expecting a table name, an array containing field names, and another array containing field values. The UPDATE statement is primarily a list of field names and values, which can be easily obtained with a for loop stepping through the $fields and $vals arrays.

Once the query has been created, it is submitted to the database. The success or failure of the update is reported back to the user.

## Deleting a Record

Deleting a record is actually pretty easy compared to adding or updating. All that's necessary is the table name, key field name, and key field value. The deleteRec() function accepts these parameters and uses them to build an SQL DELETE statement. As usual, the success or failure of the operation is returned as part of the output string.

```
function delRec ($table, $keyName, $keyVal){
  //deletes $keyVal record from $table
  global $dbConn;
  $output = "";
  $query = "DELETE from $table WHERE $keyName = '$keyVal'";
  //print "query is $query<br>\n";
  $result = mysql_query($query, $dbConn);
  if ($result){
    $output = "<h3>Record successfully deleted</h3>\n";
  } else {
    $output = "<h3>Error deleting record</h3>\n";
  } //end if
  return $output;
} // end delRec
```

## Adding a Record

Adding a new record is much like editing a record. It is a two-step process. The first screen builds a page in which you can add a record. I used techniques from the smartRToEdit() function to ensure the primary and foreign key references are edited appropriately.

```
function tToAdd($tableName){
  //given table name, generates HTML form to add an entry to the
  //table.  Works like smartRToEdit in recognizing foreign keys

  global $dbConn;
  $output = "";

  //process a query just to get field names
  $query = "SELECT * FROM $tableName";
  $result = mysql_query($query, $dbConn) or die(mysql_error());

  $output .= <<<HERE
<form action = "processAdd.php"
      method = "post">
  <fieldset>
  <dl>
```

```php
      <dt>Field</dt>
      <dd>Value</dd>

HERE;

  $fieldNum = 0;
  while ($theField = mysql_fetch_field($result)){
    $fieldName = $theField->name;
    if ($fieldNum == 0){
      //it's the primary key field.  It'll be autoNumber
      $output .= <<<HERE

        <dt>$fieldName</dt>
        <dd>AUTONUMBER
          <input type = "hidden"
                 name = "$fieldName"
                 value = "null">
        </dd>

HERE;
    } else if (preg_match("/(.*)ID$/", $fieldName, $match)) {
      //it's a foreign key reference.  Use fieldToList to get
      //a select object for this field

      $valList = fieldToList($match[1],$fieldName, 0, "name");
      $output .= <<<HERE
        <dt>$fieldName</dt>
        <dd>$valList</dd>

HERE;
    } else {
      //it's an ordinary field.  Print a text box
      $output .= <<<HERE
        <dt>$fieldName</dt>
        <dd><input type = "text"
                   name = "$fieldName"
                   value = "">
        </dd>
```

```
HERE;
   } // end if
   $fieldNum++;
 } // end while
 $output .= <<<HERE
   </dl>

       <input type = "hidden"
              name = "tableName"
              value = "$tableName">
       <button type = "submit">
          add record
       </button>
   </fieldset>
 </form>

HERE;

  return $output;

} // end tToAdd
```

The INSERT statement that this function creates uses NULL as the primary key value, because all tables in the system are set to AUTO_INCREMENT. I used the same regular expression trick as in smartRToEdit() to recognize foreign key references. If they exist, I built a drop-down list with fieldToList() to display all possible values for that field and send an appropriate key. Any field not recognized as a primary or foreign key will have an ordinary textbox.

## Processing an Added Record

The tToAdd() function sends its results to processAdd.php, which reorganizes the data much like updateRecord.php. The field names and values are converted to arrays, which are passed to the procAdd() function.

```
function procAdd($tableName, $fields, $vals){
  //generates INSERT query, applies to database
  global $dbConn;

  $output = "";
  $query = "INSERT into $tableName VALUES (";
```

```
    foreach ($vals as $theValue){
      $query .= "'$theValue', ";
    } // end foreach

    //trim off trailing space and comma
    $query = substr($query, 0, strlen($query) - 2);

    $query .= ")";
    $output = "query is $query<br>\n";

    $result = mysql_query($query, $dbConn);
    if ($result){
      $output .= "<h3>Record added</h3>\n";
    } else {
      $output .= "<h3>There was an error</h3>\n";
    } // end if
    return $output;
} // end procAdd
```

The main job of procAdd() is to build an SQL INSERT statement using the results of tToAdd(). This insert is passed to the database and the user receives a report about the insertion attempt's outcome.

## BUILDING A LIST BOX FROM A FIELD

Both smartRToEdit() and tToAdd() need drop-down HTML lists following a specific pattern. In both cases, I needed to build a list that allows the user to select a key value based on some other field in the record. This list should be set so any value in the list can be indicated as the currently selected value. The fieldToList() function takes four parameters and uses them to build exactly such a list.

```
function fieldToList($tableName, $keyName, $keyVal, $fieldName){
  //given table and field, generates an HTML select structure
  //named $keyName.  values will be key field of table, but
  //text will come from the $fieldName value.
  //keyVal indicates which element is currently selected

  global $dbConn;
  $output = "";
  $query = "SELECT $keyName, $fieldName FROM $tableName";
```

```
    $result = mysql_query($query, $dbConn);
    $output .= "<select name = \"$keyName\">\n";
    $recNum = 1;
    while ($row = mysql_fetch_assoc($result)){
      $theIndex = $row["$keyName"];
      $theValue = $row["$fieldName"];
      $output .= <<<HERE
    <option value = "$theIndex"
HERE;

      //make it currently selected item
      if ($theIndex == $keyVal){
        $output .= " selected = \"selected\"";
      } // end if
      $output .= ">$theValue</option>\n";
      $recNum++;
    } // end while
    $output .= "</select>\n";
    return $output;
} // end fieldToList
```

The `fieldToList()` function begins by generating a query that returns all records in the foreign table. I build an HTML `SELECT` object based on the results of this query. As I step through all records, I see if the current record corresponds to the `$keyVal` parameter. If so, that element is selected in the HTML.

## Creating a Button That Returns Users to the Main Page

To simplify navigation, I added a button at the end of each PHP program that returns the user to the program's primary page. The `mainButton()` program creates a very simple form calling whatever program is named in the `$mainProgram` variable, which is indicated at the top of the library.

```
function mainButton(){
  // creates a button to return to the main program

  global $mainProgram;

  $output = <<< HERE
<form action = "$mainProgram"
```

```
      method = "get">
  <fieldset class = "tiny">
    <button type = "submit">
       return to main screen
    </button>
  </fieldset>
</form>

HERE;
  return $output;
} // end mainButton

?>
```

# Taking It to the Next Level

The exercise in this chapter shows what a complete data-driven web app can do. Still, this is only the beginning. My real goal for the dbLib tool is for it to be a starting platform for your own data projects.

## Optimizing Your Data

If you can build your data design from scratch, there are a few guidelines to keep in mind. If you follow these, dbLib will be able to use your database without any modification whatsoever:

- Make the primary key of each table the table name followed by the value ID. If you use this convention, dbLib will be able to automatically recognize all primary and foreign keys in your database (even though MySQL can't always do this itself).

- Make the primary key the first field of every table. This is a common convention anyway, but it makes the dbLib's job easy when it's time to discern primary and foreign keys.

- Use auto-number for all primary keys. This isn't absolutely required, but it is a good practice, because it's an easy way to guarantee unique keys.

- Use camelCase for all field names. This will help your data work in environments that are case-sensitive.

- Describe link tables with the underscore character between the two table names (table1_table2). This allows the system to guess the queries for many-to-many joins (although I haven't yet implemented this feature).

- Specify all primary and foreign keys. Although dbLib doesn't use this feature yet, it's still useful to have these values explicitly listed in the data.

- If a table is used as a foreign reference, make sure it has a field called name. The mechanism for making a drop-down list from a foreign key looks for a name field as the information presented to the user (although you can change this behavior easily).

## Reusing the dbLib Module

The dbLib module was designed to be flexible enough to work with any database. It's really very easy to reuse this code for a completely new purpose. Here are the steps:

1. Build your database. If possible, build the database according to the section "Optimizing Your Data" earlier in this chapter. If the database has already been created according to a different scheme, you may have to modify things a bit to make it all work seamlessly.
2. Copy all the PHP files to a new directory. Take everything, and put it in a new directory in the htdocs path of your server.
3. Rename spyMaster.php to something more in keeping with your application. Give it a name that reflects the main purpose of your database.
4. Set the variables in dbLib.php. The global variables listed at the top of dbLib.php might be the only things you need to change. Use these variables to specify the location of the database, database settings, administrative password, and so on.
5. Modify the dbLib.css stylesheet. Every page in the system uses the same stylesheet, so it should be easy to create your own look and feel by modifying this stylesheet.
6. Customize the application. The basic functionality should work fine, but you may want to reorganize things to make life easier for your users. For example, it would be great to have a custom addAgent page that includes a button for adding a specialty. That way, if the user has an agent with a new specialty, that new specialty can be created on the fly.
7. Test. Things go wrong. Be sure to carefully test your application before releasing it.
8. Back up your data. Don't forget to have regular data backups. Things can go wrong, and you don't want to lose valuable data.

## SUMMARY

The details of the SpyMaster system can be dizzying, but the overall effect is a flexible design that you can easily update and modify. This system can accept modifications to the underlying database and can be adapted to an entirely different data set with relatively little effort.

Although you didn't learn any new PHP syntax in this chapter, you saw an example of coding for reuse and flexibility. You learned how to use include files to simplify coding of complex systems and how to build a library file with utility routines. You learned how to write code that can be adapted to multiple data sets and code that prevents certain kinds of user errors. You learned how to build programs that help tie together relational data structures. The things you have learned in this chapter form the foundation of all data-enabled web programming, which in turn form the backbone of e-commerce and content-management systems.

## CHALLENGES

1. Add a module that lets the user interactively query the database. Begin with a page that allows the user to type in an agent's name and returns data based on that agent. Be sure to guard against SQL injection!

2. Once the basic agent search is done, add checkboxes that allow certain agent aspects (operations and skills) to be displayed.

3. Build programs that allow searching on other aspects of the data, including skills and operations.

4. Build a program that lists each agent's skills along with that agent's other data. Note you'll need a second pass to the database for this.

5. Create your own data structure and use dbMaster to allow access to the data.

6. Make modifications to your new system specific to your data.

# INDEX

# License Agreement/Notice of Limited Warranty

**By opening the sealed disc container in this book, you agree to the following terms and conditions. If, upon reading the following license agreement and notice of limited warranty, you cannot agree to the terms and conditions set forth, return the unused book with unopened disc to the place where you purchased it for a refund.**

### License:

The enclosed software is copyrighted by the copyright holder(s) indicated on the software disc. You are licensed to copy the software onto a single computer for use by a single user and to a backup disc. You may not reproduce, make copies, or distribute copies or rent or lease the software in whole or in part, except with written permission of the copyright holder(s). You may transfer the enclosed disc only together with this license, and only if you destroy all other copies of the software and the transferee agrees to the terms of the license. You may not decompile, reverse assemble, or reverse engineer the software.

### Notice of Limited Warranty:

The enclosed disc is warranted by Course Technology to be free of physical defects in materials and workmanship for a period of sixty (60) days from end user's purchase of the book/disc combination. During the sixty-day term of the limited warranty, Course Technology will provide a replacement disc upon the return of a defective disc.

### Limited Liability:

THE SOLE REMEDY FOR BREACH OF THIS LIMITED WARRANTY SHALL CONSIST ENTIRELY OF REPLACEMENT OF THE DEFECTIVE DISC. IN NO EVENT SHALL COURSE TECHNOLOGY OR THE AUTHOR BE LIABLE FOR ANY OTHER DAMAGES, INCLUDING LOSS OR CORRUPTION OF DATA, CHANGES IN THE FUNCTIONAL CHARACTERISTICS OF THE HARDWARE OR OPERATING SYSTEM, DELETERIOUS INTERACTION WITH OTHER SOFTWARE, OR ANY OTHER SPECIAL, INCIDENTAL, OR CONSEQUENTIAL DAMAGES THAT MAY ARISE, EVEN IF COURSE TECHNOLOGY AND/OR THE AUTHOR HAS PREVIOUSLY BEEN NOTIFIED THAT THE POSSIBILITY OF SUCH DAMAGES EXISTS.

### Disclaimer of Warranties:

COURSE TECHNOLOGY AND THE AUTHOR SPECIFICALLY DISCLAIM ANY AND ALL OTHER WARRANTIES, EITHER EXPRESS OR IMPLIED, INCLUDING WARRANTIES OF MERCHANTABILITY, SUITABILITY TO A PARTICULAR TASK OR PURPOSE, OR FREEDOM FROM ERRORS. SOME STATES DO NOT ALLOW FOR EXCLUSION OF IMPLIED WARRANTIES OR LIMITATION OF INCIDENTAL OR CONSEQUENTIAL DAMAGES, SO THESE LIMITATIONS MIGHT NOT APPLY TO YOU.

### Other:

This Agreement is governed by the laws of the State of Massachusetts without regard to choice of law principles. The United Convention of Contracts for the International Sale of Goods is specifically disclaimed. This Agreement constitutes the entire agreement between you and Course Technology regarding use of the software.